Methodologically rigorous and theoretically rich, Chesson's beautifully illustrated study evocatively captures the entangled relationships between people and their things, demonstrating how dressers and delph materialize memories, knit together kin and community, and transform a house into a home. Chesson's compelling prose coupled with the direct words of household members vividly captures the intimacy and vibrancy of homemaking in the west of Ireland.

Audrey Horning, Professor of Archaeology, Queens University Belfast

Combining archaeological and anthropological research with detailed fieldwork, this comprehensive publication considers the requirements which transform a house into a home. Meredith concentrates on the dresser and its much cherished delph which form an integral part of this transformation. She draws on her broad experience to focus on rural communities in western Ireland, providing an expansive range of examples encompassing both past and present. This study affords a glimpse of the personalities who curated and cared for the wonderful collections of heirlooms.

Rachel Mc Kenna is an architect and author of publications
including, Traditional Architecture in Offaly

Irish Dressers
and Delph

Irish Dressers and Delph

HOMEMAKING THROUGH TIME

MEREDITH S. CHESSON

With contributions by Ian Kuijt,
Meagan Conway McDonald, Katherine Shakour,
Nicholas Ames, Tommy Burke
and Rachel Tracey

EST 1925 CUP CORK UNIVERSITY PRESS

CLÓ OLLSCOILE CHORCAÍ

First published in 2025 by
Cork University Press
Boole Library
University College Cork
Cork
T12 ND89
Ireland

Authorised representative: Sinead Neville. Email: corkuniversitypress@ucc.ie

Library of Congress Control Number: 2025942553
Distribution in the USA: Longleaf Servi¯ces, Chapel Hill, NC, USA

ISBN 978-1-78205-067-4

Book design and typesetting, Anú Design, Tara
Printed in Poland by BZ Graf

Dedicated to Kaatje, Ian, Dianne and Ralph Jr,

and to the people of Inishbofin, Inishturk and Inishark

Contents

List of Figures and Tables   xi

Acknowledgements   xxix

Image Permissions   xxxiii

Chapter 1

An Anthropology of Homemaking in Western Ireland

page 1

Chapter 2

Dressers, Delph and Homemaking in Western Connemara

page 39

Chapter 3

'Round the house and mind the dresser': The lives of dressers

page 95

Chapter 4

Homemaking on Inishark: Enduring houses, delph and everyday life,

c. 1780–1960

page 163

(co-authors Meredith S. Chesson, Ian Kuijt, Meagan Conway McDonald, Katherine Shakour, Nicholas Ames, Tommy Burke and Rachel Tracey)

Chapter 5

The Taste of Home: Delph, consumption and connections to the wider world

page 239

Chapter 6

'Made to grow old': Dressers, heritage and the future of homemaking

page 311

Notes   331

Bibliography   355

Index   377

List of Figures and Tables

FIGURES

Fig. 1.1:   Michael's parlour hearth, whose surround was decorated with inlaid shells, and mantelpiece displaying delph and other belongings

Fig. 1.2:   Ellen's dresser, filled with objects connected to her family's past, their present life and hopes for the future

Fig. 1.3:   Heirloom objects on Ellen's dresser: (a) lustreware milk jug and sugar bowl from the 1930s–40s; (b) green eye-wash glass dated to 1930s; (c) teapot from Price Kensington Potteries, Longport, UK, 1962 onwards; (d) her grandfather's pocketknife

Fig. 1.4:   Wall art for sale in a Mishawaka, Indiana home crafts shop

Fig. 1.5:   (a) View of Craggaunowen's crannóg in 1995; (b) tourists at exterior hearth next to the replica wattle and daub hut in the crannóg

Fig. 1.6:   CLIC archaeologists excavating an AD 1780–1820 house at the Poirtíns, Inishbofin: (a) clearing collapsed building materials to expose the floor of Room A, recording elevations on wall stones (background) and uncovering a blocked doorway (foreground); (b) clearing stone rubble to expose Room A's floor and a stone wall creating a byre

Fig. 1.7:   Archaeologist carefully exposing the floor of the Late Iron Age House 2 adjacent to the upper cashel in Mooghaun Fort, County Clare in 1995. Note the stone foundations for thick walls and the storage pit located just in front of the bucket.

Fig. 1.8:   Reconstruction of the cluster of Late Iron Age houses within and outside the Upper Cashel at Mooghaun Fort, including Hut 2 located to the right of the cashel (Artist David Hill)

Fig. 1.9:   Aerial photograph of Mooghaun Fort, with ramparts and cashels outlined (Photograph by Aoife Daly)

Fig. 1.10:   View of Craggaunowen's replica cashel in 1995 from its exterior

Fig. 1.11:   Replica buildings and features within Craggaunowen's cashel in 1995: (a) entrance into replica stone hut; (b) replica rectangular stone building, exterior hearth and hide-curing rack

Fig. 1.12:   Partially excavated early medieval house (Structure Eta) from Deer Park Farms, County Antrim. Note the double-walled construction, with space to pack insulating materials (Adapted from C. Lynn and J. McDowell, *Deer Park Farms*, Plate 7.15).

Fig. 1.13:   View of the inner wall from the replicated hut's interior, partway through construction

Fig. 1.14:   View of the outer and inner walls from the hut's exterior, with the pitched roofline rising upwards

Fig. 1.15:   Detail of the thatched roof over the woven roofline

Fig. 1.16:   Finished replica of the eighth-century house at Deer Park Farms

Fig. 1.17:   View of the main room of Patrick's home with its key elements (left to right): settle (in which Patrick sits to the left of the door), hearth, press, cooker and dresser

Fig. 1.18:   (a) View of Patrick's early twentieth-century dresser and delph in an uninhabited home in Cashel; (b) detail of Arklow jugs, matching Eternal Beau plates and tureen, and Carrigaline milk jug on the bottom shelf

Fig. 2.1:   Tourists walking the Low Road towards Inishbofin's harbour and new pier

Fig. 2.2:   Map of study region with places mentioned in the book

Fig. 2.3:   Remains of Inishbofin's late medieval church, situated within the bounds of the original early monastic shrine and covering an earlier wood church, and the island's current cemetery

Fig. 2.4:   Detail of Inishbofin parish records of baptisms, with entry stating the home of the child and family as 'Sebastapool' – a possible reference to the Crimean War (1853–6)

Fig. 2.5:   Cromwell's Barracks, situated at the mouth of Inishbofin's harbour

Fig. 2.6:   Drone's-eye view of Inishbofin's harbour at dawn, looking southeast to the mainland

Fig. 2.7:   Map of villages, harbours, churches and military barracks on Inishbofin and Inishark, 1600–1960, that have been studied archaeologically or oral historically by the CLIC team

Fig. 2.8:   Detail from the 1856–60 valuation book of residents in Fawnmore village, Inishbofin, listing Patt Lavelle as a boatwright and tenant, renting a house and adjacent land

Fig. 2.9:   1874 announcement of sale of Inishbofin and Inishark with smaller associated islands

Fig. 2.10:   Local archaeologist and historian Tommy Burke (centre, wearing a blue sleeveless jacket) leads a walking tour of significant historical and archaeological sites on Inishbofin.

Fig. 2.11:   View of Inishark's historic village, looking west along the southern coastline

Fig. 2.12:   In the spring of 1885, landlord Cyril Allies wrote to the government requesting the construction of a breakwater and pier at Inishark to facilitate landing and disembarking on the island.

Fig. 2.13:   Excavations on Inishark in 2012, with orange and blue tents in the background

Fig. 2.14:   Drone's-eye view of Inishturk's harbour

Fig. 2.15:   Map of Inishturk, 1600–1960, with key ports and historical sites

Fig. 2.16:   View of inner harbour of Inishturk, with the ferry at the pier

Fig. 2.17:   View of Clifden from the John D'Arcy Monument

Fig. 2.18:   Talking with Patrick and his friend Francis about Patrick's dresser and old home in Cashel

Fig. 2.19:   Other heirlooms in Mary's home: (a) one of her elaborate taxidermy displays in a glass case adorning her sitting room; (b) her early twentieth-century house shrine (made by her father)

Fig. 2.20:   Common terminology for dresser components that we recorded

Fig. 2.21:   Most common delph forms from dresser and delph collections that offer good comparisons with the archaeological assemblages from the seven excavated houses on Inishark

Fig. 2.22:   An assemblage of milk jugs from the Doonmore Hotel's delph collection

Fig. 2.23:   CLIC director Ian Kuijt (in black) excavating with graduate and undergraduate students in House 8 in 2014 amidst a string grid of 1-square-metre units

Fig. 2.24:   Meagan McDonald recording architectural features, including the chimney, roof, doorways and windows, in one of the still-standing houses on Inishark

Fig. 2.25:   (a) Meagan McDonald excavating a 2012 test trench at House 8 and exposing nearly complete spongeware vessels; (b) Catriona Baldwin and Erin Crowley mapping architectural features at Inishark's medieval shrine of Clochán Leo

Fig. 2.26:   Screenshots of preliminary results from (a) Ancestry.com and (b) the
              National Archives of Ireland arising from a search of the 1841 and 1851 census
              search forms for the last name Scuffle (today's Schofield) on Inishbofin in
              the nineteenth century

Fig. 2.27:   The 1838 Fair Plan map of Inishark village produced by the Ordnance
              Survey team, with houses (red rectangles), fence lines (in black),
              locations of medieval period monuments, and names of topographical
              features and coves

Fig. 2.28:   1902 valuation record map for Inishark, based on the 1898 Ordnance
              Survey map. Note the changing valuation record numbers written in
              red, sometimes crossing out earlier numbers assigned to specific plots.

Fig. 2.29:   1911 Irish census form for the Cloonan family, who resided in House 57
              on Inishark (House 13 of that year's survey)

Fig. 2.30:   Page from Inishbofin parish records of baptisms from 1870 performed
              on Inishbofin

Fig. 2.31:   Page from Inishbofin marriage records from 1867 to 1869

Fig. 2.32:   Pages from historic shop ledgers: (a) ledger entries for purchases on
              Wednesday, 23 February 1916 by an Inishbofin shopkeeper acquiring
              stock in a Westport shop; (b) ledger entries for 1930–1 purchases by the
              national school teacher on Inishbofin from a Clifden clothing shop

Fig. 3.1:   View along Sarah's dresser towards the hearth in her uninhabited home

Fig. 3.2:   View of James' and Margaret's old dresser from just inside the door into
              the home's main room

Fig. 3.3:   Top three shelves of James' and Margaret's dresser, with details of
              decorative elements

Fig. 3.4:   Delph heirlooms from Margaret's and James' mothers, displayed in
              their dresser: (a and b) a German pink-rimmed bowl with its mark,
              manufacturer unknown; (c and d) one of a set of small Arklow plates
              with a pink rose pattern with its mark, from the 1950s

Fig. 3.5:   Irish- and English-manufactured jugs from James' and Margaret's
              dresser: (a and b) jug with decal floral decoration and vertical fluting
              and (c) its maker's mark: Arklow, 1950s; (d and e) jug with floral
              decal decoration and a thin green band encircling the rim and (f) its
              maker's mark: manufactured by a cooperative post-Second World War

economic scheme by a group of British pottery manufacturers, 1945–52

Fig. 3.6:   View of Rusheen's cottages on Inishbofin

Fig. 3.7:   View of George's dresser with the etched glass doors open wide

Fig 3.8:   Detail of the shelves on George's dresser

Fig. 3.9:   George's (a) Syria pattern platter with (b) maker's mark, made by R. Cochran & Company, Verreville Pottery in Glasgow, Scotland, 1869–1917

Fig. 3.10:   Examples of George's delph: (a) Sadler teapot from the dresser; (b and c) scalloped Johnson Brothers plate in storage; (d and e) Wade mug commemorating Queen Elizabeth II's 1953 coronation

Fig. 3.11:   Old plates mended with lead staples, formerly displayed in the original dresser belonging to George's parents

Fig. 3.12:   Signature of Michael Burke inscribed on the interior of his wardrobe door in our 2012 visit to his uninhabited home

Fig. 3.13:   (a) Detail of decorative carving on Sarah's dresser in her uninhabited Inishbofin home; (b) detail of decorative carving on Julia's dresser

Fig. 3.14:   Dressers made by Inishturk craftsman John Joe O'Toole: (a) Bedelia's dresser in her uninhabited Inishturk home; (b) Celia's dresser in her Inishturk bed and breakfast; (c) Catherine's dresser in her Inishbofin restaurant

Fig. 3.15:   Detail of top two shelves of Celia's dresser showing the older-style plate rail in the uppermost shelf

Fig. 3.16:   Liam Lyons' photograph of John Joe O'Toole building a *currach* on Inishturk in 1992

Fig. 3.17:   Two dressers made for Inishturk bed and breakfasts by Mark in the 1990s: (a) Celia's second dresser; (b) Honora's dresser

Fig. 3.18:   Anne's dresser in her Clifden home, made by students at ATU in Letterfrack, County Galway

Fig. 3.19:   Sitting below a shelf of old platters, an Inishbofin elder teaches CLIC director Ian Kuijt about traditional boats and fishing while enjoying pints at Murray's, the Doonmore Hotel's bar.

Fig. 3.20:   Mary's dresser, maintained in its original position and with her father's paint scheme in her Cashel home

Fig. 3.21:   Honora's updated dresser (made by Mark), painted blue and white in 2023

Fig. 3.22:   Comparison of the delph and objects displayed on the Doonmore

Hotel dresser located in the hotel dining room: (a) 1989, with platters and bowls on top; (b) 2014, with jugs on top and platters on all three shelves; (c) 2022, hung on wall without its press and with a similar arrangement as its 2014 iteration

Fig. 3.23:   Michael's kitchen dresser, one of the older dressers in the study, includes a hanging dresser (attached shelves) extending from both sides of his dresser

Fig 3.24:   Julia's grandmother's dresser, located in her family's pub and restaurant on Inishbofin

Fig. 3.25:   Martin's and Juliana's old dresser, recently stripped and awaiting further refurbishment. Built in the early twentieth century by a local Inishbofin craftsperson, it was retrofitted with doors at some point in its life history.

Fig. 3.26:   Dressers in rental cottages: (a) Betty's dresser on Inishturk; (b) Penelope's dresser on Inishbofin; (c) Catherine's dresser on Inishbofin

Fig. 3.27:   Displayed objects in Catherine's dresser in the Galley Restaurant

Fig. 3.28:   Delph display in Michael's parlour in a glass cabinet

Fig. 3.29:   Oona's dresser and delph in Indiana: (a) Amish-made dresser with interior floodlamp to better display objects; (b) detail of displayed delph and glassware with the glass doors opened

Fig. 3.30:   Oona's delph, inherited from her aunt: (a) large jug with (b) an English registered mark indicating the vessel's manufacture on 7 February 1877 (parcel 8); (c) large transfer-printed and hand-painted platter with no identifiable maker's mark

Fig. 3.31:   Frequency (or popularity) of ceramic vessel forms in recorded dresser and delph collections. The darker the green colour, the more frequently the vessel form appeared in dresser or delph collections; the lighter the green, the rarer the form.

Fig. 3.32:   Plates from Anne's delph collection, displayed on walls in her home: (a) plate with (b) maker's mark of W.H. Lockitt, UK, 1913–19; (c) plate with (d) maker's mark from Minton Pottery, UK, 1850s

Fig. 3.33:   Delia's seven platters

Fig. 3.34:   Three of Michael's coffeepots, all made in England: (a) the Hunter coffeepot located in the parlour on the mantelpiece with (b) maker's mark by Myott (post-1976); (c) Kleen Kitchen coffeepot located on the kitchen dresser, where he kept items used daily with (d) maker's mark by Sadler Pottery (1940s–50s); (e and f) Sadler Pottery coffeepot made in 1960s (estimated age by style)

Fig. 3.35:   Older mugs made before the 1950s: (a) banded mug from hanging dresser in Michael's kitchen; (b) transfer-printed mug from Delia's delph collection, made by (c) Campbellfield Pottery in Glasgow, Scotland, *c.* 1884.

Fig. 3.36:   William's and Peggy's 2010 dresser filled with mugs, small bowls, plates and water glasses used daily

Fig. 3.37:   (a) Delia's Alexandra tureen, known as 'The Bank', held her purse when the tureen was stored in her now-discarded dresser; (b) made by Booth's, UK, early twentieth century

Fig. 3.38:   Belongings found on dressers: (a) Celia's platter with (b) mark for Hampden pattern, New Wharf Pottery, UK, 1891–4; (c) plate on Michaels' kitchen dresser made by (d) Morley Ware, UK, 1938–45; (e) mug and saucer on Michael's main room dresser with (f) mark for Golden Amber, Ridgway Potteries, UK, 1955 onwards

Fig. 3.39:   Belongings found on dressers: (a) Bedelia's rose motif and India Tree jugs made by (b) Arklow, 1950s–60s; (c) Ellen's glass and metal chicken vessel, filled with various small items; (d) Doonmore Hotel jug, early twentieth century; (e) Doonmore Hotel's small blue Willow plate made by (f) Arklow, 1940–8; (g) Celia's Cottageware teapot made by (h) Price Brothers, UK, 1931–63, likely 1945–63

Fig. 3.40:   Comparison of how many older and more recently assembled dressers contain different vessel forms

Fig. 3.41:   Bedelia's dresser in her uninhabited home on Inishturk

Fig. 3.42:   Comparison of percentages of vessel forms on nine archival dressers

Fig. 3.43:   Shelves of delph in old dressers: (a) James' and Margaret's dresser and (b) Mary's dresser

Fig. 3.44:   Comparison of percentages of vessel forms on eleven more recently assembled dressers

Fig. 3.45:   Catherine's dresser in an Inishbofin rental cottage

Fig. 3.46:   Comparison of percentages of vessel forms in nine dresser-less delph collections

Fig. 3.47:   Visual compilation of dresser stories represented by delph recorded in this study (2013–19)

Fig. 4.1:   Everyday ceramic and glass vessels, along with metal possessions, excavated in House 8

Fig. 4.2:   LiDAR map of the southern portion of Inishark village, showing seven houses excavated by the CLIC team

Fig. 4.3:   View of the excavations of House 57, the westernmost house in the village

Fig. 4.4:   Tour of House 6 showing the three standing gable walls, looking towards the sea

Fig. 4.5:   Archaeological plan of excavated House 8 remains

Fig. 4.6:   Basil Bradley's painting *Irish Cabin, Spinning* (no year) shows a hearth built against a gable wall, with a door to the left giving entrance to a second room in the home. The outer hearth is constructed of smooth pebbles set into the beaten earth floor, with a small window gifting the room with some light.

Fig. 4.7:   Niches in Inishark historic houses: (a) niche built into gable wall of House 2, as well as the blocked doorway to the far right in the gable wall; (b) detail photograph of House 20's niche

Fig. 4.8:   Glass bottles found within the spaces between dry-laid stones of a house's wall

Fig. 4.9:   View of the eastern face of House 6 with (1) exterior doorways of the central room situated opposite each other, and one doorway into the additional room added later; and (2) three windows on the front of the house

Fig. 4.10:   Ledge on the interior gable wall (noted by red dotted line) of the northernmost room of House 6 that would have supported the flooring of a loft over part of the room. Note the pile of yellowed rendering material, which would have originally coated the gable wall, resting on the ledge and still remaining on the bottom of the gable wall surface.

Fig. 4.11:   Internal northern gable wall of the central room in the Halloran house (House 6). Note (1) the interior doorway on the far right leading from the main room to the lofted small room to the north; (2) a collapsed chimney and hearth, added sometime in the latter half of the nineteenth century to this gable wall; (3) remains of interior plastering on the western wall in the corner and towards the centre of the room; and (4) a white quartz stone placed high in the gable wall.

Fig. 4.12:   House 6 chimney: (a) northern or back side of the double hearth in House 6; (b) view up the chimney stack from the hearthstone

Fig. 4.13:   Excavated back-to-back hearth in House 8 showing three identified postholes framing the hearth and likely used to support a mantelpiece or metal swing arm

Fig. 4.14:   Exterior face of southern gable wall of House 6 with smoke ventilation window

Fig. 4.15:   Exterior face of House 6's western wall, showing (1) the original doorway in the central room, and (2) the vertical seam in the stone wall created with the addition of the southernmost room

Fig. 4.16:   Reconstruction of a nineteenth-century home in Errislannan, County Galway (by artist Eric Carlson, CLIC Archives)

Fig. 4.17:   Inishark islanders carrying furniture and belongings down to the pier for transport to their new mainland homes, 20 October 1960

Fig. 4.18:   (a) Inishark islanders with a dresser for loading onto a *currach* for transport to Inishbofin and transshipment to Cleggan; (b) Inishark islanders on *The Lilly* heading to their new mainland homes in Fountainhill, Claddaghduff

Fig. 4.19:   Anthony Carey Stannus' painting *An Irish Interior* (1860s) depicts many of the humble objects of everyday life likely to have been found in Inishark's homes

Fig. 4.20:   Frances Livesay's *By the Fireside, Co. Mayo* (1875) depicts many of the more perishable objects that do not survive in the archaeological record, including basketry, clothing, foodstuff, rushes and wood objects

Fig. 4.21:   Sherds from House 20 excavations (context 132), including a brown transfer-printed rim (centre), three spongeware sherds with blue, brown, red and green decorations (right and bottom left), and a purple and brown machine-turned slipware body sherd

Fig. 4.22:   Ceramic vessel #1026, a teacup excavated from House 8. A sherd from the cup's rim is at the top of the photo, body sherds in the middle, and the base sherds below.

Fig. 4.23:   Ceramic vessel #1185, a saucer excavated from House 8, in the process of joining sherds and reconstructing the vessel

Fig. 4.24:   Schematic architectural biography for House 57, Inishark

Fig. 4.25:   Undergraduate student excavating *in situ* ceramic and glass vessels from Room 2 of House 57

Fig. 4.26:   View of excavations of House 57 from above

Fig. 4.27:   Summary of belongings found inside and directly outside of House 57

Fig. 4.28:   Child's shoe from House 57

Fig. 4.29:   Ring (left) and metal crucifix (right) from House 57

Fig. 4.30:   Metal fork (without handle) from House 57

Fig. 4.31:   Wood pully from a block and tackle, found in House 57

Fig. 4.32:   (a) Transfer-printed teacup with imagery of a boat and bridge, vessel #1101; (b) hand-painted mug, vessel #1091

Fig. 4.33:   House 57 ceramic vessels: (a) hand-painted saucer with floral motifs and a red band on rim, vessel #1088; (b) transfer-printed teacup with purple ribbon and shamrocks, vessel #1100 with interior surfaces on the left and exterior surfaces on the right

Fig. 4.34:   Two spongeware mugs from House 57, likely mid-nineteenth century: (a) vessel #1097; (b) vessel #1094

Fig. 4.35:   (a) Plate made by John Mortlock Pottery in London, *c.* 1880, vessel #1093, House 57 and (b) its maker's mark

Fig. 4.36:   Base and body of a stoneware marmalade jar made by Caledonian Pottery in Glasgow for the W.P. Hartley Jam Company, operating out of London and Liverpool, *c.* 1900–20, vessel #1124, House 57

Fig. 4.37:   A variety of partially excavated glass vessels that would have contained medicines, alcoholic beverages and food found in House 57. Note glass buoys beginning to emerge: one just above the right side of the scale bar and below the remains of a leather strap in the right foreground, the other at the top centre nestled between an alcohol bottle on its right and a food jar on the left.

Fig. 4.38:   FMF icon on the bottom of a marmalade jar excavated in a unit near St Leo's Church, not associated with any single house structure (Unit 4, context 401)

Fig. 4.39:   View of excavations of House 8 in 2014. Note the southern gable wall of House 6 meeting the field wall running behind House 8 and seen above the head of the surveyor in the background.

Fig. 4.40:   Schematic architectural biography for House 8, Inishark

Fig. 4.41:   Undergraduate student checking her dustpan for small ceramic and glass sherds while excavating a concentration of complete or nearly complete glass bottles and ceramic vessels in House 8, visible in the foreground

Fig. 4.42:   Summary of belongings found within and around House 8 during excavation

Fig. 4.43:   House 8 saucers: (a) vessel #1006; (b) vessel #1008

Fig. 4.44:   House 8 ceramic vessels: (a) plate (vessel #1182) with an 'Imperial, D M & Sons' stamped maker's mark on the base and produced by David Methven & Sons Pottery, Kirkcaldy, Scotland, c. 1870s; (b) transfer-printed platter (vessel #1019) with geometric design

Fig. 4.45   House 8 serving vessels: (a) spongeware plate (vessel #1181); (b) spongeware bowl (vessel #1193)

Fig. 4.46:   House 8 teacups: (a) hand-painted teacup sherds from vessel #1191; (b) teacup handle, rim and body sherds from vessel #1027

Fig. 4.47:   House 8 serving vessels: (a) spongeware and banded bowl (vessel #1009); (b) spongeware mug (vessel #1004)

Fig. 4.48:   (a) House 8 transfer-printed mug (vessel #1183) with Cattle pattern (top: exterior; centre: base; bottom: interior body); (b) matching example of mug from Delia's delph collection

Fig. 4.49:   (a) House 8 marmalade jar #1017; (b) base with mark details: made by Caledonian Pottery, Glasgow, c. 1900–20, for H.P. Hartley Jam Company operating out of London and Liverpool

Fig. 4.50:   House 8 crockery sherds: (a) black-glazed redware bowl rim with body sherds (context 6108); (b) cream-glazed redware crock and stoneware base fragment (context 6085c1)

Fig. 4.51:   House 8 carbonised beverage bottles

Fig. 4.52:   House 8 alcohol bottles

Fig. 4.53:   Alcohol and carbonised beverage bottles found together in House 8 alongside two blue medicine bottles (context 6079-F3)

Fig. 4.54:   1862 British halfpenny found on the floor of House 8

Fig. 4.55:   Spectacles from House 8

Fig. 4.56:   (a) Joinable fragments from the school slate found in House 8 with (b) initials FD inscribed on one side

Fig. 4.57:   (a) Joinable fragments from other side of the school slate found in House 8 with (b) initials BH inscribed twice on one side

Fig. 4.58:   House 8 pipes from Hynes of Galway

Fig. 4.59:   House 8 saucers with matching decoration (but different sizes): (left) vessel #1015; (right) vessel #1016

Fig. 4.60:   Comparison of relative frequencies of ceramic forms in Houses 8 and 57

Fig. 4.61:   Percentages of ceramic vessel forms present in the seven houses on Inishark excavated by the CLIC team, 2009–17

Fig. 4.62:   Summary of house life histories, documentary sources and oral histories associated with each home

Fig. 4.63:   Looking back at the village of Inishark after finishing CLIC's archaeological field season in 2014

Fig. 5.1:   Jugs from Honor's (right) and Thomas' (left) ancestors

Fig. 5.2:   Exterior and interior decorations of Anne's bowl

Fig. 5.3:   Maker's mark on base of Anne's bowl

Fig. 5.4:   (a) Delia's glass IV bottle with (b) mark patented and produced by Cutter Laboratories in Berkeley California in the 1940s

Fig. 5.5:   (a) Mary's favourite plate, decorated with the Broadway pattern and (b) produced by Foley Pottery in Staffordshire from 1948 to '63

Fig. 5.6:   (a) Platter displayed above the bar at the Doonmore Hotel with the (b) Lake pattern, made by G.L. Ashworth and Brothers Ltd of Hanley, Staffordshire, UK, 1862–84

Fig. 5.7:   Trends of manufacturing origins of ceramic vessels through time in ethnographic dresser and delph-only assemblages

Fig. 5.8:   Identifiable manufacturing origins of 138 ceramic vessels in dressers and delph collections

Fig. 5.9:   Graph showing the ages and manufacturing origins of forty-five ceramic vessels or sets of matching vessels with identifiable maker's marks in the earliest manufacturing period (1840–1927). Each entry represents a single or set of matching vessels with identifiable maker's marks that provide details of date range and manufacturing origins. When identifiable, entries include the name of specific decorative patterns, such as Willow or Asiatic Pheasant.

Fig. 5.10:   Transfer-printed delph examples from England made before 1928: (a) Patrick's plate and (b) mark for Ford & Sons, Burslem, Staffordshire, UK, 1893–1907; (c) Catherine's teacup and saucer made by (d) Coalport

Pottery, UK 1891–1920; (e) Delia's Dudley platter with (f) mark for Hollinshead & Kirkham, Tunstall, UK, 1900–24

Fig. 5.11:   Graph showing the ages and manufacturing origins of sixty-four ceramic vessels or sets of matching vessels with identifiable maker's marks in the middle manufacturing period (1927–69). Each entry represents a single or set of matching vessels with identifiable maker's marks that provide details of date range and manufacturing origins. When identifiable, entries include the name of specific decorative patterns, such as Cottage Rose or yellow crinoline girl.

Fig. 5.12:   Delph manufactured from 1928 to '69: (a) Patrick's banded milk jug with (b) mark from Carrigaline, Ireland, 1930–40s; (c) Michael's dinner plate made by (d) Barratt's, Staffordshire, England, 1945–53; (e) Bridget's Garland Rose platter from (f) Arklow, Ireland, 1950–60s

Fig. 5.13:   Graph showing the ages and manufacturing origins of twenty-nine ceramic vessels or sets of matching vessels with identifiable maker's marks in the most recent manufacturing period (1970–2000s). Each entry represents a single or set of matching vessels with identifiable maker's marks that provide details of date range and manufacturing origins. When identifiable, entries include the name of specific decorative patterns, such as Willow or Eternal Beau.

Fig. 5.14:   English transfer-printed delph produced after 1970: (a) Catherine's Finlandia teacup from (b) Myott Pottery, England, 1982 onwards (matching saucer and small bowl not pictured); (c) Michael's chequered bowl by (d) Staffordshire Tableware, England, 1990–2000; (e) Penelope's blue Willow plate from (f) Grindley Pottery, UK, 1970s onwards

Fig. 5.15:   Dates and manufacturing origins of nineteenth- and early twentieth-century ceramic vessels from excavations on Inishark

Fig. 5.16:   Comparison of manufacturing origins of ceramic vessels with maker's marks in the ethnographic (1840–1969) and archaeological (1820–1960) assemblages

Fig. 5.17:   (a) One of Patrick's five matching plates made in (b) Helsinki, Finland by the Arabia Pottery factory, 1932 to mid-1940s

Fig. 5.18:   *The Country Shop* by Jack B. Yeats (1912) depicts a shopkeeper with her day ledger.

Fig. 5.19:   Excerpt from a more specialised shop: purchases of clothing, boots, needles, elastic, buttons and caps from a Clifden clothing and clothing supplies shop on 7 November 1921 with the purchased goods to be sent to an Inishbofin customer by post (delivered to Cleggan and then to Inishbofin by boat)

Fig. 5.20:   Inishbofin fishing ledger from 1932, showing shellfish caught by Inishbofin and Inishark fishermen, who sold their catches to an intermediary based on the mainland who managed the transfer of shellfish to France. Note that the intermediary paid for catches by individual fishermen as well as for any labour provided by crewmen.

Fig. 5.21:   Early twentieth-century ledger entries from a Westport general shop showing purchases by Pat Murray, Pat Burke and Patrick Lavelle, three Inishbofin shopkeepers who acquired stock in Westport: (a) the bottom half of the page shows the 10 March 1910 entry for Pat Murray, who sailed to Westport and purchased goods, to have delivered to his boat at the port; (b) this ledger page from 25 November 1915 shows two orders of goods, one by Pat Burke and the other by Patrick Lavelle, to be delivered to Pat Burke's boat at the port

Fig. 5.22:   The right side of George's dresser with the etched glass door open, displaying delph manufactured in England and purchased from shops in the mid-twentieth century

Fig. 5.23:   (a) Honora's modern Willow pattern plate, made by (b) English Ironstone Tableware company, Staffordshire, UK, 1973–94

Fig. 5.24:   (a) Michael's matching teacup, saucer and small plate from a larger set, manufactured by (b) Ridgway Potteries in the UK, 1955–64

Fig. 5.25:   Bottom shelf of James' and Margaret's dresser with more recently purchased items

Fig. 5.26:   (a) Anne's chinoiserie pedestalled bowl displayed in her home with (b) maker's mark from John Tam's Crown Pottery, 1875–1903, Longton, Staffordshire, UK

Fig. 5.27:   Three Scottish-produced vessels from the Doonmore Hotel delph collection: (a) blue Willow platter made by (b) J. & M.P. Bell Co. Ltd, Glasgow, 1850–70; (c) Damascus platter made by (d) David Methven & Sons, Kirkcaldy, Scotland, 1870–1928; (e) Syria platter in blue with (f) mark from Britannia Pottery, Glasgow, 1855–96

Fig. 5.28:   Spongeware vessels: (a) spongeware vessel from the Doonmore Hotel delph collection; (b) spongeware bowl (vessel #1007) excavated from Inishark House 8 in 2012

Fig. 5.29:   Catherine's teacups and saucers, gifts to her from her grandmother who emigrated to the US on visits back home to Ireland: (a and b) made in England by Johnson Brothers, Staffordshire, 1913–1930s; (c and d) transfer-printed and hand-painted Lowestoft Border pattern, made by Booth's, 1906–1920s

Fig. 5.30:   (a) Vessels from a Japanese tea set, made by (b) Moriyama Pottery, founded in 1911 in Morimachi, Japan, for the export market to Europe and the US, given as a wedding gift to Julia's grandparents for their wedding

Fig. 5.31:   (a) Portion of the full dinner set given to Delia's mother-in-law as a wedding gift with (b) mark from Colclough & Company, 1908–28

Fig. 5.32:   Honora's glass and metal chicken vessel proudly displayed on her dresser on Inishturk. It was gifted to her on her twenty-first birthday by the original proprietress of the Doonmore Hotel on Inishbofin.

Fig. 5.33:   Religious belongings and mementoes in Sarah's dresser: (a) Mary and Child of Prague statues; (b) plastic bottle of holy water from Lourdes

Fig. 5.34:   Everyday belongings associated with dressers and delph collections: (a) a pocket watch, spectacles and an old lighter in Michael's house with a banded mug resting behind them; (b) Bedelia's very large blue medicine bottle, from which she frequently dispensed milk of magnesia to ailing Inishturk residents

Fig. 5.35:   Souvenir delph from (a) Michael's parlour and (b) Julia's parents' dresser

Fig. 5.36:   Souvenir mugs from (a) Denmark and (b) Zagreb, Croatia in Honora's dresser

Fig. 5.37:   Dressers and delph as vehicles to transport people to different places and times

Fig. 5.38:   Purple transfer-printed teacup from House 5/ (vessel #1100)

Fig. 5.39:   (a) Hand-made and stamped mug from Michael's hanging dresser in his outshot kitchen with (b) maker's mark from Greece

Fig. 5.40:   Inishbofin parish records of Easter and Christmas station masses 1890–1 with transcription

Fig. 5.41:   Percentages of decoration techniques on the minimum number of decorated serving vessels from Inishark's excavated post-medieval houses (n=356 vessels; stoneware and crockery vessels not included)

Fig. 5.42: Vessels from the early period in delph assemblages: (a) Mary's Asiatic Pheasant platter with (b) mark from Thomas Cone Ltd, UK, 1912–35; (c) Patrick's green Argyle pattern tureen, which was accompanied by five matching plates and a second tureen, (d) made by Ford & Sons in Burslem, Staffordshire, UK, 1893–1907

Fig. 5.43: Delph styles from period 2 (1928–69): (a) Michael's English-made plate with floral and gild decoration, made by (b) Alfred Meakin after 1945; (c) Catherine's Irish-made Willow pattern teacup with gilded rim and handle, made by (d) Arklow, 1949–1950s; (e) Patrick's Irish-made jug with the woman in the yellow dress (yellow crinoline girl), made by (f) Arklow, 1949–1960s

Fig. 5.44: Two English-made transfer-printed plates made after 1970: (a) Ellen's plate with The Post House design, made by (b) Alfred Meakin; (c) a plate from Julia's family with the Olde England design, made by (d) Royal Tudor Ware

Fig. 5.45: (a) Michael's Homemaker plate; (b) the backstamp codes indicate its production in the second half ('2') of 1962 ('62')

Fig. 5.46: Anne's flow blue tureen: (a) view from the side; (b) base interior and (c) maker's mark: W.H. Grindley & Company Ltd 1880–1914, Staffordshire UK; (d) lid exterior and (e) maker's mark on interior: Co-Operative Wholesale Society Ltd Staffordshire UK, 1911–20

Fig. 5.47: The contents of Michael's dresser in the main room of his uninhabited home

Fig. 5.48: Teacup, saucer and coffeepot from Michael's German coffee set displayed in his parlour

Fig. 5.49: Percentages of vessel forms in dressers whose contents are displayed but rarely used and in dressers whose contents are used daily

Fig. 5.50: Dresser designed with a bursting abundance approach, with every cubic centimetre filled with objects: second and third shelves of Mary's dresser

Fig. 5.51: Dressers designed to be full, but not overflowing: (a) Bedelia's dresser; (b) Penelope's dresser

Fig. 5.52: Dresser designed with elegant restraint and fewer pieces arranged artfully: Catherine's rental cottage dresser

Fig. 5.53:   Dresser display grouping certain vessels by form, and with attention to symmetry and colour: second and third shelves of the Doonmore Hotel dresser on Inishbofin

Fig. 6.1:   Drone's-eye view of the village of Inishark
Fig. 6.2:   *Currach*-making as part of home: Jane's son in his workshop making a *currach* and *currach* models
Fig. 6.3:   Richard and his *currach* in Auburn, Alabama
Fig. 6.4:   Martin inspecting a *currach* he was painting on the beach below the Inishbofin House Hotel
Fig. 6.5:   Stephen's Irish dressers: (above) found in a Chicago antique shop; (opposite page) purchased from a Connecticut estate sale
Fig. 6.6:   Drone's-eye view looking to the northwest over Inishbofin's Old Pier, Inishbofin House Hotel, The Beach and St Colman's Church (all in the foreground) with Middlequarter, Fawnmore and the Westquarter commonage spreading to the horizon
Fig. 6.7:   Breakfast in the Doonmore Hotel dining room
Fig. 6.8:   View looking eastwards towards the main harbour of Inishturk from the road leading to the community centre
Fig. 6.9:   Inishturk dresser and delph in bed and breakfasts: (opposite page) Honora's dresser in the dining room; (right) Celia's delph displayed above the kitchen sink in view of bed and breakfast guests
Fig. 6.10:   Discarded dresser in the east end of Inishbofin
Fig. 6.11:   A closer view of the discarded dresser
Fig. 6.12:   Screenshot of a portion of Michael Fortune's Facebook page, with 89,000 followers
Fig. 6.13:   Detail of jugs on the Doonmore Hotel's dresser, including a blue transfer-printed Melrose pattern vessel, produced by Barkers and Kent Ltd in Staffordshire, England (1889–98; Godden mark 264, 266; Kowalsky and Kowalsky mark B177, B180)

TABLES

Table 2.1:   Location, age and counts of ceramic (n=1,232) and glass (n=327) vessels in dressers recorded in this study

Table 2.2:   Location, context and counts of ceramic (n=365) and glass (n=67) vessels recorded outside of dressers for this study

Table 2.3:   Transcription of Inishbofin parish records for 1870 baptisms from May to July

Table 2.4:   Transcript of 1867–9 marriage records from Inishbofin parish registry

Table 3.1:   Counts and percentages of delph by vessel form

Table 4.1:   1855 Griffith's Valuation to assess land and holdings of Inishark village, owned by Henry Wilberforce

Table 4.2:   Minimum Number of Vessel (MNV) counts for seven excavated houses on Inishark

Table 4.3:   Minimum Number of Vessel (MNV) counts for excavated Houses 8 and 57 on Inishark

Table 5.1:   Maker's marks by country of origin on ceramic vessels (or matching sets of vessels) in ethnographic dresser and delph assemblages

Table 5.2:   Summary of manufacturer origin by country, popular vessel forms, and most frequent decorative motifs and techniques through time

Acknowledgements

I learned a tremendous amount from all of the participants in this research project, and I owe everyone involved profound thanks and appreciation for their generosity, hospitality, patience and indulgence in gifting to me their expertise in dressers, delph and homes. The participants shared their wondrous heirlooms with me, along with insights into their heritage and hopes for the future. While specific participants in the study necessarily remain anonymous to maintain the ethical standards of anthropology, I am able to thank the dozens of people who welcomed me and my team to Inishbofin and Inishturk over the last decade. Not only did they help make this research possible, but they enriched our lives with friendship, laughter, amazing food and support.

Inishbofin's Doonmore Hotel, the Dolphin Hotel and Inishbofin House Hotel have housed us over the years, offering us a base to explore the islands. I greatly appreciate staff members' enormous work, hospitality, patience and willingness to accommodate archaeological and ethnographic research needs. Over the last several years we have rented wonderful cottages from Tommy Burke, Cathy Coyne, Marie Coyne, Maureen and Brian Hamilton, and Frances Ní Gráinne and Kieran O'Halloran. We have also stayed in lovely bed and breakfasts, hosted by Mary Day Lavelle, Emma Cunnane, Eimear Goggins, Mary Jo Prendergast and Mary Catherine Heanue. The staff at the Inishbofin Community Centre consistently offered support for the larger archaeological team over many years, and I thank Kevin Abeyta, Brenda Burke, Gráinne Coyne, Mary Day Lavelle, Hugh McMahon, Ann Prendergast, Simon Murray, Tuuli Rantala, Imelda Reidy and Margaret Schofield for their generosity, logistical help, and space to process artefacts from excavations and host community events.

Several excellent establishments kept my family, my team members and me fed while working on this research. Profound thanks go to the staff at the Doonmore Hotel and Murray's, The Galley, Inishwallah, The Saltbox, Day's Tea Shop,

Dolphin Restaurant, The Beach and Inishbofin House Hotel. Tremendous thanks go to the Inishturk Community Centre where I ate many lovely meals with one of the most glorious views in Ireland. Upstairs Downstairs in Clifden provided wonderful breakfasts, lunches and snacks over the years, and the Clifden Bookshop has always provided a welcoming and inspiring place to browse and acquire books on Connemara. We could not have survived without the Bofin Shop, now in the community centre, and we thank John Adams, David Anderson, Gráinne Coyne, Enya Day, Imelda Reidy and Annieka Ward for their service and logistical support over the years.

For transportation to and from Inishbofin, Inishturk and neighbouring islands we rely on Inishbofin Ferry's services. I thank Charlie, Dermot, Dylan, Harry, Kitty, Luis, Nikola, Pat and Seamus Concannon, and their staff and crew members, for excellent and dependable service on the main ferries and the fast ferry. This research could never have happened without their support. I also thank Jack Heanue for bringing us to and from Inishturk on his mail runs to Cleggan. Over the years, Sky Taxi and O'Neill Taxi of Clifden and Justin Mortimer of Letterfrack offered excellent transportation service to and from Dublin and Galway to Cleggan and around Clifden, getting us from point A to B safely and with lovely conversations. They were often our first welcome back and final farewell to Connemara, and I cannot thank them enough. CityLink also provided essential transportation for us and our team members for many years.

I truly appreciate the assistance of several people in documenting dressers and delph over the years: Nicholas Ames, Kat Chesson, Ryan Lash, AnnMarie Lindzy, Sara Morrow, Katie O'Halloran, Katie Shakour and Rachel Tracey all took turns in carrying cameras, photographing delph, taking notes, holding ledger pages and chatting with participants.

Over more than a decade many people in Inishbofin, Inishturk and Clifden have graciously welcomed us into their homes, businesses and lives, offering us friendship, lively conversation and support for our research. Enormous and enthusiastic thanks are due to Tommy Burke; Simon Murray and Mary Ward; Aileen Murray; Andrew Murray and Donna Dever; Patrick Murray and Roisin Pryce; Fiona Murray; Audrey and Michael Murray; Caroline Coyne and Dermot Concannon; Nikola and Pat Concannon and family; Seamus Concannon and Michelle Carey; Ann Prendergast and family; Margaret Schofield and Michael Joe O'Halloran; Mary Jo Prendergast;

Mary Catherine Heanue and family; Michael John and Mary Ann O'Toole; Nora Faherty; Emma Cunnane and Aidan Day; Alice O'Halloran; Mary Day Lavelle and family; Francis and Kathleen O'Halloran and family; Adrian Herlihy, Orla Day and family; John Adams; Marie Coyne; Orla Smithwick, Declan Sheppard and family; James and Patsy Coyne (in fond memory) and family; Kartika Menon and Austin Coyne; Mirella Murray; Declan O'Halloran and Olive Brennan; and Margaret Lavelle and all the other island nurses over the years.

As a relative newcomer to post-medieval archaeology and post-medieval pottery studies, several experts have listened to my queries and answered my questions, provided advice and encouraged my exploration of dressers and delph. Listing them in alphabetical order, I thank Nick Brannon, Tommy Burke, Caroilin Callery, Meagan Conway, Marie Coyne, Anthony Donoghue, Maria Franklin, Erin Gibbons, Audrey Horning, Ned Kelly, Claudia Kinmonth, Ryan Lash, Rosa Meehan, Franc Myles, Kieran O'Conor, Rachael Ritchie, Krysta Ryzewski, Katie Shakour, Rachel Tracey and Laurie Wilkie.

I thank Tony Moore on behalf of the estate of Padraic Colum for permission to use the poem 'The Fire Bringer' and remember his late wife Clíona Ní Shuilleabháin, grandniece of the author. I am likewise very grateful to Eleanor Wilner for permission to use part of her poem 'Emigration', which inspired me to think about those who waved farewell to their loved ones as they departed for other shores.

Several images were reproduced courtesy of the following institutions and individuals: Jack Yeats' *The Country Shop* (1912) © Estate of Jack B Yeats. All rights reserved, DACS / ARS 2023; Anthony Carey Stannus, *An Irish Interior*, (1860s) © National Museums of Northern Ireland Ulster Museum; photograph of Francis Livesay's *By the Fireside, Co. Mayo* (1875) © deVeres 2011; photograph of Basil Bradley's *Irish Cabin—Spinning* (no year) © Christie's, 1994; Photographs from Deer Park Farms replica medieval house (2011) © Christopher Lynn and Jacqueline McDowell, Northern Ireland Department for Communities, Human Environment Division; Tommy Burke leading a heritage walking tour (2025) © Ryan Lash (2025); Late Iron Age house and site reconstruction (1999) © Eoin Grogan 1999, *Mooghaun*, The Discovery Programme; *Inishbofin, Co. Galway – Interior – Doonmore Hotel*, 1989, Fáilte Ireland Tourism Photographic Collection, Dublin City Library and Archive; Liam Lyons photograph *Inishturk Currach Builder John Joe O'Toole* (1992) Liam Lyons Photographic Archive in County Mayo

Library and Fidelma Lyons; sale advertisement for Inishbofin and Inishark (1874), governmental correspondence about the Inishark pier (1885), census records (1851 and 1911), and Ordnance Survey Map (1838) reproduced by kind permission of the Director of the National Archives of Ireland; Inishbofin Parish records (1868–1870, 1888, 1889–1891) National Library of Ireland; photographs documenting the forced abandonment of Inishark (1960) © Getty Images; Valuation records and maps (1856–1860, 1921) © Tailte Éireann; film stills of currach making (2019) © Ian Kuijt and William Donaruma; photographs of Inishbofin, Inishark, Clifden, and Inishturk (1995–2022) © Ian Kuijt; anthropological research photographs (2008–2022) © Cultural Landscapes of the Irish Coast, University of Notre Dame. Funding for the ethnographic and archaeological research was provided by the John Tynan family, Wenner-Gren Anthropological Foundation, National Science Foundation, and the University of Notre Dame's Franco Family Institute for the Liberal Arts and the Public Good, Keough-Naughton Institute for Irish Studies, Nanovic Institute for European Studies, and Office of Research. Financial support for publication came from Notre Dame's Franco Family Institute and the Nanovic Institute for European Studies. Several generous friends read earlier drafts of parts or the entire manuscript, helping me immensely to refine the narrative, correct errors of fact, and clarify the scope of this story about homemaking. In particular, I owe Tommy Burke, Ian Kuijt, Ryan Lash, Ciarán Ó Mathúna, Meagan McDonald, Simon Murray, Franc Myles, Diarmuid Ó Giolláin, Katie Shakour and Rachel Tracey profound thanks for their careful reading and insightful suggestions to improve the book. Likewise my colleagues at Notre Dame helped me to hone this narrative through several public lectures, chats in offices and at dinner parties and receptions. In particular, this research could not have been possible without the assistance, astute listening and workshopping of ideas by Mary O'Callaghan, Aedín Clements, Diarmuid Ó Giolláin, Donna Glowacki, Ian Kuijt and Mark Schurr.

Lastly, I offer profound thanks and appreciation to my family, especially Ian Kuijt, Kaatje Chesson and Dianne and Ralph Chesson, who have nurtured my passion for investigating how people use their possessions, heirlooms and spaces to craft homes for the present and future.

Image Permissions

Copyrighted images courtesy of:

Christie's: 4.6

Pat and Nikola Concannon: 5.20

Crown Department for Communities, Historic Environment Division, Northern Ireland: 1.12, 1.13, 1.14, 1.15, 1.16

Cultural Landscapes of the Irish Coast Project, University of Notre Dame: 2.13, 2.23, 2.25b, 4.1, 4.4, 4.7a, 4.7b, 4.12b, 4.16, 4.28, 4.29a, 4.29b, 4.30, 4.31, 4.32a, 4.32b, 4.33a, 4.33b, 4.34a, 4.34b, 4.35a, 4.35b, 4.36, 4.38, 4.39, 4.41, 4.43a, 4.43b, 4.44a, 4.44b, 4.45a, 4.45b, 4.46a, 4.46b, 4.47a, 4.47b, 4.48a, 4.48b, 4.49a, 4.49b, 4.50a, 4.50b, 4.51a, 4.51b, 4.51c, 4.52a, 4.52b, 4.52c, 4.53, 4.54, 4.55, 4.56a, 4.56b, 4.58, 4.59, 5.28b, 5.38

deVeres Art Auctions: 4.20

Marty Fahey: 6.5a, 6.5b

Fáilte Ireland Tourism Photographic Collection, Dublin City Library and Archive: 3.22a

Eoin Grogan: 1.8, 1.9

James and Susan Kelly of Peter J. Kelly & Sons, Westport: 2.32b, 5.21a, 5.21b

Ian Kuijt: 1.5, 1.6, 1.7, 1.10, 1.11, 2.1, 2.3, 2.6, 2.11, 2.14, 2.17, 2.24, 2.25a, 3.1, 3.6, 3.12, 4.3, 4.25, 4.37, 4.63, 5.34, 6.1, 6.2, 6.6

Ian Kuijt and Bill Donaruma: 6.3, 6.4

Ryan Lash: 2.10

Fidelma Lyons and the County Mayo Photographic Archives: 3.16

National Archives of Ireland: 2.9, 2.12a, 2.12b, 2.26a, 2.26b, 2.27, 2.29

National Gallery of Ireland: 5.18

National Library of Ireland: 2.4, 2.30, 2.31, 5.40

John and Sue Stanley: 2.32a, 5.19

Tailte Éireann, Irish Valuations Office: 2.8, 2.28

The Trustees of National Museums Northern Ireland: 4.19

1

An Anthropology of Homemaking in Western Ireland

You are not from here. You grew into it, stone by stone, plant by plant.
You knotted with it through marriage, through your longing,
and your soul sings here, knowing as many do
that home is not always the place your birth gives you.

Robyn Rowland[1]

W hat distinguishes a house from a home? How do we transform a building, like a house, into a place we feel, in our bones, is *our* home? As an archaeologist, I have always been fascinated by how people perform this piece of alchemy, converting an architectural space into a meaningful place that nurtures both body and soul. Countless poets, historians, novelists, sociologists, ethnographers, architects and cultural theorists have grappled with this profound human endeavour.[2] Combining archaeological and anthropological research, this book explores how some Irish people living today in island and coastal communities in western counties Galway and Mayo remake houses into homes that nourish them in all aspects of life by devoting time, finances, labour, materials and memories to personalise their place (Fig. 1.1). Michael's parlour hearth on Inishbofin (Inis Bó Finne – The Island of the White Cow) exemplifies the creative effort devoted to homemaking, with his handcrafted hearth surround embedded with local shells.[3]

Our homes speak to us from deep within ourselves, evoking a full spectrum of emotions, memories, desires and hopes for the future. Homes gather residents

1

and visitors throughout their lifetimes to accumulate personal histories, lived experiences, emotions, stories and possessions. As the quote from Robyn Rowland's poem 'Unbroken Stone in a Stubborn Sea – Epic of Inishbofin' describes, we craft homes from our experiences and histories. In turn, homes nurture us, our friends and our families. Homes grow, learn, and collect people, stories, histories, memories and our hearts' deepest desires: safety, stability, longevity, health and happiness. While this volume focuses on western Irish homes, we can apply the concept of homemaking more broadly to any place at any time someone establishes and works to maintain and improve a home.

A reader might then ask which critical aspects differentiate homemaking from housemaking and houses from homes, two questions residing at the crux of this book. The very nature of home expands beyond the walls enclosing a residence, encompassing more than the structure we inhabit and its furnishings. Any description of a home must include the places through which we move in our daily paces, sounds and scents of everyday life, people with whom we live and interact, and other creatures populating the world around us. Homes exude these rhythms of movements, interactions, emotions and memories in a dynamic relationship between living beings, landscapes, things and memories. They are simultaneously complex and simple: we know when we feel at home, and we know when we find ourselves outside of that context. That knowing emerges from a mental, sensual and emotional calculus in which our bodies, movements, senses and memories coalesce to produce an intrinsic knowledge that grows and shifts as we age and change, whether we live in one home for all of our life or move from one to the next.

Houses themselves cannot encompass all of these complicated and intertwined aspects of home because homes are not just an edifice: many people make their homes in other types of residences that are more or less permanently situated (for example, yurts and houseboats). Homes expand far beyond the walls of a residential structure, imbued with architectural, object and life histories situated within specific environmental contexts and cultural communities. Archaeologist Nicholas Wolff aptly describes homes as 'constituted by the cumulative weight of experience and the formative relationships that animate the spaces we inhabit. Home is the fulcrum of our daily existence, a fundamental means of relating to the world around us and establishing a sense of self; it is the distillation of dwelling.'[4] Homes thus encompass physical and social realms. In his 1970s study of a Northern Ireland community in County Fermanagh, folklorist Henry Glassie argues that community

Fig. 1.1: Michael's parlour hearth, whose surround was decorated with inlaid shells, and mantelpiece displaying delph and other belongings

is the space connected by hearths. For him, the hearth symbolises one of the most crucial anchor points in homes, both in the literal sense of the building which someone inhabits and of the community in which they reside and participate.[5] This more expansive understanding of home concurs with what I learned in talking with participants in this project: home is never separated from the wider community and countryside in village, island or town spheres.[6]

The concept of homemaking, and not housemaking, engages with the diversity of ways people inhabit and dwell in places that they make, inhabit and maintain for future generations, whether we speak about a prehistoric stone hut, medieval cashel or crannóg, early twentieth-century cottage or twenty-first-century residence. The frame of homemaking affords us the ability to consider home both at larger community and smaller, more focused spheres, such as specific rooms or spaces within a residential building, affording an essential flexibility of scope: people inhabit space in multiple ways simultaneously – a chair, placed in a room within a building, situated in a neighbourhood or village, that is found within a region in a country.[7]

Viewing homemaking through multiple focal points exemplifies an anthropological approach to understanding human behaviour. At its heart, anthropology is a comparative discipline, and we learn a great deal from juxtaposing varying case studies to investigate similarities and differences. As an anthropologically trained archaeologist,[8] I have contemplated the alchemy of homemaking while excavating and studying ancient and not-so-ancient homes in Jordan, Italy, Ireland, Canada, Cyprus and the United States. Regardless of the vastly different cultural, chronological and environmental contexts, all the homes investigated included a suite of similar features: areas to prepare meals, places to store foodstuffs and tools, shelter from the elements, and places for residents and guests to gather together to share food and stories while building memories, relationships and histories. Drawing on decades of experience, I have learned that homemaking involves three key practices.[9] First, people invest physical and mental labour and resources to establish a home (placemaking).[10] Next, residents inhabit that place, filling it with belongings, movements and sounds of everyday life; in other words, they live and add their own experiences, memories and possessions (dwelling). Lastly, people work to maintain homes for the next generation into some uncertain but imagined future in which the home's residents will flourish (resiliency).[11] To homemake, people must store the necessary tangible materials, like food, tools, vessels, clothing and heirlooms, as well as the crucial intangible memories that index social connections, joyful events and even enduring loss. Thus, homes offer a place from which we may relate to the rest of humanity, simultaneously grounding ourselves and expanding outwards in our daily and seasonal movements, interactions and engagements with the wider world.

As a topic, homemaking encompasses an immense scope of scholarship from many disciplines. To narrow the focus onto a well-defined set of practices as a vehicle to explore the much larger set of behaviours, I chose a traditional homemaking practice: dresser- and delph-keeping, in which people stored material expressions of the past, present and in some cases aspired-for future to nourish their families. Historically and recently, these possessions, associated architecture and other material culture comprise a powerful part of a homemaking toolkit for some people in western Irish rural communities. However, these furnishings are not the only tools.[12] This book presents my insights and perspectives on how people turn their houses into homes by examining the materiality (the tangible aspects of homes: buildings, possessions, furniture, gardens and outbuildings) of this never-ending endeavour.

I utilise dressers, delph and other material culture in archaeological and ethnographic cases as focal points to build an anthropological approach to homemaking in western Ireland. As a practice, dresser- and delph-keeping incorporate a dizzyingly broad spectrum of ordinary and extraordinary activities, buildings, belongings and human interactions that establish homes as meaningful places to be maintained into some undefined future point. While presenting research on dressers, delph and other related furnishings, this book does not offer a social history of these items, nor does it aim to address regional and chronological variations in Irish dresser styles. Similarly, this volume does not present an ethnographic study of island and coastal communities in western Ireland, nor does it explicitly engage with the problematic mythologising of the west of Ireland as a sphere of Irish cultural authenticity.[13]

This book immerses readers into the material and intangible dimensions of placemaking, dwelling and resiliency through the lens of dressers and delph that Irish people living in small island and coastal communities in Connemara use to transform their residences into homes. To begin this exploration, I discuss the anthropological approach to materiality that grounds this study before transitioning to aspects more closely examined in the work: archaeological examples of Irish homemaking in the past; rationales for situating the study in western parts of counties Galway and Mayo and for focusing on dressers and delph; and a brief overview of the chapters in the book.

Thinking about homemaking: thing-heavy worlds, sticky belongings and difference

Archaeology is a magpie discipline employing a suite of methodologies and theoretical frameworks, frequently borrowed from humanities and social science disciplines. This book gathers insights from the disciplines of anthropology, sociology, archaeology, Irish folklore, social geography, oral history, history, vernacular architecture, decorative arts and material culture studies to explore western Connemara homemaking practices today and in the past. More specifically, I investigate how and why people acquired and used dressers, delph and other homemaking materials to craft strong attachments to places and possessions that enact the magic of homemaking. What types of spaces did residents need to create in their homes, and what kinds of furnishings facilitated this alchemical process? I take particular inspiration from ethnographers, social geographers, social theorists, folklorists and archaeologists investigating relationships between ourselves and our belongings, especially how we understand and engage with the world through and with those furnishings and how people inscribe dressers, delph and other belongings[14] with meanings, memories and values.[15]

We use our belongings as tools to complete specific tasks and live as the person we strive to be. Anthropologist Susan Kus reminds us that everyday possessions are more than simple functional tools:

> Microscale observances of awls, plants, spindle whorls, cooking fires, domestic space, baskets and other mundane materials in the archaeological record and in ethnoarchaeological studies allow us to understand that not only is the private the political, but that technology and the quotidian are the materials of our poetries and our philosophies.[16]

In a sense, we employ these possessions in the daily pursuit of a life well lived in terms of our well-being and our ethical footprint in our homes, communities and the greater world. Anthropologist Kenneth George asserts, 'Just as recognition and pursuit of the human good take place in language and action, so to[o] do they unfold in encounters with the material and visual.'[17] We fill our homes and lives with furnishings that act as powerful testaments to who we think we are and often who we want to be. Our belongings, however prosaic, help us express our personhood, tell stories, and connect with people and places that are important to us; in other words, these possessions allow us to engage in placemaking, dwelling and resiliency.

Archaeologist John Robb argues that once Neolithic people began building homes and villages more than 6,000 years ago, life became more 'thing-heavy'.[18] Human beings accumulated tools for building, farming, fishing and herding; ceramic vessels and tools to make those pots, furniture, baskets, grinding stones, ropes, jewellery and clothing. The earliest farmers and herders raised livestock and built houses, fences, storage sheds, barns, kilns and forges, filling each of these places with the material necessities of everyday life. People's relationships with things, animals, buildings and the wider landscapes in which they lived fundamentally shifted.

This connection between a place we call home, things, landscapes and ideas features heavily in anthropology because human beings engage with material objects as both mediators in and tools of social interactions.[19] In other words, our possessions can carry a variety of meanings, and each person may engage differently with that potential set of meanings depending on personal history and cultural context. For example, belongings in our homes signify in several ways: pointing to something else, as smoke from a chimney indicates a fire lit within the hearth (thing as index); standing as a sign of some future event, as a doormat on the threshold symbolises the welcome arrival of a guest or resident who wipes their feet and helps to maintain the cleanliness of the home (thing as symbol); and representing past experiences, as an Irish pound coin may represent economic life and networks before the Republic of Ireland adopted the euro currency (thing as icon).

Cultural theorist Sara Ahmed proposes that the potent ability of objects to act as signs and carry emotions, feelings, memories and associations demonstrates a quality of 'stickiness': our possessions hold the power to affect us. An object that may make us happy, sad or anxious may also continue to evoke that emotion long after our initial encounter. Moreover, that feeling or memory may 'stick' to other associated objects:

> We are moved by things. And in being moved, we make things. An object can be affective by virtue of its own location (the object might be *here*, which is *where* I experience this or that affect) and the timing of its

appearance (the object might be *now*, which is *when* I experience this or that affect). To experience an object as being affective or sensational is to be directed not only toward an object, but to 'whatever' is around that object, which includes what is behind the object, the conditions of its arrival.[20]

Thus, if we furnish our homes with ordinary and extraordinary belongings that carry memories and ideas, they may affect our emotional state of being, for good or ill. Those feelings or memories may 'stick' to other things around that possession or to the very place in which it is situated. As we move through our lives, the stickiness of those meaningful furnishings may fade or even disappear (we no longer feel happy, sad or frustrated when we see a specific thing, as we always have), or that set of feelings may intensify through time. Sticky belongings make us feel and remember by telling stories, and some may tell these stories better than others. Archaeologist Siân Jones speaks of the 'voicefulness' of objects and their potent ability to evoke relationships with past places and peoples.[21] In other words, some of our possessions resonate more loudly and clearly with people, depending on the physical, chronological and cultural setting, differing in content and potency from person to person and through time. Citing this strong connection between people and their belongings, archaeologists Jane Webster, Louise Tolson and Richard Carlton suggest that belongings themselves can act like interviewers, eliciting stories and memories.[22]

In our thing-heavy worlds, homemakers utilise sticky, voiceful materials to furnish homes and establish a sense of style, personality and hominess. In personalising homes, people present elements of themselves to visitors and residents alike. For instance, Ellen's dresser greets anyone entering her kitchen on Inishbofin (Fig. 1.2). Built in 1999 by Westport craftsman Tony O'Toole, this varnished dresser fits perfectly into the room.

Despite its recent vintage and smaller size, the dresser ably embraces its multiple functions. Ellen displays heirlooms that belonged to her parents and grandparents; her children's, nieces' and nephews' medals, trophies and artwork; and family photographs of loved ones, some still alive and others no longer with us. Each belonging contains one or more stories, thereby linking past to present (Fig. 1.3): her grandfather's eye-wash vessel, her grandparents' lustreware glass milk jug and sugar bowl used for station mass when it occurred in their home, her grandparents'

Fig. 1.2: Ellen's dresser, filled with objects connected to her family's past, their present life and hopes for the future

teapot, and family photographs. The pocketknife recalls her maternal grandfather to mind strongly, recounting that he used it mostly for cutting tobacco. In her mind's eye, she sees him holding his pocketknife while reaching into his pocket as he prepares to smoke his pipe: 'It's pretty worn. I remember watching him do it [cut tobacco], and he sharpened it on a stone on the wall.'

These sticky possessions celebrate Ellen's ancestors' perseverance and her family members' dreams and ambitions today. These heirlooms index important occasions, such as hosting a station mass in their home, which would have garnered

Fig. 1.3: Heirloom objects on Ellen's dresser: (a) lustreware milk jug and sugar bowl from the 1930s–40s; (b) green eye-wash glass dated to 1930s; (c) teapot from Price Kensington Potteries, Longport, UK, 1962 onwards; (d) her grandfather's pocketknife

esteem within the community, as well as everyday acts of hospitality, like serving tea to visitors. Anchored by the dresser, Ellen's kitchen acts as the heart of this home, collecting memories, telling stories and providing nourishment and an arena for family members to reconnect. On the wall above the kitchen table, family photographs are hung of her husband and sons fishing and of the well-preserved ruins of her family's ancestral home on Inishark (Inis Airc[23] – Island of the Piglet or Island of Earc, a personal name). The room hums with life's necessities: food and the tools to prepare it tidily stored on shelves or in the presses lining one wall; appliances for cooking and food storage; and a place to gather for meals to talk over the day.

The powerful combination of these memories, senses of heritage, stories about the past, and the mundane, tangible necessities of life transforms Ellen's house into a home. Her family home, like many others, gathers together the humble and voiceful belongings we need every day, including tools, food, storage spaces and clothing, and bundles them metaphorically within an ever-increasing blanket of personal experiences, memories, emotions, stories and a family's heritage within the broader community. These stories traverse time and space, linking people together through a history of endurance and communicating the resiliency of family members to meet life's challenges.

Recently, archaeologists have attempted to include past peoples' senses and lived experiences into scholarly understandings and reconstructions of the past. As a trailblazer in sensory archaeology, Susan Kus called for archaeologists to pay attention to lived experience and what she called 'sensuous human practice' in 1997.[24] Her research focused on the emergence and fluorescence of a seventeenth- to nineteenth-century AD state in central Madagascar. At that time in archaeology, researchers normally investigated the rise of state societies from a top-down approach by focusing on governmental buildings, large temple complexes, palaces and massive infrastructure (e.g. fortification walls, irrigation systems and roadways). Instead, she urged archaeologists to include an ethnographic sensibility by considering how a state forms from the bottom up by investigating regular people's everyday lives in their homes, surrounded by belongings:

> Doing ethnography not only helps one to appreciate the potency of cultural meaning in ritual activity, but also allows one to understand how such meaning is dependent upon the taken-for-grantedness of daily

activities and how it is firmly rooted in personal experience. The house is comfort and refuge and order. The family is the source of identity and ultimate source of both support and obligation. One comes to understand the intense pride and satisfaction, as well as relief, of the extended family as they view the fruits of their arduous labor in the slowly accumulating piles of rice at harvest time, and how the sense of family well-being is linked to such cooperative ventures that exhaust the body physically but fill the senses. With the end of the harvest season come festivities of marriage and of thanksgiving to the ancestors for intercessions in the health and wellbeing of the family. There is not only music and company at such celebrations, but also copious servings of 'rice with much grease'. Through ethnographic fieldwork that demands patience and participation, one comes to have some appreciation of the positive sensuality and poetry of other lives.[25]

Kus encouraged us to think seriously about how people experienced and met change in their lives, both at the level of sweeping political developments in a region and in the daily and seasonal rhythms of life in local communities. Her approach highlights the material aspects of everyday life and strong connections to how we feel, think and interact with other people with and through our possessions and places. Her notion of sensuous human practice lays the groundwork for more recent approaches to understanding the connections between people's thing-heavy lives, sticky and voiceful belongings, and daily life.[26]

From this brief discussion of how we can think about belongings affecting us, I want to emphasise three key points that will feature prominently in this book about Irish homemaking, dressers and delph. First, context and people's personal histories influence how a thing or space resonates with them. Different people may encounter the exact same object or place that evokes completely different ideas or memories. Context may also shape how someone engages with an object and the ideas it may awaken. From individual life experiences and resources emerge personalised engagements with things, and therefore how we use those furnishings in our homes and what emotions and recollections they inspire will also vary.[27]

Second, belongings and their different sets of meanings involve people's relationship to time: indexing something in the present (a blazing fire in the hearth), symbolising something in the future (a visitor's or family member's arrival at a home), and being an icon of times past (the Republic of Ireland economy before shifting to the euro currency).[28] In this way, everyday possessions, like delph and dressers, act as both storytelling devices and time-travelling machines, invoking memories of the past, experiences of the present and hopes for the future. Each dresser or piece of delph possesses a unique biography, combining disparate origins as distinct raw materials to the belonging's crafting, use and eventual disposal. The place where a dresser or piece of delph resides and the people interacting with it also embody specific life histories, present existences and future potentials. A possession's stickiness and voicefulness help people travel in their minds through time and across space to consider a person's metaphorical, literal and possibly even metaphysical place in the world.

Lastly, just as everyday life involves the risk of failure, misstep or unintended consequences along with successes and triumphs, so too do people's use of their belongings to tell stories and recount memories.[29] Symbolic associations with an object may vary from person to person, generation to generation or place to place. The series of decisions involved in furnishing a home with certain belongings to achieve a particular feel or style may resonate as successful with one person while failing entirely with another. Moreover, we change as we age, experience new events and confront new challenges, and grow into these places we make for ourselves – we grow into difference. For instance, the goals, resources and context of furnishing one's home at twenty-five may differ vastly from the scope of homemaking at forty-five or sixty-five years of age, even within the same building.[30]

Despite these shifting parameters of placemaking and storytelling, we want our homes to be resilient and offer a safe place to endure life's vicissitudes. My perspective on homemaking and difference draws from my engagement with many US-based Black feminist writers, cultural theorists and poets, including bell hooks and Barbara Smith. Inspired by bell hooks, archaeologists Whitney Battle-Baptiste, Maria Franklin, Nedra Lee, Annalise Morris and Laurie Wilkie have written of homeplaces as powerful sources of inspiration and profound testaments to the strength and resiliency of African and African American ancestors to endure centuries of oppression, enslavement and racialised structural violence.[31]

Seeing through the lens of homeplace and difference, I think about homemaking as an enterprise that requires making and maintaining meaningful places through the labour of our bodies, minds and hearts. To use anthropological terms, this ongoing endeavour requires people to engage in placemaking, dwelling, memory work (making, curating and sharing memories), and resilient and sustainable practices. Employing the tools and resources local to them in any given cultural context, people strive to craft a durable and enduring safe place for themselves and their family and community. This homemaking toolkit finds expression in diverse ways in different places, unfolding as universal in general and infinitely diverse in practice.

Residences as homes: diverse through time and across space

Both the ideals and realities of home encompass multiple, overlapping spheres, and thus, anthropologists often investigate the nature of homemaking from many angles, one of which is a physical abode. From the earliest times thousands of years ago, a residence fulfilled many necessary functions for survival: shelter for occupants, storage for food and tools, a place to prepare and eat meals, and a space in which and from which to interact with the broader world. Homes as dwellings cannot be separated neatly from the biological necessities of life, encoding cultural ideas about how to be a human being in any given context. When people build or move into houses, they draw upon established ideas of how a home needs to be organised, types of necessary furnishings, spaces or features to hold these possessions, and which people belong where. Speaking of vernacular architecture, Henry Glassie asserts that

> Buildings, like poems and rituals, realize culture. Their designers rationalize their actions differently. Some say they design and build as they do because it is the ancient way of their people and place. Others claim that their practice correctly manifests the universally valid laws of science. But all of them create out of the smallness of their own experience.
>
> All architects are born into architectural environments that condition their notions of beauty and bodily comfort and social propriety. Before they have been burdened with knowledge about architecture, their eyes have seen, their fingers have touched, their minds have inquired into the wholeness of their scenes. They have begun collecting scraps of experience without regard to the segregation of facts by logical class. Released from the hug of pleasure and nurture, they have toddled into space, learning to dwell, to feel at home.[32]

Glassie notes that even before formal training, architects have already accrued a lifetime's experience with architectural design, theory and practical engagement. All people can be considered experts in this realm, drawing on personal history of living within and surrounded by homes in a specific cultural context. We understand which spaces need to be in a home, how the home should be organised, and what types of furnishings are required to make a home 'work'. Even if we may not understand the engineering and architectural intricacies of physically constructing a residence, we all possess a wealth of lived experience within them and thus have definite ideas about what they mean to us. Homes, then, are a form of material culture, which Glassie defines as culture-made-material.[33]

Thus, homemaking is grounded, literally and figuratively, in culture as an ongoing and emerging process. I like to think of homemaking as a verb, 'to homemake', a continual set of behaviours we perform for ourselves, families, friends, neighbours and community. How we design and outfit our homes speaks to us and any visitors about our access to resources, style, sense of aesthetics, and our values of hospitality, generosity and belonging. As our ideas about homes shift, we adopt, adapt and invent new homemaking practices while moving through the daily, seasonal and annual rhythms of our lives.[34] This intricate connection between culture and homes as meaningful places materialises in the first stages of construction and extends throughout the life history of a home as inhabitants settle in, renovate and dwell. Homemaking takes effort, labour, funds and thought, whether in the past or today. Moreover, homes emerge from a continuing engagement of people, place, local environment, and personal histories and tastes.[35]

More than a century of anthropological, sociological, archaeological and folklore research demonstrates that how we homemake varies widely from culture to culture across space and time.[36] Yet in all places, a home's specific physical and symbolic elements emerge from the here and now: the crucible of cultural traditions, local histories, technological know-how, access to materials and an understanding of how to be a person in a specific community. Even with persistent challenges of inequality and people's varying abilities to acquire materials and land to build houses and outfit their dwellings, our sense of home resides literally and figuratively in culturally constructed ideas particular to place and time.

Frequently, the never-finished aspect of homemaking finds realisation in how we furnish our residences, and homewares sections of many stores in North America and Europe exemplify the influence of culture on our ideas of home. Consumers

Fig. 1.4: Wall art for sale in a Mishawaka, Indiana home crafts shop

may choose among an extraordinary variety of furnishings, often displaying idealised messages about the nature of home: 'Home Is Where You Hang Your Hat', 'Home Sweet Home', 'Home Is Where the Heart Is' or 'A House Is Not a Home Without Paw Prints' (Fig. 1.4). These signs demonstrate Glassie's idea that homes truly are forms of material culture, combining the possessions of our everyday lives with cultural ideas of who we want to be and what we believe a home should feel like to us and visitors.

As an endeavour, homemaking involves both physical and cultural labour to make a meaningful place and an enduring commitment to nurturing that place and the people who dwell there, often over many generations. While building materials, tools and construction techniques differ from place to place, overarching tasks necessary to homemaking, including establishing an essential-to-life place with storage and living spaces and maintaining that place over generations, remain broadly the same. Beyond constructing, renovating, organising and outfitting a place, considerable amounts of intangible labour contribute to turning that place into a home, including nourishing intensive social aspects that coalesce through daily human interactions. Stories and memories arise through collective food preparation and meals; cooperative work in daily tasks inside and outside the home; relaxing with friends and family members; celebrating milestones like births, weddings and personal accomplishments; engaging in disputes and arguments; and mourning the loss of loved ones. We personalise our homes with furnishings, decorations and belongings to organise and utilise the space as best we can. We grow houseplants, bring pets into our lives, maintain gardens, argue and laugh with each other and entertain family members and friends. In our daily tasks, we constantly and actively energise our homes with routine movements and personal interactions. We refresh or even remake the home by restocking supplies, cleaning, reorganising and renovating over time. In extraordinary moments of celebration or loss, our homes act as arenas for knitting together community. As Rowland's poem suggests, we weave ourselves into our homes, attaching significant memories of life's triumphs and tribulations to home as an ever-growing and continually changing physical, mental and spiritual place.

At the University of Notre Dame, I teach an introductory course called The Anthropology of Your Stuff, and the first assignment requires students to design a future home for themselves. Students choose at what age to reside in that home, the specific location, whether it will be a detached or semi-detached residence or a flat, and its occupants. Students specify building materials, organise the space, provide details on the furnishings, and speak to the home's feel and stylistic dimensions, describing choices to make this space a meaningful home in a chosen future. Each semester, students initially approach this topic uncertainly and without confidence. By the end of this assignment, they recognise their own expertise as users of homes and consumers of the materials within them, developing a sense of style and taste, and an ability to discern which elements of the home speak most powerfully to each student.

Many ethnographers and archaeologists in Ireland and elsewhere have described how people make and maintain homes – and how they did so in the past.[37] Ireland's archaeological and architectural heritage offers spectacular examples of this undertaking through the millennia. Before continuing with a discussion of Irish homes in the past, I offer three caveats. First, in comparing the past to the present, in no way do I intend to invoke the timelessness of rural Irish homes and their inhabitants or an innately primitive nature of western Irish islanders and rural peoples, both damaging tropes which Mark Gardiner, among others, has aptly critiqued.[38] Second, these comparisons should never lose sight of the modern reality of unhoused peoples, the realities of refugees seeking a home in today's uncertain and often frightening world, and the too-often unremarked privilege of possessing a home. In the United States, the state of being unhoused enacts a frightening cascade of disenfranchisement, marginalisation and negative health consequences. Globally, homelessness afflicts people everywhere, particularly at this time, with displaced people seeking a better life elsewhere. The sweeping scale of refugees risking life and limb to find a better home for themselves and their families speaks volumes to people's desire to homemake, whether in a refugee camp, government migrant facility or within a resettlement community.[39] While I celebrate homemaking in this book, I do not take its existence for granted in any context, past or present.

Third, anthropology as a comparative discipline seeks to understand the diverse ways of being human in any given place and time without effacing differences under the guise of some false sense of universality. Homemaking is an endeavour practised globally; however, appeals to universals should never compromise the glorious diversity of methods, values and beliefs emanating from this very human and cultural venture. An anthropology of homemaking centres on celebrating connections, not in erasing differences of cultural approaches to being a human in the world. With an eye towards those human connections, placemaking, dwelling and resiliency, we turn now to a brief discussion of Ireland's rich prehistory and history of homemaking.

Irish homemaking through time: making meaningful places

A brief survey of ancient and historic homes in Ireland demonstrates how people achieved the combination of satisfying functional needs arising from biology and economics while simultaneously nourishing the minds and souls of those residing within its boundaries. To understand homemaking in the past, archaeologists often begin their investigations with the building itself and the initial placemaking process: How was the house constructed? Where and how did the builders situate

Fig. 1.5: (a) View of Craggaunowen's crannóg in 1995; (b) tourists at exterior hearth next to the replica wattle and daub hut in the crannóg

the house within its local environment? What types of material did people use, and from where did these resources come? How much physical labour was required, and what types of expertise and tools were employed? Using a variety of methods, we can reconstruct the local climate, available resources and surrounding ancient landscape to determine the environmental setting of a house and the construction materials available to builders to make a home place.

Some of the best historical and archaeological evidence for placemaking in Ireland's past can be found in the medieval period, particularly crannógs: human-built islands on a body of water, accessed by raised causeways and enclosed by wooden fence lines. Early medieval people constructed these islands with a foundation of stone, wood beams and other materials gathered and transported from the local environment, an engineering feat requiring massive amounts of human labour and engineering expertise.[40] Early medieval villagers built structures, including houses and sheds, on these small islands and furnished these spaces with their belongings. Craggaunowen Castle and Crannóg Park in County Clare offers a 'Living History Experience' with replicas of houses and structures within a crannóg and a cashel.[41] Visitors to Craggaunowen today can cross the bridge onto a replicated crannóg, stoop to enter through the very small door to sit within a circular wattle and daub hut with a thatched roof and follow the wood enclosure surrounding this miniature island's farmstead (Fig. 1.5).

These replicas rely on archaeological evidence to provide details of the building blocks of these homes, especially the architectural footprint of excavated buildings. While excavating, archaeologists record the locations of features, like hearths, storage pits, postholes (into which wooden beams were secured in the ground) or other installations inside and outside of structures to understand the organisation of residential space. Over the past fifteen years, the Cultural Landscape of the Irish Coast Project (CLIC), led by Dr Ian Kuijt of the University of Notre Dame in the US, has surveyed villages and excavated homes on the County Galway islands of Inishark and Inishbofin. One of our primary objectives centres on understanding the floor plan, spatial layout and extent of the interior and exterior spaces of buildings we survey and excavate. For example, in the excavations of two late eighteenth- and early nineteenth-century homes at Inishbofin's abandoned village of the Poirtíns, the partially exposed stone walls of these homes helped us determine where we needed to excavate (Fig. 1.6).

In a more ancient example, Figure 1.7 shows the 1995 excavation of a Late

Fig. 1.6: CLIC archaeologists excavating an AD 1780–1820 house at the Poirtíns, Inishbofin: (a) clearing collapsed building materials to expose the floor of Room A, recording elevations on wall stones (background) and uncovering a blocked doorway (foreground); (b) clearing stone rubble to expose Room A's floor and a stone wall creating a byre

Fig. 1.7: Archaeologist carefully exposing the floor of the Late Iron Age House 2 adjacent to the upper cashel in Mooghaun Fort, County Clare in 1995. Note the stone foundations for thick walls and the storage pit located just in front of the bucket.

Fig. 1.8: Reconstruction of the cluster of Late Iron Age houses within and outside the Upper Cashel at Mooghaun Fort, including Hut 2 located to the right of the cashel (Artist David Hill)

Iron Age (early first millennium AD) house (House 2 in Site D) at Mooghaun Fort, County Clare. The stone foundations of the roughly oval hut behind the archaeologist and the small storage pit located directly in front of the bucket in the foreground can be seen. The house's internal dimensions were roughly 3 x 3.8 metres, with an entrance facing south.[42] The builders had local access to the stones for the walls and hearth, thatch for the roof, and wooden internal features like roofing beams, in-built storage bins, benches and beds.

This house was situated just outside Mooghaun's Upper Cashel, a small, circular stone enclosure that itself was ringed by two other much larger stone-built ramparts radiating out from the innermost enclosure now containing the site's viewing platform (Figs 1.8 and 1.9). These ramparts were initially constructed by the site's inhabitants during the Late Bronze Age, around 950 BC, as defensive structures surrounding their homes, fields and pastures. The excavators estimate that local people moved over 90,000 cubic metres of stone (or roughly 500,000 tonnes) to build these massive ramparts.[43]

The entire site of Mooghaun exemplifies the placemaking aspect of homemaking. The original Late Bronze residents, likely an influential or ruling family in the local area, directed this massive project of building ramparts, recruiting labourers from the surrounding region. Approximately 1,500 years later, people from the Late Iron Age reused the site to build homes, constructing two cashels and several stone houses within the bounds of the already existing middle and outermost ramparts built in

Fig. 1.9: Aerial photograph of Mooghaun Fort, with ramparts and cashels outlined (Photograph by Aoife Daly)

Labels on image: Langough hilltop enclosure; to Newmarket; car park; outer rampart; upper cashel; outer cashel; viewing platform; inner rampart; middle rampart; lower cashel; outer rampart

the Late Bronze Age. In both cases, they altered the very landscape surrounding their home, dedicating hours of labour and thousands of metric tons of stone to create this place.

Craggaunowen also offers a replicated cashel that illustrates how Mooghaun Fort's innermost cashel might have appeared during the early medieval period (Fig. 1.10).[44] In this replica, builders constructed a stone enclosure wall, covered with earth, and with a wooden palisade on top of it. Within this enclosure, visitors may stand within a stone house or a shed, sit at a shared hearth outside the houses, walk alongside the earthen embankment enclosing these houses and outbuildings,

Fig. 1.10: (top) View of Craggaunowen's replica cashel in 1995 from its exterior

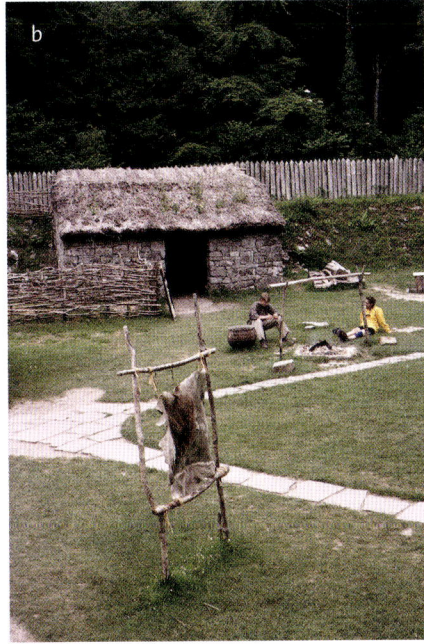

Fig. 1.11: Replica buildings and features within Craggaunowen's cashel in 1995: (a) entrance into replica stone hut; (b) replica rectangular stone building, exterior hearth and hide-curing rack

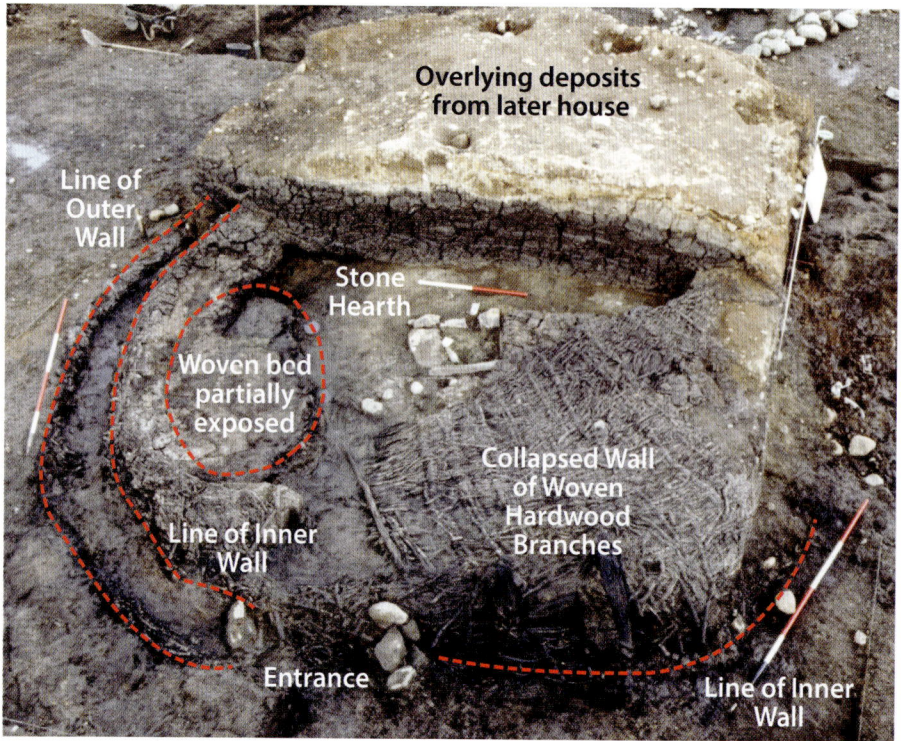

Fig. 1.12: Partially excavated early medieval house (Structure Eta) from Deer Park Farms, County Antrim. Note the double-walled construction, with space to pack insulating materials (Adapted from C. Lynn and J. McDowell, *Deer Park Farms*, Plate 7.15).

and get a sense of the scale and feel of life within this farmstead (Fig. 1.11). Like cashels, in other parts of the country, builders constructed enclosures of earthworks (called raths), with one or more concentric rings of earthen ridges surrounding a homestead with a single entrance into the compound.

While we may never know with certainty the details of why people dedicated their time, labour and effort to such massive placemaking endeavours as creating a crannóg, cashel or rath, archaeologists seek to learn how they managed these feats of engineering without modern, mechanical equipment that we may take for granted. Some researchers use a type of reverse engineering to replicate a house, often called experimental archaeology, which is a subset of the broader discipline of ethnoarchaeology (combining contemporary ethnographic methods with archaeological investigation to gain insights into the lives of past peoples). Analysing the archaeological record for details of technology, materials, size and organisation, we can determine how people built a house (or made a ceramic vessel, a stone knife, a bone awl or a metal needle) and then recreate that building or object.

In 2005, the Navan Centre in Armagh commissioned the archaeology team led by Christopher Lynn and Jackie McDowell to reconstruct an eighth-century early Christian dwelling based on several extraordinarily well-preserved early medieval buildings uncovered during excavations at Deer Park Farms in County Antrim (Fig. 1.12).[45] Based on what they learned by excavating several huts at Deer Park Farms, Lynn and McDowell's team gathered raw materials (in this case, straight hazel rods of the right length and thicker stakes for anchoring the woven walls, thatch and insulation), transported them to the buildings site, laid out the line of inner and outer walls, and established the location of the entrance. The archaeologists used replicas of early medieval tools to cut stakes and rods, and to collect insulating materials and thatch. The team began with the inner wall construction, sinking stakes into the ground and weaving the hazel rods around them (Fig. 1.13). At the desired height for the roof, the team shifted the angle of the wall inward, approximately 45 degrees, to create a pitched roofline. By this time, the outer wall was finished, and builders worked from the interior of the hut to weave the remainder of the roof (Fig. 1.14). Before roofing with thatch, they added insulating material between the outer and inner walls. The team thatched the roof using traditional techniques with replicas of early medieval tools (Fig. 1.15). Once the structure was completed, they built a central stone-lined hearth and finished the door with wood jams (Fig. 1.16). The houses at Deer Park Farms showed no evidence of using daub for insulation. Instead, the excavators propose that the inhabitants developed the double-walled construction technique for insulating their homes without covering the walls with daub.

By building a life-size replica of an early medieval house, team members learned what these houses looked like, the amount of effort and technical expertise required, and the feel of being within this type of dwelling. Increasingly, archaeologists strive to expand these types of public-facing opportunities for archaeological engagement with the general public. Experimental archaeology offers an excellent chance for non-specialists to participate in these types of endeavours. For instance, in 2015, students from the Centre for Experimental Archaeology and Material Culture at University College Dublin constructed their own early medieval roundhouse based on excavated examples from well-preserved sites like Deer Park Farms and Moynagh Lough in County Meath.[46]

(from left to right) **Fig. 1.13**: View of the inner wall from the replicated hut's interior, partway through construction; **Fig. 1.14**: View of the outer and inner walls from the hut's exterior, with the pitched roofline rising upwards; **Fig. 1.15**: Detail of the thatched roof over the woven roofline; **Fig. 1.16**: Finished replica of the eighth-century house at Deer Park Farms

Constructing replicas demonstrates that builders of ancient Irish farmsteads invested tremendous amounts of material, labour and expertise in the homemaking process. These experiments offer an opportunity to tangibly and experientially recreate the technical knowledge, the gathering and use of a large amount of building materials, and the immense investment in labour required to construct a farmstead in a crannóg, cashel or rath.

Archaeologists know that homemaking did not conclude with the initial construction of the place: homemaking requires people to dwell and interact within these places. For those contexts associated with historical sources, archaeologists can infuse their reconstructions of homes and daily life with information gleaned from texts and imagery. For instance, researchers of Ireland's early medieval period draw on rich documentary sources describing daily life. O'Sullivan and Nicholl argue that the organisation of early medieval settlements reflected the complex legal codes and cultural practices that governed the status of different categories of people living in or around these communities, including kings, lords, free commoners, tenants and enslaved people.[47] Differences from age, kinship and gender further influenced which types of people possessed access to spaces, materials, buildings and status within and outside enclosure sites like cashels and crannógs. These early

homesteads acted as bustling arenas for daily cooking chores, wool and textile production, blacksmithing, dairying, and tool and furniture making, all involving social interactions between people of varying status.[48] O'Sullivan and Nicholl describe how non-elite adult women and men, and likely children as well, shared many daily tasks, including ploughing, planting, harvesting and caring for livestock. They note that textual sources also designate women as primarily responsible for child-rearing, feeding the family and making textiles of various types; men, in turn, were primarily responsible for heavy labour in farming, blacksmithing, stonework and masonry, construction and carpentry.

Post-medieval archaeology, which investigates lifeways from the sixteenth century onwards, offers insights into homemaking and placemaking in the more recent past. Excavations of residential and industrial contexts contribute to our understanding of life in both urban and rural places and the complicated intersections of human labour, economic forces and political systems.[49] People's homes and their daily lives formed the foundation of these bigger spheres of interaction, and excavations of post-medieval residences and associated spaces demonstrated that people still engaged in activities centred around placemaking, dwelling and persevering.[50] Archaeologists also gain insights into the rhythms of everyday life within and around people's homes in the recent past through the autobiographies of rural people, such as those from the Blasket Islands.[51]

By many people's standards today, life in prehistoric, early medieval or more recent eras may have been very difficult, but it was no less rich than our own lives

Fig. 1.17: View of the main room of Patrick's home with its key elements (left to right): settle (in which Patrick sits to the left of the door), hearth, press, cooker and dresser

as we socialise, confront challenges, endure tragedy and celebrate triumphs. Glassie urges us to remember that ancient peoples produced art as well as the prosaic materials in their homes: music and musical instruments, paintings, carvings, textiles, and the profound pleasure of a well-ordered home:

> We have to strain to see the reality of the alternative through curtains of rhetoric, some dropped by the nostalgic, more by the apologists for capitalism. The old life was simple, we are told. Absurd. Life was anything but simple when people in small groups, interrupted by storms and epidemics and marching armies, managed to raise their own food, make their own clothing, and build their own shelter, while creating their own music, literature, art, science and philosophy.[52]

Fig. 1.18: (a) View of Patrick's early twentieth-century dresser and delph in an uninhabited home in Cashel; (b) detail of Arklow jugs, matching Eternal Beau plates and tureen, and Carrigaline milk jug on the bottom shelf

Ultimately, any reconstruction of the past requires us to recognise the humanity, richness and complexity of our ancestors' lives, however many generations back. Replicas and artistic reconstructions encourage us to engage our senses of sight, sound, smell and touch to offer a feel for past peoples' lives and bring the past alive. Reconstructions of the past invite people to suspend reality and use their imagination to place themselves in some long-gone setting and way of life in order to consider the intangible qualities of what makes a house a home. Today, these same senses and emotional resonances enrich our appreciation for our homes: the smell of good food, the soft, smooth touch of fabrics or wood furniture, the murmurs of voices or the sound of music. Dresser- and delph-keepers often recounted that they found immense pleasure and creativity in handling, cleaning and displaying delph and dressers as part of the homemaking process.

Why dressers and delph?

This book explores the complex interplay between our homes, possessions and our understanding of who we are and who we hope to be by focusing on homemaking in a specific case study: how people use Irish dressers and delph to transform houses into homes. I do not attempt to answer the question 'How Does a Home Feel?' because every home feels different. Instead, I strive to show how people in western Connemara use their belongings, especially dressers and delph, to make a home feel as they wish, be that welcoming, austere, edgy or even off-putting to others. This book describes how contemporary people utilise these furnishings to personalise homes and then compares these efforts today with archaeological evidence for nineteenth- and early twentieth-century homemaking from excavations in the historic village on Inishark.

In many ways, dressers and delph exemplify the sticky voicefulness of everyday belongings. Many dresser- and delph-keepers recounted that until thirty or forty years ago, dressers and delph graced the kitchens or sitting rooms of most western Irish homes. In older homes, especially those built before the mid-twentieth century, the main room contained the hearth for cooking and warmth, a dresser, table, chairs and stools, and perhaps a settle bed, bench or wardrobe for storage.[53] Glassie argues that an old Irish house's hearth and dresser acted as key features of order and welcome: 'The old house has two wishes, comfort and generosity. It holds them in balance between closed rooms and open kitchens, and symbolizes their easy coexistence on hearth and dresser.'[54] Together, hearths and dressers anchored the home, symbolising hospitality, generosity and constancy despite changing seasons and years.

In many old houses, this pairing of hearth and dresser endures. Patrick's old home in Cashel, County Galway offers a fine example (Figs 1.17 and 1.18). Dresser and hearth stand on opposite sides of the main room, embracing the room's contents like bookends. Upon entering the home, the first thing one encounters is the old dresser on the right, beyond which is a blue-painted door leading to one of the side rooms. Situated against the back wall, a small cooker with a hanging dresser for ready access to cooking tools and vessels stands adjacent to a wardrobe, in front of which a table has been placed. Turning more to the left, one sees a very large hearth with built-in stands supporting hot kettles and pans. On the far side of the hearth, another blue door leads into a bedroom. Turning again to face towards the front of the house, a generous window sits above a settle. Most of life's necessities and comforts abide within this room. Even though no one has resided in the house for many years, the feel of home still lingers – due primarily to the well-maintained dresser, its displayed heirlooms, the hearth and settle.

Like others in countless older homes, Patrick's dresser offers an extraordinary wealth of information about the life histories of this home and its former residents. Though the house was uninhabited at the time, Patrick had carefully covered the dresser shelves with plastic sheeting to keep the dust off the delph.[55] Patrick and his friend Francis recounted that the dresser originated with the construction of this house around 1914. They did not know if the residents acquired the dresser as a gift or made it themselves, but described that it was always part of the home. Plate by plate, jug by jug and shelf by shelf, Patrick's dresser and his delph tell intimate histories of his family's life in Cashel, evoking a rich and abiding sense of heritage. Matched sets of blue Finnish plates, green English plates and hexagonal tureens, and Johnson Brothers' Eternal Beau pattern plates and tureen, two Carrigaline milk jugs and four Arklow jugs testify to the dresser-keeper's aesthetic style and engagement with international markets and fashions in homewares through the early and mid-twentieth century.

Researching dressers and delph taught me to nourish a profound appreciation for the potency of people's everyday decisions to craft meaningful lives and overcome social, economic and political challenges, both great and small. Moreover, I discovered that the ways people use and fill dressers and furnish homes change through time, offering insights into shifting ideas of creating and maintaining a proper home, to uphold social, economic and moral responsibilities to oneself and one's family, and to preserve their sense of personal, community and even national identity.

Dressers, like the delph and other possessions held within, tell stories. People utilise the power of these sticky, voiceful belongings to make a place meaningful and full of memories arcing through time and across space to connect people. Dressers themselves evoke multiple ideas and culturally constructed ways of understanding the world. First, they symbolise hospitality, generosity, family histories and community heritage. Next, dressers index traditional (and now often changed) gender roles and valued contributions that men and women make, and made, to their island and coastal communities: especially men as boatwrights and carpenters to make dressers and women as orchestrators of home, overseeing cooking, baking, cleaning, weaving, gardening, milking cows, bringing water from wells and keeping dressers. Lastly, these furnishings stand as icons of the past, linked together with once-ubiquitous large open hearths. In other words, Irish dressers turn houses into homes by weaving together the tangible and intangible aspects of a family's and a community's history.

Dressers and delph, like Patrick's and Ellen's, also recount fascinating microhistories of their owners, families, the broader community in which they live(d), economic and social networks expanding outwards through emigration, migrant labour networks, and kinship connections spanning continents and oceans. These furnishings in Connemara homes represent material footprints of social relations in two spheres: (1) regional longstanding economic labour networks, including pathways of industrialised manufacturing and distribution of consumer goods, and the histories of international migration, and (2) local and family histories of marriages, deaths, christenings, graduations, moves, pilgrimages, visits from relatives who moved away, and other small and large happenings that enrich or challenge people throughout their lives. For dresser- and delph-keepers, these possessions offer anchoring points that strengthen a sense of self and fortitude to persevere through difficulties, including those at a personal level and those arising from region-wide social, economic, religious and political forces. For this reason, Stephen, a curator specialising in Irish art and furniture and working for an Irish American private collector, aptly calls dressers 'the furniture of the self'.

Thus, dressers and delph serve as both time machines and travel devices: their stories encompass the world, past and present, and welcome people into the embrace of a home grounded in one place and connected to many others. At the same time, these furnishings demonstrate how all consumption (the act of people acquiring goods through gift, loan, barter, serendipity or purchase, and then using and sometimes discarding those items) emerges from a specific time, place and sets of relationships.[56] When people consume goods from both local and distant sources, they infuse these belongings with meanings and values, personalising relationships with furnishings in a specific physical, historical and cultural Here. For me, this paradox of being simultaneously local and distant, and present and past, imbues dressers and delph with sticky, voiceful potency.

Moreover, studying dressers and delph refutes the denigrating tropes of marginality and impoverishment often applied to these communities and their inhabitants in the past and present. While inhabitants of western Connemara communities may have resided in seemingly remote areas, they nevertheless acquired and displayed goods similar to those living closer to seats of political and economic power. Participants in this project, including those long-departed individuals who created the archaeological remains we have excavated on Inishark and Inishbofin, acquire, use and discard possessions linked to global economic networks. Consumers evaluate popular regional trends to acquire, gift, display or store specific delph styles and vessel forms, acting as arbiters of good taste in a community.

Homemaking is a never-ceasing, emerging practice, and dressers and delph collections currently in use embody this constancy of change linked as they are to people's lives over their life course. Engagement with regional and global styles and good taste continues with today's dresser- and delph-keepers, who update parts of dresser ensembles over time, adding pieces as families grow and lose members to death or emigration, and evaluating new tastes and fashion trends. Dressers may be repainted in a new style or maintained with the older paint scheme remembered from the past. If delph-keepers display heirlooms outside of a dresser, they may shift pieces from one room to the next, add new belongings to the collection, and 'freshen up' displays of these pieces by swapping delph that has not been seen for a time. Dressers and delph are preserved to store aspirations and memories while paving a household's path to the future. In this way, there exists a great deal of flexibility for how dresser-keepers update their dressers by combining elements of the dresser's heritage with emerging elements of the hoped-for future.

Overview of volume

This book invites readers to consider Irish dressers and delph through an anthropologist's eyes. By combining traditional ethnographic and archaeological practices to analyse the built environment, craft production and consumption inherent in people's daily lives and homes, the work employs more socially oriented anthropological, folkloric and sociological research approaches. I strive to demonstrate that thinking about and through homes empowers readers to span multiple spatial and social spheres (bodies, houses, neighbourhoods, communities, kin groups and regions), temporal rhythms (moments, days, months, seasons, years, life histories and generations) and cultural realms (life course, gender, age, religion, migration, class, race, education, sexuality, politics and personhood) to build a richer understanding of different ideals of home and homemaking practices.

The volume's second chapter welcomes the reader to the western islands of County Galway (Inishbofin and Inishark) and County Mayo (Inishturk – Inis Turk, Island of the Wild Boar[57]), as well as the County Galway coastal communities of Clifden and Cashel. I offer a very brief history of these communities to situate this research and then describe the scope, goals, guiding research questions, methods and the types of participants in this ethnoarchaeological project. With that background context and methodological foundation set, the third chapter describes what I learned in studying dressers and delph in contemporary contexts, including homes and businesses. I present how people keep dressers and delph to ground homes, hotels, restaurants and rental cottages by telling stories about themselves, their families and communities. This chapter also demonstrates how people use these sticky, voiceful furnishings to maintain a sense of belonging, hospitality and heritage in western Irish communities.

The fourth chapter transports readers back in time to examine homemaking practices on Inishark in the nineteenth and early twentieth centuries, based on analysis of the village's archaeological, archival and oral historical records. I reorient our perspective from ethnography and the contemporary world to the archaeological past to explore how much we can learn about people's lives through the houses and belongings left behind. This chapter recounts how archaeologists read the architectural remains, excavated artefacts, oral histories and archival documents to reconstruct homemaking on Inishark. I begin with the buildings themselves, drawing on archaeological and documentary evidence, including valuation and census records, as well as ethnographic and folklore studies. When possible, I interleaf oral histories with these evidentiary lines to give a more human voice to our understanding of village life on Inishark and consider the life histories of homes on the island.

The fifth chapter compares the archaeological, archival, oral historical and ethnographic records to place the contemporary world of today and that of Inishark's past into conversation with each other. I present evidence to demonstrate how people use delph and other belongings to make and maintain connections across space and time and the various pathways dressers and delph took to arrive in these communities over the last two centuries. In considering how consumption patterns shifted through time, I discuss identifiable manufacturing origins, modes of arrival and changing trends of style and taste through time to consider how people attach stories, emotions and memories to pieces of delph and other heirlooms as part of their homemaking practices.

Finally, I discuss why people continue to keep dressers and delph as part of their homemaking endeavour in contemporary Ireland. I discuss the elements of dressers and delph that make them such powerful tools for homemaking, especially the ability to personalise how people use these possessions in a way that speaks specifically to themselves and their family history. These home furnishings act as powerful testaments to who we think we are or who we want to be. I conclude by discussing the future of dressers and delph in western Ireland and beyond by considering why community and family heritage, in this case materialised in dressers and delph, help people today to build a pathway to a sustainable future for themselves and their descendants, starting at home and expanding outwards into the broader world.

2

Dressers, Delph and Homemaking in Western Connemara

It's part of our heritage, isn't it? I'd love if somebody came to the door and said 'I'm O'Halloran, I'm from Pittsburgh, I'm from wherever I'm from, and my ancestors were from here [Inishark] or Inishbofin.' It's great to think that somebody can instil a passion for a place into someone, that maybe fifty, sixty, eighty, a hundred years down the line someone in that line will decide 'Yes, I'm going back to see this place.'

Ellen, visiting Inishark, 2012[1]

W hen Ellen speaks about this linkage between heritage and place, she highlights how strongly our personal histories may connect to specific places, even if we have never travelled there. I believe that part of this connection emerges from the weaving of history, places, landscapes, memories and people that anchor people's homes and contribute to the alchemy of homemaking. For the Dresser Project, focused on homemaking with dressers and delph, these sticky and voiceful places, buildings and belongings help forge and strengthen connections crucial to establishing and maintaining our homes.

One of the most common questions people ask about the Dresser Project is why I conducted this research in western Ireland. My answer is twofold. First, on Inishturk and Inishbofin, those connections and the appreciation for local heritage infuse every aspect of life, making these communities the perfect place for this project. While I am neither an islander nor Irish, Inishbofin, in many ways, feels like a home to me in Rowland's sense of growing into a place[2] (Fig. 2.1).

My relationship with home is complicated and finds its roots in my childhood and family, particularly my parents. My mother is a lifelong avid collector of pottery and early American rustic furniture. By collector, I mean to say that since the 1960s she has scoured every antique and thrift shop, flea market, estate and car boot sale and dilapidated barn hosting a sale throughout Virginia, North Carolina, South Carolina, Mississippi, Louisiana and Alabama. She has an excellent eye for deals and hidden gems that need only a bit of care to shine. My parents' home has always been filled with delph and furniture, including eighteenth- and nineteenth-century dressers and tall presses. My father served in the Navy, and we moved every three years from one military base to another in the southeastern United States. The common adage in military communities, 'you make your home where you are', taught me to find home wherever we settled. However, in military communities, a sense of transience lingers when thinking about home – home always carries a sense of being temporary and a knowledge that one will never sink deep roots into a house, place or landscape. Until my husband and I moved to the landlocked state of Indiana twenty-four years ago, I never lived more than six months away from the sea nor resided in any one place for more than four years.

Due to the combination of Ireland's wonderful archaeological heritage, my passion for pottery and old homes, the lovely people I have met over many years, and being on the ocean, Inishbofin speaks to me as one of my home places. Experiencing

Fig. 2.1: Tourists walking the Low Road towards Inishbofin's harbour and new pier

the visceral combination of glorious land- and seascapes, island community life, island heritage, amazing food and good friends over many years grounds me in a way I have never thoroughly felt in Indiana. Our privileged ability to spend roughly four weeks every summer on Inishbofin, with two of those weeks often camping on Inishark while conducting archaeological research, has earned us the status of regular visitors. More importantly, during these repeated sojourns we built stories of life on Inishark and Inishbofin for our family, especially revolving around our daughter: making lifelong friendships with Inishbofin children, learning to ride a bike, taking swimming lessons in the harbour, and embracing her independence. I believe these experiences and familial memories enhance our feelings about Inishbofin and often make it feel more like a home than Indiana. This strong connection to people, place and memories often fuels homemaking endeavours, as people reflect on the past to build their here-and-now with an eye towards the future.

Returning to the question of 'Why western Ireland?', the genesis of the Dresser Project emerged from my experiences of the gracious hospitality offered by many of Inishbofin's and Inishturk's residents with invitations to call in, take tea and chat. Welcomed into their homes, enjoying scones, cups of tea and the occasional hot whiskey, I saw many complete examples of nineteenth- and early twentieth-century pottery vessels in dressers, sitting on shelves and mounted on walls. These vessels captured my attention, allowing me to see what the bits and pieces of pottery sherds collected in our archaeological excavations would have looked like when originally brought as complete vessels to Inishbofin, Inishturk and Inishark some three or four generations past. Inishbofin's and Inishturk's hotels, cafes, pubs, bed and breakfasts and rental cottages display delph to customers, often in dressers, to evoke and invoke the island's heritage of hospitality and specific ideas about islanders' identities and histories. As storage receptacles of family and community histories, dressers and delph ground and enliven a home and imbue a business with a sense of hominess, hospitality and family connections. As readers will learn, the wonderful diversity of dressers and delph on these islands and in the County Galway mainland communities of Cashel and Clifden celebrate the heritage of their residents, demonstrating how ably these furnishings facilitate the alchemical process of homemaking. This chapter provides a brief overview of these communities and the research methods and specific objectives of this anthropological study of homemaking – to offer the reader a feel for the research area and how my team and I learned about delph, dressers and homemaking.

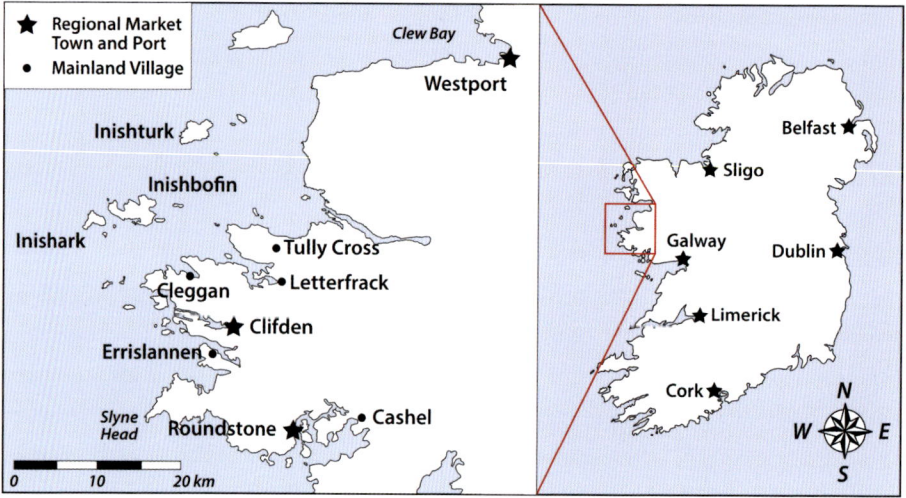

Fig. 2.2: Map of study region with places mentioned in the book

Island and coastal communities, landscapes, histories and homes[3]

My team (usually consisting of a graduate student, undergraduate student or a postdoctoral researcher and myself) spent several weeks each summer in island and coastal communities in western counties Galway and Mayo (Fig. 2.2). Most of our time we documented dressers and delph in Inishbofin and Inishturk, conducting ethnographic and oral historical research, recording dressers, delph and shop ledgers and comparing our findings to the archaeological remains excavated from Inishark's eighteenth- to twentieth-century homes. This section offers readers a brief introduction to these island communities.

People made homes on these three islands since the Bronze Age period (roughly 1500–600 BC), and remains of prehistoric houses, promontory forts and field systems are still visible today.[4] Bronze Age residents raised cattle and farmed to support their families, making homes in circular buildings whose remains appear as large stones outlining an oval or circular foundation, called hut circles by archaeologists. Scholars have also documented extensive evidence for medieval communities (AD 650–1200) from both excavations and textual accounts,[5] and tourists and residents alike can explore medieval Christian shrines and churches, cemeteries and holy wells, many of which served as *turas* monuments for eighteenth- to twentieth-century islanders living on Inishbofin, Inishark and Inishturk (Fig. 2.3).[6] Many medieval monastic communities built homes on other islands in the area, including nearby Caher, Omey and High (Ard Oileán), whose remains still serve as key pilgrimage destinations.

More recently, during the post-medieval period (AD 1600 to roughly 1950), residents of Inishbofin, Inishturk and Inishark experienced 350 years of tumultuous change and challenges as regional, national and international political, religious and economic transformations profoundly affected their communities. During this period, military conflicts in Ireland, England and Europe involved islanders in one form or another: as soldiers, nurses and provisioners of daily essentials like meat, dairy products and everyday necessities. For instance, the Inishbofin parish records document the baptism of Thomas Scuffle on 5 August 1888, with his parents, Edward Scuffle and Mary Lacey Scuffle, as living in 'Sebastapool' (Fig. 2.4). Oral history on Inishbofin recounts that a section of land between the North Beach harbour and the Blow Holes was known historically as Sebastapool, named after the Crimean city, because two Crimean War veterans and brothers returned from the war to Inishbofin and lived there in the mid-nineteenth century.

These trans-European connections are particularly clear when arriving by boat to Inishbofin, as everyone is greeted by the island's most prominent and imposing

Fig. 2.3: Remains of Inishbofin's late medieval church, situated within the bounds of the original early monastic shrine and covering an earlier wood church, and the island's current cemetery

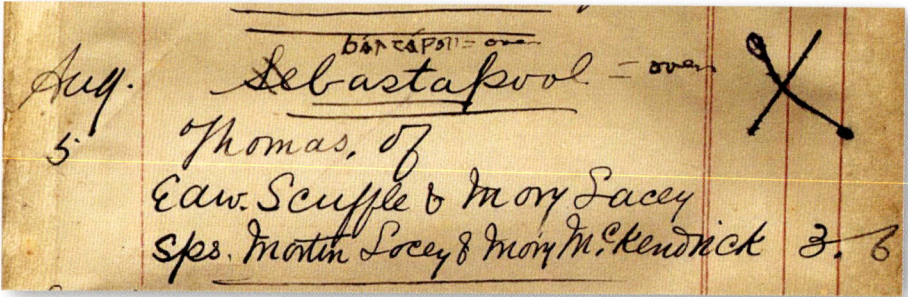

Fig. 2.4: Detail of Inishbofin parish records of baptisms, with entry stating the home of the child and family as 'Sebastapool' – a possible reference to the Crimean War (1853–6)

monument to life in the seventeenth century: the remains of Cromwellian barracks, which served as both military garrison and prison for political prisoners, situated at the harbour's entrance (Fig. 2.5). This garrison was built atop the foundations of an earlier fort, called Don Bosco's Castle, constructed during the first half of the seventeenth century.[7] Throughout the seventeenth to early nineteenth centuries, Inishbofin hosted a series of military barracks, including the eighteenth- and nineteenth-century Clanricarde barracks and the Royal Irish Constabulary – while located geographically at the edge of Europe and the last point of departure into

Fig. 2.5: Cromwell's Barracks, situated at the mouth of Inishbofin's harbour

Fig. 2.6: Drone's-eye view of Inishbofin's harbour at dawn, looking southeast to the mainland

the Atlantic Ocean moving west, the residents of Inishbofin, Inishark and Inishturk experienced first-hand many of the economic, social and political consequences of these regional and international policies and engagements.

Inishbofin, County Galway (Fig. 2.6)

Inishbofin, whose name translates to Island of the White Cow, is situated approximately nine kilometres from the pier at Cleggan, the primary point of departure from the mainland for today's residents and tourists (Fig. 2.7). In the early stages of the dresser research, roughly 160 full-time residents called these historic villages home. The island's population has grown over the last few years to 184 souls, particularly with young islanders returning home to cocoon during the pandemic and staying on to raise their families.[8]

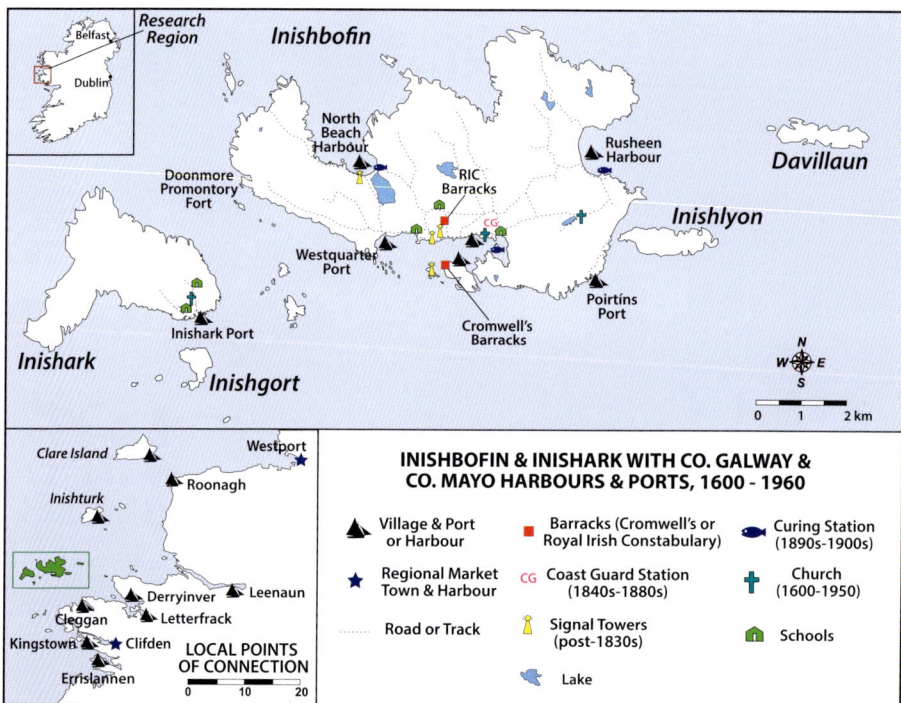

Fig. 2.7: Map of villages, harbours, churches and military barracks on Inishbofin and Inishark, 1600–1960, that have been studied archaeologically or oral historically by the CLIC team

In the eighteenth and nineteenth centuries, landlords owned Inishbofin and Inishark as a combined property, collecting rents from tenant farmers, fishermen, boatwrights, weavers and their families. From 1842 until the mid-twentieth century, valuation records document five main villages on Inishbofin, from east to west: Cloonamore, Knock, Middlequarter, Fawnmore and Westquarter (Fig. 2.8). Until 1873, Inishbofin and Inishark belonged to County Mayo, and were owned by the marquis of Sligo, George John Brown, whose nearest residence was Westport House in Westport, County Mayo.[9] Henry William Wilberforce purchased Inishbofin and Inishark in 1854 for £11,000, relying on his land agent Henry Hildebrandt to collect rents. After approximately two decades, a quick succession of landlords followed over the next few years, including Reverend Sir William Palmer and Reverends Edward Coldridge and Thomas H. Newman, with Thomas Allies purchasing both islands in the mid-1870s (Fig. 2.9). His son Cyril inherited ownership shortly afterwards and served as the final and only resident landlord until 1905, with his house on Inishbofin on the site of what is now Inishbofin House Hotel. The

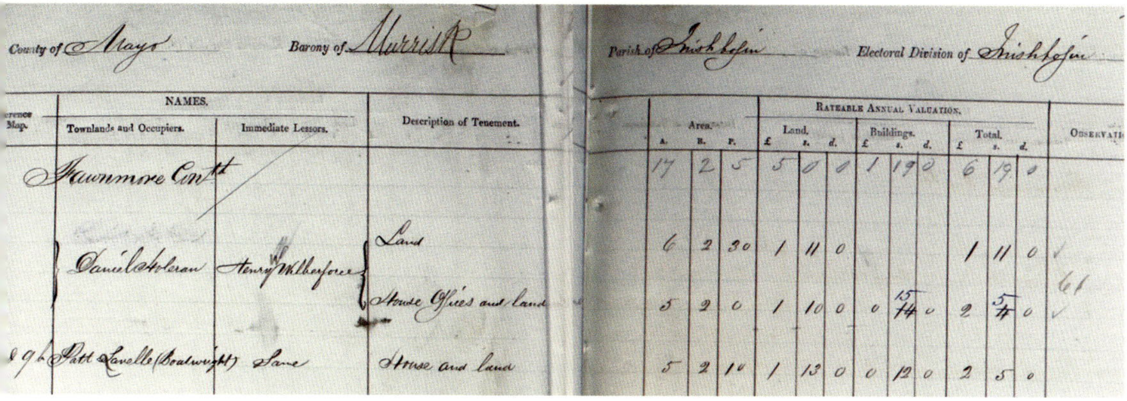

County of Mayo Barony of Murrisk Parish of Inishbofin Electoral Division of Inishbofin

Reference to Map	Names: Townlands and Occupiers	Names: Immediate Lessors	Description of Tenement	Area: A.	R.	P.	Land: £	s.	d.	Buildings: £	s.	d.	Total: £	s.	d.	Observations
	Fawnmore Contd			17	2	5	5	0	0	1	19	0	6	19	0	
	Daniel Holeran	Henry Wilberforce	Land	6	2	30	1	11	0				1	11	0	
			House Offices and land	5	2	0	1	10	0	0	15/14	0	2	5/4	0	
9b	Patt Lavelle (Boatwright)	Same	House and land	5	2	10	1	13	0	0	12	0	2	5	0	

Fig. 2.8: Detail from the 1856–60 valuation book of residents in Fawnmore village, Inishbofin, listing Patt Lavelle as a boatwright and tenant, renting a house and adjacent land

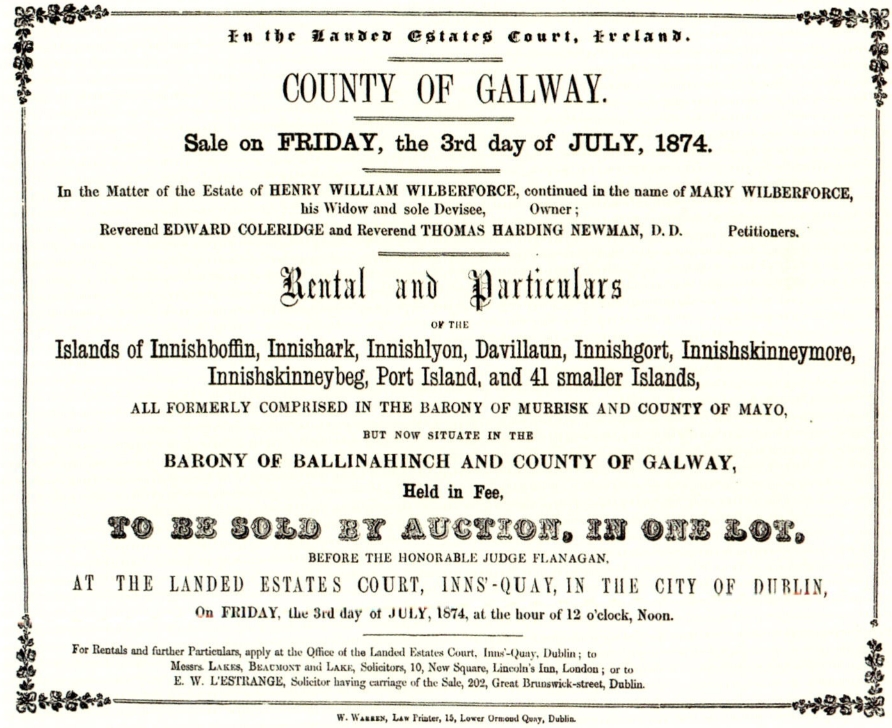

In the Landed Estates Court, Ireland.

COUNTY OF GALWAY.

Sale on FRIDAY, the 3rd day of JULY, 1874.

In the Matter of the Estate of HENRY WILLIAM WILBERFORCE, continued in the name of MARY WILBERFORCE, his Widow and sole Devisee, Owner;
Reverend EDWARD COLERIDGE and Reverend THOMAS HARDING NEWMAN, D. D. Petitioners.

Rental and Particulars

OF THE

Islands of Innishboffin, Innishark, Innishlyon, Davillaun, Innishgort, Innishskinneymore, Innishskinneybeg, Port Island, and 41 smaller Islands,

ALL FORMERLY COMPRISED IN THE BARONY OF MURRISK AND COUNTY OF MAYO,

BUT NOW SITUATE IN THE

BARONY OF BALLINAHINCH AND COUNTY OF GALWAY,

Held in Fee,

TO BE SOLD BY AUCTION, IN ONE LOT,

BEFORE THE HONORABLE JUDGE FLANAGAN,

AT THE LANDED ESTATES COURT, INNS'-QUAY, IN THE CITY OF DUBLIN,

On FRIDAY, the 3rd day of JULY, 1874, at the hour of 12 o'clock, Noon.

For Rentals and further Particulars, apply at the Office of the Landed Estates Court, Inns'-Quay, Dublin; to Messrs. Lakes, Beaumont and Lake, Solicitors, 10, New Square, Lincoln's Inn, London; or to E. W. L'ESTRANGE, Solicitor having carriage of the Sale, 202, Great Brunswick-street, Dublin.

W. Warren, Law Printer, 15, Lower Ormond Quay, Dublin.

Fig. 2.9: 1874 announcement of sale of Inishbofin and Inishark with smaller associated islands

Congested Districts Board (CDB, 1891–1923) purchased all lands on Inishbofin and Inishark in 1905, and from that point on, the islanders gained the right to purchase land and homes.

From the 1840s to the late nineteenth century, residents of Inishbofin and their Inishark neighbours survived repeated years of famine arising from potato blight and fishing and kelp industry collapses, like many other rural western communities.[10] A correspondent from *The Irish Times* travelled to Inishbofin in 1886, reporting that:

> The condition of these people is one of great poverty, and in the case of the vast majority it is one of downright misery. In nearly every instance all the potatoes which they had grown last year were eaten before January, save occasionally a modest store reserved for sowing … In another house an old woman was lying on some boards – her only bed – and all the food she had was a few diminutive potatoes scarcely fit for food.[11]

Inishbofin and Inishark were not alone in struggling with these challenges. Through the CDB, administered by the chief secretary of Ireland, Arthur Balfour, and a series of Land Acts and Labourers Acts passed from the 1880s to the 1900s, the government attempted to address chronic poverty, unemployment and poor housing conditions in rural areas throughout Ireland in the late nineteenth century and pre-Civil War twentieth century.[12] CDB officials travelled throughout the poorer, rural counties of Ireland to document the economic realities of daily life, including how people made a living, their living conditions, and the existing markets and trade. In turn, these reports were collated, studied and used to enact development projects that included the construction of schools, housing, roads, field walls, drainage features and fishing infrastructure (e.g. piers, breakwaters and curing stations), as well as introducing agricultural sciences to modernise stock-raising and farming techniques. Valuation records for both Inishbofin and Inishark document increasing numbers of land purchases from the landlord, and later the CDB, from the 1890s onwards. In purchasing lands, people sometimes built new homes, following the very specific governmental guidelines for the number of windows, height of ceilings, and flooring requirements – designed to promote better air quality and cleanliness.[13] Many historians of vernacular architecture have documented houses built before and after CDB reforms, including regional

Fig. 2.10: Local archaeologist and historian Tommy Burke (centre, wearing a blue sleeveless jacket) leads a walking tour of significant historical and archaeological sites on Inishbofin

variations. Many Bofiners today still live in CDB-style homes, which have often been renovated and modernised.

A century later, Inishbofin's residents still farm and fish, supplementing the island's main economic engine: tourism. The thriving tourism economy offers a variety of accommodation and wonderful restaurants in the villages of Cloonamore, nearby Rusheen, Middlequarter, Fawnmore and Westquarter, a justifiably famous Irish traditional music scene, daily ferry service between Cleggan and the island, and a general shop. The island also features a community centre, St Colman's Catholic church, a medical clinic with a full-time nurse and weekly physician office hours, a national school, and a heritage museum established by local historian Marie Coyne. During the tourist season of April through mid-October, tourists enjoy endless opportunities to explore Inishbofin and the nearby islands, including hiking, sea kayaking, bird watching, pony-trekking, scuba diving, sailing, walking heritage tours (Fig. 2.10), seal colony tours by boat, and a chance to unwind from life's daily rigours and stresses. Yearly festivals, including the Bia Bó Finne Food Festival, Walking Festival, Regatta, Half Marathon, Storytelling Festival, Set Dancing and Trad Weekend, and the Arts Festival, celebrate the island community's heritage and efforts to build a sustainable future.

Inishark, County Galway (Fig. 2.11)

While the ethnographic and oral historical components of the Dresser Project required trips to several communities throughout the region, the archaeological component focused on Inishark, where the CLIC team conducted surveys and excavations from 2008 until 2017.[14] Located about one kilometre as the crow flies from Inishbofin (and approximately four kilometres from pier to pier), Inishark lies approximately twelve kilometres by boat from the Cleggan pier. Similar to Inishbofin, the material footprints of Inishark's three main periods of occupation dominate the island's landscape: Late Bronze Age stone field wall systems and foundations of stone hut circles built by farmers and herders, early medieval monastic shrines and monuments, and post-medieval historic village and field systems (AD 1750–1960).[15]

Landing on Inishark historically and especially now presents challenges to the most skilled boater: her pier is situated in a narrow inlet on the southern coastline, offering little protection during high seas and wind, especially those coming from the southeast. In poor weather and sea conditions, Inishark islanders were

Fig. 2.11: View of Inishark's historic village, looking west along the southern coastline

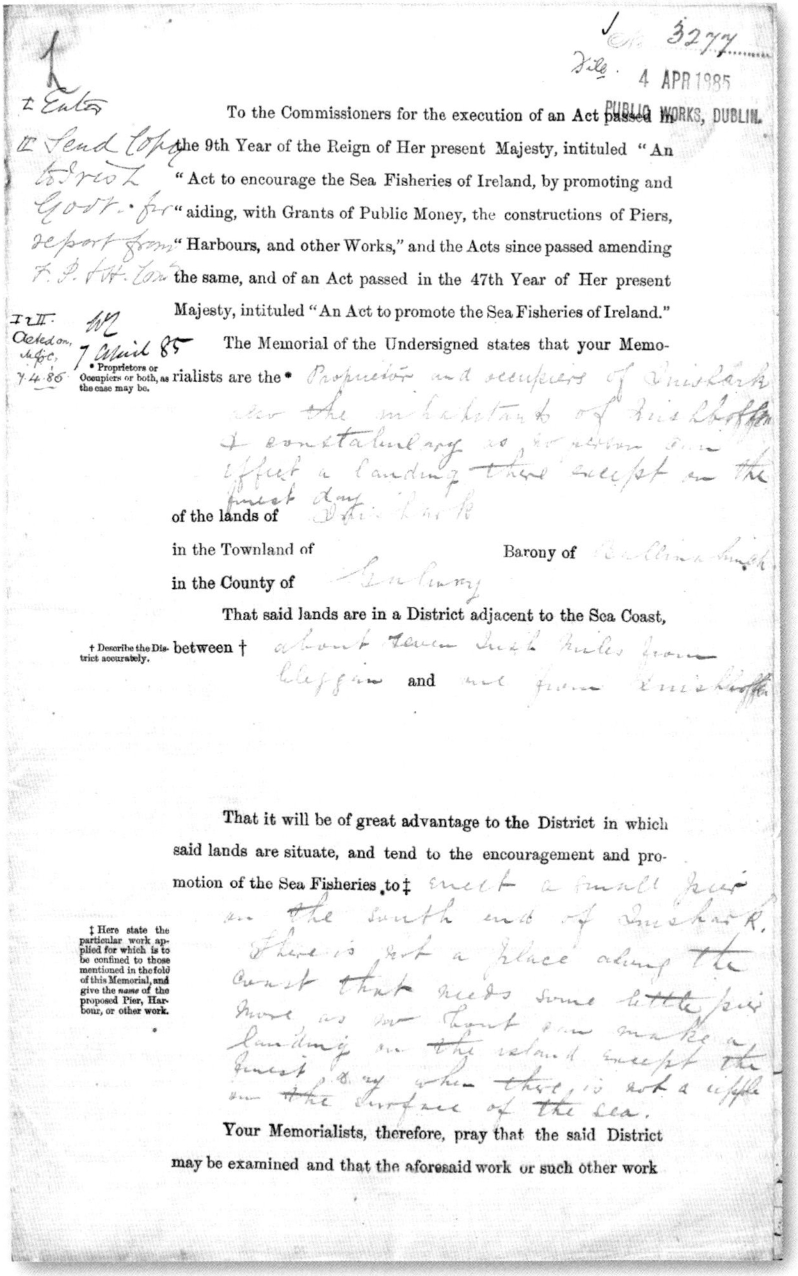

To the Commissioners for the execution of an Act passed PUBLIC WORKS, DUBLIN.

the 9th Year of the Reign of Her present Majesty, intituled "An

"Act to encourage the Sea Fisheries of Ireland, by promoting and

"aiding, with Grants of Public Money, the constructions of Piers,

"Harbours, and other Works," and the Acts since passed amending

the same, and of an Act passed in the 47th Year of Her present

Majesty, intituled "An Act to promote the Sea Fisheries of Ireland."

The Memorial of the Undersigned states that your Memo-

*Proprietors or Occupiers or both, as the case may be.

rialists are the * *Proprietors and occupiers of Inishark*

also the inhabitants of his Shark

& constabulary is to return the

effect a landing there except in the

finest day

of the lands of *Inishark*

in the Townland of   Barony of *Ballinahinch*

in the County of *Galway*

That said lands are in a District adjacent to the Sea Coast,

†Describe the District accurately.

between † *about seven Irish miles from*

Cleggan and   from Inishbofin

That it will be of great advantage to the District in which

said lands are situate, and tend to the encouragement and pro-

motion of the Sea Fisheries to‡ *erect a small pier*

‡Here state the particular work applied for which is to be confined to those mentioned in the fold of this Memorial, and give the name of the proposed Pier, Harbour, or other work.

on the south end of Inishark.

There is not a place along the

coast that needs some little pier

more as we cont one make a

landing on the island except the

finest day when there is not a ripple

on the surface of the sea.

Your Memorialists, therefore, pray that the said District

may be examined and that the aforesaid work or such other work

Fig. 2.12: (above and over leaf) In the spring of 1885, landlord Cyril Allies wrote to the government requesting the construction of a breakwater and pier at Inishark to facilitate landing and disembarking on the island

3

in lieu thereof as the said Commissioners shall deem fit, may be executed under the said Acts.

Dated at

this   day of   188

Present when signed by *Cyril Allen J.P.*

Michael Halloran
Michael + Murray   his mark
Patt + Cloonane   his mark
Thomas + Murray sen.   his mark
William + Cloonane   his mark
Thomas + Murray Jun.   his mark
John + Cacy   his mark
Michl + Cacy   his mark
Anthony + Faris   his mark
Patt + King   his mark
Patt + Cloonane   his mark
Michl + Cacy   his mark
John + Cloonane   his mark
Patt + Cloonane   his mark

P.S. I deem that there is no place that needs the erection of a little pier more than Inishark as it is impossible to harbour any boat there in rough weather. The boats must be hauled up on the land otherwise they would be broken against the rocks. Two only a few weeks ago the sea rightaway attempted a landing which nearly would be the loss of their lives. Rev. Martin Collaran

cut off from the mainland and Inishbofin for weeks and sometimes months at a time, without a way to contact the mainland or neighbouring islands.[16] For many generations, residents coming and going to the island have faced the challenges of poor weather, high seas and a southeast wind. In 1885, landowner Cyril Allies wrote a letter, composed on a government form, to request that the authorities invest in a pier for the islanders (Fig. 2.12).

A transcription of Allies' letter and the postscript from the Inishbofin priest reads (with handwritten responses italicised):

To the Commissioners for the execution of an Act passed in the 9th Year of the Reign of Her present Majesty, intituled 'An Act to encourage the Sea Fisheries of Ireland, by promoting and aiding, with Grants of Public Money, the construction of Piers, Harbours, and other Work', and the Acts since passed amending the same, and of an Act passed in the 47th Year of Her present Majesty, intituled 'An Act to promote the Sea Fisheries of Ireland'.

The Memorial of the Undersigned states that your Memorialists are the

Proprietor and occupiers of Inishshark also the inhabitants of Inishboffin & constabulary as no person can effect a landing there except on the finest day

Of the lands of *Inishark*
in the Townland of [left blank] Barony of *Ballinahinch*
in the County of *Galway*

That said lands are in a District adjacent to the Sea coast between a*bout seven Irish miles from Cleggan* and *one from Inishboffin*

That it will be of great advantage to the District in which said lands are situate, and tend to the encouragement and promotion of the Sea Fisheries to

erect a small pier on the south end of Inishark. There is not a place along the coast that needs some little pier more as no boat can make a landing on the island except the finest day when there is not a ripple on the surface of the sea.

Your Memorialists, therefore, pray that the said District may be examined and that the aforesaid work or such other work in lieu thereof as the said Commissioners shall deem fit, may be executed under the said Acts.

Present when Signed by *Cyril Allies J.P.*

> *Michael Halloran*
> *Michael Murray (his mark X)*
> *Patt Cloonane (his mark X)*
> *Thomas Murray Senior (his mark X)*
> *William Cloonane (his mark X)*
> *Thomas Murray Junior (his mark X)*
> *John Leacy (his mark X)*
> *Michael Leacy (his mark X)*
> *Anthony Davis (his mark X)*
> *Patt King (his mark X)*
> *Patt Cloonane (his mark X)*
> *Michael Leacy (his mark X)*
> *John Cloonane (his mark X)*
> *Patt Cloonane (his mark X)*

P.S. I deem that there is no place that needs the erection of a little pier more than Inishark as it is impossible to harbour any boat there in rough weather. The boats must be hauled up on the land otherwise they would be broken against the rocks. Too, only a few weeks ago the [undecipherable] *attempted a landing which nearly resulted in the loss of their lives.*

Rev'd Martin Colleran [priest on Inishbofin 1884–6][17]

Comparing the handwritten postscript and the other portions of the document, it is clear that Reverend Martin Colleran served as the principal scribe for this correspondence. However, the signatures differ: landowner Cyril Allies signed his name, but all of the men's signatures below are in the same hand. The only signature that does not include 'his mark X' is that of Michael Halloran, who held the position of king of Inishark, an individual who often spoke for the villagers, resolved disputes, and helped to organise collective labour endeavours.[18] If we are correct, Michael Halloran, in his position of representative of the Inishark villagers, wrote each man's name, and every man placed an 'X' as their mark just above it.[19] The margin notes, stamped and written by staff members of the Office of Public Works in Dublin, indicate that the request was received on 4 April 1885, given the document number 3277, and amended on 7 April 1885. The construction of a breakwater, finally completed in 1932, did help Inishark's residents, but not enough to support a thriving and growing community.[20] Due to prolonged economic hardship, emigration and decades-long infrastructural neglect by first British and then Irish governing bodies, the population declined steadily through the early and mid-twentieth century until Inishark's islanders were forced to leave home in 1960.[21] In addition to the development of the small harbour in 1932, the government also invested in improved housing during the first two decades of the twentieth century through relief efforts administered by the CDB. Simultaneously, the valuation records document many residents purchasing homes and lands from landlord Allies. For the first time, residents owned their homes and the land they worked and farmed.

Unlike Inishbofin, however, Inishark's village no longer rings with the sound of people and daily life. After decades of declining population, emigration of young people to find work in England and America, and several drownings and fatal medical emergencies, on 20 October 1960 the Irish government removed Inishark's remaining twenty-four residents to the mainland, settling them in Fountainhill, Claddaghduff, County Galway – where they could look out across the sea to their former island home.[22]

Today, local farmers graze sheep on the island, and the corncrake conservation teams visit to assess the established preservation habitats and take a census of these endangered birds. Inishark's current full-time residents include sheep, rabbits, snails, corncrakes, skuas, black-backed gulls and a variety of other birds and insects that move through the uninhabited buildings in the village, atop cliffs and hills, in the bogs and along the coastline. The lives of these non-human residents are occasionally encroached upon by sheep farmers, birdwatchers, hikers and day-trippers. From 2008 to 2017, our team camped on Inishark for approximately two and a half weeks (Fig. 2.13), with a resupply trip halfway through the season, when we gratefully returned to Inishbofin to enjoy the pleasures of a comfortable hotel bed, hot showers, electricity and pubs.

Fig. 2.13: Excavations on Inishark in 2012, with orange and blue tents in the background

Inishturk, County Mayo (Fig. 2.14)

Like Inishbofin and Inishark, people have lived on Inishturk for the last few thousand years (Figs 2.14 and 2.15). Members of the Ordnance Survey team (1830s), Dr Charles Browne (1898) and Clare Island surveyors (1910) reported both prehistoric and historical monuments and sites on the island, including the remains of three prehistoric forts and house sites, as well as scanty remains of a medieval church dedicated to St Columba.[23] Interestingly, none of these sources mentioned the Martello tower, erected (but never finished) on a prominent hilltop on Inishturk's northwestern portion during the Napoleonic Wars. In an 1820s engineering report commissioned by the Commissioners of Fisheries, a surveyor and engineer reported the need for a jetty in the main harbour.[24]

Ownership of Inishturk in the nineteenth century was more complicated than in the case of Inishark and Inishbofin. In the 1855 Griffith's Valuation, the earl of Lucan was listed as the landowner of only one township on Inishturk: Bellavaum (composed only of grazing land), whose sole tenant, Henry P. Hildebrande, was the land manager who collected rents for the marquis of Sligo from residents of Inishbofin and Inishark. He also owned the small surrounding islands of Caher, Ballybeg and Inishdalla – all with a single tenant: himself. Interestingly, for Inishturk's townlands of Craggy (grazing land), Garranty and Ballyheer (both with houses and associated gardens and fields), Hildebrande is also listed as the owner ('lesser'). Finally, in the township of Mountain Commons, composed only of grazing land, the marquis of Sligo is listed as owner of one parcel, with Henry Hildebrande possessing the majority of that township until the late 1870s. At that point, the valuation records list James McDonnell as the owner of all Inishturk except for a plot in Mountain Commons held by Lucan. In 1903, the earl of Lucan is listed as the owner of Caher Island, and McDonnell's heirs, the Misses McDonnells, held their father's portions until 1908 when the fourth earl of Lucan purchased all of these islands. His ownership ended in 1909 when the CDB held all townlands, commonage and small islands.

While oral histories describe Hildebrande as an unsympathetic character,[25] historical documents and local oral history describe Lucan as a ruthless landlord

Fig. 2.14: Drone's-eye view of Inishturk's harbour

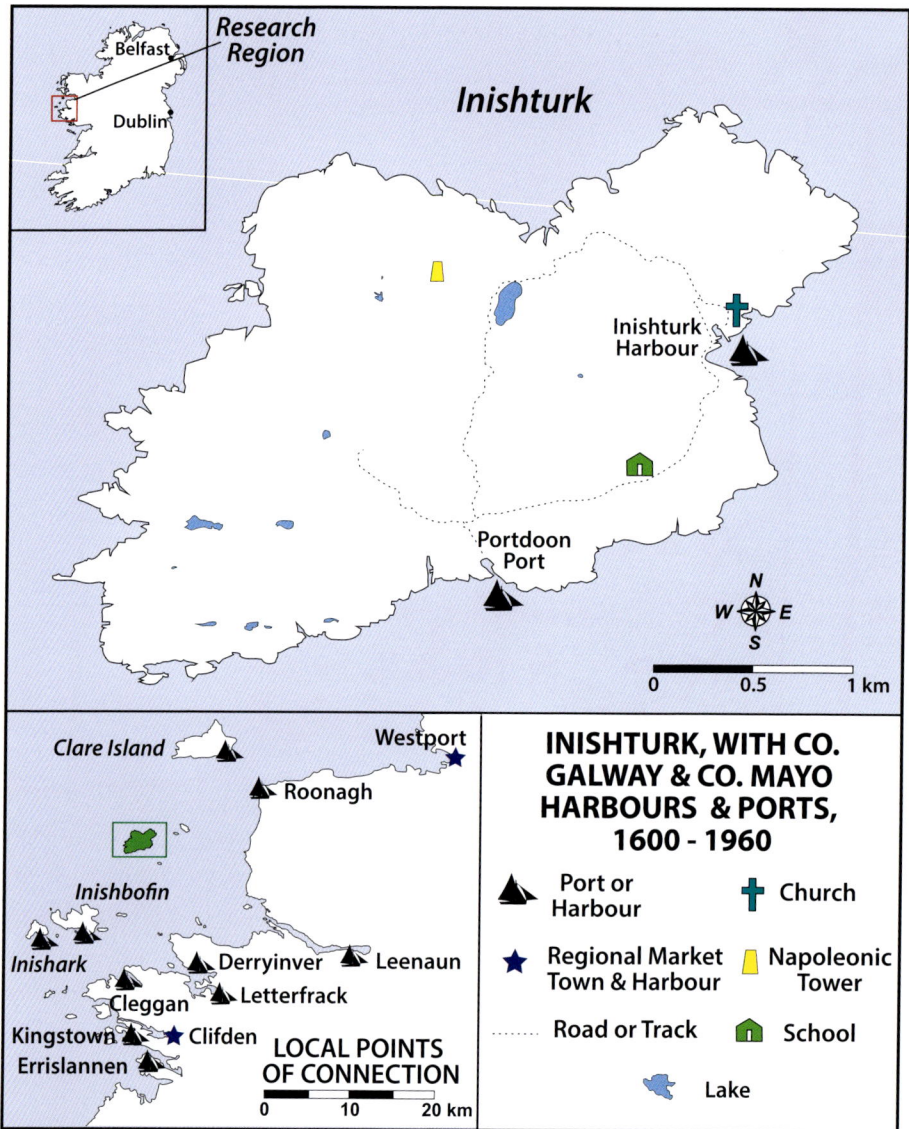

Fig. 2.15: Map of Inishturk, 1600–1960, with key ports and historical sites

responsible for thousands of people being evicted from his mainland properties.[26] In a series of letters written by Finlay Dun, a reporter sent by *The Times* to Ireland to assess the state of land ownership and estate management in 1880–1, he described the state of properties owned and managed by the third earl of Lucan (1800–88):

Lord Lucan has 60,570 acres in Mayo, part of it around Castlebar, where his substantial old house stands; part of it at Cloona Castle, near Ballinrobe. Griffith's valuation of the estate is £12,940. It presents some contrasts to most of the large neighbouring estates. From several parishes extensive evictions were made from 1846 to 1850; throwing together the smaller holdings, several large grazing and a few considerable tillage farms were made. Lord Lucan, in his terse, incisive style, asserted that 'he would not breed paupers to pay priests'. Some townlands, nevertheless, still remain greatly overcrowded. With a sort of military despotism, he has endeavoured personally to rule his estates.[27]

Throughout the nineteenth and twentieth centuries, longstanding economic and kinship ties connected the residents of Inishturk, Inishbofin and Inishark. When talking with Inishturk and Inishbofin islanders, they often reference siblings, aunts and uncles, cousins and in-laws who connect these islands to this day. Today, it is relatively easy to arrange to travel to Inishturk. A daily ferry service from Roonagh, County Mayo, with the O'Malley Ferry Company, serves the island community, and one can also hire the Inishbofin Ferries fast ferry directly from Inishbofin to arrive in Inishturk in less than an hour. At the time of this research, Inishturk's full-time residents numbered around sixty people. Similar to Inishbofin, the island hosts gracious bed and breakfast accommodation, self-catering cottages, a community centre, a small shop, a medical clinic with a full-time nurse, St Colomba's Catholic church, a national school and one of Ireland's most amazing sports pitches nestled into the surrounding hills. Visitors, many of whom return yearly, travel to the island to hike, rock climb, birdwatch, deep sea fish and sail. Like Inishbofin, Inishturk also hosts yearly festivals, including TurkFest[28] and a pattern day festival with traditional Irish music, dancing and a sheep-shearing contest (Fig. 2.16).

Fig. 2.16: View of inner harbour of Inishturk, with the ferry at the pier

Clifden, Cleggan and Cashel (County Galway), Westport (County Mayo)

While situated for the majority of the Dresser Project on Inishbofin and Inishturk, my team and I also spent time on the mainland in Clifden talking with people about dressers and delph, including a furniture shop owner and dresser and delph collector, Anne. Founded in the early nineteenth century by the local landowner John D'Arcy,[29] today Clifden is a bustling market town with a brisk tourism industry, full of pubs, restaurants, hotels, bed and breakfasts, shops, the home of the Connemara Pony Breeders Society and the yearly Arts Festival. From 2006 to 2008, before the Dresser Project was ever conceived, Clifden served as the CLIC team's home base when we conducted archaeological surveys on the mainland surrounding the town (Fig. 2.17).

While in the town documenting Anne's dresser and delph, I enjoyed the great fortune of meeting with a Carna-based archaeologist, who, in turn, introduced us to local people who possessed historical shop ledgers. My team and I photographed four shop ledgers in Clifden to better understand how past islanders and mainland

Fig. 2.17: View of Clifden from the John D'Arcy Monument

residents acquired their home furnishings and personal possessions. One of Clifden's shopkeepers introduced us to Francis from Cashel, who knew of two dressers whose owners had heard of and wanted to participate in the Dresser Project. With that connection, off we went to Cashel to document two fascinating dressers.

We have also learned from participants about shopping and local economies in three other mainland communities by documenting historical shop ledgers in Cleggan and Tully Cross (County Galway) and Westport (County Mayo). Based on conversations with dresser, delph and ledger owners, I realised that we needed to visit Westport, the primary port frequented by islanders historically to purchase goods. In 2016, we travelled to the town to speak with shopkeepers and documented purchases by Inishbofin islanders from an old shop ledger. We also made two side-trips, one to speak with a curator at the Museum of Country Life in nearby Castlebar, and the second to document portions of a shop ledger in Tully Cross, County Galway.

These communities and inhabitants form the heart of this story about homemaking in the past and present. My team and I spoke with thirty-five people about dressers, delph collections and the types of belongings kept safely stored or displayed in or outside of dressers. Claudia Kinmonth argues that studying the material culture in people's homes, including dressers and delph, requires an interdisciplinary approach.[30] In her decades-long studies of Irish rural furniture and homes, she examines a wide variety of historical documents, artworks, museum collections and private homes with extant pieces, where she also collects oral histories of homes, inhabitants and furnishings. Following in Kinmonth's footsteps and building on her exhaustive research, this project investigates homes, dressers and delph with an anthropologist's eyes. It focuses on a smaller region by utilising three main methods: ethnography and ethnoarchaeology, archaeology, and archival research. The following section offers brief overviews of these methodological approaches, describing each component's scope, goals and research workflow.

Documenting ethnographic voices and ethnoarchaeological dressers and delph

This type of study is often called ethnoarchaeology because it combines ethnography (the study of contemporary peoples) with archaeology (the study of past peoples through their material possessions, residences and places). Ethnoarchaeologists

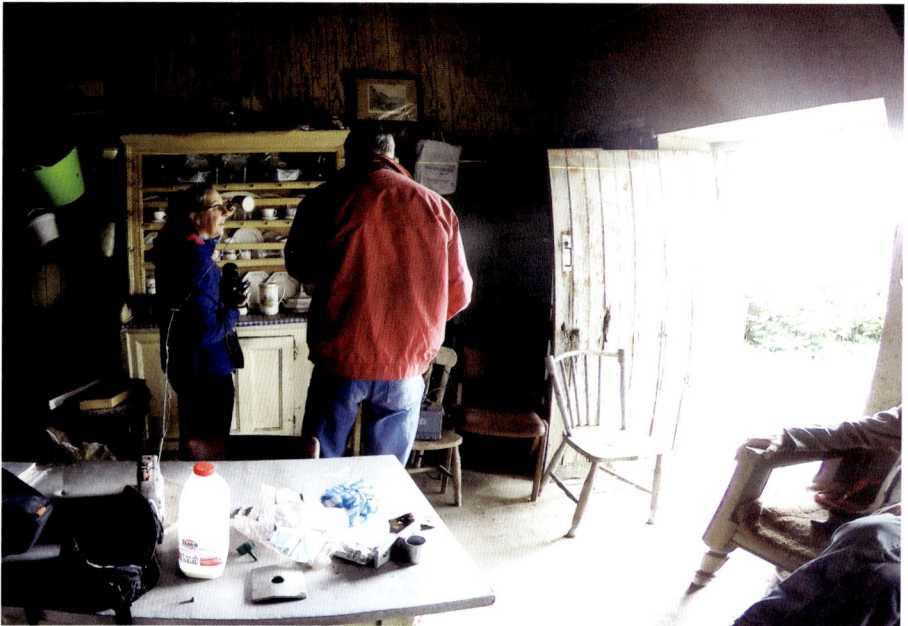

Fig. 2.18: Talking with Patrick and his friend Francis about Patrick's dresser and old home in Cashel

research people's interactions with belongings, living spaces and surrounding landscapes to gain insights into changing manufacturing technologies, expertise, styles and designs, and uses of buildings. More recently in Europe and North America, some scholars consider this research as part of the burgeoning field of contemporary archaeology – the archaeology of the now, or at least the more recent past. Whatever name one bestows on this research, it focuses on people's belongings and places within specific historical and cultural contexts (Fig. 2.18). By studying their historical and current relationships with dressers and delph, I explore how people employ these furnishings to transform a house into a home and how these practices change or stay the same through time. Comparing contemporary dressers and delph to archaeological remains of Inishark's and Inishbofin's nineteenth- and twentieth-century homes, this study also engages with perspectives from history, decorative arts, vernacular architecture, island studies, material culture studies, folklore and critical heritage studies, particularly when these disciplines intersect with rural Irish settings. In many ways, I use a 'kitchen sink' approach, bringing the tools and insights from several disciplines to understand people's relationships with dressers, delph and homes.

Social geographer Peter Jackson encourages scholars to interrogate how we interact with our belongings because these linkages often provide insights into people's multi-faceted relationships with other people.[31] I believe that the same claim can be made about people's homes. Together, our possessions and homes often display how we understand ourselves and our aspirations in life. People adorn and outfit homes with belongings that may speak to a family's history, social and geographical context in a broader community, heritage and the surrounding landscape. Unlike traditional ethnography or archaeology, which situates the researcher as the 'expert', I follow more recent approaches in North American anthropology that situate me as a 'learner', listening to delph- and dresser-keepers' understanding, experiences and beliefs about homemaking. Dresser Project participants taught, and I learned, documented and compared dressers and delph and reflected on the results of the knowledge about homemaking that we produced together.[32] To offer a sense of this process, I start by describing the scope and details of the research in each of the communities where we conducted research, including the Dresser Project's relationship with the University of Notre Dame's CLIC project.

Ethnographic investigations

This project relied on ethnographic methods, such as interviews and participant observation, to learn about homemaking with dressers and delph. Before describing the process, I need to briefly address the troubling history of relationships between anthropologists, especially ethnographers, and rural Irish people and communities who have been the subjects of study. Irish people have welcomed anthropologists into communities for more than a century. Despite generations of these interactions, in many places a justifiable sense of distrust still lingers due to an unfortunate history of many prominent ethnographers failing to conduct research and publish results in a comprehensively ethical manner.[33] Michael Viney's 1983 scathing editorial in *The Irish Times*, 'The Yank in the Corner: Why the ethics of anthropology are a worry for rural Ireland', concisely and accurately illustrated the moral injury at the crux of this fraught history: the harm brought by anthropologists who did not protect subjects from the consequences emerging from the process of knowledge production and publication of any research.[34] Community members recognised themselves, family members and neighbours in these ethnographies, in which the researchers both exposed and judged the most private and personal aspects of these people's lives, decisions and beliefs.

The last few decades have witnessed a transformation in how anthropologists must conduct research. I am not so naïve to believe that the power-laden approach to ethnographic research, grounded in an unshakeable sense of academic entitlement, a false sense of neutral objectivity and a purely extractive and invasive process, does not still occur. While the majority of ethnographers of Irish communities conduct research grounded in ethical practices and with empathy,[35] I acknowledge the harm wrought and the distrust sown by less ethically sound anthropologists. In many ways, I follow in their footsteps and must step softly and gently, always with an eye towards self-reflection and awareness of my position as a researcher. For me, these earlier ethnographies provide anthropologists with a set of guidelines for how not to conduct research. For example, one key aspect of the Dresser Project centred on approaching the research process as a learner and a listener, sharing what I learned, and basing the entire endeavour on informed consent and permission.

Anthropologists in many countries are now governed by ethical review boards that require us to submit our research design for approval before ever speaking to a single person. For example, US-based researchers interviewing, observing and learning from people must follow ethical standards established by the 1974 Belmont Report.[36] These guidelines protect anyone who agrees to participate in 'human subjects' research, whether taking part in medical research, pharmaceutical testing or ethnographic interviews. Three key ethical concepts guide all research involving living human subjects: Autonomy, Beneficence and Justice. Autonomy, also called Respect for Persons, ensures that research participants understand the scope and methods of the research, give informed consent to participate and maintain control over any data collected from them. Beneficence requires researchers to accomplish two tasks – first, scholars must minimise all risks to participants as much as possible; second, the study must ensure that all benefits and risks to participants are distributed equally: no one set of participants may be at more or less risk than others. The third Belmont Principle is Justice, or the just distribution of the research benefits according to the participants' needs, societal contributions and efforts. Researchers must incorporate all three principles into any research design involving living human participants. This system of guidelines is not perfect because it relies on human beings making judgements about the nature of consent, risks, benefits and just distributions. However, it provides a crucial foundation for protecting the people who help us learn more about the experience of being human in the world.

Working within the framework of these three principles, researchers must devise an ethical protocol – a research plan – that will protect the project's participants from any risks while maximising the benefits to them. In turn, we submit this protocol to our institution's Institutional Review Board (IRB; in this case, at the University of Notre Dame) for assessment. Based on how well or poorly a researcher follows the three Belmont Principles, the IRB panel will approve, deny or ask for corrections and resubmission of the research plan. I completed this same process for the Dresser Project, whose IRB protocol (#14-03-1623) requires that all participants be offered anonymity; those who chose to be identified despite that protocol will be named (generally, these are people whose dressers and delph are displayed in more public venues, like pubs and restaurants). To help maintain the anonymity of the participants, I used pseudonyms[37] for everyone in this book unless that participant was associated with a public entity (the Museum of Country Life or the Doonmore Hotel), an historical figure, or asked that their actual name be used. Whenever possible, I also checked with people to make sure they were comfortable with the pseudonym assigned to them.

Situating myself as a learner and always mindful of this troubling history of anthropological research in Ireland, I sought to always respect and honour the dresser- and delph-keepers who opened their homes to me. Recording someone's dresser and/or delph required anywhere from two to eight hours, using photography to document dressers, delph and any other belongings; measuring and describing dressers;[38] and interviewing dresser- and delph-keepers to learn about these possessions, life histories and homes. When anthropologists take photographs of museum objects, they rarely use flash photography, instead employing photography stands that possess movable lighting sources and cloth backdrops, like velvet. The goal in these instances focuses on representing an object and its key features in a standardised fashion by producing professional-quality photographs with even lighting that accentuates key features of the pottery vessel, painting or any other object framed by a non-distracting background. Photographing delph and dressers for this study involved a very different set of methods, contexts and standards. At least half of the homes in which we recorded dressers and delph were uninhabited and without electricity. Lighting was generally less than optimal for photography, and we added light by opening doors and windows, using flash photography and moving pieces outside. Instead of a tasteful and evenly textured velvet backdrop, we often used one of our jackets in whatever colour contrasted best with the recorded possessions. In some cases, large pieces of furniture had to be shifted to gain access to dressers and then moved carefully back into place to leave the home in the same state as before our arrival.

In all instances, we worked under strict time limits: people graciously dedicated time from very busy daily schedules to share their homes, dressers and delph with us, and we wanted to impose as little as possible. Sometimes, we worked within the added constraint of the ferry schedule between Inishbofin and the mainland. For example, recording dressers in Cashel required us to work as quickly as possible: Francis, Patrick and Mary all had other obligations that day, and we were pushed to meet the taxi for our trip to Cleggan to catch the ferry home to Inishbofin. In every case, documentation involved a feeling of urgency: we were quick, as efficient as possible, and always strove to inconvenience our hosts as little as possible.

I started the Dresser Project research by speaking with people whom I knew through long stays on Inishbofin, and from those participants I learned about other dresser- and delph-owners to contact.[39] Choosing people to approach for this research represented only the first and smallest step – after all, many people keep dressers and delph. The next step was to enquire if they would agree to participate in this research. In contacting each potential party, I explained the project's scope, objectives, methods and ethical standards. Understandably, several people declined the somewhat dubious pleasure of having a nosy anthropologist root around in their homes, businesses and family histories. Despite that intrusive element, thirty-five people generously agreed to contribute to this research project, sharing dressers, delph, shop ledgers, histories and expertise with my research assistants and me. In total, we recorded twenty-one dressers and ten delph collections in these communities (Tables 2.1 and 2.2).

The ethnographic and ethnoarchaeological research components included ethnographic and oral historical interviews (ranging from slightly formal to very informal), as well as participant observation (what anthropologists sometimes call 'deep hanging out' where an ethnographer spends time doing whatever other people are doing – farming, fishing, cooking, gardening or going to the pub).[40] Interview and documentation processes were framed by two overall research questions:

1. How and why did people make and keep dressers and delph over the last 150 years in these island and coastal communities?
2. How and why do people continue to use delph collections and dressers to transform houses or businesses into welcoming and homey places?

Dresser-Keeper	Location	Context when Recorded	Origin	Number Ceramic Vessels	Number Glass Vessels
Doonmore Hotel	Inishbofin	Hotel dining room	Made on the mainland, maker unknown, early twentieth century; press had to be discarded in 2017 due to woodworm infestation; dresser shelves now mounted on dining room wall with the same delph displayed	61	1
Sarah	Inishbofin	Main room in an uninhabited home	Inishbofin-made by Willie or Peter Burke, early to mid-twentieth century; house bought and renovated in 2017, and dresser moved to family shed	58	17
William and Peggy	Inishbofin	Shed adjacent to the home	Inishbofin-made by Peter Burke, early to mid-twentieth century	65	9
William and Peggy	Inishbofin	Home kitchen	New; bought in Westport in 2010, maker unknown	132	37
George and Nicholas	Inishbofin	Home main room	Prefabricated set bought in Clifden at Stanley's in 1960s, assembled at home by the homeowner in 1960s when purchased	84	4
James and Margaret	Inishturk	Home main room	Inishturk-made by homeowner's grandfather Pat McHale, late nineteenth century	109	2
Bedelia	Inishturk	Main room in an uninhabited home	Inishturk-made by John Joe O'Toole, early to mid-twentieth century; dresser discarded because too infested with woodworm to save	83	6

Dresser-Keeper	Location	Context when Recorded	Origin	Number Ceramic Vessels	Number Glass Vessels
Celia	Inishturk	Dining room in a bed and breakfast	Inishturk-made by John Joe O'Toole, 1980s	109	20
Celia	Inishturk	Dining room in a bed and breakfast	Inishturk-made by Mark, 1990s (taught by John Joe O'Toole)	32	120
Michael	Inishbofin	Kitchen in an uninhabited home	Inishbofin-made, unknown craftsperson, late nineteenth century	4	3
Michael	Inishbofin	Main room in an uninhabited home	Unknown (off island), mid-twentieth century	52	3
Catherine	Inishbofin	Main room in the Galley Restaurant	Inishturk-made by John Joe O'Toole for the restaurant in 1995, transported to Inishbofin	57	1
Ellen	Inishbofin	Home kitchen	Westport-made by Tony O'Toole, 1999; brought to Inishbofin from mainland	7	10
Julia	Inishbofin	Side dining room in The Beach pub	Inishbofin-made by Peter Burke, early to mid-twentieth century	50	3
Anne	Clifden	Home kitchen	Letterfrack woodworking institute students, 1980s	14	0
Patrick	Cashel	Main room in an uninhabited home	Cashel-made for 1914 house, never moved; maker name unknown	62	5
Mary	Cashel	Home main room below stairs (built into space below stairs next to house altar)	Cashel-made by the owner's father, early twentieth century	97	6

Dresser-Keeper	Location	Context when Recorded	Origin	Number Ceramic Vessels	Number Glass Vessels
Catherine	Inishbofin	Rental cottage main sitting room	Inishbofin-made, unknown craftsperson, first half of twentieth century?	38	0
Penelope	Inishbofin	Rental cottage main sitting room	Unknown (previous long-term cottage owners from Clifden)	32	1
Honora	Inishturk	Dining room of bed and breakfast	Inishturk-made by Mark, 1999 (taught by John Joe O'Toole)	8	44
Betty	Inishturk	Main room in an old home (now rented)	Inishturk-made by Johnny Faherty, mid-nineteenth century or older; repaired in 2018 and treated for woodworm	78	35

Table 2.1: Location, age and counts of ceramic (n=1,232) and glass (n=327) vessels in dressers recorded in this study

I usually started our conversations with participants by asking them about their favourite or most voiceful belongings, the histories behind various pieces, and any stories associated with the heirlooms or particularly voiceful possessions they exhibited in homes. When possible, I spoke with each owner about the dresser's life history, including its provenance (history of ownership): who made it, where it came from, how frequently it has been repainted, stripped or varnished, how often the delph within it was used, and how often and who cleans its contents. I made similar enquiries about the possessions placed on the dresser's shelves, photographing them and asking the owners about the life histories of each piece. If participants wanted to share other important items outside of dressers and delph, we recorded these furnishings (Fig. 2.19). All interviews were conducted without video- or audio-recording, in accordance with local sensibilities and concerns. Handwritten notes were taken of each conversation, and later, these notes were transcribed.

Delph-Keeper	Location	Current Context	Number Ceramic Vessels	Number Glass Vessels	Assemblage Provenance
Doonmore Hotel	Inishbofin	On walls and in the dresser in the hotel dining room; on shelves or mounted on walls in two sitting rooms and pub	121	15	Many pieces, especially platters, were inherited from family; assemblage increased by purchase or gifts from friends, customers and family members over the decades
George	Inishbofin	In kitchen press	8	0	Belongings handed down through the family
Celia	Inishturk	On shelves and above upper kitchen cabinets, bed and breakfast	31	1	Some possessions were inherited from family; others were acquired by purchase or gifts from friends, customers and family members over the decades
Michael	Inishbofin	On walls, mantelpieces and tables; in sideboards, bars and kitchen sink; in the main room, kitchen and parlour of uninhabited home	115	47	Specifics unknown
Catherine	Inishbofin	Recently added to an old dresser in a rental cottage	14	0	Most of the original delph contents were taken from an old dresser; now filled with post-1980s tablewares and remaining vessels

Delph-Keeper	Location	Current Context	Number Ceramic Vessels	Number Glass Vessels	Assemblage Provenance
Bridget	Inishbofin	Stored in kitchen press and dining room sideboard in a bed and breakfast	7	3	Belongings handed down through family
Delia	Inishbofin	Stored in cabinets and presses in the home	59	1	Possessions inherited from family
Anne	Clifden	On walls and bookshelves in the living room and kitchen area of the home	7	0	Bought in antique stores and markets over the last twenty years
Honor and Thomas	Inishbofin	In windowsills of home	2	0	Gifted as heirlooms from family members
Mary	Cashel	Kitchen press	1	0	Her favourite breakfast plate, inherited from her father

Table 2.2: Location, context and counts of ceramic (n=365) and glass (n=67) vessels recorded outside of dressers for this study

We documented dressers by measuring and photographing them, taking notes on details of style, decoration and construction (Fig. 2.20). Measurements of dressers, notes on dresser features and manufacturing, and counts of dresser contents were recorded during the interviews, and extensive photographs of dressers and delph completed the initial documentation process. In a few cases, it was necessary to work from photographs of dressers to make counts of the belongings and to make contact with the dresser owner if any queries subsequently arose. These documentation methods, where the only things we take away are notes and photographs, are sometimes referred to as 'catch-and-release' survey approach.

In recording the ceramic vessel forms found on dressers, in delph collections and in the archaeological record, I categorised them into common types (Fig. 2.21).[41]

Fig. 2.19: Other heirlooms in Mary's home: (a) one of her elaborate taxidermy displays in a glass case adorning her sitting room; (b) her early twentieth-century house shrine (made by her father)

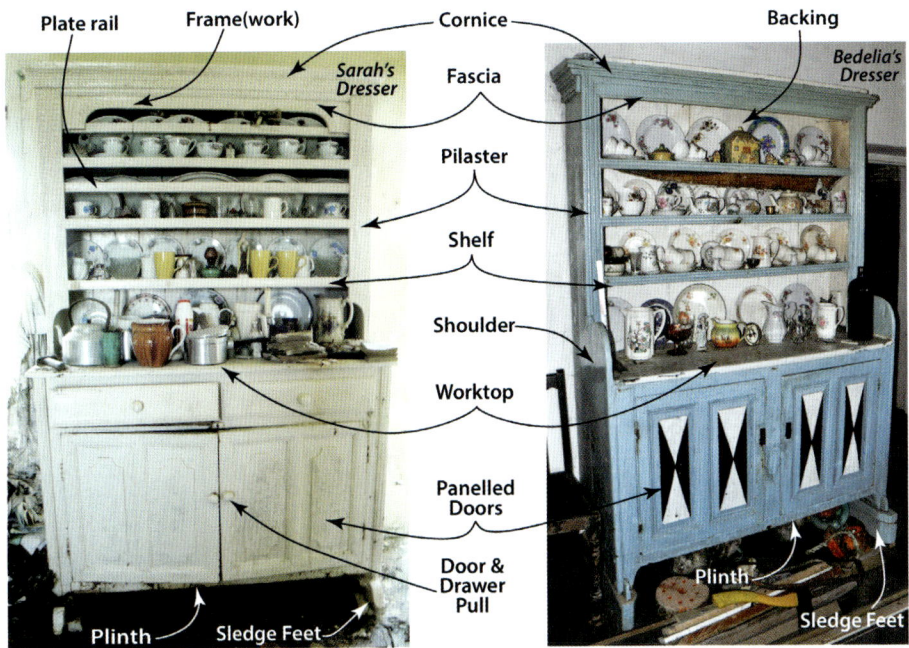

Labels on figure:
Plate rail — Frame(work) — Cornice — Backing
Sarah's Dresser — Fascia — Bedelia's Dresser
Pilaster
Shelf
Shoulder
Worktop
Panelled Doors
Door & Drawer Pull
Plinth — Sledge Feet — Plinth — Sledge Feet

COMMON TERMS TO DESCRIBE DRESSER ELEMENTS IN THIS STUDY

Fig. 2.20: Common terminology for dresser components that we recorded

For the most part, these vessels included tablewares, like refined earthenware and porcelain plates, platters, bowls, teacups, saucers, mugs, teapots, milk jugs, jugs and tureens.[42] Additionally, many delph and dresser collectors kept old crockery, particularly large redware bowls and basins, and stoneware food and beverage jars. I noted information on fabric (clay and temper components of the body), maker's marks on the base of vessels, decoration, size and state of preservation for each vessel and matching sets, taking photographs of as many objects as possible.

Each set of belongings, whether from a specific dresser or a delph collection, comprised a discrete assemblage (a group of objects). Archaeologists use the term to describe all or a subset of materials under study (Fig. 2.22). For example, the Doonmore Hotel possessed many milk jugs in their delph collection, and together they formed an assemblage for this place and form. Alternatively, I grouped dressers into assemblages based on age of construction (e.g. dressers made before 1950) or context (e.g. within a private home or a business).

As a rule, we documented belongings only from the top, open portion of dressers; we only opened presses or drawers if the owner asked us to examine their contents. In

Fig. 2.21: Most common delph forms from dresser and delph collections that offer good comparisons with the archaeological assemblages from the seven excavated houses on Inishark: (A) Platter, (B) Plate, (C) Jug, (D) Bowl, (E) Teacup and Saucer, (F) Milk Jug, (G) Mug, (H) Tureen, (I) Teapot, (J) Crockery Jar, (K) Large Redware Bowl or Basin

cases of delph stored in presses or closets, we recorded possessions owners wanted us to document; we specifically did not ask to see anything in storage. We maintained this rule for two reasons. First, I wanted to focus on how visible dressers and delph present stories to people living in or visiting a home, and therefore concentrated on those belongings people displayed openly. Second, I wanted to respect people's privacy as much as possible. In recording openly shown belongings and those the owner wanted to share from storage areas, I built a systematic and comparative dataset that did not rely on whether or not an owner allowed me to see possessions enclosed and hidden in the press. I also concentrated our documentation on ceramic vessels since they offer a robust comparative assemblage of belongings in dressers, delph collections, and archaeological assemblages from Inishark and Inishbofin.[43]

Upon return to Notre Dame, I compiled data on all recorded delph to ascertain origins and production dates based on decoration, fabric, maker's marks and information gathered from interviews. Forms, ages and provenance of glass vessels, statues or other objects were not analysed or recorded as systematically as the ceramics. Once the transcription of interviews and analysis were completed, I sent each participant a note of appreciation, thanking them for their time and knowledge, and included a copy of the interview transcript and dresser and delph analysis results for corrections, possible redactions and follow-up comments. A few participants asked that I redact information or photographs from the record, which is a right under IRB guidelines. In all cases, I happily complied with the requests: all participants maintained control over personal information, even years after the initial interview. Next, I wrote

Fig. 2.22: An assemblage of milk jugs from the Doonmore Hotel's delph collection

a 71-page illustrated synthesis of the comparative analysis of the recorded dressers and delph. I sent the report to all participants to share my findings and allow them to make comments, request redactions and add any other information they felt was important.

In sharing dressers, delph, homes and businesses with us, the Dresser Project's participants taught me a tremendous amount about homemaking in these communities today, as well as the history of residents' lives over the last 150 years. As one research element of the longstanding CLIC project, the dresser and delph research compares what we learned from dresser- and delph-keepers today with the results from the CLIC team's archaeological excavations on Inishark. In this next section, I discuss how the archaeological research on Inishark complements and enhances the Dresser Project research.

Archaeological and oral historical investigations of Inishark's homes and delph

For over a decade, CLIC's archaeological investigations on Inishbofin and Inishark have employed architectural survey and excavation methods to investigate past lifeways on these islands. An intensive survey of standing architecture in Inishark's

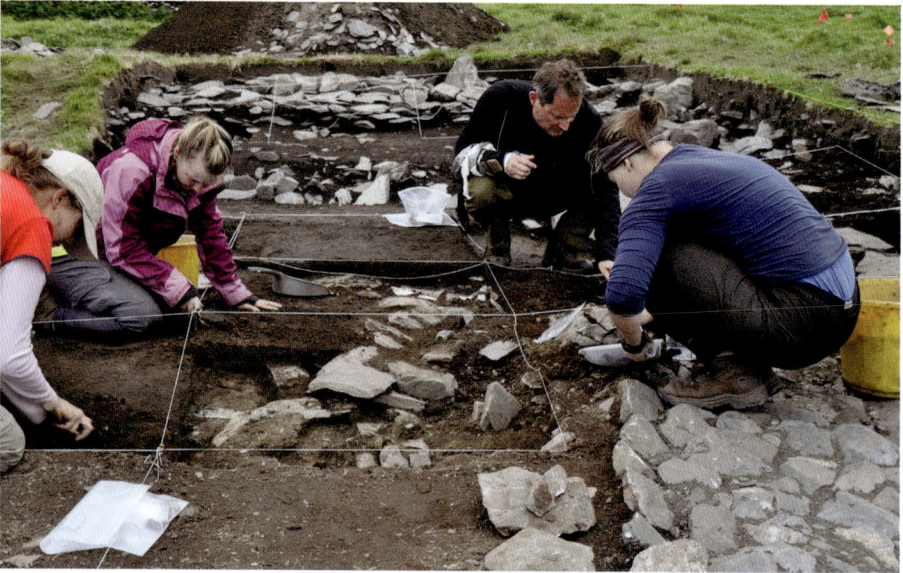

Fig. 2.23: CLIC director Ian Kuijt (in black) excavating with graduate and undergraduate students in House 8 in 2014 amidst a string grid of 1-square-metre units

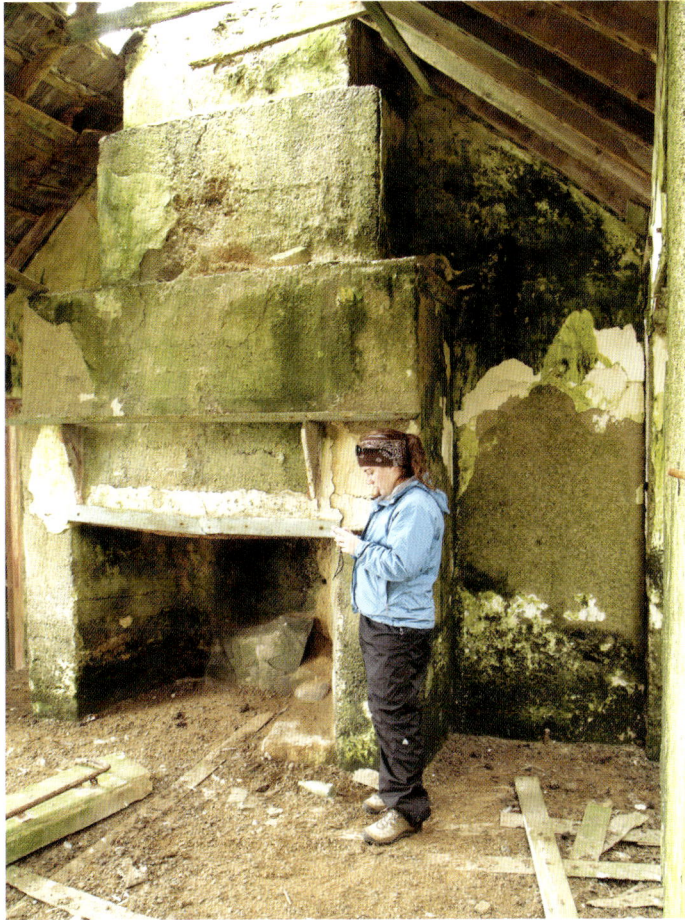

Fig. 2.24: Meagan McDonald recording architectural features, including the chimney, roof, doorways and windows, in one of the still-standing houses on Inishark

historic village (Figs 2.23 and 2.24) established a foundation for further excavation of the island's post-medieval homes. Survey team members recorded and photographed construction materials, phases of building and renovation, home features (such as windows, chimneys, doors, floors and hearths), and the state of preservation for each extant building.

Based on this survey and the results from remote sensing techniques, such as ground-penetrating radar and LiDAR scanning, several Inishark historic homes were selected for archaeological excavations. Remote sensing allows archaeologists to glimpse buried features below the surface without digging. In this case, using these techniques allowed the team to determine the location of houses and other buildings that were completely buried below the surface and guided our selection of which houses to excavate. During

Fig. 2.25: (a) Meagan McDonald excavating a 2012 test trench at House 8 and exposing nearly complete spongeware vessels; (b) Catriona Baldwin and Erin Crowley mapping architectural features at Inishark's medieval shrine of Clochán Leo

excavation, CLIC archaeologists recorded architectural plans of buildings and the locations (what we call provenience or the find-spot) of all artefacts uncovered (Fig. 2.25). One of the major goals of excavating these homes is to reconstruct the life history of a house, recording the sequence of construction and renovation events, as well as the types and locations of belongings we recover. We draw plans and take photographs of architectural features and artefacts *in situ* (where they were uncovered), adding information on the site formation processes (how the possessions and buildings came to be buried). All artefacts are then placed into bags with provenience information to await cleaning, labelling, analysis and further photography in the laboratory once excavations for that season have concluded.

Drawing on the detailed documentation from seven of Inishark's excavated houses, some with walls still standing and others buried completely, I studied the architectural life histories of these homes to gain a sense of when they were constructed, if and how inhabitants renovated them over the generations, and how long people lived in them. Using provenience information for artefacts, I also studied the pottery, glass vessels and other belongings that were found within or around these houses. To enable a comparison with the delph we recorded ethnographically, I analysed the ceramic vessel forms, decorations, origins and chronologies of the 4,800 pottery sherds, dating to roughly AD 1780–1960, recovered from these seven homes.[44] I tracked what types of pottery vessels people acquired, used and preserved in their (now long abandoned) homes as part of homemaking practices and how these practices changed over time on Inishark. For nearly whole or reconstructable glass vessels, I recorded forms, decorations, origins (when possible) and potential functions (e.g. food jar, alcohol bottle, medicine bottle).

Like many historical archaeology projects around the world, the CLIC team also collects oral histories from descendant community members (those whose ancestors lived in the place under investigation).[45] Within the scope of the CLIC project, descendant community members may reside in the surrounding region, in the same community, or on different continents (if their ancestors emigrated to somewhere distant). For instance, interviewing former inhabitants of Inishark plays a crucial role in our team's reconstruction of life on the island. Over the years, our team has toured the village with several of them, conducted interviews in Fountainhill homes, and collaborated with filmmakers (Inishbofin's Kieran Concannon and Notre Dame's Bill Donaruma) to document life on Inishark. These ethnographic details and oral histories supplement the archaeological evidence in often astonishing and always enlightening ways. Descendant community members graciously and generously gift us with precious time and incredible insights about life on the islands and often offer us very specific information to help us flesh out the life histories of Inishark's houses and the experiences of former inhabitants.

Archival research about life on Inishbofin, Inishark and Inishturk

To augment our understanding of past lifeways in these communities, the Dresser Project and the CLIC team investigate archived records whenever possible. Increasingly, many governmental records are available on the Internet, facilitating

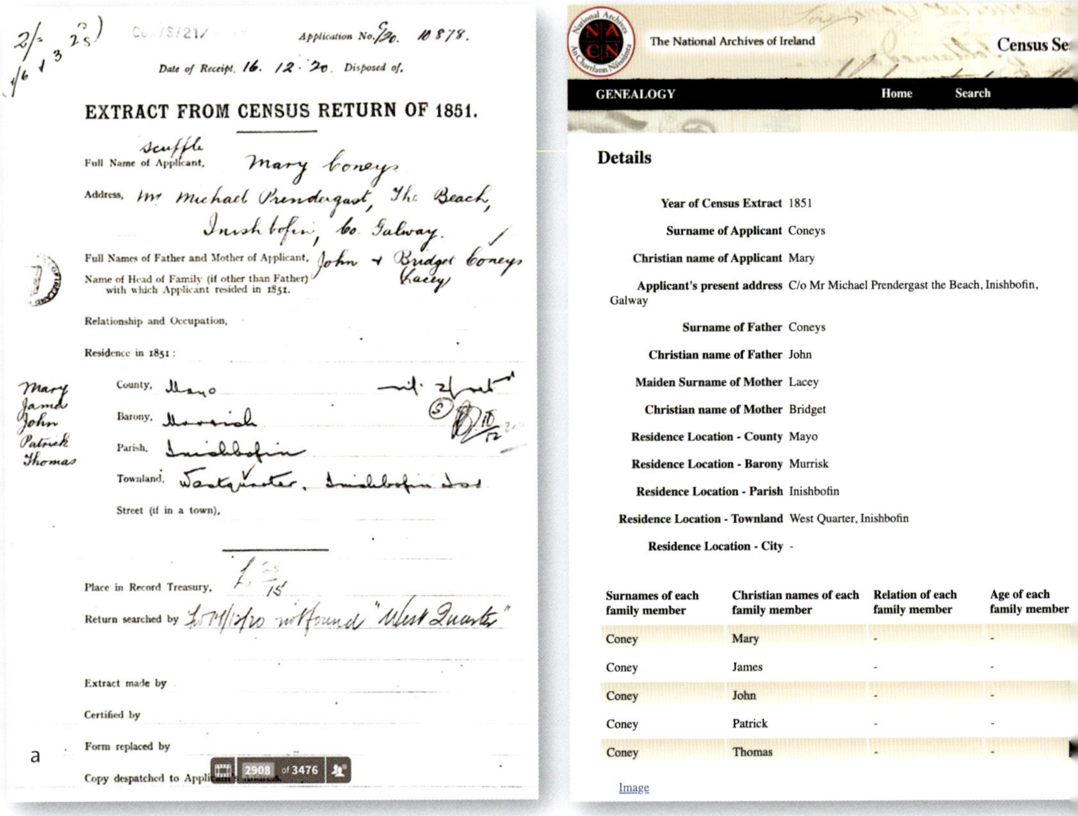

2908 of 3476

a

Application No. 10878.

Date of Receipt, 16 . 12 . 20. Disposed of,

EXTRACT FROM CENSUS RETURN OF 1851.

Full Name of Applicant, Mary Coneys (Scuffle)

Address, Mr Michael Prendergast, The Beach, Inishbofin, Co. Galway.

Full Names of Father and Mother of Applicant, John + Bridget Coneys (Lacey)

Name of Head of Family (if other than Father) with which Applicant resided in 1851.

Relationship and Occupation,

Residence in 1851:

County, Mayo

Barony, Murrisk

Parish, Inishbofin

Townland, West Quarter, Inishbofin

Street (if in a town),

Place in Record Treasury,

Return searched by

Extract made by

Certified by

Form replaced by

Copy despatched to Applicant

Mary
James
John
Patrick
Thomas

The National Archives of Ireland

Census Se

GENEALOGY Home Search

Details

Year of Census Extract 1851

Surname of Applicant Coneys

Christian name of Applicant Mary

Applicant's present address C/o Mr Michael Prendergast the Beach, Inishbofin, Galway

Surname of Father Coneys

Christian name of Father John

Maiden Surname of Mother Lacey

Christian name of Mother Bridget

Residence Location - County Mayo

Residence Location - Barony Murrisk

Residence Location - Parish Inishbofin

Residence Location - Townland West Quarter, Inishbofin

Residence Location - City -

Surnames of each family member	Christian names of each family member	Relation of each family member	Age of each family member
Coney	Mary	-	-
Coney	James	-	-
Coney	John	-	-
Coney	Patrick	-	-
Coney	Thomas	-	-

Image

Fig. 2.26: Screenshots of preliminary results from (a) Ancestry.com and (b) the National Archives of Ireland arising from a search of the 1841 and 1851 census search forms for the last name Scuffle (today's Schofield) on Inishbofin in the nineteenth century

genealogical, historical and archaeological research (Fig. 2.26). We compare what we learn from archaeological excavations, oral histories and ethnographic interviews to many of these archival documents to help us understand the history of life on Inishark and Inishbofin, especially as we attempt to trace family histories and link them to specific Inishark houses. For the Dresser Project, where I could interview dresser- and delph-owners, participants often knew specifically the craftspeople who made old dressers and who originally lived in their homes. People also frequently knew the names of the people who initially brought delph heirlooms to these communities. As we lack the ability to interview residents of excavated houses on Inishbofin and Inishark, archival records contribute crucial information when reconstructing homemaking practices on these islands during the nineteenth century.

While oral histories provided to us by the Inishark islanders and residents of Inishbofin and Inishturk offer a wealth of information about who lived where and with whom, most of their memories and histories reside within the twentieth century and do not encompass every house on these islands, especially those no longer standing for the last eighty or more years. The most commonly helpful records include folklore accounts, maps (especially the Ordnance Survey maps of the islands[46]), Irish census records, property valuation records and maps, church parish records (including marriage and baptismal records), Clifden court records, ship

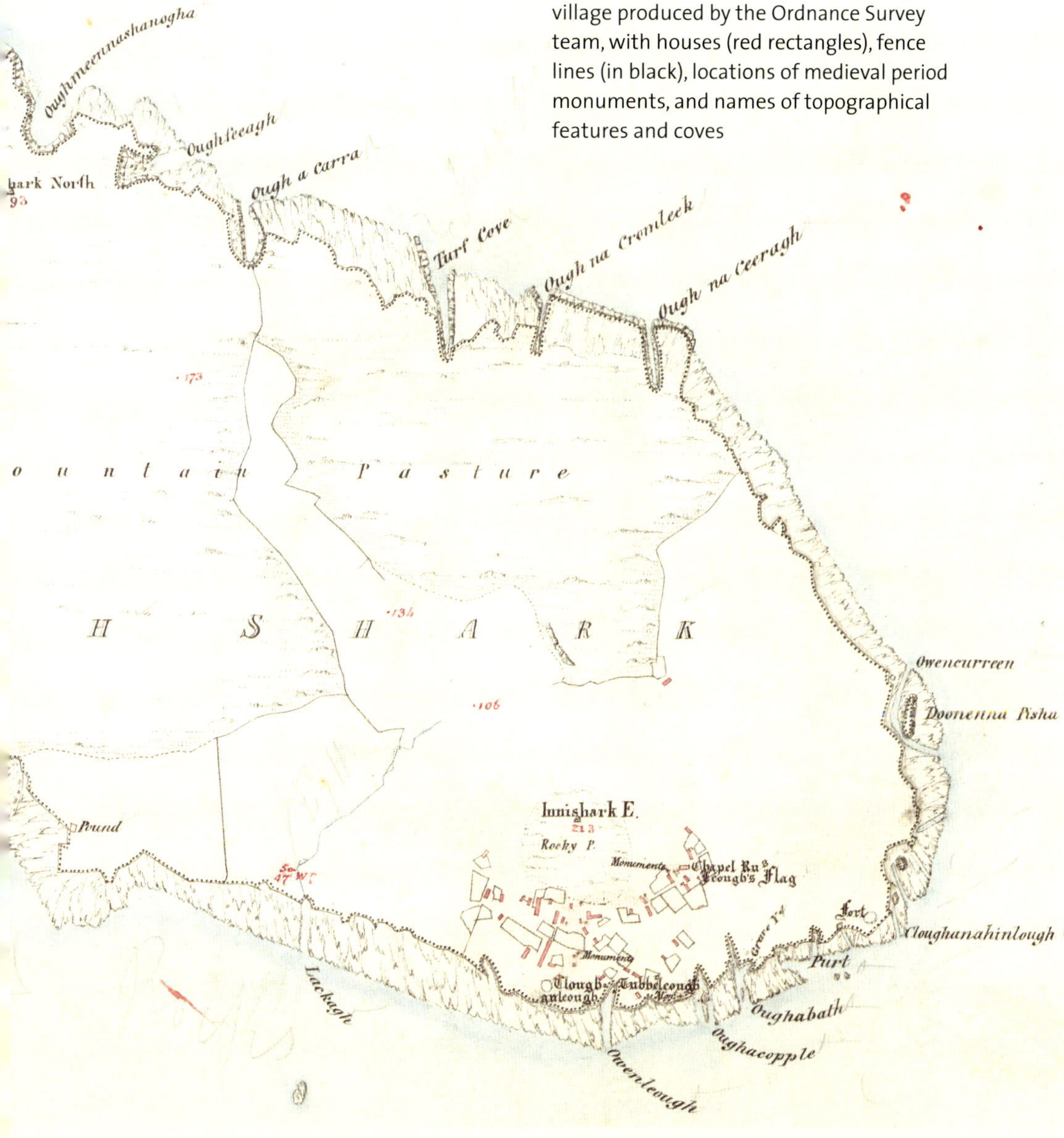

Fig. 2.27: The 1838 Fair Plan map of Inishark village produced by the Ordnance Survey team, with houses (red rectangles), fence lines (in black), locations of medieval period monuments, and names of topographical features and coves

manifests listing emigrants, and US Immigration records. For the Dresser Project, I mainly utilised the maps, census, valuation and church parish records, all available to varying degrees from online databases. In addition to these sources, the Dresser Project added one category of archival documents to this list: local shop ledgers.

Historical maps offer a snapshot of community organisation and how past islanders used the landscape around them. For instance, the Fair Plan of the first-edition Ordnance Survey map, published in 1838, depicts red-coloured outlines of village houses, the field walls surrounding garden plots as black lines, and the main historical monuments and geographical features (Fig. 2.27). Later, survey teams

Fig. 2.28: 1902 valuation record map for Inishark, based on the 1898 Ordnance Survey map. Note the changing valuation record numbers written in red, sometimes crossing out earlier numbers assigned to specific plots.

updated Ordnance Survey maps periodically (for instance, in 1898), and often they were in turn utilised by governmental bodies like the Valuation Office to track and assess residency, tenancy, ownership and taxes (Fig. 2.28). Valuation records also included a list of all head-of-household tenants and owners of houses, outbuildings (called offices), plots of land, and financial assessments in these communities. Valuation records were compiled in 1855 under the direction of Richard Griffith (and therefore called the Griffith's Valuation).[47] These cadastral (i.e. tax-related) records were updated annually or semi-annually, and for amateur and professional researchers today these documents provide a wealth of information about which families lived and worked on specific plots of land.

This oversimplified explanation makes this documentary source seem clear as crystal. However, as the reader will see in Chapter 4, the linkages between valuation records and families are not always transparent to researchers.[48] While we may know the names of heads-of-households, we often do not know who resided with them in that home, nor can we consistently correlate that household with a building on a historical map. The 1901 and 1911 census records can sometimes add clarity to the process of matching homes to inhabitants in early twentieth-century island villages. Census records are available on the Internet through the National Archives of Ireland; each house's inhabitants are listed by age, sex, occupation and ability or inability to read and write.[49] Figure 2.29 shows an example of a 1911 census recording for the westernmost house in the village; CLIC researchers named it House 57 and excavated a large portion of its buried foundations in 2017. Correlating the 1910 valuation records with the 1911 census, oral histories and archaeological evidence, we know that this home was inhabited by Thomas Cloonan, his wife Jane and their children Bridget, Mary, Julia, Patrick, John, Maggie, Ellen, Michael and Kate.

I supplemented the valuation and census records with church parish records as they became available online in order to pinpoint key life history moments for island residents. For instance, parish records of some baptisms and marriages performed in St Colman's Church on Inishbofin from 1867 to 1911 were digitised and recently posted online by Ancestry.com. These records help us track marriages and christenings during periods when census records were lost to fire. Figure 2.30 shows a page from these records detailing baptisms performed by Father John O'Boyle from May through June 1870, listing the names of the child, parents (including the mother's maiden name) and sponsors (Table 2.3 for transcription). From this record, we can see that both Inishbofin and Inishark children were christened in

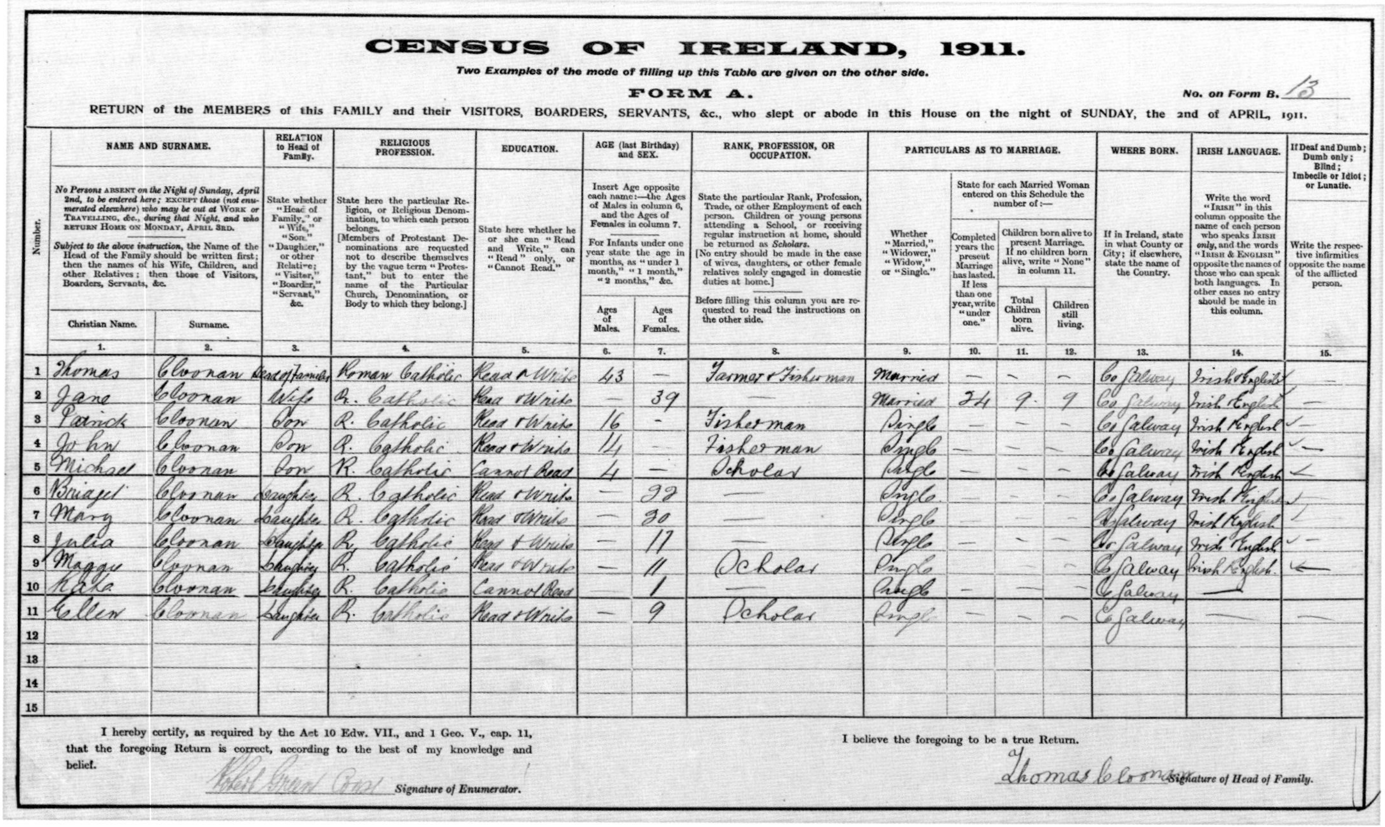

IRISH DRESSERS AND DELPH: HOMEMAKING THROUGH TIME

Fig. 2.29: 1911 Irish census form for the Cloonan family, who resided in House 57 on Inishark (House 13 of that year's survey)

St Colman's, with the first two entries including Edmund Scuffle on 1 May 1870 (assumed of Inishbofin) and John Lacey of Inishark on 3 May 1870.

Interestingly, these listings appear as ledger entries, with fees paid or waived in each case. Through Ancestry.com, other archival parish records are also available online. Figure 2.31 shows a listing of marriages performed by Fathers O'Boyle and O'Connor from late 1867 through November 1869 for residents of both Inishbofin and Inishark (Table 2.4 for transcript). This admittedly partial set of archival records includes the names of the wedding couple, their witnesses and officiant; sometimes the village in which they resided; the ceremony date; and the cost of the ceremony. The top entry displays the record of the 18 November 1867 marriage of John Baker to Bridget Lavelle of Middlequarter, Inishbofin, witnessed by James Tierney and Penelope Lavelle. Lower down in the register, two Inishark marriages were recorded in October 1869: on 21 October, Inishark islanders Patrick Cloonan and Mary Murray were married, the ceremony witnessed by Colman and Margaret Walsh; four days later, Patrick Murray of Inishark married Bridget Davis of Westquarter, Inishbofin with Thomas and Mary Holleran standing as witnesses.

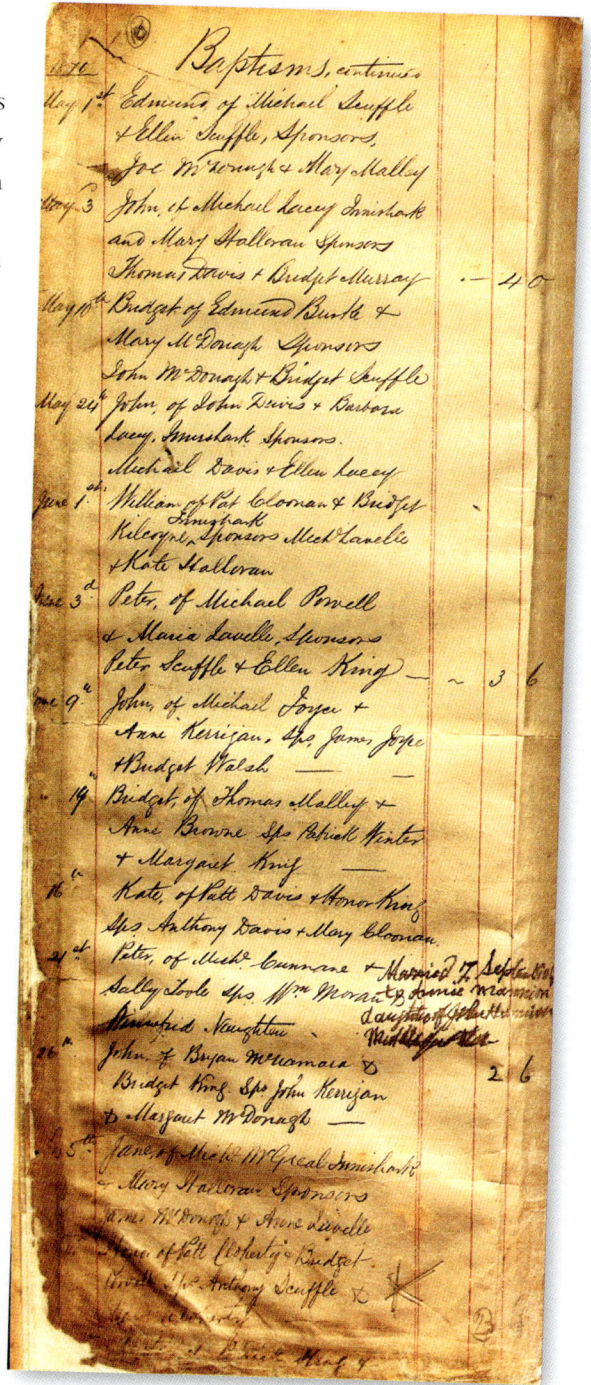

Fig. 2.30: Page from Inishbofin parish records of baptisms from 1870 performed on Inishbofin

Date	Child's Name	Parents	Sponsors
May 1	Edmund	Michael Scuffle and Ellen Scuffle	Joe McDonough and Mary Malley
May 3	John	Michael Lacey and Mary Halloran	Thomas Davis and Bridget Murray
May 10	Bridgct	Edmund Burke and Mary McDonough	John McDonough and Bridget Scuffle
May 24	John	John Davis and Barbara Lacey	Michael Davis and Ellen Lacey
May 1	William	Pat Cloonan and Bridget Kilcoyne	Michael Lavelle and Kate Halloran
June 3	Peter	Michael Powell and Maria Lavelle	Peter Scuffle and Ellen King
June 9	John	Michael Joyce and Anne Kerrigan	James Joyce and Bridget Walsh
June 19	Bridget	Thomas Malley and Anne Browne	Patrick Winter and Margaret King
June 16	Kate	Patt Davis and Honor King	Anthony Davis and Mary Cloonan
June 21	Peter	Michael Cunnane and Sally Toole	William Moran and Winnifred Naughton
June 26	John	Bryan McNamara and Bridget King	John Kerrigan and Margaret McDonough
July 5	Jane	Michael McGreal and Mary Halleran	James McDonough and Anne Lavelle
July X	Honor	Patt Cloherty and Bridget Powell	Anthony Scuffle and Mary Cloherty

Table 2.3: Transcription of Inishbofin parish records for 1870 baptisms from May to July

The final category of archival materials important to the Dresser Research includes eight shop or business ledgers we photographed page-by-page. These ledgers fall broadly into two categories: general and speciality shops. We have recorded ledgers or portions of ledgers from general shops in Cleggan, Inishturk, Tully Cross and Westport (Fig. 2.32). The other four photographed ledgers come from more specialised businesses in Clifden, and a fishing ledger from Inishbofin. We have conducted only preliminary investigations of these ledgers and hope to focus on them in future research. Within the guidelines established by the Belmont Principles, I strive to keep specific individuals' names anonymous when I present these ledgers. I revealed identities in the few cases where early twentieth-century, well-known Inishbofin shopkeepers appeared in the Westport general shop ledger purchasing stock for island shops. Even at this early stage in working with these ledgers, I have learned a great deal about how people acquired goods to furnish homes and nurture families.

Date	Newlyweds	Witnesses	Residency
Nov. 18, 1867	John Baker & Bridget Lavelle	James Tierney & Penelope Lavelle	Inishbofin: Middle-quarter
Feb. 19, 1868	Peter Scuffle to Anne King	John Scuffle & Bridget Scuffle	Inishbofin: Middle-quarter
Dec. 23, 1868	John Malley to Mary Halloran	Francis Halloran & Mary Halloran	not listed: Inishbofin?
Jan. 30, 1869	Michael Kerrigan to Mary Naughton	Joseph Halloran & Anne Naughton	not listed: Inishbofin?
Mar. 1, 1869	Patt Lavelle to Bridget Hughes	Michael Lavelle & Margaret Tierney	not listed: Inishbofin?
Apr. 4, 1869	Martin McCann to Mary Halloran	John Halloran & Catherine Corbett	not listed: Inishbofin?

Date	Newlyweds	Witnesses	Residency
July 14, 1869	John Price to Biddy Cunane	W. John McCormack & Ellen Powell	not listed: Inishbofin?
Oct. 21, 1869	Patrick Cloonan to Mary Murray	Colman M. Walsh & Margaret Walsh	Inishark
Oct. 25, 1869	Patrick Murray to Bridget Davin [Davis?]	Thomas Halloran & Mary Holleran	Inishark & Inishbofin: West-quarter
Nov. 1, 1869	Peter Joyce to Mary Cunnane	Patrick Cunnane & Annie McCormack	not listed: Inishbofin?
Nov. 17, 1869	Michael Gleshem to Sally Groden	John Halloran & Mary Halloran	not listed: Inishbofin?
Nov. 20, 1869	William McNamara to Mary McCormack	Michael McNamara & A---[Anne?] ----lliard /---lliant?	not listed: Inishbofin?

Table 2.4: Transcript of 1867–9 marriage records from Inishbofin parish registry

Combining the archival documents, archaeological research, ethnographic interviews, oral histories and ethnoarchaeological recording of dressers and delph creates a rich foundation for understanding past and present homemaking in these communities. In juxtaposing these sources, I compare the different views of the past and present in order to build a more comprehensive and nuanced understanding of the varieties of ways people make homes meaningful and useful to them and their families. When I encounter inconsistencies between different lines of evidence, such as the archaeological and documentary records, I approach these moments as opportunities to explore the nuances of human experience. Each methodology offers a fresh perspective on people's lives today and in the past, and my goal centres on encompassing all of these inconsistencies and congruencies alike. Ultimately, the weaving together of several perspectives on the past and present allows me to consider the history and future of homemaking in these communities.

Anthropological research as service to communities: significance of the Dresser Project

That 'passion for a place' that Ellen describes at the beginning of this chapter arises from the potent combination of personal histories, community heritage and homeplaces. The Dresser Project explores a single facet of this complex mix of past, present and future that creates and nurtures such a passion: how some islanders and residents of coastal mainland communities transform houses into homes. This line of inquiry offers insights into these places' broader historical and current context. I learned how people of these communities sustained themselves and their families through more than a century of immense social,

Fig. 2.31: Page from Inishbofin marriage records from 1867 to 1869 performed on Inishbofin

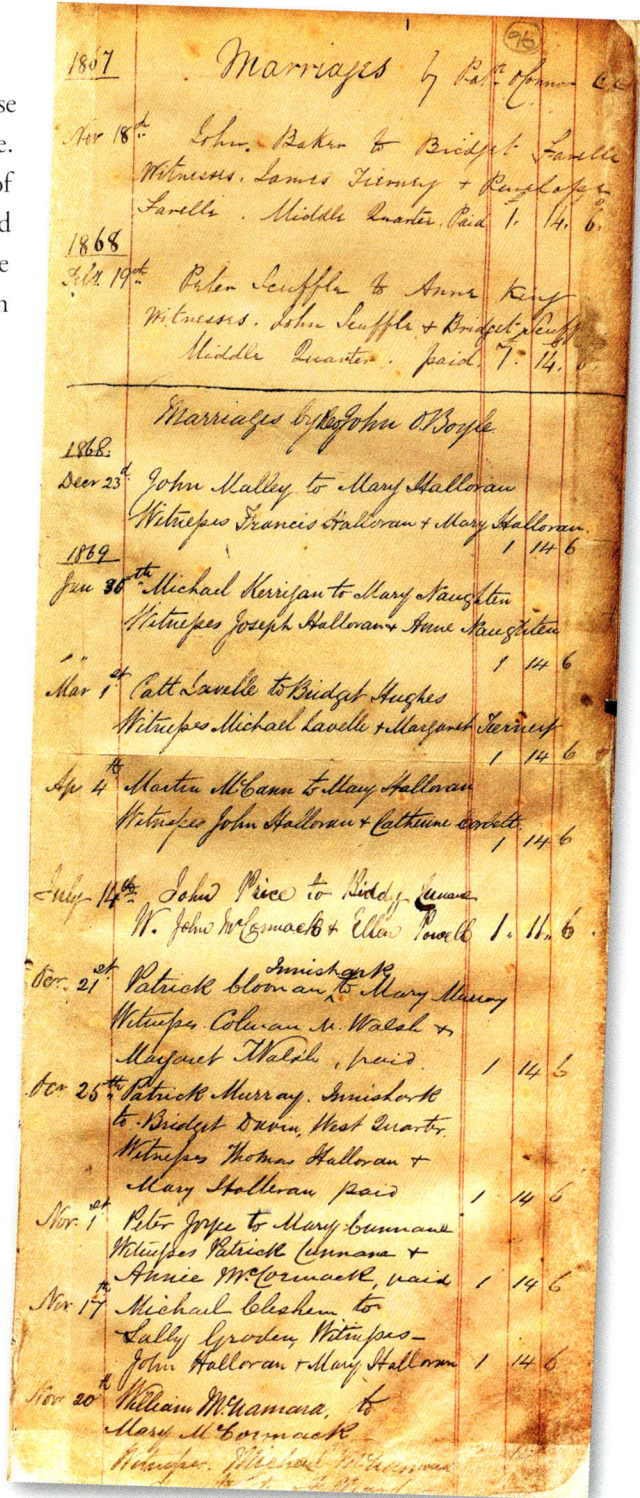

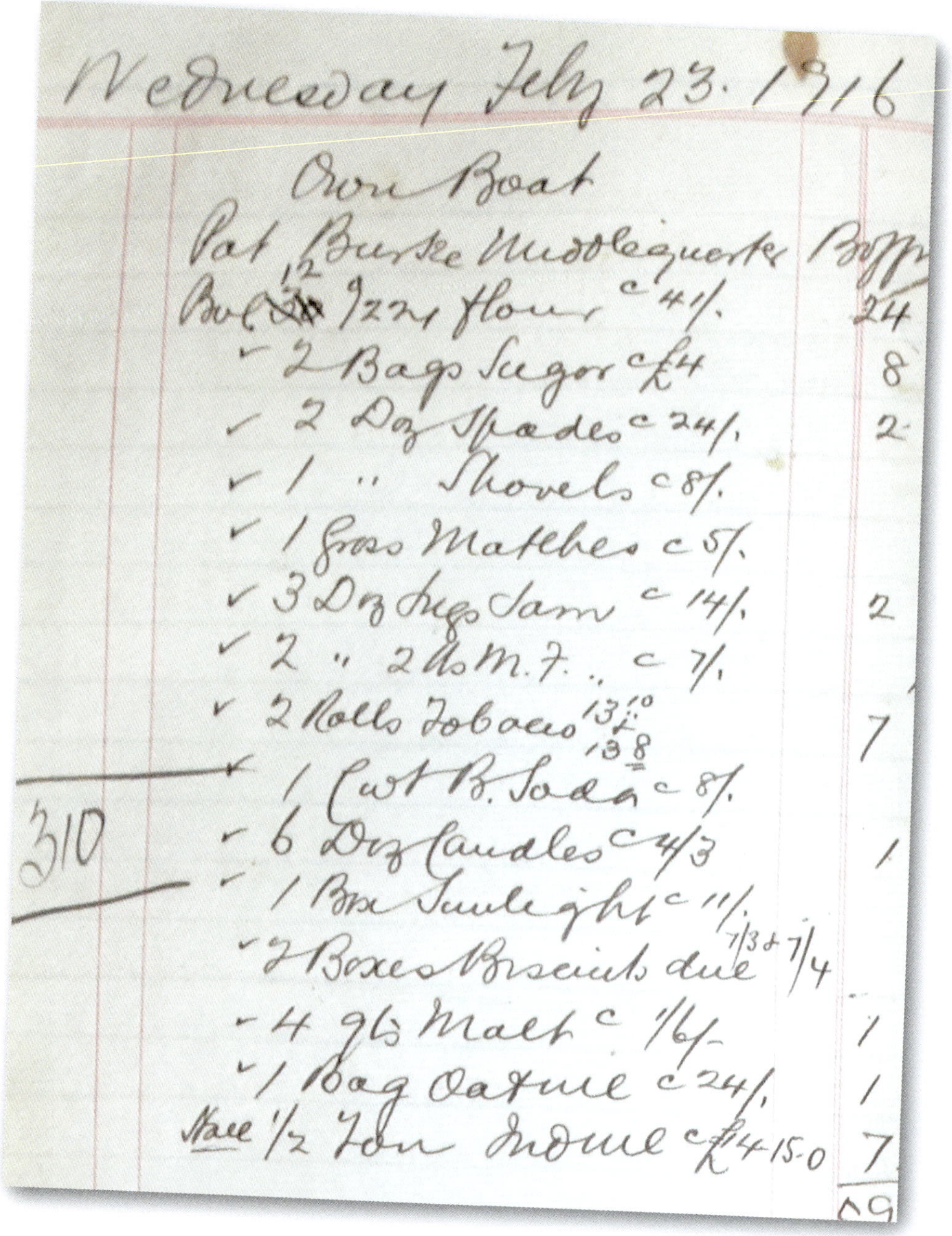

Wednesday Feby 23. 1916

Own Boat
Pat Burke Middlequarter Boffin

Bol.... 9zzs flour c 4/.		24
✓ 2 Bags Sugar c£4		8
✓ 2 Doz Spades c 24/.		2
✓ 1 ,, Shovels c 8/.		
✓ 1 gross Matches c 5/.		
✓ 3 Doz hugs Jam c 14/.		2
✓ 2 ,, 2 lb M.7. ,, c 7/.		
✓ 2 Rolls Tobacco 13 10 / 13 8		7
✓ 1 Cwt B. Soda c 8/.		
✓ 6 Doz Candles c 4/3		1
✓ 1 Box Sunlight c 11/.		
✓ 2 Boxes Biscuits due 7/3 & 7/4		
✓ 4 gls Malt c 1/6/–		1
✓ 1 Bag Oatmeal c 24/.		1
Nall ½ Ton Indmeal c £4 15-0		7

310

Fig. 2.32: Pages from historic shop ledgers: (above) ledger entries for purchases on Wednesday, 23 February 1916 by an Inishbofin shopkeeper acquiring stock in a Westport shop; (overleaf) ledger entries for 1930–1 purchases by the national school teacher on Inishbofin from a Clifden clothing shop

political and economic transformations. Through the dressers, delph and ledgers, participants taught me the many innovative ways that islanders and coastal community members creatively met the challenges of famine years, British occupation, emigration, cycles of boom and bust in fishing, revolution and civil war, two world wars, and the rigours and dangers of living with and off the ocean's bounty.

In today's world of climate change, economic crises, pandemics and increasingly polarised political arenas, many comm-unities across the globe struggle to sustain themselves. The history and present-day efforts of islanders and coastal community members who participated in the Dresser Project testify to the resiliency of people to contrive solutions to often overwhelming challenges, often starting in their homes and home communities. While the specific trials people face today may or may not differ from those faced by ancestors, these hurdles are no less grave or complex. In some ways, the big question faced by people in the past and in the future remains the same: how can people craft a life and future for themselves and their descendants in a particular place?

I hope the Dresser Project demonstrates that efforts to craft sustainable futures can utilise memories, belongings, stories and places from a community's past and present. This desire emerges from the CLIC project's approach to research: we want our research findings to help current and future inhabitants of Inishbofin, Inishturk, Fountainhill, Clifden, Cashel and other nearby places to nurture communities for generations to come. We use a particular set of tools and methods to help construct a picture of the past and present, a product we hope residents find meaningful and useful. We may be experts in anthropology and archaeology, but the residents of these communities are the true authorities in their livelihoods, landscapes and heritage. Ultimately, we work for them and strive to honour participants' trust in us as we investigate the rich heritage, ways of life and innovative solutions to life's complications, both large and small.

Increasingly, anthropologists and archaeologists transform research endeavours to become more than traditional academic projects: we redesign our scholarly work to incorporate pathways to service by creating knowledge collaboratively and offering relevant information that can be harnessed to celebrate heritage in local communities where the research occurs.[50] For example, as part of our service to the descendant communities in this area, the CLIC project has hosted several community events on Inishbofin to share with locals and tourists alike the results of our archaeological, ethnographic and archival research. These events are one small way to share our findings with the descendants of community members and to thank islanders for longstanding support and generosity of time and expertise. For these occasions, we invite all residents and tourists to see the research results, and we strive for a combined show-and-learn and show-and-tell approach. Everyone is encouraged to handle and discuss displayed objects that were uncovered in archaeological excavations on Inishark and Inishbofin. Presentations of archival research consistently elicit questions and more detailed discussions of ancestors and current kin. In less formal settings, we have extended an open invitation to residents to visit us while we work in our laboratory space on Inishbofin and excavate on Inishark. Formal and informal opportunities to collaborate with islanders significantly enhance the science, allowing us to craft more comprehensive and nuanced understandings of life in these communities. By sharing our findings, listening to and involving community members in the research, we learn more and become better scholars.

Ultimately, we see our research in these communities as a way to provide a service to the people with and for whom we work and from whom we learn. We hope to contribute valuable tools which islanders may utilise to build sustainable futures. We aspire for our research to resonate powerfully with contemporary islanders' and coastal community members' lives because the knowledge we produce offers them a grounding of where they came from and undeniable proof of their resiliency, validity and future potential to survive in a rapidly changing world. More specifically for the Dresser Project, I hope that inhabitants of these communities today, and descendants of those who emigrated long ago, find inspiration in how people used – and still use – dressers and delph to create meaningful homes for themselves.

3

'Round the house and mind the dresser': Lives of dressers

For many generations, dressers have offered a powerful tool for people in rural, western Irish communities to transform their houses into homes, crafting a space from which to overcome life's challenges. Often, dressers are paired with hearths in older homes (Fig. 3.1) or near cookers in more modern dwellings. This linkage between hearths and kitchens is no accident, because dressers store possessions that fulfil biological, functional and emotional needs in life: vessels for preparing and serving food and for maintaining critical emotional and familial memories, as well as photographs and heirlooms that recall social connections, joyful events and enduring loss. Whether placed on dressers or kept safely in presses, delph and other sticky belongings act as material expressions of people's past, present and, in some cases, aspired-for future, to make their homes and nourish their families.

Dressers carry stories of weddings, gifts, family histories, losses and perseverance. Like traditional, hand-crafted settles and settle beds, chairs, beds, presses, tables, house shrines, cradles and stools, dressers are often categorised as vernacular furniture. The term 'vernacular' is generally associated with everyday language and architecture traditionally situated within a particular time, place and people.[1]

Fig. 3.1: View along Sarah's dresser towards the hearth in her uninhabited home

When anthropologists speak of the vernacular, whether referencing speech, buildings or furniture, they specifically emphasise how people's understanding of the world both relies on and emerges through their daily cultural activities and landscapes. Vernacular evokes the everyday, the local, and the material scaffolding of people's lives. The close connection between vernacular furniture and vernacular architecture in Ireland's recent history emanates from the makers themselves: Bernard Cotton argues that the same craftspeople who built houses were also those who built shop fronts, settle beds, tables, chairs and dressers, working within their communities with materials locally ready to hand.[2] They produced items designed for specific spaces, most often homes, that addressed the needs of their consumers and made tangible local technological know-how and cultural understandings of what a house, chair, settle bed or dresser should be functionally and stylistically.

Old or new, and regardless of origin, dressers and delph contribute gravitas to the very nature of a home, weaving together tangible furnishings with the intangible sense of place and personhood. Inishbofin's local archaeologist and historian, Tommy Burke, taught me an old saying: 'Round the house and mind the dresser', which cautions people to take care during kitchen parties as musicians play music in people's homes.[3] While the tables, chairs, stools, settles and other pieces of furniture could be moved to create more room for dancers, musicians and revellers, dressers and their contents must remain untouched as treasured storehouses of heirlooms that herald a family's heritage, their present reality, and spoken and unspoken future desires.

This chapter describes how people use dressers and delph to turn houses into homes, with special attention to how they value these belongings. As storage receptacles of family and community histories, dressers and delph ground and enliven a home or imbue a business with a sense of hospitality, generosity and family connections. Fewer people keep dressers and delph today than thirty or forty years ago. As the older generations passed on and their homes were inherited by younger family members or sold, dressers were often placed in sheds and never reinstalled in the home. Honor, who no longer possesses her old home's original dresser, noted that many people felt a strong sense that Ireland was changing rapidly in the 1980s and therefore abandoned dressers with the idea of 'out with the old and in with the new'. She recounted to me that many people's old dressers became infested with woodworm and were discarded to prevent the infestation from spreading. Even today, people must decide whether to keep a dresser or discard it depending on its condition and their sense of how they wish to create a feeling of home for themselves.

To begin describing the participants' dresser and delph collections, I introduce readers to two dressers with very different life histories, the delph they store and the homes they grace. We start with James' and Margaret's dresser on Inishturk, built over a century ago. We then travel to Inishbofin with George's pre-fabricated dresser, which was bought from a shop in the market town of Clifden in 1965.

James' and Margaret's dresser on Inishturk, County Mayo

Upon entry into James' and Margaret's home on Inishturk, the visitor is greeted with a resounding welcome by the family's dresser, situated opposite the entryway: a large, painted, nineteenth-century dresser filled to the brim with delph (Fig. 3.2). Family photographs adorn the top of the dresser, as if to invite the guest to visit with absent kin as well as those who dwell in the home. Their dresser emanates hospitality, kinship and the family's and island's heritage.

Fig. 3.2: View of James' and Margaret's old dresser from just inside the door into the home's main room

Viewing James' and Margaret's dresser for the first time, one recognises the truth behind Henry Glassie's description of a County Fermanagh dresser: 'The dresser's beauty is its gift to the visitor …'[4] Glassie's accounting continues, noting that '[the dresser's] more important dimensions abide invisibly. One is social association. The Belleek plate that seems pretty to you and to her also means a wedding to her, a gift, a lost friend.' In talking with James and Margaret about their dresser and its delph, they confirmed Glassie's assessment from decades ago and kilometres distant.

James' and Margaret's dresser stands over seven feet in height and measures four and a half feet wide. Describing that it has always been in this position, they declined to even guess its weight, laden with 109 ceramic vessels, multiple glass vessels (including several lidded casserole dishes), framed and unframed photographs and countless layers of paint. The light blue and white paint, lovingly and dutifully maintained over the past century by the family, accentuates carved seashell-inspired corners and a sunburst motif of alternating pie-shaped blue and white segments on the two door panels of the press. The press' three drawers are also painted white and blue, with metal door pulls and signs that the central drawer may have featured a lock at one time. The dresser's upper portion contains four shelves, each with a beaded edge and framed by sloping shoulders. The side pilasters are also carved with horizontal beads, and the fascia board (the horizontal board linking the topmost shelf to the cornice) is decorated with dentil moulding. Interestingly, the cornice was carved to represent bricks, a motif matching the hearth situated on the adjacent wall, seen in a 1980s photograph by Liam Lyons displayed in the Inishturk Community Centre. This same motif also appears in some older Inishbofin homes with painted hearth surrounds, such as Sarah's former home (Fig. 3.1). This shared decoration was not surprising because a longstanding and strong web of kinship and economic networks connect these two islands. Many families share ancestral links between Inishturk, Inishbofin and Inishark. In fact, I first met James and Margaret on Inishark, where they travelled by a *currach* outfitted with an outboard motor across the open sea for over an hour's journey to picnic at James' ancestral home one fine day in 2012.

While James, Margaret and their ancestors have lovingly preserved this dresser for more than a century, its contents have changed over the decades. Their dresser displays the family's rites of passage and life histories through generations. Currently, the top shelf holds James' mother's ceramic set from the 1950s,[5] whiteware decorated with a popular rose pattern. While the rose set unfortunately lacks a maker's mark, James' and Margaret's wedding set on the second shelf proclaims to have been manufactured in the 1970s by Broadhurst Pottery in Staffordshire, England (Fig. 3.3).

On the third shelf, James and Margaret store a combination of heirlooms: a gilt-edged partial set of Arklow-produced whiteware plates, teacups and saucers from Margaret's mother's wedding set; a few pressed- or cut-glass bowls; and what Margaret identified as the dresser's oldest vessel: a small whiteware bowl, decorated with a light pink band below the exterior rim and a 'Made in Germany' green maker's mark on its base (Fig. 3.4). The bowl belonged to Margaret's mother, and

Fig. 3.3: Top three shelves of James' and Margaret's dresser, with details of decorative elements

she did not offer more details of its provenance: for Margaret the key meanings reside with her mother's memory. Next to this bowl sits a 1979 mug commemorating Pope John Paul II's visit to Ireland.

The fourth shelf contains large, upright platters forming a backdrop for casserole dishes, a teapot, teacups, saucers and three old jugs made in Ireland or England and dating to the 1940s and '50s (Fig. 3.5).[6] James and Margaret purchased two of the platters in Springfield, Massachusetts while visiting James' six older brothers and sisters, all of whom had emigrated and settled in the US to raise families. Both of these platters are bright, hand-painted and totally different in style from the other delph; Margaret loves them for their bright colours and the cherished memories they evoke of annual family visits.

Dresser-work often coincides with traditional gendered practices: men as carpenters and boatwrights often make dressers, and women and girls keep them as part of their homemaking practices. This dresser is no exception: James recounted that his ancestor, Patrick McHale, built it sometime around 1870 as a wedding gift for another of James' ancestors, at the time when the house was originally constructed. Margaret acts as the primary dresser-keeper, removing delph and other objects three times a year for cleaning at Christmas, Easter and during the summer. She does not permit anyone to help her, as she worries about accidental breakage.

Fig. 3.4: Delph heirlooms from Margaret's and James' mothers, displayed in their dresser: (a and b) a German pink-rimmed bowl with its mark, manufacturer unknown; (c and d) one of a set of small Arklow plates with a pink rose pattern with its mark, from the 1950s

She and James have discussed the idea of stripping the dresser to follow the more recent fashion of varnished finishes, but she remarked that such a finish would darken the room. Moreover, she asserted that a stained old dresser is not 'proper'. They both strongly value keeping the dresser as is, within their family and in their home.

Fig. 3.5: Irish- and English-manufactured jugs from James' and Margaret's dresser: (a and b) jug with decal floral decoration and vertical fluting and (c) its maker's mark: Arklow, 1950s; (d and e) jug with floral decal decoration and a thin green band encircling the rim and (f) its maker's mark: manufactured by a cooperative post-Second World War economic scheme by a group of British pottery manufacturers, 1945–52

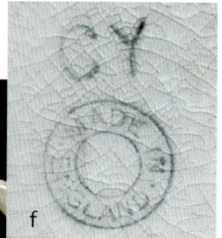

About two decades ago, someone offered them a great deal of money for the dresser, presumably to be sold to antique dealers or collectors. They refused to relinquish it.

The dresser remains where it was first placed in the home, then a two-room cottage with a thatched roof and large double-sided hearth serving both rooms. In the intervening century, James' family renovated these original rooms and expanded the house around them, installing two large skylights in the original sitting room and adding a modern kitchen, an enclosed porch and several bedrooms to the home. Reading the home's life history of architectural additions, conversions and renovations requires a similar attention to detail as that used to investigate the dresser and delph maintained by the family who have dwelled in this home for more than a century.

James' and Margaret's dresser and delph exemplify the stickiness and voicefulness of their belongings, reminding the visitor, as well as themselves, of the decades of challenges and triumphs of their ancestors and current family members. Values of family and heritage echo through the heart of their home, with two generations of displayed ceramic wedding sets as well as the dresser itself, whose life history began as a wedding gift. The Arklow pieces resound with Irish history, while the recent platters from Springfield speak directly to the Irish diaspora and the grief of missing loved ones. The papal commemorative mug evokes their Catholic faith, and the British-made pottery testifies to their longstanding participation in international trade markets, and their discerning engagement with popular ceramic fashions. Every vessel references a story of their family over five generations and conjures their ancestors, family members separated by emigration and death, and their past and present hopes for future generations.

Moreover, the dresser's contents change with time and life: Margaret keeps her dresser current, rejoicing in the blossoming of her family's heritage. In June 2019, I called into their home again and noted that she had added new family photographs to the dresser's top and reorganised the shelves with a few new items. Just as James' and Margaret's home accumulated new rooms and renovated spaces, so too does their dresser, as family members carry on their lives in places nearby and distant. In this regard, dressers embody dynamic qualities, including what anthropologists call emergent properties in which something more coalesces from an assemblage of many parts.

James' and Margaret's dresser provides an accurate snapshot of many of the other dressers we documented. The life histories of the displayed delph and dresser offer intriguing and powerful testaments to how people use seemingly prosaic belongings to endure and nurture their families through good times and bad, anchoring their homes in the past and present. We now travel over the open sea to George's dresser, situated in the home of an Inishbofin bachelor, to illustrate a slightly different perspective on dressers and delph.

George's dresser on Inishbofin, County Galway

George lives in the east end village of Rusheen in a cottage he inherited from his parents. The village's homes are nestled closely together, facing the horseshoe-shaped harbour (Fig. 3.6). He recounted to me that he had recently reinstalled his father's dresser into the main room of the house, after it had been stored for a long time in a shed behind the house, where it held his father's tools. Like most dressers, his is located so it is one of the first things a visitor sees when entering the cottage (Fig. 3.7), situated on the wall adjacent to the hearth. Together, the dresser and fireplace frame the main room and emanate that intense feeling of home and family heritage.

While James' and Margaret's dresser radiated a profound sense of age and history, George's felt more recent and sported a more modern finish: it had been stripped and varnished and featured glass panel doors etched with a floral design. Furniture historian Claudia Kinmonth noted that glass doors were often installed in older Irish dressers or built into new dressers from the 1930s onwards in line

Fig. 3.6: View of Rusheen's cottages on Inishbofin

Fig. 3.7: View of George's dresser with the etched glass doors open wide

with greater concerns for hygiene in Ireland.[7] The press contained two drawers and two doors, and the profile of the footings was clean and straight: gone were the sledge feet we saw in James' and Margaret's dresser on Inishturk and common to many older dressers. Several other features marked this dresser as more recently fashioned: the cornice was uncarved, and the dresser contained only three shelves and lacked shoulders to frame the worktop. Finally, the backing was formed of one sheet of wood rather than a series of vertical boards. Regardless of its relative youth of roughly sixty years, George's dresser functions similarly to its older siblings: it evokes the heritage of the home and the family whose members nourished the dresser and the delph, welcoming guests and displaying a history of hospitality, generosity and community connections.

Fig. 3.8: Detail of the shelves on George's dresser

When George inherited the house after his father passed away, he decided that it needed a dresser to make it 'feel right', to feel more like a home – and he immediately thought of his father's dresser in the shed. Originally, the dresser had been painted brown, but George wanted to brighten up his main room, and thus, he refinished it. He had to replace the worktop, bottom doors and hardware, but other than those changes the dresser remains largely as his parents had kept it. Many of the eighty-four vessels displayed now had previously been in the dresser, with the exception of a few pieces that were damaged or could not be fit without crowding the contents, and including a few new additions purchased by George.

George arranged his delph with symmetry, colour and balance in mind. Teacups and saucers are neatly stacked, plates and platters barely overlap, creating a tidy horizon line for each shelf. He placed small statues or glass vessels to frame each shelf, and focal pieces, like the jug and teapot on the middle shelf and the small wood stand with a gilded teapot and teacup situated in the centre of the top shelf. Splashes of yellow plates and cat statues, red roses and blue Willow platters and teacups invite the eye to linger on each shelf to appreciate his display's artistry and aesthetic (Fig. 3.8).

As he filled his refinished dresser, George recounted that he realised that he needed more blue vessels to complement the old Willow platters on the top shelf. He purchased some modern renditions of blue Willow teacups and saucers from SuperValu in Clifden, updating the collection while still anchoring the dresser and its contents with older heirloom pieces. While we chatted about the dresser, George rang his uncle Nicholas to see if he might be willing to stop by and talk more about the dresser. He arrived at George's house soon after the invitation and described the

Fig. 3.9: George's (a) Syria pattern platter with (b) maker's mark, made by R. Cochran & Company, Verreville Pottery in Glasgow, Scotland, 1869–1917

original dresser that this newer one replaced. Nicholas purchased this dresser on behalf of his brother, ordering it from Stanley's in Clifden in 1965, along with two wardrobes and a bed. Large old platters graced the top shelf on that older dresser, supported by plate rails. Nicholas remembers these vessels filled with potatoes at large family dinners and special occasions. These platters are not currently displayed because they have been damaged over the last century. George keeps these vessels safely stored in the kitchen press with other old delph heirlooms.

All three of these old platters were decorated with brown transfer-printed designs and possessed maker's marks on their bases: two matching platters with Syria pattern marks (Fig. 3.9) and one with the Damascus pattern mark. The Robert Cochran & Sons Verreville Pottery in Glasgow, Scotland produced the Syria pattern platters between 1869 and 1917.[8] David Methven & Sons of Kirkcaldy, Scotland produced Damascus pattern platters from 1870 to 1928.[9] By the time I concluded the dresser study, I had documented examples of these same platters on several other dressers and delph collections. Our archaeological team also found sherds from them while excavating historic period houses on Inishark. These patterns were clearly popular additions to people's homes.

As we photographed the platters, Nicholas noted that he was unsurprised that they were made in Scotland. He recalled stories of people from Inishbofin and Inishark travelling to Scotland seasonally to work in the potato fields. He called this practice 'bothy work' and noted that the agricultural labourers were called 'tattie hoakers'. Archaeologist Franc Myles has suggested that the archaeological excavations on Inishark and Inishbofin have produced so many Scottish-made pottery because of this labour connection between this region and Scotland.[10] While we do not know the exact circumstances of how George's ancestors acquired these platters, they do communicate a few key pieces of information: (1) these people had access to Scottish-made ceramic vessels, in particular platters, the largest vessel to grace dressers and dinner tables; (2) they assessed and followed popular ceramic fashions of the late nineteenth and early twentieth centuries, acquiring the same vessels as many of their neighbours and kin; (3) they displayed and used these vessels in their home, showing good taste in ceramics and the ability to acquire and maintain them; and (4) family members kept these possessions for at least a century and over many generations, prizing them as precious heirlooms.

In addition to these platters, George's dresser and its earlier incarnation contained three vessels with maker's marks from British Staffordshire factories: a

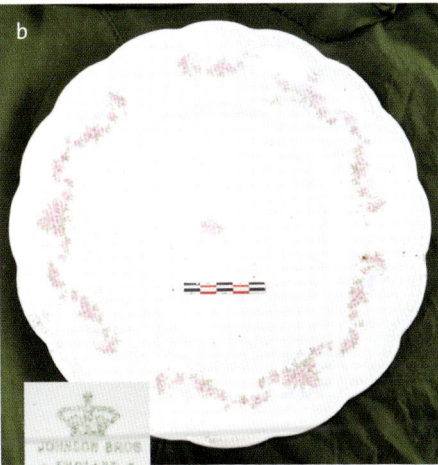

Fig. 3.10: Examples of George's delph: (a) Sadler teapot from the dresser; (b and c) scalloped Johnson Brothers plate in storage; (d and e) Wade mug commemorating Queen Elizabeth II's 1953 coronation

Fig. 3.11: Old plates mended with lead staples, formerly displayed in the original dresser belonging to George's parents

Johnson Brothers plate with pink roses encircling the rim, a teapot with a red rose pattern made by Sadler Pottery,[11] and a mug commemorating the 1953 coronation of Queen Elizabeth II made by Wade Pottery (Fig. 3.10).[12] George believes that the Sadler teapot came from one of his grandmother's trips to England. Another saucer, decorated with a pink rose pattern similar to the Johnson Brothers plate, was manufactured in Carrollton, Ohio.[13] George reported that his mother travelled to the US frequently to visit family, and he believed that she brought this saucer back from one of those trips.

George stored two other plates from his parents' dresser in his kitchen press: a blue Willow plate and a white plate with a brown hand-painted and stamped design. Neither vessel had a maker's mark, but both had been repaired with lead staples (Fig. 3.11). George recounted how these vessels had been precious enough to mend rather than discard. To him, they spoke of hardship, perseverance and heritage, and he keeps them safe in his home.

George's dresser is filled with belongings for display, and he does not use them daily. He occasionally adds possessions to the dresser, generally as mementoes of the past or his experiences. For instance, on the middle shelf he has placed a small clay pipe and a baby spoon found while digging in his garden, as well as small pieces of sea delph (pottery sherds gathered from the seashore) that he has discovered while walking around Inishbofin. In many ways, George designed the dresser to link with his parents and grandparents, anchoring his home with his ancestors while adding pieces of his present to the tableau. As we witnessed with James' and Margaret's dresser, the displayed heirlooms reference greater political and economic realms, such as the migrant labour of his ancestors, the coronation of Queen Elizabeth II, and his ancestors' struggles and successes in surviving poverty, generations of English occupation and the loss of loved ones to emigration and death. If James' and Margaret's dresser exudes 'here-ness' and a firm resolution to stay in place, George's sticky dresser and delph speak to the mobility of everyday life in the past and present.

Dresser-makers and dresser- and delph-keepers

George's and James' and Margeret's dressers and delph exemplify how people use their belongings to enliven their homes, celebrate their families, remember loved ones distant and gone and express personal values and taste.[14] Both personal and personalised, they celebrate specific people, places and events. To create that special sense of 'home', these objects traverse islands, oceans, continents and generations to bring memories, people and heritage together. We can see these journeys by thinking about the similarities and differences in the biographies and contexts of these furnishings.

Let's begin with similarities. First, both dressers act as focal points in their homes, located in the central room, and draw the eye due to their size, position and bright colours. George filled his dresser with his parents' delph, updating the display with items found on his beloved island and adding his own touches, such as the blue Willow saucers and teacups from SuperValu. James' and Margaret's dresser also contains family heirlooms, particularly those celebrating three generations of weddings, beloved vessels from their parents, and pieces they have acquired while visiting family who emigrated to America. Furthermore, the displayed possessions on these dressers are used sparingly, if ever. Finally, both of their homes mirror this deft, personalised combination of old and new, with additions and renovations indexing the life histories of the inhabitants as new people arrive and others depart.

Like cooking or baking, the differences between these Inishturk and Inishbofin dressers demonstrate how dresser- and delph-keepers are not constrained by strict, never-changing recipes of where they place dressers in a home, what they display on that dresser and how often they use belongings stored on a dresser. James' and Margaret's venerable old dresser was made locally and has occupied the same place in their home since its construction and emplacement. George's much younger dresser has enjoyed a more peripatetic life history: purchased from a mainland store in Clifden as a pre-fabricated dresser. The identity and location of its craftspeople are lost to time: we have no concept of where or who made this dresser originally, likely in a mainland shop or factory. At some point, George's father moved it from the house to a shed to store his tools. George, in turn, reestablished his father's dresser back into the home, lovingly restoring it to its former place near the hearth.

Framing these similarities and differences, the biographies of these dressers and their delph (like those in many other homes, rental cottages, restaurants and bed and breakfasts) testify to multiple connections through time and travel within and between these island and mainland communities. For instance, when visiting with George and Nicholas on Inishbofin, we learned how Nicholas' grandparents came from Inishturk and some of his family still reside there. Similarly, James' and Margaret's dresser was built as a matrimonial gift for the marriage of two young

Inishturk residents, though one of James' ancestors lived on Inishark. These stories of kinship and connections between these small communities represent common themes we heard from multiple dresser- and delph-keepers as they showed us their favourite sticky and voiceful teacups, saucers, jugs and platters, all of which reminded them of friends and family members, whether living down the road or absent due to emigration or mortality. Returning to folklorist Henry Glassie's description of dressers in County Fermanagh in the early 1970s, he describes that delph vessels remind us powerfully of the importance of kin and community:

> While I was gone, they say, I thought of you. My mind did not abandon our home. The gift compensates for the loss of company. Become an ornament, it becomes company, a continual memento of the one who remembered the one whose responsibility was staying home to keep the home alive.[15]

Thus, dresser-makers and dresser- and delph-keepers play crucial roles in a family's and community's sense of heritage and in their efforts to pave pathways towards the future. While we may not think of skilled carpenters as agents who can change the world, I argue differently. Dresser-makers may not exert influence globally, but the furnishings they create act as tools for everyday people to craft memories of the past, celebrate the present, and overcome present and future challenges in their own world, bounded by the sea, land and the inexorable passage of time. Dresser-makers enable people to enact change, to make their lives more connected to the past and present, and their homes more nurturing – in other words, they offer powerful placemaking tools to homemakers.

Bernard Cotton has argued that furniture makers lived within the communities that used their products and therefore shared an intimate understanding of how furniture should fit within homes and serve its owners. Moreover, these 'makers saw their creations as objects which would enliven the home'.[16] On Inishbofin, participants identified several craftspersons who were noted for making dressers, including Peter, Willie and Michael Burke - all talented local furniture-makers (Fig. 3.12).[17] Sarah, Peggy and William, and Julia recounted that their dressers were made by Peter or Willie Burke. Interestingly, the decorative carving on the pilasters and fascia of Peggy's and William's dresser resembles that of Sarah's and Julia's, suggesting that both may have been built by the same maker (Fig. 3.13).

Fig. 3.12: Signature of Michael Burke inscribed on the interior of his wardrobe door in our 2012 visit to his uninhabited home

Fig. 3.13: (a) Detail of decorative carving on Sarah's dresser in her uninhabited Inishbofin home; (b) detail of decorative carving on Julia's dresser

On Inishturk, we recorded Bedelia's (the former island postmistress) and Celia's dressers, both made by craftsperson John Joe O'Toole, a well-respected carpenter and boatwright. We also documented one of O'Toole's dressers on Inishbofin: Catherine commissioned him to make her a dresser for her business, the Galley Restaurant, which opened in 1999 (Fig. 3.14). A comparison of Bedelia's dresser, made by O'Toole approximately seventy years ago, with his later dressers made in the 1990s demonstrates that, like all good makers, he kept current with stylistic preferences and changing tastes. Bedelia's dresser possesses the key elements of older dressers in this region: sledge feet, painted decoration, wide backing boards and a cornice with crown moulding. This dresser had no plate rails nor evidence that they had ever been part of it. Celia's and Catherine's dressers conform to more recent styles: varnished and not painted, narrow backing boards, cornices with cupid bow moulding, and bases lacking sledge feet. Moreover, the two more recent dressers were purpose-built to serve in business settings: a bed and breakfast and a restaurant. Both of these more recent dressers have three drawers and were bespoken for specific spaces within these establishments. All three dressers made by O'Toole possess low, hemispherical shoulders bounding the worktop, two panelled doors in the press, and a raised plinth allowing for a relatively low space below the press. Interestingly, the top shelf on Celia's more recent dresser includes a plate rail, although none of the other documented dressers by O'Toole contained them (Fig. 3.15).

O'Toole also built *currachs* (Fig. 3.16) and, later in his life, trained another local craftsperson, Mark, to make both dressers and *currachs*. Mark's dressers currently grace the dining rooms of two bed and breakfasts on Inishturk (Fig. 3.17). Both of his dressers have rounded shoulders, two drawers, two doors and cornices with crown moulding. He fashioned the fascia board on Celia's dresser with a carved wave while he crafted an elegantly simple fascia board for Honora's dresser. Like O'Toole's dressers made in the 1990s, these dressers are both varnished, lack sledge feet, and utilise narrow backing boards. The Museum of Country Life in Turlough Park, Castlebar, County Mayo also displays one of Mark's fine *currachs*. In talking with me about dressers made by his mentor O'Toole, he described them eloquently as 'made to grow old': well-crafted to endure for generations, designed to serve many owners, and endowing a home or business with messages of hospitality, generosity and perseverance while displaying belongings that tell stories of family, community, connections and heritage.

Honor, Thomas, Catherine, Celia, Peter and Martin all lamented the loss of the craft and expertise of dresser-making; they noted that fewer men (or women) learn dresser-making today. Most new dressers are now store-bought and brought to the island from other places and cannot be connected to any specific craftsperson. This process of importing dressers started with pre-fabricated kits in the 1950s or

a

Fig. 3.14: Dressers made by Inishturk craftsman John Joe O'Toole: (a) (opposite page) Bedelia's dresser in her uninhabited Inishturk home; (b) Celia's dresser in her Inishturk bed and breakfast; (c) Catherine's dresser in her Inishbofin restaurant

Fig. 3.15: Detail of top two shelves of Celia's dresser showing the older-style plate rail in the uppermost shelf

Fig. 3.16: Liam Lyons' photograph of John Joe O'Toole building a *currach* on Inishturk in 1992

1960s (such as George's dresser), and of course many houses today do not host a dresser at all. Some participants noted that the recent, kit-built dressers missed something. Still others believed that it was more important to have a dresser than not; hand-crafting and knowing the craftsperson was not essential to dresser-keeping. However, all participants still feel a reverence for old dressers, and others truly appreciate the craft and knowledge materialised in a well-built dresser built by a true craftsperson for a specific home or business.

Mark, dresser- and *currach*-maker, is not the only skilled carpenter of more recent generations. Over the years, I have met several young men from Inishbofin, including Peter, who continue to work in wood as part of their full-time employment or as a hobby. The nearby coastal village of Letterfrack hosts the National Centre for Excellence in Furniture Design and Technology, an arm

Fig. 3.17: Two dressers made for Inishturk bed and breakfasts by Mark in the 1990s: (a) Celia's second dresser; (b) Honora's dresser

of the Atlantic Technological University,[18] training the next generation of skilled craftspeople.[19] Anne's dresser, located in a Clifden home, was one of the earliest dressers made by students at the institute's campus in Letterfrack (Fig. 3.18). Now painted light blue, it combines classic elements of older and more recent dressers. The wide backing boards, the panelled press doors, four shelves and open shelving are more commonly associated with older, traditional dressers. The dresser-maker's choice to not frame the worktop with shoulders and to finish the top with rounded edges and no formal cornice gives the dresser a more modern feel. Anne recounted how she purchased it with much persuasion and exertion from the Clifden shop owner, who wanted to keep it as a unique and historically important piece.

On the other side of the dresser–delph equation reside the dresser- and delph-keepers, who accept the responsibility to openly display or safely store the heirlooms and belongings speaking of a family's historic and present accomplishments and

memories. They create tableaus in dressers and on walls and shelves that communicate a home's or a business' generosity, hospitality, history, community, connections and heritage. Even if visitors to these spaces do not know the specific details of each heirloom's biography, they know what they mean collectively: be welcome in this place, where we value you as guests and fulfil our obligations as hosts. The residents or owners of that establishment will be the ones to fully appreciate the intimate and personal stories connected to these objects that inspire memories of loved ones lost to death or emigration, as well as important life milestones like births, christenings, graduations, pilgrimages, marriages, birthdays, anniversaries and deaths.

In this study, all participants told stories about their mothers, aunts, grandmothers and themselves as the primary dresser-keepers. Margaret recounted that in her youth, older female relatives required her help semi-annually to clean the delph and other belongings kept in the family's dresser. By helping keep these objects clean, she acted as an apprentice to the craft of dresser- and delph-keeping. She learned to value these heirlooms and the dresser itself, or at least understand why her older kin treasured them. These cleaning episodes often accompanied storytelling events, as dresser-keepers narrated the biographies of each vessel, statue or photograph, teaching Margaret about family, community, connections and heritage. Most men and women in this study narrated stories similar to Margaret's memory of learning dresser-keeping from her older female relatives.

However, dresser-keeping is not only the realm of women and young girls acting in apprentice roles. Four of the dressers in this project belonged to men: readers have already learned about George's dresser, and Martin, Peter and Patrick kept dressers located in their homes for many years. Dressers travel across generations as well. For example, a husband-and-wife team launched the Doonmore Hotel over the June bank holiday weekend of 1969, and she collected delph vessels over many decades. Many of the hotel guests were and continue to be repeat customers, and over the years they brought delph vessels as gifts to the owner and her husband. The sons and daughter who now run the Doonmore Hotel inherited their mother's delph and dresser collection, which is by far the most extensive in this study. They, in turn, train their children, nieces and nephews to care for these precious objects, particularly the old platters above the bar in the hotel's pub (Fig. 3.19). One of the younger family members told me cleaning these platters was one of the most stressful tasks at the hotel: they were terrified that they would break a treasured heirloom in the process of removing it from the narrow shelf, cleaning it and then replacing it.

Fig. 3.19: Sitting below a shelf of old platters, an Inishbofin elder teaches CLIC director Ian Kuijt about traditional boats and fishing while enjoying pints at Murray's, the Doonmore Hotel's bar

Fig. 3.20:
Mary's dresser, maintained in its original position and with her father's paint scheme in her Cashel home

Interestingly, several people told me of their childhood memories of dressers – not as receptacles of family heritage and memories but of places of childhood play. Ellen remembered that as children they used to role-play a game of 'Confession' in the enormous two-door press of her family's very large, old dresser. They would empty out the linens stored there, including a funerary shroud, and one child played the priest by climbing into one side of the press while the other assumed the role of the penitent coming to seek forgiveness. For many years, she and her family referred to the dresser as the 'Confessional dresser'. Several other people recounted how their older relatives stored biscuits and treats for children and that, to this day, they maintain strong associations with treats when they see dressers.

Folklorist and photographer Michael Fortune produces an annual calendar celebrating Irish people and their old dressers in various counties.[20] Each month features one or two dressers from a home, offering a snapshot of information about the dresser's biography and owners. As an introduction to the calendar, Fortune speaks about 'the importance of such objects as receptacles of life stories and the deep connection between them and their owners'. Similar to what I learned from participants in this study, this calendar features both men and women as dresser-keepers, with younger generations maintaining the practice when they inherit a home or a dresser.

Mary, who lives alone in Cashel, maintains her home's dresser as her father had by honouring his aesthetic choices and dedication to this heirloom and her family legacy. The dresser was his to keep and use to display their family history. She faithfully keeps the same paint scheme he did, repainting the dresser occasionally to keep it fresh and looking clean and keeping everything dusted and ready for viewing (Fig. 3.20). Her dresser connects her to her father and her past while grounding her in the present to face future challenges.

Even as dresser- and delph-keepers strive to maintain the heritage of their older dressers, they nevertheless update their displays over time, regardless of whether the dressers are situated in homes or businesses. As families achieve major life milestones, such as births, christenings, or trips to visit kin or on holidays, they add mementos to their home's dressers. For instance, two dressers contained plastic bottles of holy water from pilgrimages, one to Knock (Sarah) and the other to Lourdes (Martin and Juliana). Martin and Juliana also had placed a christening candle on the shelves to celebrate a granddaughter's baptism. Ellen's dresser exhibited sports medals earned by her now-grown children, as well as wedding photographs of her eldest son, all arranged amid her family heirloom delph and glassware.

In 2023, Honora dedicated much thought and care to considering how to update the dresser Mark made for her to grace the dining room of her bed and breakfast on Inishturk. She felt that the varnished wood made the room feel darker, especially in combination with the wood panel on the ceiling. She debated over colours, wanting to reference tradition with a white and blue colour scheme but also wanting it to feel a bit more contemporary. In the end, she combined a darker blue and a whiter white than was traditional and used blue and white creatively to

Fig. 3.21: Honora's updated dresser (made by Mark), painted blue and white in 2023

Fig. 3.22: Comparison of the delph and objects displayed on the Doonmore Hotel dresser located in the hotel dining room: left to right – (a) 1989, with platters and bowls on top; (b) 2014, with jugs on top and platters on all three shelves; (c) 2022, hung on wall without its press and with a similar arrangement as its 2014 iteration

accent and frame the shelves, drawers and doors. She recounted that she had been nervous about taking such a big step in recasting the dresser from its original style but was very pleased with how it turned out.

Sometimes, dresser updates take the form of moving the piece to another position or separating the press from the shelves. The Doonmore Hotel's dresser, used for decades in the dining room, offers a good example (Fig. 3.22). This late nineteenth- or early twentieth-century dresser contains a large collection of delph

spanning many generations. Comparing a 1989 photograph of this dresser from the Dublin City Archives with ones of the dresser in recent years, it is clear that during the intervening two decades the dresser's vessels have changed position or been moved to other locations in the hotel for display, or stored as a new belonging took its place. Three especially notable changes occurred with the dresser: (1) in 1989 the dresser had been lifted off the press and hung on the wall, creating another shelf space and increasing the size of the worktop; (2) jugs dominated the top of the dresser in 2014, while the platters and teapots are seen in that same place in 1989; and (3) in 2019 the dresser top was mounted on the dining room wall again after it was removed from the press, which suffered from a woodworm infestation.

The durability of dressers and delph enhances their sticky voicefulness. Built to last, dressers are constructed to endure for decades, if not centuries. By combining this lasting presence of dressers with the ability for dresser- and delph-keepers to display meaningful belongings and update a dresser's offerings, people are able to forge connections with others, whether they reside with the dresser and delph or encounter them as guests in a home or business.

Made to grow old: personalisation through time

The ability to update a dresser display contributes to its longevity while also bestowing the powerful tool of personalisation onto dresser- and delph-keepers. Moreover, it contributes to placemaking, one of the three crucial aspects of homemaking. In addition to the variation in which possessions grace a dresser's shelves, dressers vary significantly in their construction, style, decoration and placement; similarly, the types and arrangement of belongings can also differ to greater or lesser degrees. Of the twenty-one dressers and ten delph collections we investigated, I discovered that four elements most influenced variations among them: the location, when the dresser contents were assembled, a combination of specific vessel forms, and frequency of use of the displayed items.

The dressers in this study were constructed as early as the mid- to late nineteenth century and as recently as 2010 (Fig. 3.23). Not surprisingly, dresser-makers added features or changed styles over the decades. Older dressers built by local craftspeople often shared a regional style with common decorative flourishes: crown moulding on their cornices; carved decorations on pilasters and fascia; one or two doors in the press; zero to three drawers in the press above the doors; plate rails; shoulders flanking the worktop; hooks set into shelf fronts to suspend teacups, mugs and small milk jugs; sledge footings; and painted decoration with a creamy white-lemon or light blue colour (sometimes both on the same dresser). Those built mid-century (from the 1950s onwards) were either painted or varnished and typically fronted with glass doors. Two old dressers, one owned by Martin and Juliana and the other by Julia's grandmother, had been retrofitted in the past to add glass doors and then stripped and varnished. The dresser originally owned by Julia's grandmother now adorns a bright room in The Beach restaurant on Inishbofin (Fig. 3.24). Of the most recently made dressers from the 1990s onwards, island-crafted ones were open (without glass-fronted doors) and varnished. The youngest dresser, purchased new

Fig. 3.23: Michael's kitchen dresser, one of the older dressers in the study, includes a hanging dresser (attached shelves) extending from both sides of his dresser

in 2010 from a Westport store, was painted white and sported two glass-fronted doors for the top two shelves with the bottom two left open.

Fewer homes today contain old dressers, or in fact any dresser at all. John, a furniture seller on the mainland, noted that he does not see many old dressers on the market anymore: most have been sold off or destroyed before making it to the commercial market. Twenty years ago or more, he frequently used a large acid vat for dipping dressers to prepare them for sale in national and international

Fig. 3.24: Julia's grandmother's dresser, located in her family's pub and restaurant on Inishbofin

markets. He told me that this process was very time-consuming due to the thick coats of paint on older dressers. He would dip them, find ten or more coats of paint remaining, and start the arduous task again. He recounted that the local 'younger folks' had no interest in old furniture, and upon inheriting a dresser that had been held in a family for several generations, they wanted to be rid of it. He believed that their taste had turned to purchase 'brand new furniture, especially IKEA-style, modernist furniture, without a heritage or past attached to it'.[21] Stephen, a curator for a private collector of Irish furniture and art in Chicago, argues persuasively that the 'country kitchen' craze of the 1980s and '90s created such demand for Irish dressers in England and the US that many Irish people sold their dressers to antique dealers eager for these items. Either way, many Irish homes updated their kitchens during those decades. The dressers were removed and countless numbers of Irish dressers emigrated to the UK and America, following in the footsteps of generations of Irish people. Despite the sense that dresser-keeping is less common, many people still keep dressers and delph in their homes and businesses. The next few sections describe the variation I found in dressers and their contents in Inishbofin, Inishturk, Clifden and Cashel.

Placemaking with dressers and delph

Regardless of their age, dressers and delph collections in this study were located in four general contexts: (1) inhabited and uninhabited homes; (2) sheds behind homes; (3) rental cottages; and (4) businesses, including hotels, bed and breakfasts, pubs and restaurants. Thirteen dressers were located in homes, either currently inhabited or uninhabited. In instances where old dressers and their delph have been maintained assiduously in the owners' home, often in the original location (e.g. James' and Margaret's dresser on Inishturk and Mary's dresser in Cashel), participants expressed strong hopes that their heirs would continue to maintain the dresser and delph as they have for decades. In most cases, these dressers stand in the main room of the original house and had been repainted so many times that owners expressed concern that the dressers could not be moved due to their weight and age. One old dresser, originally owned by William's and Mark's parents, Martin and Juliana, is stored safely in a well-ventilated and dry shed awaiting repair and eventual reinstallation into the main room of William and Peggy's home (Fig. 3.25).

Three older dressers were stored in uninhabited homes for many years and have recently been restored and placed in long- or short-term rental cottages to accentuate the feeling of home for guests (Fig. 3.26). In these cases, the dresser stands in the cottage's main room and holds the tableware, cutlery and kitchen implements to be used by renters. Rental cottage owners said they wanted a dresser to offer guests

Fig. 3.25: Martin's and Juliana's old dresser, recently stripped and awaiting further refurbishment. Built in the early twentieth century by a local Inishbofin craftsperson, it was retrofitted with doors at some point in its life history.

that same sense of welcome and hospitality that they might encounter in their own or in family or friends' homes.

Finally, eight dressers were located in hotels or pubs, an Inishbofin restaurant, and Inishturk bed and breakfasts (Fig. 3.27). These dressers are kept in excellent condition and contain old and new delph. All proprietors reported utilising the dressers and delph to highlight the sense of hospitality, heritage and a home-away-

Fig. 3.26: Dressers in rental cottages: left to right (a) Betty's dresser on Inishturk; (b) Penelope's dresser on Inishbofin; (c) Catherine's dresser on Inishbofin

from-home atmosphere. For example, Catherine positioned her beautiful dresser directly across from the entrance to the Galley Restaurant, which is one of the first things to catch your eye upon entry. She has filled it with colourful old and new delph vessels, and the entire display brightens the room and invites customers to enjoy tea, lunch or some dessert.

In addition to the delph and other heirlooms found in the twenty-one recorded dressers, ten participants stored or exhibited a total of 365 ceramic vessels in their homes or businesses outside of dressers. In the Doonmore Hotel and in Michael's home, the delph collections far exceeded their dressers' capacities; therefore vessels festooned the walls, mantelpieces, windowsills, bookshelves, display cases and shelves (Fig. 3.28). In three cases, the owners discarded their dressers long ago but kept the delph stored carefully in presses or wardrobes.

The most extensive delph collection outside of a dresser is located throughout the Doonmore Hotel on Inishbofin, with 121 vessels displayed on shelves or hung

Fig. 3.27: (above) Displayed objects in Catherine's dresser in the Galley Restaurant

Fig. 3.28: (left) Delph display in Michael's parlour in a glass cabinet

on walls in the dining room, pub, parlour, sitting room and hallways. The original owners' son and daughter now own the hotel and keep the dresser and delph displayed for guests and themselves to enjoy. Regardless of where people keep dressers, delph and heirlooms, they strive to communicate a sense of hospitality, welcome, generosity, family or community history, and heritage.

Dresser age: substance over style

The emergent quality of a dresser arises from the coalescence of all its elements: the design and age of the dresser itself, quantities and types of displayed belongings, display design, location, aesthetic qualities, the stories associated with these furnishings, and how often those belongings are used. Likely due to this dizzying range of variation, I found no strong patterns in how dressers are used in terms of the actual age of the dresser. Old and new dressers functioned similarly in homes and businesses, and their style, decoration and context did not alter their functionality. The newest dressers in this study fulfilled the same tasks as the oldest ones: imbued spaces with a feeling of home, immersed in an atmosphere redolent with stories, memories, community and heritage. For instance, after emigrating to America, Oona's dresser in her dining room evokes her family's old dresser in Cork, despite being only a few years old and purchased from an Amish craftsperson in Indiana (Figs 3.29 and 3.30). Its presence references her family's heritage and dresser- and delph-keeping practice, even thousands of kilometres away. Oona inherited the delph from her aunt, who loved these pieces, and she told me that her aunt would have been thrilled that she was keeping up the tradition. Only one of the vessels contained a maker's mark, proclaiming it to have been produced in England in 1877.[22]

Diving deeper into each dresser, we find the dynamic and fascinating process of personalisation, of how people craft a dresser and delph display: which stories are told and which memories are invoked, and how the owners believe that the dresser and delph should function in different types of spaces. Sometimes, the intended use of the displayed possessions or their context produces a great deal of variation in what types of items are visible, which ones are stored away, and which are to be used frequently or never. In the next section, I present the results of analysing what people display in their homes and businesses to consider how people utilise the sticky nature of dressers and delph to endow a space with a powerful sense of home.

Fig. 3.29: Oona's dresser and delph in Indiana: (a) Amish-made dresser with interior floodlamp to better display objects; (b) detail of displayed delph and glassware with the glass doors opened

Fig. 3.30: (opposite page) Oona's delph, inherited from her aunt: (a) large jug with (b) an English registered mark indicating the vessel's manufacture on 7 February 1877 (parcel 8); (c) large transfer-printed and hand-painted platter with no identifiable maker's mark

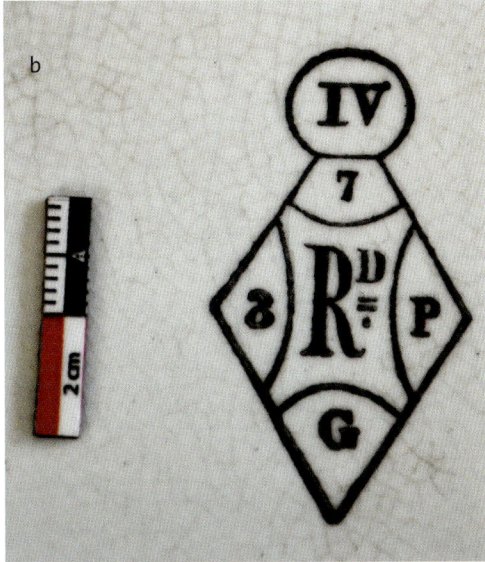

Personalisation and storytelling with dressers and delph

If asked about the function of a dresser, on first impression one could answer that its job is simple and straightforward: it stores useful belongings. However, considerations around what 'useful' might mean or what role a dresser might fulfil quickly develops into more complicated and nuanced inquiries than one might initially expect.[23] As an anthropologist, part of my job is to examine familiar things we take for granted, like dressers or delph, and explore the intricacies of how human beings use them in both symbolic and tangible ways throughout their lives. In Claudia Kinmonth's wonderful book on rural Irish furniture,[24] she describes accounts of people's dressers and delph from songs, stories, articles in popular magazines, probate accounts, government reports, insurance evaluations, oral histories, autobiographies and journals she found in her exhaustive archival research. These examples may vary over centuries and throughout the entire island of Ireland. Still, one thing is clear: the people involved, regardless of whether they were rich, poor or of middling class, all cared greatly for their dressers and delph. As curator Stephen explained, dressers are interwoven with people's sense of themselves.

In the previous sections, I discussed how each dresser's or delph collection's age and location may or may not influence what any particular dresser achieves in a specific context. I now consider what kinds and how many possessions are exhibited in dressers, on walls and shelves, or stored in presses. Ceramic vessels by far comprise the largest category of belongings displayed on dressers or in other areas of homes and businesses, especially serving dishes associated with meals and tea drinking. Table 3.1 provides the numbers of vessels and the relative overall percentages for all twenty-one dressers and ten delph assemblages stored or displayed outside of dressers.

While the age of the dresser itself did not necessarily make a difference as regards what belongings were displayed, I discovered that the year when the owners created the delph display (often with other belongings) was significant. Therefore, I divided the dressers into two basic categories: archival dressers (for those whose displayed possessions were primarily arranged before 1980) and post-1980 dressers (whose delph had been selected and placed on the dresser after 1980).

We recorded 1,597 ceramic vessels and analysed 1,596 of them (excluding the single gravy boat, which had no other comparative vessels in both ethnographic and archaeological assemblages).[25] The most common vessel types were plates, teacups, saucers and mugs. Small plates, bowls, teapots and milk jugs were the next most

Vessel Type	Delph on All Dressers (n=21)		Pre-1980 Archival Dressers (n=10)		Post-1980 (Re)assembled Dressers (n=11)		Non-Dresser Delph (10 collections)		TOTALS OF ALL ETHNOGRAPHIC DELPH	
	#	%	#	%	#	%	#	%	#	%
Platter	43	3.5%	27	4.3%	16	2.7%	36	9.9%	79	4.9%
Dinner Plate	185	15.0%	97	15.5%	86	14.6%	76	20.8%	261	16.4%
Small Plate	114	9.3%	52	8.3%	57	9.6%	32	8.8%	146	9.1%
Saucer	200	16.2%	121	19.3%	76	12.9%	52	14.2%	252	15.8%
Teacup	211	17.1%	130	20.8%	78	13.2%	46	12.6%	257	16.1%
Tea- & Coffeepot	31	2.5%	19	3.0%	12	2.0%	29	7.9%	60	3.8%
Mug	183	14.9%	53	8.5%	128	21.7%	27	7.4%	210	13.2%
Milk Jug	62	5.0%	39	6.2%	19	3.2%	28	7.7%	90	5.6%
Jug	69	5.6%	62	9.9%	10	1.7%	15	4.1%	84	5.3%
Small Bowl	109	8.9%	19	3.0%	90	15.2%	20	5.5%	129	8.1%
Large Bowl	9	0.7%	1	0.2%	9	1.5%	1	0.3%	10	0.6%
Tureen	11	0.9%	5	0.8%	6	1.0%	3	0.8%	14	0.9%
Eggcup	4	0.3%	1	0.2%	4	0.7%	0	0.0%	4	0.3%
TOTAL	1,231		626		591		365		1,596	

Table 3.1: Counts and percentages of delph by vessel form

frequently recorded vessels. Teapots were found throughout the assemblage but in low numbers, and large bowls, tureens and ceramic eggcups[26] were the least common vessel forms in dressers and delph collections. Figure 3.31 depicts the relative frequency of vessel forms exhibited on dressers and in delph collections, which allows us to visualise which ceramic vessels dresser- and delph-keepers prefer to collect.

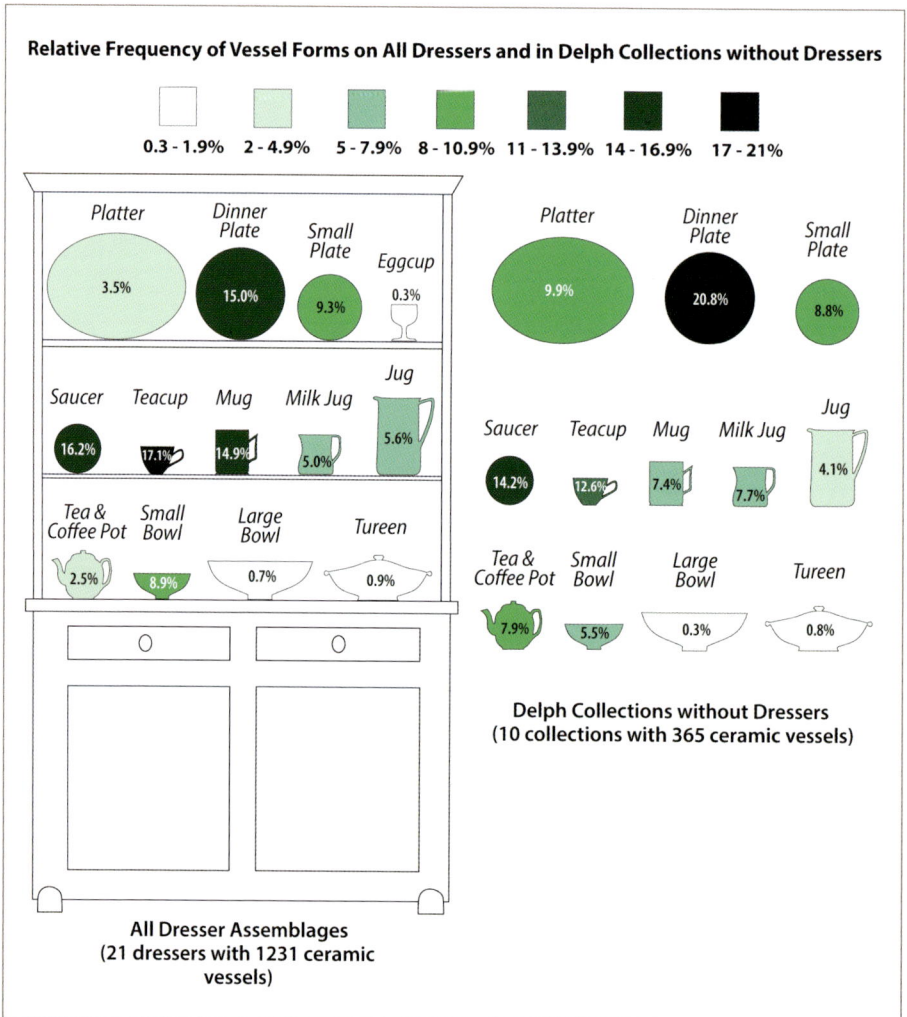

Relative Frequency of Vessel Forms on All Dressers and in Delph Collections without Dressers

0.3 - 1.9% 2 - 4.9% 5 - 7.9% 8 - 10.9% 11 - 13.9% 14 - 16.9% 17 - 21%

All Dresser Assemblages
(21 dressers with 1231 ceramic vessels)

Platter 3.5% | Dinner Plate 15.0% | Small Plate 9.3% | Eggcup 0.3%
Saucer 16.2% | Teacup 17.1% | Mug 14.9% | Milk Jug 5.0% | Jug 5.6%
Tea & Coffee Pot 2.5% | Small Bowl 8.9% | Large Bowl 0.7% | Tureen 0.9%

Delph Collections without Dressers
(10 collections with 365 ceramic vessels)

Platter 9.9% | Dinner Plate 20.8% | Small Plate 8.8%
Saucer 14.2% | Teacup 12.6% | Mug 7.4% | Milk Jug 7.7% | Jug 4.1%
Tea & Coffee Pot 7.9% | Small Bowl 5.5% | Large Bowl 0.3% | Tureen 0.8%

Fig. 3.31: Frequency (or popularity) of ceramic vessel forms in recorded dresser and delph collections. The darker the green colour, the more frequently the vessel form appeared in dresser or delph collections; the lighter the green, the rarer the form.

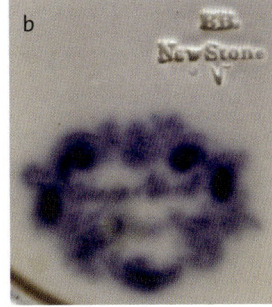

Fig. 3.32: Plates from Anne's delph collection, displayed on walls in her home: (a) plate with (b) maker's mark of W.H. Lockitt, UK, 1913–19; (c) plate with (d) maker's mark from Minton Pottery, UK, 1850s

Both dresser assemblages and delph collections contained dinner plates, small plates, saucers and jugs in roughly the same proportions. Often, delph-keepers displayed plates on walls and bowls on bookshelves and mantelpieces as both pieces of artwork and heirlooms, such as Anne's plates which were manufactured in England (Fig. 3.32).[27]

Interestingly, while plates were the most common item to display, the preference for platters differed significantly, comprising only 3.5 per cent of vessels on dressers but nearly 10 per cent of all delph collections. For instance, Delia, who recently passed away at almost a century of age, kept seven beautiful platters (or 11.9 per cent of her collection of fifty-nine vessels in her delph collection) (Fig. 3.33). All but the two smallest delph collections contained platters: Honor kept only two jugs from her family's delph collection, and Mary kept her father's treasured plate in her kitchen. Platters are a valued form exhibited in dressers or on walls or stored away for posterity, and whose very size and weight enhance the visual impact of any delph display, drawing the eye and inviting appreciation. Many participants told me that these large vessels resonate with memories of family feasts and hospitality and symbolise a family's ability to feed many people and a spirit of generosity.

Fig. 3.33: Delia's seven platters

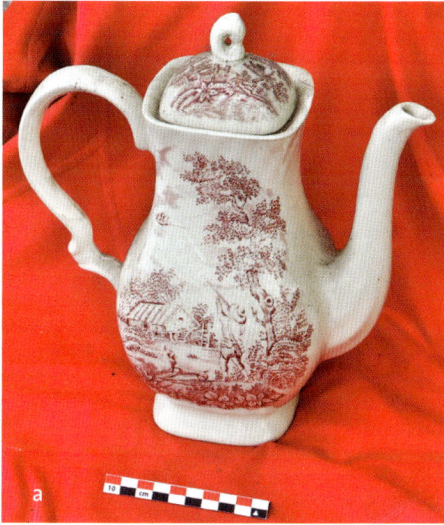

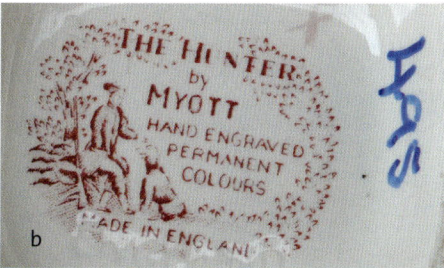

Fig. 3.34: Three of Michael's coffeepots, all made in England: (a) the Hunter coffeepot located in the parlour on the mantelpiece with (b) maker's mark by Myott (post-1976); (c) Kleen Kitchen coffeepot located on the kitchen dresser, where he kept items used daily with (d) maker's mark by Sadler Pottery (1940s–50s); (e/f) Sadler Pottery coffeepot made in 1960s (estimated age by style)

Similarly, nearly 15 per cent of vessels on dressers were mugs, making up only 7 per cent of all delph collections. People were three times more likely to keep tea- and coffeepots in their dresser-less delph collections than display them on dressers. Like platters, tea- and coffeepots symbolise hospitality and home, connecting to the everyday practice of drinking caffeinated beverages during breakfast, an afternoon break in the day, or welcoming a guest into a home. Only four delph collections possessed both tea- and coffeepots, and together these vessels occurred thrice more often in delph collections than in dressers. Michael's delph collection shines in this regard: it contained three teapots and four mid-century coffeepots,[28] the largest number in any delph collection (Fig. 3.34). One participant recounted that Michael's home was renowned during its heyday for excellent hospitality and proper etiquette, especially when serving tea and coffee to guests.

The last significant difference between dressers and delph collections revolves around the presence of mugs. In this study, I recorded two types of mugs: old ones

Fig. 3.35: Older mugs made before the 1950s: (a) banded mug from hanging dresser in Michael's kitchen; (b) transfer-printed mug from Delia's delph collection, made by (c) Campbellfield Pottery in Glasgow, Scotland, c. 1884

Fig. 3.36: William's and Peggy's 2010 dresser filled with mugs, small bowls, plates and water glasses used daily

manufactured before the 1950s such as Michael's banded and Delia's Cattle transfer-printed mugs (Fig. 3.35),[29] and more recent ones that we are most familiar with in our own daily lives.

Interestingly, the inclusion of mugs in dressers and delph collections varies by the age of the mug and dresser assembly, and the frequency of vessel use. Dressers owned by Celia and by William and Peggy both contained thirty-six mugs, the highest number of mugs in all the dressers and the highest or nearly the highest percentage of vessel types in all dressers. William and Peggy's dresser is located in their kitchen addition, built off the back of the family's original CDB cottage on Inishbofin.

The couple purchased this dresser in Westport in 2010, and it is filled with the busy family's everyday cutlery and dishes (Fig. 3.36). The most numerous and frequent vessel form in their dresser is the small bowl (forty-six bowls, or 34.8 per cent of the dresser's vessels). Celia's primary dresser, made by John Joe O'Toole in the 1990s, sits proudly in the dining room of her bed and breakfast on Inishturk, with the majority of the vessels used to feed guests. Her dresser also contained the second largest group of twelve small bowls, although that number was much lower than displayed in William and Peggy's new dresser. In both cases, we counted many more modern mugs and small bowls in newer dressers whose contents are used frequently for serving food.

Small bowls and mugs highlight how several factors may influence how often any vessel form is included in dressers or in delph collections, particularly frequency of use, relative ease of acquisition, and popularity as a workhorse in serving foodstuffs. Both small bowls and mugs often hold common breakfast foods, like hot porridge or cereal, and hot tea and coffee. Modern mugs tend to be less fragile and less likely to be broken by children or guests in their daily use in busy households, and are also more easily obtainable in local shops or online. Conversely, teacups are an older style of vessel associated with tea and coffee drinking, and we documented them more commonly on older dressers.

Beyond the pottery and glass vessels, people keep an astonishing number of belongings on dressers: mementoes from important rites of passage like weddings and birthdays, photographs, old clay pipe and cherished letters from absent kin and friends. Several participants recounted how their parents or grandparents kept wills, land deeds and money inside vessels, teapots, jugs and bowls on dressers, such as Delia's early twentieth-century tureen made by British manufacturer Booth's[30] and called 'The Bank' since it held her purse (Fig. 3.37).

Religious items, including vials of holy water and medallions from Irish and continental shrines, crucifixes, statuettes of Mary, prayer cards for various saints, christening candles, memorial cards and rosaries, also graced the shelves of many dressers we recorded.

Everyday life spills over into both old and more recently assembled dressers, many of which abound with small ornaments, particularly statues featuring stylised children, dairy maids, angels, cats, geese and lighthouses; bud and flower vases; candlesticks and tea lights; travel souvenirs; salt and pepper shakers; small crocks; and cookie jars. Vessels hold children's athletics medals, loose coins, buttons, batteries and pens and pencils. Suncream, school notebooks, prescription medicines, eyeglasses, watches, notepads, paperback books, calendars and iPads are tucked into dressers, ready at hand for use, and keys hang on hooks attached to the side or front of dressers. Even when a home is uninhabited for a time, dressers

Fig. 3.37: (a) Delia's Alexandra tureen, known as 'The Bank', held her purse when the tureen was stored in her now-discarded dresser; (b) made by Booth's, UK, early twentieth century

often become useful storage or working surfaces, continuing in service by holding carpentry tools and supplies, farming chemicals, screwdrivers and spanners set alongside the original delph.

Archaeologists are often keen to divine an object's function as the most important element of their analyses. However, dressers demonstrate why our emphasis on mechanical function restricts our understanding of people's relationships with their belongings in the past and present. In describing a dresser owned by a woman in County Fermanagh, Glassie describes the stickiness and voicefulness of dressers and delph:

> Standing before the dresser, confounded by the idea that things that can be used must be used, that useful things cannot be art, you would see it as an open toolbox. Letting its order and glow enter your mind, hearing people compliment its loveliness, you would be persuaded that it is an exhibit, an untouchable work of art. Neither is quite the case. Stay awhile.

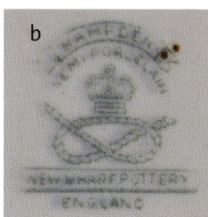

Fig. 3.38: Belongings found on dressers: (a) Celia's platter with (b) mark for Hampden pattern, New Wharf Pottery, UK, 1891–4; (c) plate on Michaels' kitchen dresser made by (d) Morley Ware, UK, 1938–45; (e) mug and saucer on Michael's main room dresser with (f) mark for Golden Amber, Ridgway Potteries, UK, 1955 onwards

Fig. 3.39: Belongings found on dressers: (a) Bedelia's rose motif and India Tree jugs made by (b) Arklow, 1950s–60s; (c) Ellen's glass and metal chicken vessel, filled with various small items; (d) Doonmore Hotel jug, early twentieth century; (e) Doonmore Hotel's small blue Willow plate made by (f) Arklow, 1940–8; (g) Celia's Cottageware teapot made by (h) Price Brothers, UK, 1931–63, likely 1945–63

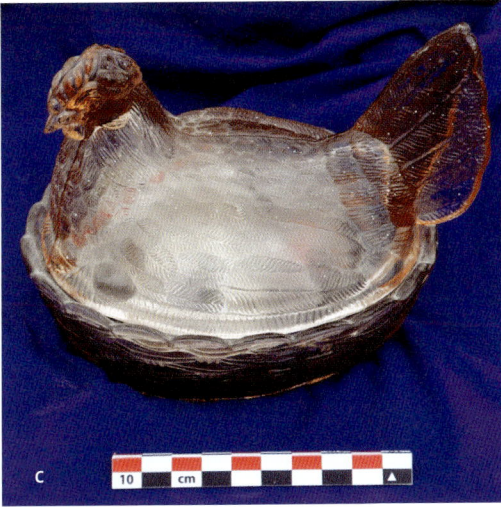

Though most of the crockery put daily to use hides in the pantry, you will see some of the dresser's side plates break out for service at dinner, and other of its pieces constantly at work. At the upper end of a row of unusable Belleek mugs stands the one and only cup Mrs. Cutler uses for all the day's many teas. The resplendent dresser is a work of art, but it gracefully incorporates utility too. The ratio of display to use, art to tool, varies greatly from dresser to dresser, but all stand through time as beautiful.[31]

Dressers contain many things, including people's precious heirlooms, to be used only on the most special of occasions (if ever) or daily as their favourite belongings (Figs 3.38 and 3.39).[32] The variation between dressers, even in the same community, demonstrates the personalisation arising from private family and personal histories and a dresser-keeper's sense of style and aesthetics.[33] The beauty, memories, stories and sentiments that dressers evoke are in the eye of the beholder and expressed in vessels that transcend oversimplified categories of useful and decorative. In this next section, I will walk the reader through how long ago a dresser's contents were assembled, which may affect which types of vessels and other types of possessions people display or store.

Variations in dresser and delph displays across time and space

Generally, archaeologists are interested in what belongings people use and then discard during their lives and in tracking how these practices change or remain stable over generations. In order to ask these same archaeological questions of the vessels we recorded, I divided the counts of vessel forms on each dresser or delph collection into two broad assemblages based on the age of assembly for twenty well-preserved dressers: dressers with archival assemblages from before 1980, and dressers built or reassembled after 1980.[34] The first round of analysis involved a simple presence-absence count: which types of vessels appeared on dressers in these two assemblages. I found that 100 per cent of the nine older archival dressers contained dinner plates, milk jugs and teacups, while eight also contained saucers (Fig. 3.40). Seven archival dressers exhibited teapots, small bowls, jugs, small plates and platters. Mugs were displayed on six of the nine archival dressers, followed by tureens on three dressers, and large bowls only on one.

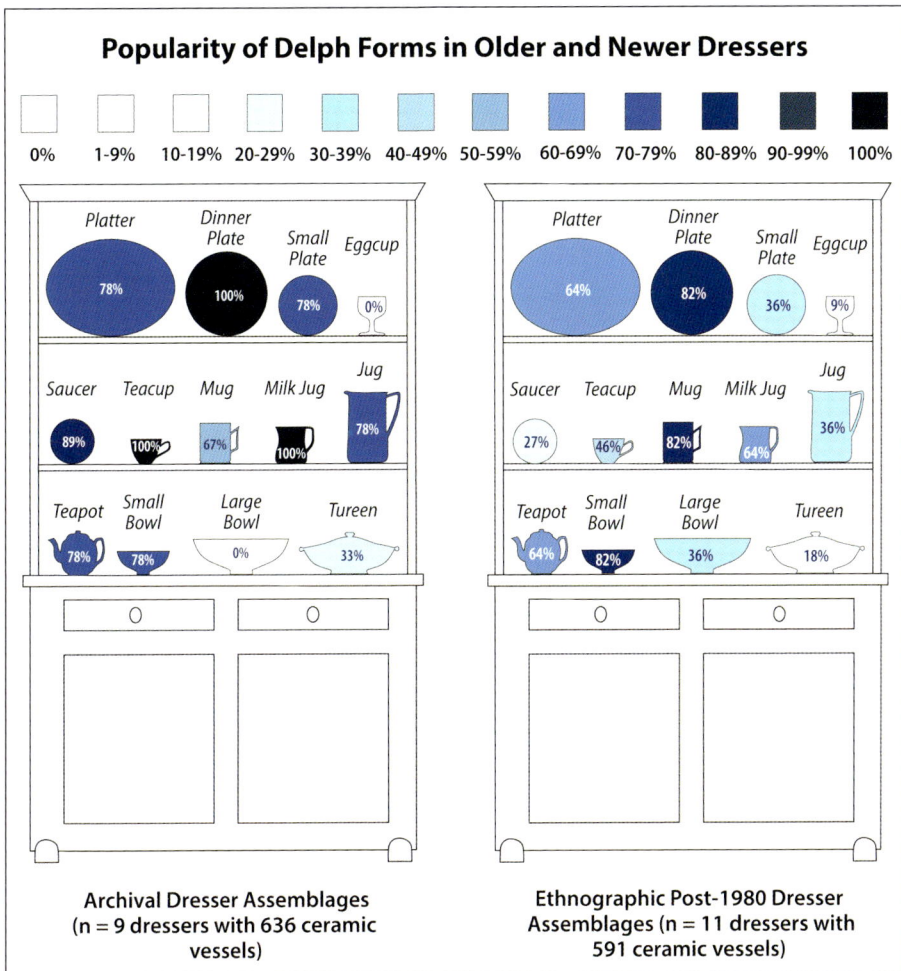

Popularity of Delph Forms in Older and Newer Dressers

| 0% | 1-9% | 10-19% | 20-29% | 30-39% | 40-49% | 50-59% | 60-69% | 70-79% | 80-89% | 90-99% | 100% |

Left dresser (Archival):

Platter 78% | Dinner Plate 100% | Small Plate 78% | Eggcup 0%

Saucer 89% | Teacup 100% | Mug 67% | Milk Jug 100% | Jug 78%

Teapot 78% | Small Bowl 78% | Large Bowl 0% | Tureen 33%

Archival Dresser Assemblages (n = 9 dressers with 636 ceramic vessels)

Right dresser (Ethnographic Post-1980):

Platter 64% | Dinner Plate 82% | Small Plate 36% | Eggcup 9%

Saucer 27% | Teacup 46% | Mug 82% | Milk Jug 64% | Jug 36%

Teapot 64% | Small Bowl 82% | Large Bowl 36% | Tureen 18%

Ethnographic Post-1980 Dresser Assemblages (n = 11 dressers with 591 ceramic vessels)

Fig. 3.40: Comparison of how many older and more recently assembled dressers contain different vessel forms

Bedelia's dresser on Inishturk exemplifies the archival dressers we recorded, with its tidy display of dinner plates, small plates, teacups and saucers (Fig. 3.41). Like her dresser, all nine archival dressers contained dinner plates, teacups and milk jugs. Though all archival dressers followed a general guideline for what types of belongings should be displayed, the frequency of those vessel forms varied significantly (Fig. 3.42).

Ubiquitous teacups (in light blue) occur consistently, accounting for between 10 and 37 per cent of vessels in each dresser. However, dinner plates (in red) vary

Fig. 3.41: Bedelia's dresser in her uninhabited home on Inishturk

more in frequency, accounting for between 1½ and 33 per cent of vessels in older dressers. Among archival dressers, we see the greatest variation in vessel forms with dinner plates (red), platters (blue), jugs (bright green) and saucers (purple). For an archival dresser to be adorned in a socially acceptable way, the owner needed to exhibit plates, teacups, saucers and milk jugs – literally or actually be prepared to host guests for tea and a meal. On the other end of the spectrum, tureens and large bowls seem to have been least necessary for a 'proper' display. These rules may never have been written down, but people taught them to their children, who learned to read dressers from a very early age.

This learning process underpins what anthropologists call a 'community of practice': a group of people who practise a craft, share a body of knowledge and teach younger generations to follow in their footsteps.[35] When adults involve their children, nieces and nephews in cleaning a dresser and its delph, or use certain

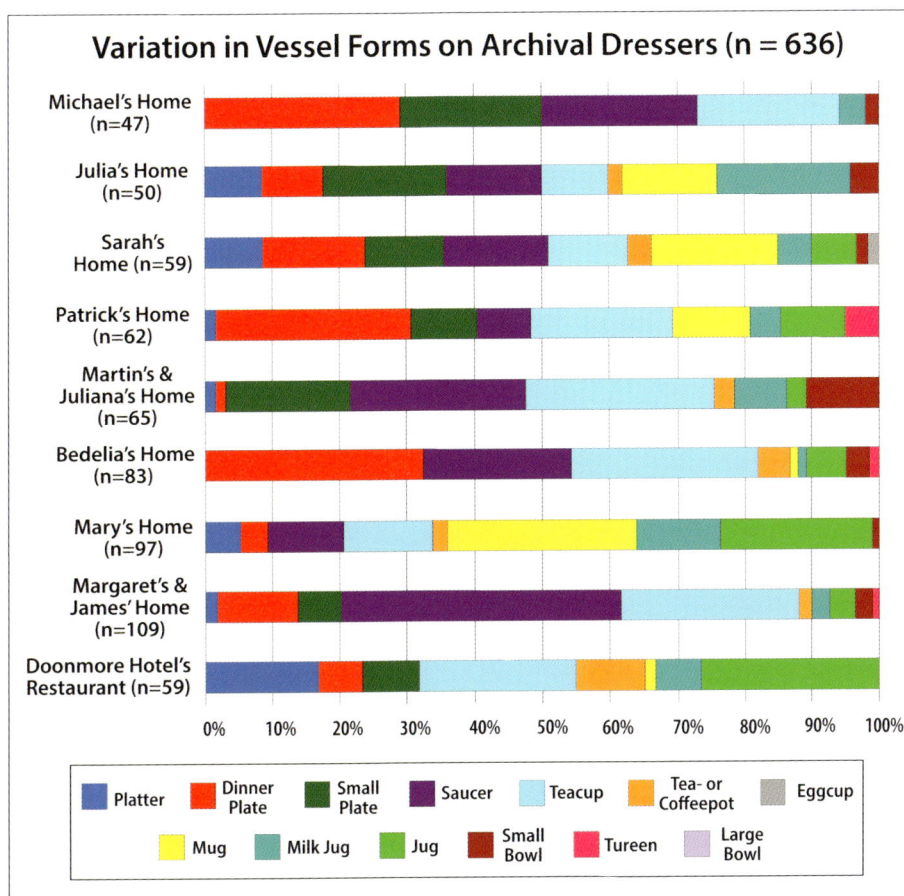

Fig. 3.42: Comparison of percentages of vessel forms on nine archival dressers

vessels daily or only on special occasions, they inculcate ideas around valuing these possessions. The younger generation learns, through practising the art of dresser- and delph-keeping, how to assemble a dresser display, as well as how dressers anchor homes, tell family stories, keep connections between kin lost to emigration and death, and communicate the crucial values of home, hospitality and generosity.

While there may exist a common guiding sense of what belongings should appear on a dresser, dresser-keepers interpret these guidelines according to their own personal history of delph- and dresser-keeping, style, frequency of use and aesthetics. For example, in comparing vessel types on James' and Margaret's dresser with Mary's, we see the variation between these two archival assemblages filled with

Fig. 3.43: Shelves of delph in old dressers: (a) James' and Margaret's dresser and (b) Mary's dresser

delph that is less often, if ever, used (Fig. 3.43). They also took different approaches to dresser- and delph-keeping in these homes. Both dresser-keepers utilised the top of the dresser to display objects, but the belongings themselves are fundamentally different: Margaret and James exhibited family photographs, while Mary placed teapots, old glass buoys, an old hand-painted milk jug, several modern mugs, a small bowl and a ceramic cookie jar. Both sets of items speak to family connections, but the types of possessions they use to communicate these values vary greatly. Working our way downwards, the top two shelves on Margaret's and James' dresser contained ceramic wedding sets given to themselves and their parents. Mary's top two shelves contained very old platters resting against plate rails. These platters are family heirlooms, once belonging to her parents and grandparents, and are accompanied by smaller objects, such as mugs, matching teacups and saucers, two bud vases, two cut-glass vessels, an old plate, and a working clock positioned in the middle on the third shelf and a chicken vessel set in the centre on the fourth shelf.

The third and fourth shelves on James' and Margaret's dresser contained more delph from their parents and relatives. The third shelf in the photograph looks slightly empty and uneven because we had removed several pieces for documentation: her grandmother's bowl from Germany is missing from the view, as well as their Cottageware teapot. In contrast, Mary's collection of twenty-two old jugs dominates her bottom two shelves, lined up neatly and tightly, forming a ceramic backdrop to each of these shelves. She placed a yellow cut-glass lustreware pedestalled bowl in the centre of the third shelf, below the clock and the chicken vessel. Her fourth shelf, the worktop, contains family photographs, memorial cards for loved ones who have passed away, flower vases, a blown glass rooster, a ceramic chicken vessel, and a centrally positioned iron stand fashioned from horseshoes and supporting brightly coloured plastic flowers.

These two dressers demonstrate the prominent influence of taste and personalisation in practising dresser- and delph-keeping using old family dressers. James' and Margaret's dresser celebrates Inishturk's heritage and their family, linking past and present members represented by wedding sets, heirloom vessels and photographs, with an approach that values symmetry, colour and openness, allowing all possessions to be seen easily. Mary's dresser, festooned with mugs, teacups and milk jugs on hooks across the shelf fronts and pilasters, literally bursts with delph in an exuberant overabundance which speaks to her family's history in Cashel. Each of the centrally situated belongings lends a sense of symmetry,

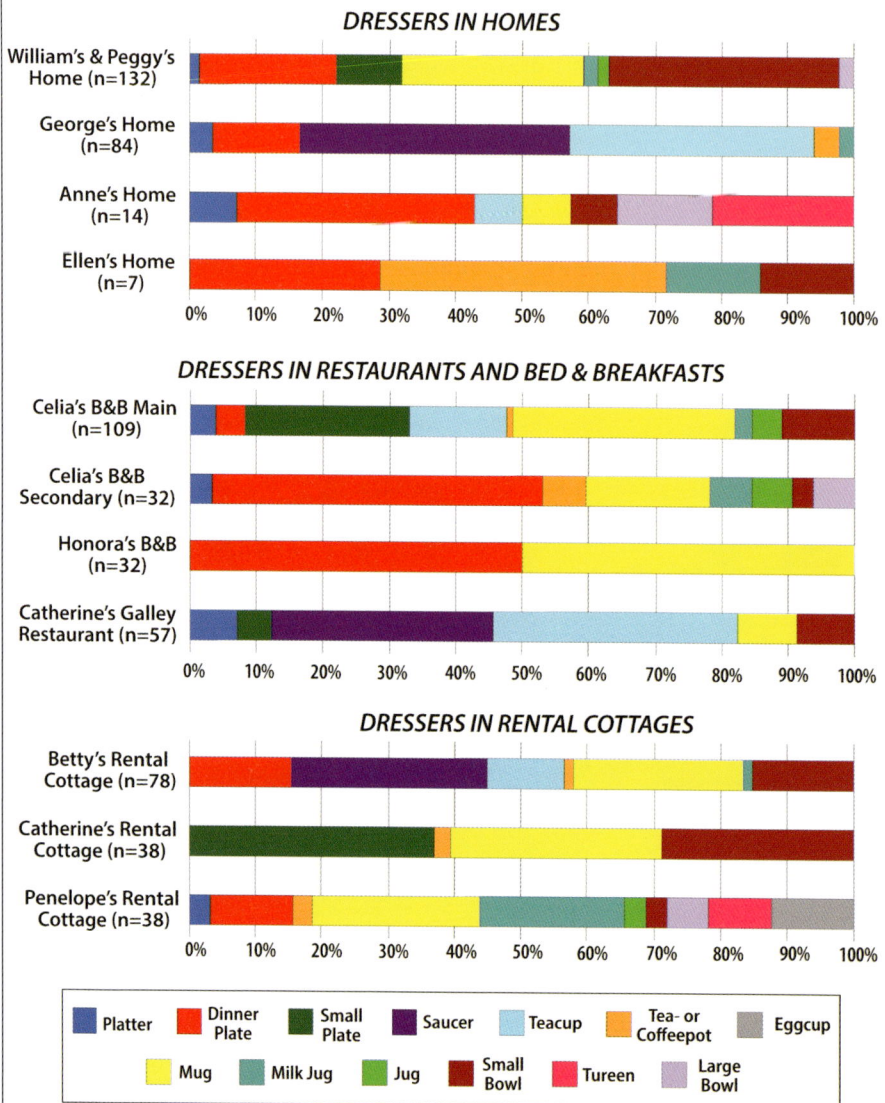

Vessel Form Variation in More Recently Assembled Dressers

DRESSERS IN HOMES

- William's & Peggy's Home (n=132)
- George's Home (n=84)
- Anne's Home (n=14)
- Ellen's Home (n=7)

DRESSERS IN RESTAURANTS AND BED & BREAKFASTS

- Celia's B&B Main (n=109)
- Celia's B&B Secondary (n=32)
- Honora's B&B (n=32)
- Catherine's Galley Restaurant (n=57)

DRESSERS IN RENTAL COTTAGES

- Betty's Rental Cottage (n=78)
- Catherine's Rental Cottage (n=38)
- Penelope's Rental Cottage (n=38)

Legend: Platter, Dinner Plate, Small Plate, Saucer, Teacup, Tea- or Coffeepot, Eggcup, Mug, Milk Jug, Jug, Small Bowl, Tureen, Large Bowl

Fig. 3.44: Comparison of percentages of vessel forms on eleven more recently assembled dressers

Fig. 3.45: Catherine's dresser in an Inishbofin rental cottage

allowing the eye to repose a moment before moving on to take in the other shelves. Both dressers are kept painted in traditional styles and have never moved from the spot where they were originally installed. These heirloom furnishings stand as works of art and tools for homemaking, and the visitor delights in each dresser-keeper's aesthetic sensibilities.

Unlike archival dressers, there are fewer general guidelines for what vessel types people should display on more recently assembled dressers, with greater variation in the frequency of forms and no one form displayed on the eleven more recently assembled dressers (Fig. 3.44). While dinner plates, small plates, saucers, teacups, small bowls and mugs are the most frequent vessels on these dressers, their presence varies enormously from dresser to dresser, especially when we consider a dresser's context. While we might expect dressers in bed and breakfasts to be more similar to each other, that hypothesis does not bear fruit. Similarly, the assemblages on Catherine's, Penelope's and Betty's dressers, all located in rental cottages, vary greatly in terms of which forms and how many of each vessel type they hold. For instance, Catherine's dresser contains thirty-eight vessels, most of which are small plates (green), small bowls (burgundy) and mugs (yellow) (Fig. 3.45). Betty's dresser contains more than twice the number of vessels and a greater variety of forms, as it is situated in a long-term rental home instead of a holiday rental cottage. Instead of small plates, one of the most common forms are saucers – which likely serve the same purpose: serve snacks and small meals.

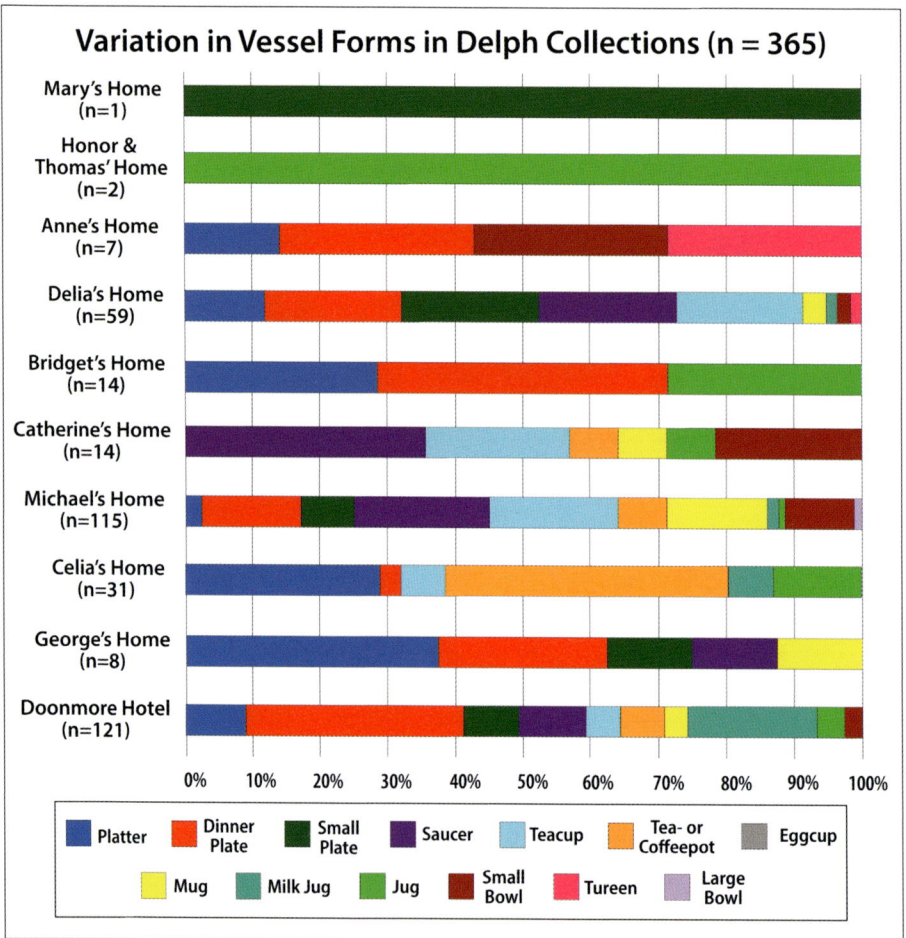

Fig. 3.46: Comparison of percentages of vessel forms in nine dresser-less delph collections

While rental cottages and bed and breakfast dressers and their contents are not currently and exclusively linked to any specific family, these furnishings imbue these spaces with a sense of home and island heritage. The dresser-keepers have positioned the vessels for functional use and with an eye towards aesthetics and colours. Consider Catherine's dresser, assembled in 2019 for her recently purchased rental cottage. Her dresser greets its visitors with clean symmetry, a balance of dark and light, the bud vase with fresh cut flowers, and the photograph of an interior corner in the home before it had been restored. The old dresser and the photograph of the pre-restoration furnishings evoke past occupants of the cottage. The new dishes herald the future of contented residents on holiday, enjoying all Inishbofin has to offer during the tourist season.

Regardless of the age of the dresser, when it was assembled or specific combinations of objects on display, dressers serve their owners in a variety of ways, including as storage receptacles for belongings, home furnishing and decoration, and a tangible receptacle for family history and heritage. People displaying delph outside of dressers also demonstrated a deeply personalised approach to their delph collections (Fig. 3.46). For instance, most participants displayed or stored platters and plates, and no single vessel form appeared in all ten delph collections.

Whether delph is displayed on or outside of dressers, these vessels offer the chance for people to travel across time and space and connect past lives to present ones. These belongings tell stories about the community in which we find them, recounting personal histories of the people who inhabit these homes and manage these businesses. Dresser-keepers always instil something of their own aesthetic sensibilities, values and ideas about homemaking into each dresser. To wrap up this chapter, the next section briefly discusses stories that emerge from dressers and delph in these communities.

Storytelling about the past, present and future with dressers and delph

By now, I hope readers appreciate the stickiness and voicefulness of dressers and delph, telling stories through visual and tactile media. Moreover, dresser- and delph-keepers carefully curate which stories they will share with others, personalising those stories with these belongings. As an anthropologist, I think of these furnishings as a form of expressive culture, like poetry, prose or dance. I see a beautiful dresser, lovingly crafted by a skilled carpenter and filled with colourful ceramic vessels and glass objects, and I know that these possessions contain past and present worlds, almost like a painting or a collection of short stories. People's lives and experiences reside within dressers and delph collections, and it is our privilege and responsibility to discern, learn and pass on their stories faithfully. The metaphor of language offers another way to think about dressers and delph. I sometimes believe that they act like a shared language to express ideas about home and heritage. People today encounter dressers and delph in their own or others' homes, learning which stories are appropriate to tell with these furnishings and how to tell those stories, and practising that language as they craft and update displays at home.

Alternatively, if we invoke a dramatic metaphor, dressers and the walls and shelves displaying delph may be understood as the stages on which stories of life, loss and success are told and retold by dresser- and delph-keepers to their audiences. However one thinks of dressers and delph, they tell stories. Like any narrative genre, be it oral or written, dressers and delph typically focus on a common set of themes that frame stories. In this context, stories about family and kin networks, community history, emigration, religious devotion, resiliency, daily life and heritage feature prominently (Fig. 3.47). Because dresser-keepers and delph collectors draw on their own and their family's histories, combined with their own aesthetic sense and style, each display is unique and personalised. Each story may speak to shared themes and experiences, but the material manifestation and the specific outcomes of the story will always be fresh, personal and distinctive. The most powerful of these stories celebrate the here and now while evoking the departed and the past.

By telling these stories and preserving family memories, dressers anchor homes as they aid in placemaking, protecting and embracing memories of loved ones lost to death or emigration, as well as important life milestones like births, christenings, graduations, pilgrimages, marriages and deaths. Acting as symbols of hospitality, family history and community heritage, dressers and delph provide a visually engaging and prominent manifestation of how people turn houses into homes by storing material aspects of a family's and a community's history. In this way, dressers and delph serve as vehicles for travelling through time and making connections across space. The next chapter transports the reader into the past to examine the material remains of that heritage by learning about delph recovered in the excavations of seven post-medieval houses on the island of Inishark. Even broken bits of delph possess the power to tell stories about people in the past, though their dressers may have long been lost to woodworm, decay or disinterest.

One of Mother's treasured platters

Clay pipe found when digging in the garden

Their favorite plate, used for breakfast to start each day with their departed parent (whose plate it was)

Grandmother's German-made Bowl

A favourite old British-made bowl

British-made coffeepot & favorite mug, used daily

Grandmother's Japanese wedding tea set

Devotional Statue

Mother's plate acquired on a US trip

Own and parents' wedding sets

Grandparents' lustre ware milk jug & sugar bowl, used for Christmas & Easter Stations at their home

Platter holding heaping servings of potatoes

Grandfather's medicinal eyewash glass vessel

Gift from grandmother who emigrated to America on visit to family in Ireland

Small medicinal bottle dug up in the garden

Family Heirloom: plate repaired with lead staples, evoking memories of hardship & resiliency

Large blue medicinal bottle that typically held milk of magnesium, owned by aunt who often acted as nurse

US-made jug: gift from aunt who emigrated to America on visit to relatives in Ireland

21st birthday gift (from another delph collector in this study)

The Bank: tureen keeping their mother's wallet

Fig. 3.47: Visual compilation of dresser stories represented by delph recorded in this study (2013–19)

4

Homemaking on Inishark: Enduring houses, delph and everyday life, *c.* 1780-1960

Co-authors: Meredith S. Chesson, Ian Kuijt,
Meagan Conway McDonald, Katherine Shakour,
Nicholas Ames, Tommy Burke and
Rachel Tracey[1]

In this cold barn we dream
A universe of humble things –
and without these, no memory
no faithfulness, no purpose for the future
no honor to the past.

Adrienne Rich, from Part 12 of 'Natural Resources'[2]

In the previous chapter, we saw how humble possessions, like dressers and delph, tell powerful stories about people, families and communities to anchor homes and maintain a sense of belonging, hospitality and heritage in western Irish communities. In this chapter, I turn from the present to the past, reorienting our perspective from ethnography and the contemporary world to the archaeological past to explore how much we can learn about past peoples' lives through the houses and furnishings left behind. Namely, if people today use sticky and voiceful possessions to create a sense of home and craft memories and stories, what might we learn from discarded belongings and abandoned houses that we uncover through excavation? While we cannot interview these people directly about their lives, homes and possessions, we can still gain significant insights by combining the material footprints of life with documentary records and oral histories gathered from members of the descendant community.

Archaeologists tell stories about past peoples' lives. We rely on scientific methods learned in university and fieldwork settings, a profound ability to embrace

Fig. 4.1: Everyday ceramic and glass vessels, along with metal possessions, excavated in House 8

the often-tedious aspects of excavation and laboratory analysis, and a keen passion for imagining the daily challenges and triumphs of human experiences. Adrienne Rich's 'universe of humble things' exactly describes the kinds of archaeological evidence that we use to discern and narrate these stories of homemaking on Inishark and Inishbofin – the everyday ceramic vessels, cast-iron pots, glass bottles and abandoned homes we uncover (Fig. 4.1). We strive in our reconstructions to honour the long-departed islanders whose homes and possessions we excavate and study and to offer tangible contributions to island heritage and to the descendants who work to build their own futures.

The move from ethnography to archaeology means a change in the nature of evidence and a shift in what types of questions we can and cannot answer. First and foremost, we lose the rich tapestry of contemporary people's voices about their delph, dressers, homes and the physical dressers themselves. Despite forfeiting these lines of evidence, the archaeological remains of delph, glass bottles, a variety of other household possessions and the homes themselves offer a wealth of information about people's lives on Inishark from roughly 1780 to 1960 (when inhabitants were forced to abandon the island). Drawing on the results of a decade of excavations inside and outside of seven houses in Inishark's historic village; oral histories

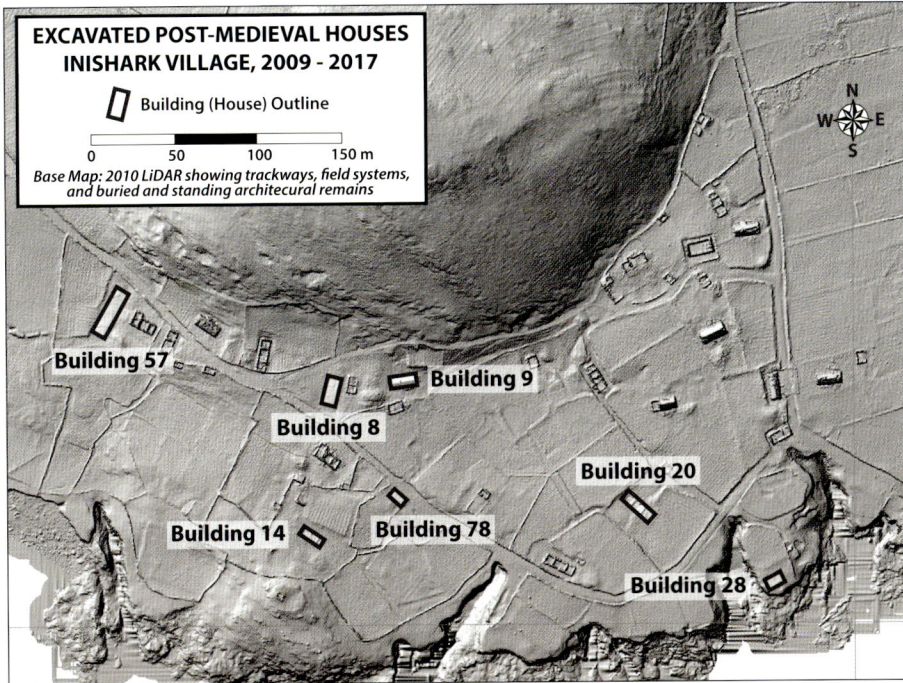

**EXCAVATED POST-MEDIEVAL HOUSES
INISHARK VILLAGE, 2009 - 2017**

Building (House) Outline

0   50   100   150 m

Base Map: 2010 LiDAR showing trackways, field systems, and buried and standing architecural remains

N W E S

Building 57

Building 9

Building 8

Building 20

Building 14   Building 78

Building 28

Fig. 4.2: LiDAR map of the southern portion of Inishark village, showing seven houses excavated by the CLIC team

from several of the island's last residents, descendant community members and neighbouring islanders; folklore accounts; and archival records, in this chapter we examine how people built houses and furnished them with the belongings needed to nourish and nurture their families (Fig. 4.2). In fact, we found that Inishark islanders employed the same key homemaking tools of placemaking, sticky house furnishings and flexibility to persevere over the centuries.[3]

Homemaking in Inishark, 1780–1960: building a home, making a place

When archaeologists excavate, we are not only interested in finding people's belongings. We are also keen to understand how people constructed, maintained and renovated houses, fences, pasturelands, gardens, sheds, trackways, drains and piers – what archaeologists call the 'built environment'. The founders of Inishark's historic village established an enduring place to raise families, tell stories and make memories attached to homes, fields, landscapes and way of life. Like ceramic and glass vessels, houses act not only as receptacles for stories of change and resolve, but also physically testify to inhabitants' lives in their walls, floors, hearths, niches and doorways: they are both sticky and voiceful. Between 2009 and 2017, the CLIC team excavated large portions of the remains of four Inishark homes: House 28 on the southern coastline, Houses 8 and 57 tucked under the lee of the mountain, and House 78, located to the south of the main trackway that crosses the village diagonally from southeast to northwest. We also conducted limited test excavations in three other Inishark homes (Houses 9, 14 and 20). Our team recovered 4,800 ceramic sherds, thousands of sherds from glass vessels and windows, dozens of corroded and often unidentifiable metal objects, and many other possessions people used daily. These structures and belongings offer fascinating insights into life in this rural island community and attest to how islanders turned their houses into homes over almost two centuries of life in the village.

Fig. 4.3: View of the excavations of House 57, the westernmost house in the village

This chapter describes what we have learned about islanders' homes by excavating these seven houses, constructed during the nineteenth and early twentieth centuries, with particular attention to Houses 8 and 57 and their recovered furnishings. While I include insights from the excavated and surveyed homes, there are four good reasons to concentrate on these two homes. First, Houses 8 and 57 contained the highest number of reconstructable glass and ceramic vessels,[4] and the preservation of other belongings and architectural remains was excellent. Second, broad horizontal excavation units allowed the team to uncover most of these buildings, giving us a good sense of how residents maintained and renovated homes through the generations (Fig. 4.3). Third, we have identified these houses and life histories of occupancy in the valuation and census records. We can also link them to oral histories we collected from previous residents of Inishark and people living in Inishbofin. Last, these houses and furnishings compare well with the architecture and materials uncovered throughout the village at other excavated houses: they are generally representative of other residences and their contents on Inishark.

We begin our exploration of homemaking in Inishark with placemaking and the built environment: people needed to build houses in order to transform them into their homes. The first five quatrains of Padraic Colum's 1907 poem 'The Fire Bringer' evoke many stages of house construction:

Who will bring the red fire
Unto a new hearth?
Who will lay the wide stone
On the waste of the earth?

Who is fain to begin
To build day by day?
To raise up his house
Of the moist, yellow clay?

There's clay for the making
Moist in the pit,
There are horses to trample
The rushes thro' it.

Above where the wild duck
Arise up and fly,
There one may build
To the wind and the sky.

There are boughs in the forest
To pluck young and green,
O'er them thatch of the crop
Shall be heavy and clean.[5]

The archaeological record contains evidence of these features and activities, particularly the more durable stone walls, floors and hearths, in both excavated and still-standing houses on Inishark. One of the best-preserved houses in the village is House 6, locally known as the Halloran House. It was here that I first met Inishturk islanders James and Margaret, keepers of the blue and white dresser described at the beginning of the previous chapter. Every year, the couple embarks on a pilgrimage picnic, travelling by *currach* from Inishturk to visit his ancestors' home on Inishark. James and Margaret wait for appropriate weather and sea conditions and a break from daily tasks, packing a picnic basket full of Margaret's homemade scones and jams and travelling to visit House 6. Inhabited by the Halloran family from the mid- to late nineteenth century, the house retains the family's name today even though the Coursey family moved into it in the late nineteenth century. The house appears on the 1838 Fair Plan Ordnance Survey map, and oral histories of the house indicate that at least one of its rooms was in use in the 1950s. This three-room home exemplifies many of the common building practices we see throughout the village in houses built before 1900. An archaeological tour of House 6 will demonstrate how archaeologists discern the life history and stories of a building's life through its architectural features.

Today, House 6 stands invitingly despite its roofless state (Fig. 4.4). Lichen now decorates the slanting lines of its gable roofs, and its once-bold fireplace and mantel have collapsed in the main room. Most of the exterior walls stand to full height where the thatched roof would have rested on beams. While many observers may denounce it as a ruin due to its currently roofless state, archaeologists appreciate its stark beauty, estimable durability, and its gift of knowledge. With its stone masonry exposed, we may track the house's history through its renovations that testify to the

Fig. 4.4: Tour of House 6 showing the three standing gable walls, looking towards the sea

skill of the people who built, adapted and maintained this home. Like many of the village's earliest homes, House 6 is oriented roughly north–south and situated in the lee of the mountain. Indeed, it is clear that builders intentionally and repeatedly employed two key design features to adapt to local environmental conditions: a north–south orientation to minimise a house's exposure to rainwater flowing off the mountain, and east–west opposing doors to maximise airflow from the westerly prevailing winds.[6]

In the late eighteenth and nineteenth centuries, the majority of people living in western, rural Ireland were Catholic tenant farmers who owned neither homes nor land. Instead, Irish Catholic tenants were forced to obtain permission from landowners or their estate agents to build a house and work the land leased from the English landlord. Our team members have not been able to locate any archival documents specifying who built House 6 or any of the earliest houses in Inishark's village, constructed before the initial Ordnance Survey map of the island was published in 1838. Irish archaeologist Audrey Horning notes that people frequently obtained verbal permission from the land agent or landowner to build a house (to be leased to them by the landowner) and to begin working the land.[7] We believe this scenario most likely describes what happened with Inishark when the scale of the village expanded significantly in the late eighteenth and early nineteenth centuries.

The oldest archival document listing tenants in the village is the 1855 Griffith's Valuation, a survey of all buildings and lands owned or leased by people in the village for Britain's tax purposes (Table 4.1).[8]

Map Reference Number	Tenant's Name	Description of Tenement	Rateable Land (£, s., d.)	Rateable Buildings (£, s., d.)	Rateable Total (£, s., d.)
1	Lacy, Matthias	House and land	2,8,0	0,5,0	2,13,0
2	Davis, Thomas	House, offices and land	2,12,0	0,8,0	3,0,0
3	Davis, Anthony	House, offices and land	2,7,0	0,8,0	2,15,0
4	Davis, Patrick	House, offices and land	1,15,0	0,8,0	2,3,0
5	Lacy, Patrick	House and land	3,0,0	0,8,0	3,8,0
6	Cloonan, Patrick (Thomas)	House and land	1,3,0	0,5,0	1,8,0
7	Murray, Mary	House and land	0,18,0	0,5,0	1,3,0
8	Linnaun, Patrick	House, offices and land	2,7,0	0,8,0	2,15,0
9	Murray, Thomas (Ml. [Michael])	House and land	2,8,0	0,7,0	2,15,0
10	Cloonan, John (Jas. [James])	House, offices and land	2,3,0	0,7,0	2,10,0
11	Cloonan, Pat. (James)	House, offices and land	1,8,0	0,7,0	1,15,0
12	Courcey, John	House, offices and land	3,10,0	0,10,0	4,0,0
13	Holleran, Ellen	House, offices and land	4,10,0	0,10,0	5,0,0

Map Reference Number	Tenant's Name	Description of Tenement	Rateable Land (£, s., d.)	Rateable Buildings (£, s., d.)	Rateable Total (£, s., d.)
14	Lavelle, Michael	House and land	1,15,0	0,7,0	2,2,0
15	Holleran, Edward	House and land	0,18,0	0,7,0	1,5,0
16	Dimond, James	House and land	3,10,0	0,5,0	3,15,0
17	Toole, John	House and land	1,3,0	0,5,0	1,8,0
18	McGreale, John	House and land	2,13,0	0,7,0	3,0,0
19	Baker, John	House and land	1,15,0	0,7,0	2,2,0
20	Baker, James	House and land	1,15,0	0,5,0	2,0,0
21	McGreale, Patrick	House and land	1,15,0	0,8,0	2,3,0
22	Lacy, Edward	House and land	2,7,0	0,7,0	2,14,0
23	Murray, John	House and land	3,10,0	0,10,0	4,0,0
24	Holleran, John	House and land	2,10,0	0,8,0	2,18,0
25	Murray, James	House and land	1,3,0	0,7,0	1,10,0
26	Murray, John	House and land	1,15,0	0,7,0	2,2,0
27	Murray, Thos. (Thos [Thomas])	House and land	3,0,0	0,10,0	3,10,0
28	Holleran, Jno. (Michl. [Michael])	House and land	2,7,0	0,10,0	2,17,0
29	Anthony, Patk [Patrick] (Davis)	House and land	1,17,0	0,5,0	2,2,0
30	National school	House	NA	0,10,0	0,10,0

Table 4.1: 1855 Griffith's Valuation to assess land and holdings of Inishark village, owned by Henry Wilberforce

The first thing one notices in the list are the names of the heads-of-households. We tend to attach a type of human gravity to names, and these powerfully resonate since many continue to be in use: Cloonan, Holleran, Lavelle, Murray and Toole are common surnames today on Inishbofin and Inishturk. Until the second half of the twentieth century, Lacy, Davis and Courcey were also common last names on Inishbofin, and still appear frequently in nearby coastal communities.

The second key piece of information attached to these names is the description of the assessed land and holdings. Most entries included a house and attached land, which encompassed garden plots associated with each house. Approximately one third of the plots in 1855 included offices (farm outbuildings including small barns and sheds) on the leased properties. Many, though not all, of the 1855–1941 valuation records list offices on plots of land.[9] Frequently, Inishark islanders constructed these small buildings, often less than half or a third of the size of village homes, along property lines and adjacent to stone field walls separating plots. By comparing maps from 1838, 1898 and 1925, we can track roughly when these offices were built and when they were taken down. Sometimes, when an office structure disappeared from one place on the plot, another one appeared in a different location. Oral histories from previous Inishark residents and Inishbofin descendant community members describe how islanders sometimes used older, uninhabited houses as storage sheds and barns.

The third interesting, though not surprising, bit of information regards the gender of the heads-of-households. Of the twenty-nine homes listed here, men appear as the head-of-household in all but two: Mary Murray (number 7) and Ellen Holleran (number 13). The overwhelming number of men as head-of-households throughout the 1855 to 1941 valuation records attests to the way British, and later Irish, governments counted its citizens, assessed their lease holdings, and recognised certain categories of persons while often omitting others, such as women and children, as below notice. Throughout the valuation records, assessors often noted the name of the deceased husband of the widows. Therefore, we can sometimes track residences that were passed down within families, from husband to widow and sometimes to a child.

In any given culture, people design homes within a general rubric of idealised floor plans, construction techniques, interior features and common building materials. In his overview of the architecture of rural houses in the northern portions of the island of Ireland, Alan Gailey notes that 'those who built traditional houses did so according to norms that were widely known and accepted'.[10] In this way, building a house was akin to following a recipe for a commonly known dish. We all know that cooks and bakers may choose to follow recipes exactly, replace certain ingredients, scale up or down the recipe depending on the number of people to feed, or make additions to the recipe by adding ingredients or new elements to any dish. With this analogy, I believe that it is most likely that the original builders constructed houses with a general framework in mind (e.g. a home with one or two rooms, thick stone walls, gabled construction and thatched roofs) and incorporated specific features with their families, and future families, in mind.

Using Gailey's terminology, all of Inishark's eighteenth- and nineteenth-century homes began as direct-entry houses, and many, if not all, were originally designed as byre-dwellings, with designated spaces for cattle or sheep.[11] Most were constructed with two rooms and built with stone walls, opposing doors on the long axis to maximise ventilation, two small windows on the lee side of the structure, below-floor drains, and at least one hearth placed along a gable wall. Builders oriented many houses to minimise exposure to flooding during heavy rains and to provide the home's inhabitants with an adjacent garden area, often enclosing that space with stone fences. Floors within the home were created with flat stone pavers or with a beaten earth surface. Hearths were often made of large flat stones flanked either by posts to support a mantel, likely made of a large wood beam salvaged from one of the island's beaches or inlets, or large and flat stones set on edge. A street was built of stones and rubble to create a raised, narrow, paved platform extending along one or both of the long sides of the house. A thatched roof was supported by wooden beams, which most likely would have been salvaged after washing up on the island's shores.

The main room of each house contained a large hearth, which provided warmth for inhabitants and guests and on which meals were prepared.[12] As seen in House 8, both rooms sometimes contained hearths placed on opposite sides of the same gable wall (Fig. 4.5). Like dressers today and in the past, hearths literally anchored the home by enlivening the space with warmth, providing the means to nourish its inhabitants with food and hot beverages, and offering a crucial backdrop to everyday tasks, meals, celebrations and losses. As Glassie argued in his ethnography of Ballymenone, these hearths helped people build and maintain a sense of community.[13] Inishark's hearths welcomed family members and visitors from within the village and from other neighbouring communities like Inishbofin

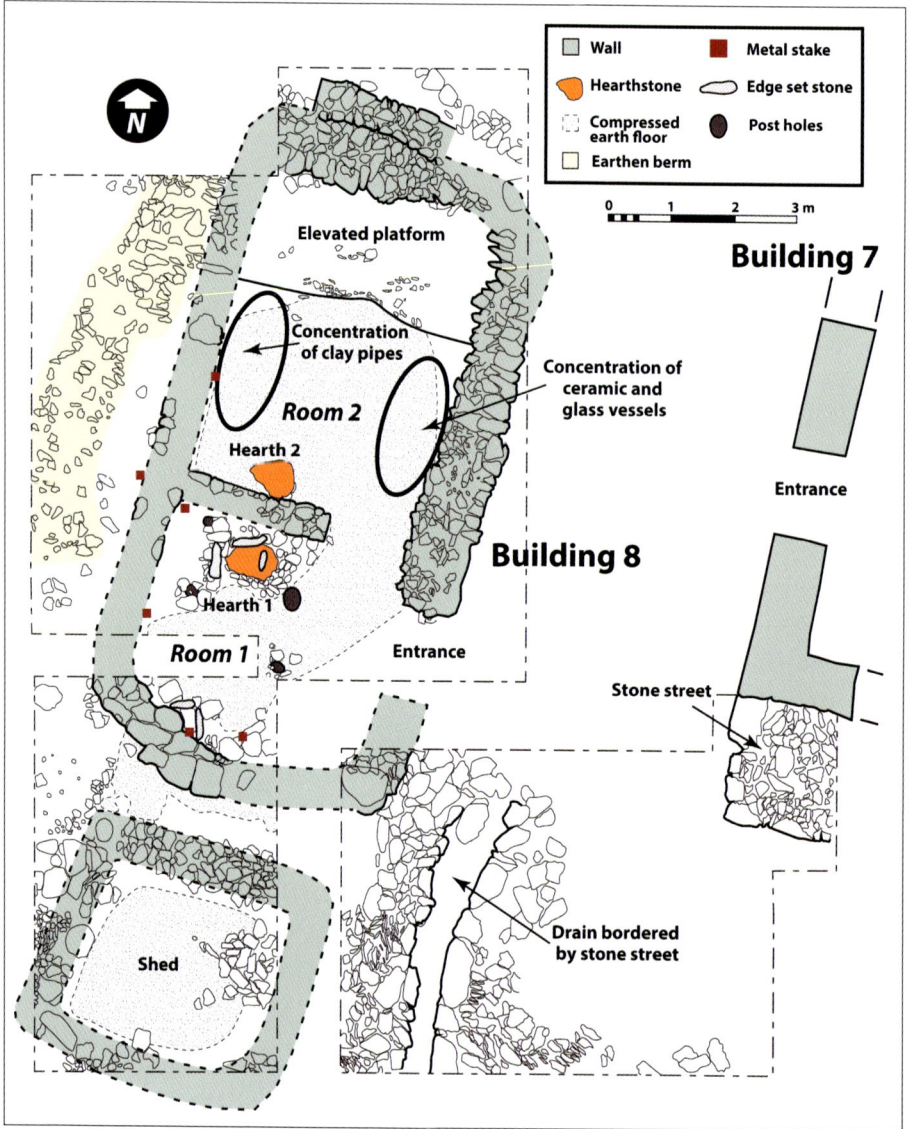

Legend:
- Wall
- Hearthstone
- Compressed earth floor
- Earthen berm
- Metal stake
- Edge set stone
- Post holes

0 1 2 3 m

Building 7

Entrance

Elevated platform

Concentration of clay pipes

Room 2

Concentration of ceramic and glass vessels

Hearth 2

Building 8

Hearth 1

Room 1

Entrance

Stone street

Drain bordered by stone street

Shed

Fig. 4.5: Archaeological plan of excavated House 8 remains

and Inishturk. Countless cups of tea, loaves of soda bread, scones, cakes and meals were prepared on these hearths; children learned to set and feed the fires, bake and cook, and warm themselves here; residents and guests traded stories of life and death on the island; and musicians and dancers celebrated the community and its members as hearth fires lit the rooms.

In her comprehensive book on Irish rural homes and furnishings, Claudia Kinmonth synthesises a wide range of documentary, architectural and artefactual evidence to present a detailed overview of eighteenth- to twentieth-century rural Irish homes and furnishings.[14] She describes how the main room offered space for daily tasks and interactions. It provided the setting for socialising with friends, family members and guests; contained furniture for storing clothing, food, delph, glass bottles and other tools used in preparing and serving meals; and provided space for spinning wool, sewing and knitting, and making fishing nets and other household necessities. Basil Bradley's painting of three women spinning near the hearth of a nineteenth-century Irish cottage illustrates many features commonly found in a home's main room (Fig. 4.6), including the ability to store possessions above their heads by suspending ropes or metal wires from the roof timbers. During inclement weather, cattle, chickens, geese, dogs and cats would also take shelter in

Table 4.6: Basil Bradley's painting *Irish Cabin, Spinning* (no year) shows a hearth built against a gable wall, with a door to the left giving entrance to a second room in the home. The outer hearth is constructed of smooth pebbles set into the beaten earth floor, with a small window gifting the room with some light.

the main room. Walking through the doorway to the side of the hearth into the second room, a person would have entered a more private space used for storing belongings and for sleeping.

Inishark's houses conformed to this same general recipe but often included other features, like storage niches (Fig. 4.7) and loft spaces. Niches like the ones we documented in Houses 2 and 20 are particularly interesting, showing how people purposefully created a small press into the very walls of their homes to store belongings safely. Additionally, the variety we see in house features on Inishark suggests that the landlord or land agent gave little input into the specific details of how people designed and built houses on the island. Had the island's owner (initially the marquesses of Sligo, many of whom lived in Westport, County Mayo) and his agents exerted more oversight and management of construction, we would expect to see greater standardisation of features in the village's homes constructed in the early and mid-nineteenth century.

Thus, islanders built houses to suit themselves within the general scope of a generalised architectural recipe for a home using available resources. Builders laid the stones without mortar, constructing well-built walls that have stood the test of time and weather for nearly two centuries. Inishark's residents gathered the stone locally, often borrowing from earlier post-medieval or even earlier medieval structures in an age-old form of recycling. For example, the walls of one house in the village contained what appears to be an almost-metre-long medieval shouldered cross as part of the masonry, and many of the houses our team has excavated show signs where inhabitants removed stones for reuse to construct later houses, stone fences, sheds and barns.

As part of our survey, we found instances where glass bottles had been inserted into the crevices of walls. In one house alone, we found three small bottles in the same wall (Fig. 4.8). Local archaeologist and historian Tommy Burke offered two explanations for the location of these bottles. The first, and most likely, arises from when farmers find glass bottles on the ground and often place them onto windowsills or into wall crevices to keep the sheep and cows from stepping on them and harming themselves. It is not uncommon to see whole or almost-whole glass

(opposite) **Fig. 4.7**: Niches in Inishark historic houses: (a) niche built into gable wall of House 2, as well as the blocked doorway to the far right in the gable wall; (b) detail photograph of House 20's niche

bottles leaning against windowsills in areas where cattle and sheep graze. Today, several farmers keep sheep on Inishark, and they are careful to remove such hazards from the ground. A second option may be the practice of sealing a bottle of holy water into the wall during its construction or renovations in order to bless and protect the home's occupants, similar to installing a bottle of holy water into the bow of a *currach*. The smallest bottle of the three could only be retrieved by the hands of an eight-year-old child, and it's not clear how easily it could have been installed into the wall by someone with larger hands.

Fig. 4.8: Glass bottles found within the spaces between dry-laid stones of a house's wall

In his 1893 report on Inishbofin and Inishark, Charles Browne[15] noted that builders often used mortar or plaster to plug holes and coat the walls' interior faces. In the few photographs of islanders standing in front of buildings, it is clear that residents also covered exterior wall surfaces with render.[16] The roofs were thatched, and Browne noted that the thatch had to be refreshed on a yearly basis. He also described how many of the islanders brought farm animals into homes for shelter at night and during inclement weather if no space in a barn was available or if the family did not have a barn or shed on their property.[17] Late eighteenth- and early nineteenth-century House 2 in the Poirtíns on Inishbofin contained a stone byre in the corner of Room A for stabling a cow or a few sheep (Fig. 1.6). On Inishark, House 78's central room showed evidence of stabling animals on its eastern side, and House 57 included a raised platform with a dedicated drain for that same purpose.[18] In addition to cattle and sheep, oral histories recount islanders raising chickens, geese, ducks, donkeys and horses, as well as sheepdogs, some of whom might also have been brought into the house as needed.

Let's return to House 6. While we cannot be absolutely certain, our reading of the archival 1855–1941 valuation records from Inishark suggests that Ellen Holleran (valuation plot reference number 13) may have been head-of-household for the family who dwelled in House 6 in 1855.[19] The central room contained two doors, located directly opposite each other, to allow air to circulate through the house with

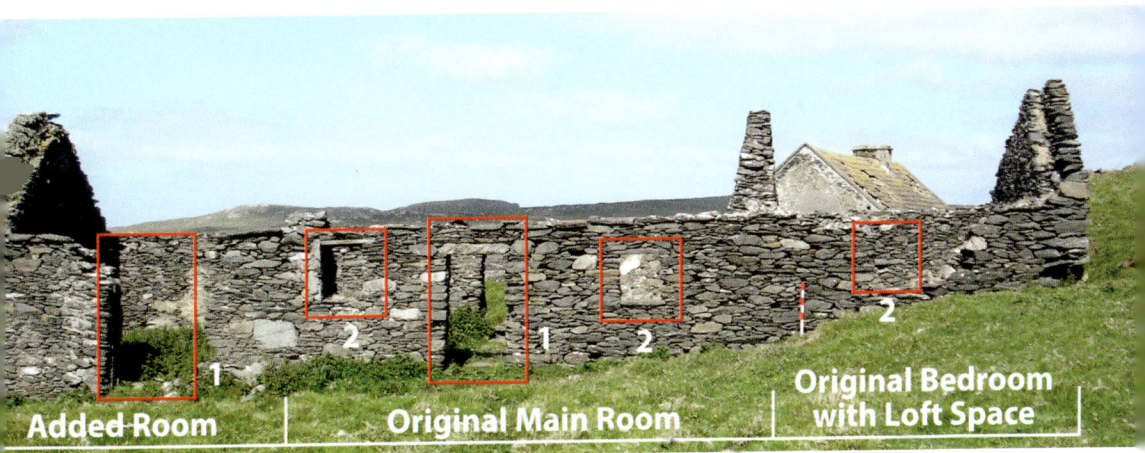

Fig. 4.9: View of the eastern face of House 6 with (1) exterior doorways of the central room situated opposite each other, and one doorway into the additional room added later; and (2) three windows on the front of the house

help from the prevailing westerly winds. On the front of the house on its eastern side, two windows flanked the central room's door, and one window in the northern room allowed light and air to flow into the smaller northernmost room (Fig. 4.9). The house was originally constructed with these two rooms: what we see now as the central room and the room upslope to the right. The central room functioned as the home's main room, with a hearth and workspace for cooking, baking, eating, spinning, sewing and relaxing with friends and family. To increase the interior space, many houses included loft spaces. House 6's northern gable wall on the far right contains a ledge to support a loft partially covering the room adjacent to the main kitchen room (Fig. 4.10). This space would have been for sleeping and storing clothing and other possessions.

Lofts were constructed by laying down planks perpendicularly on top of the roof's supporting tie-beams and with the ends tucked up against a gable wall. Based on the lack of any archaeological and architectural evidence for cruck and

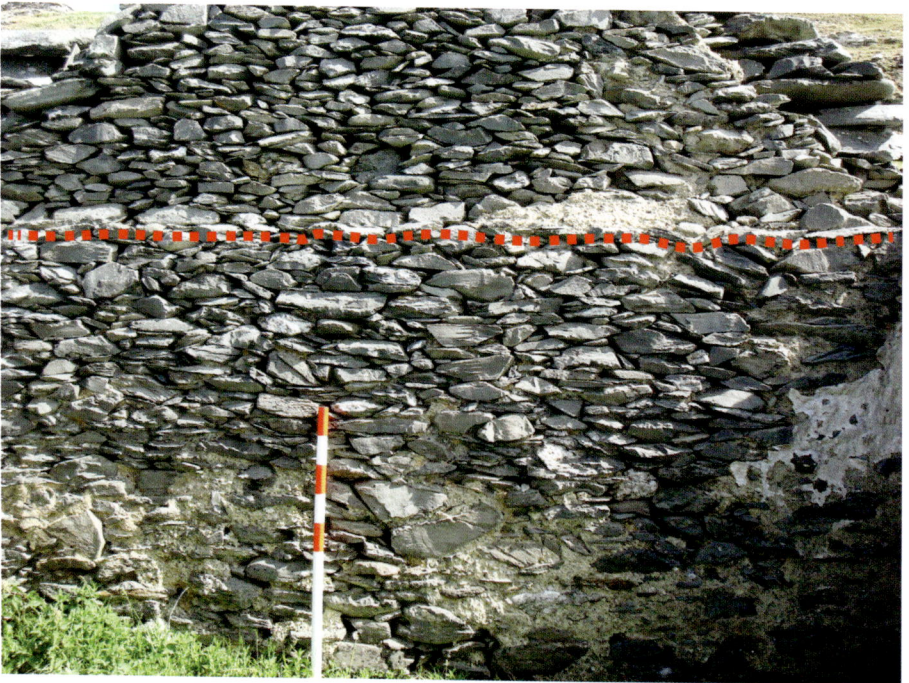

Fig. 4.10: Ledge on the interior gable wall (noted by red dotted line) of the northernmost room of House 6 that would have supported the flooring of a loft over part of the room. Note the pile of yellowed rendering material, which would have originally coated the gable wall, resting on the ledge and still remaining on the bottom of the gable wall surface.

collar-beam trusses sunk into the ground or built into the stone walls, we believe that early and mid-nineteenth-century builders on Inishark roofed their homes with purlin roofs: wood beams set parallel to the gable walls were reinforced with horizontal tie-beams. On top of this framing, they set purlins (long beams running parallel with a building's long axis, which in turn supported the thatched roof). A series of large metal stakes were found in House 8, distributed along the interior base of long-axis walls of the western and southern portion of the home, with each stake set against the interior wall face. These stakes suggest that the builders may have constructed rope-thatch roofs, with metal stakes used as tie-downs for ropes securing a thatched roof.[20] Thatched roofs required a great deal of labour and expertise, from growing and harvesting the materials, establishing the roof initially, and then yearly maintenance and repair.[21] In Anne O'Dowd's encyclopaedic volume on the use of straw, hay and rushes in traditional Irish homes and communities, she offers a detailed description of the process of thatching a home:

> The most popular thatching method in Ireland is pinned or scalloped thatch. To thatch a roof for the first time, a layer of scraws[22] cut from a grassy field or from a bog was rolled over the roof, vegetation side uppermost, and secured to the roof timbers with twisted ropes of straw and animal hair. To thatch the roof, the thatcher worked on the side of the roof moving from right to left and from eave to ridge in strips or strokes about sixty centimetres apart. He took a bundle of straws and laid it in place either over the foundation layer of scraw, or the previous layers of straw, with the ear ends up and the cut ends down. The successive bundles were secured in place with a straight scollop,[23] which was in turn secured with two to three scollops twisted into a hairpin shape.[24]

In the early twentieth century, islanders built new or updated their homes, switching from thatched roofs to asbestos-tiled roofs supported by milled lumber beams, collared beams and asbestos roof tiles. As of 2021, all of the asbestos roofs on Inishark's homes have now collapsed after six decades of the homes being uninhabited. While the thatched and tiled roofs no longer exist, the stone walls of Inishark's durable and enduring homes still stand, some for almost 200 years. The remains of these homes and sheds testify to the expertise of the builders and their descendants, who repaired, renovated and maintained these structures.

We have not excavated House 6 and do not have any direct evidence of the original flooring or any renovations to the surfacing of any of its rooms. In his overview of Irish vernacular houses, Gailey describes flooring options, two of which we found evidence for in other Inishark homes our team has excavated: earthen floors and flagstone floors.[25] In oral histories, older residents of Inishbofin described how the earthen floors were created. Builders walked to nearby peatbogs to collect 'mortar', a yellowish sediment that lay below the peat, and laid down this material across a room and beat it until it was very hard. When excavating these well-preserved floors, a trowel actually rings as if striking a metal surface. While floors were not composed of cement or concrete, they were clearly durable. Over decades and even a century of use, any floor could be patched or rebuilt if damaged by hard use or water damage. In some cases, floors were actually paved with large flat

Fig. 4.11: Internal northern gable wall of the central room in the Halloran house (House 6). Note (1) the interior doorway on the far right leading from the main room to the lofted small room to the north; (2) a collapsed chimney and hearth, added sometime in the latter half of the nineteenth century to this gable wall; (3) remains of interior plastering on the western wall in the corner and towards the centre of the room; and (4) a white quartz stone placed high in the gable wall.

stones set into the yellowish mortar material: Houses 57 and 78 contained flagstone floors in at least one room. In these two cases, our team uncovered evidence that inhabitants housed animals in these rooms, likely cattle, sheep, donkeys or horses, during inclement weather.

House 6's original two rooms offer views of some typical interior features: a doorway from one room to the next, a back-to-back hearth built into a gable wall (later retrofitted with a stone chimney), and plaster on the interior walls (Fig. 4.11). Hearths served as the most important and central feature in homes, especially in the main kitchen room, offering warmth to visitors and residents. A significant portion of daily tasks and activities revolved around this feature: meals were prepared here, water boiled for tea, and meals eaten within the bounds of its warmth. As Padraic Colum's 1907 poem 'Old Woman of the Road' highlights in its first quatrain, hearths and their productive and soothing warmth embodied the home:

> O, to have a little house!
> To own the hearth and stool and all!
> The heaped up sods against the fire,
> The pile of turf against the wall![26]

Claudia Kinmonth has demonstrated that hearths also represented an opportunity to enhance one's home by adding a chimney, a formal mantelpiece, shelving, a wood clevy (spit rack), or a crane (a metal swing arm to suspend a pot above the fire).[27] While wood mantelpieces, clevy racks and posts for cranes are not preserved on Inishark, the CLIC architectural survey of the fifty-nine standing structures on the island documented chimneys in fourteen buildings – all residences or school houses. House 6's chimney is the only one showing that the residents retrofitted an existing gable wall to insert a chimney stack, likely at some point in the second half of the nineteenth century. Occupants removed portions of the gable wall to create a space for a chimney stack and built a protruding hearth and mantel into the central room (Fig. 4.12).

All houses built before 1900 originally contained either a single hearth located against a gable wall of the main room or back-to-back hearths sharing a gable wall and servicing both rooms (like in House 6). The retrofitted chimney in House 6 originally began its life as one of those back-to-back hearths before being converted to a shared chimney open to both rooms. House 8 contained a back-to-back hearth

Retrofitted
Chimney

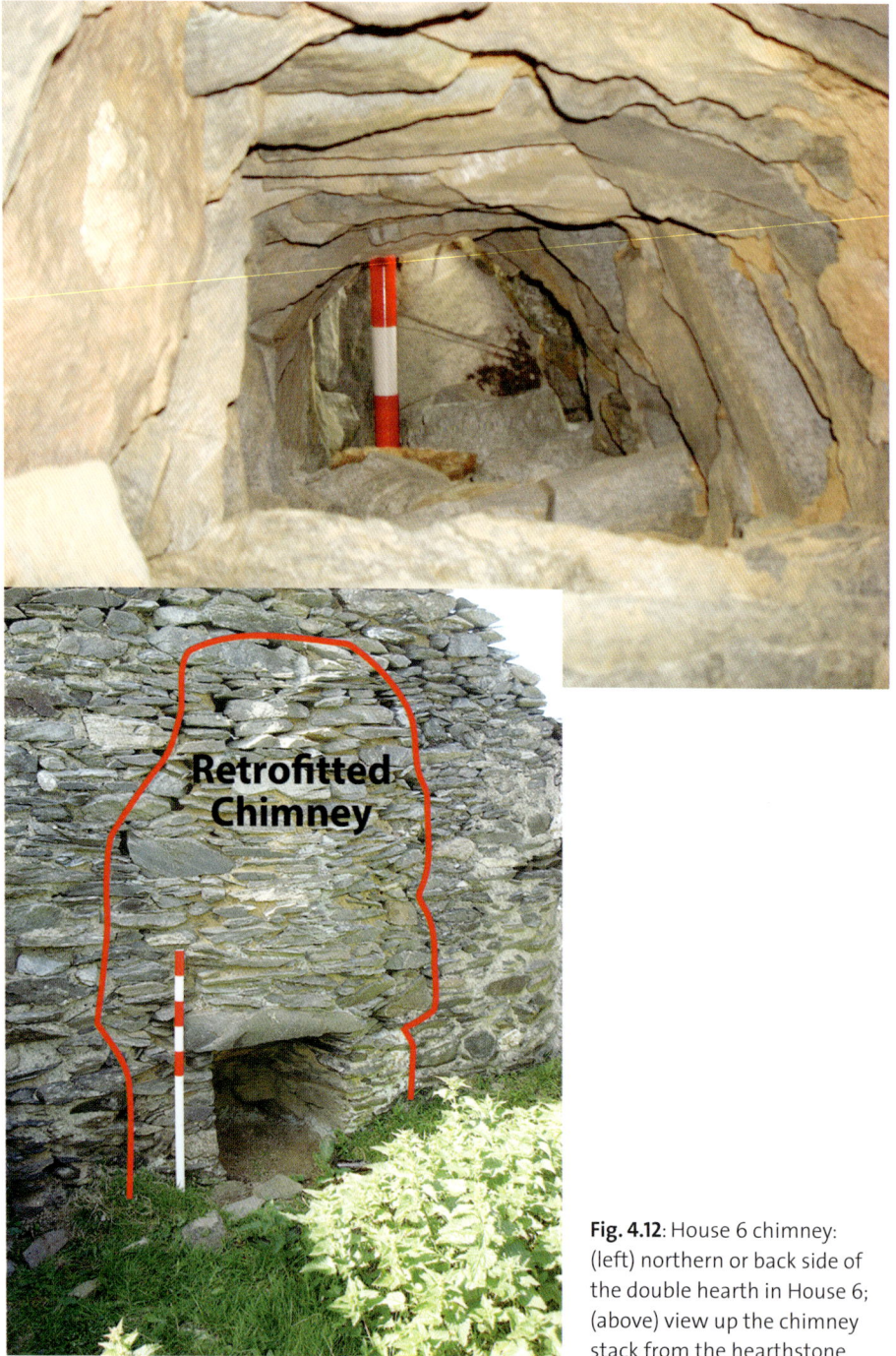

Fig. 4.12: House 6 chimney: (left) northern or back side of the double hearth in House 6; (above) view up the chimney stack from the hearthstone

built into the gable wall separating the main room from a smaller room located upslope (Figs. 4.13). House 8's double hearth contains two typical features we found in other houses: an outer hearth surface of smoothed oval pebbles set into the floor and an inner hearth of a large, flat hearthstone often reddened with use. While many of House 8's building stones seem to have been recycled for later building projects, the archaeological evidence suggests these two hearths were entirely separated by a solid gable wall. The hearths in the main rooms of Houses 8 and 78 were flanked by postholes, which likely contained upright beams to support the corners of a wood mantelpiece, which was not preserved in the archaeological record. An absence of archaeological evidence in these early structures means that we cannot know if builders may have constructed wood and clay canopies over open hearths to help funnel smoke from the interior of the house, and Browne does not describe any homes with such a feature.[28]

Based on archival documents, we believe that Inishark islanders constructed the earliest building with a chimney in 1862 for a new national school on the island.[29]

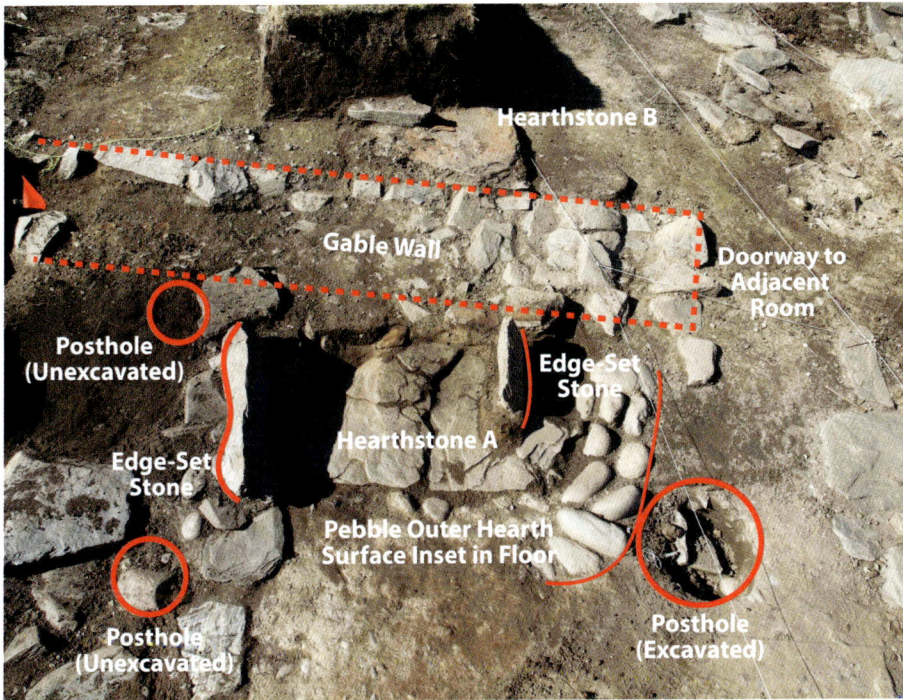

Fig. 4.13: Excavated back-to-back hearth in House 8 showing three identified postholes framing the hearth and likely used to support a mantelpiece or metal swing arm

Before that time, smoke from all hearth fires escaped the room through a hole in the thatched roof located above the hearth. In 1893, Browne noted that in some cases, hearths were constructed against an exterior gable wall, and smoke escaped through a small window placed near the apex of the gable.[30] The added southern room of House 6 contains one of these small windows, likely for a hearth now buried under collapse and so undiscernible on the surface (Fig. 4.14).

Walking outside and around the southern end of House 6, we can see by the vertical seam in the exterior western wall of the house that its southernmost room was added after its original construction (Fig. 4.15). As families grew in size, adding children, spouses, grandchildren and boarders over generations, they often added rooms to their homes. Like many later additions, a room's function may have changed over several decades, alternatively acting as a bedroom, storeroom and barn as needed.

Fig. 4.14: Exterior face of southern gable wall of House 6 with smoke ventilation window

Fig. 4.15: Exterior face of House 6's western wall, showing (1) the original doorway in the central room, and (2) the vertical seam in the stone wall created with the addition of the southernmost room

Interestingly, our team discovered two 'hidden' aspects to these homes, only visible through excavation. First, when builders dug foundation trenches into which the lowest courses of a home's stone walls were laid, they also constructed subterranean drains to manage rain and groundwater below beaten earth or paved floors. At the start of the construction process, builders assessed the lay of the building site, evaluated it for drainage and water flow, and dug shallow channels and then lined and filled them with smaller stones, usually capping this drain with flat flagstones. House 78 offers the most extensive set of sub-floor drains we've encountered in Inishark's historical houses, indicating both an awareness of the need to manage water flow and the expertise in building these features to maintain the integrity of the house itself. This house was oriented roughly northwest–southeast, unlike earlier houses, which were situated north–south. One must appreciate the technical knowledge and considerable additional effort to install extensive sub-floor 'French drains' throughout the house's foundation to keep water from seeping into the floor from below.[31] These most humble of architectural features testify to the people's commitment to providing the best and most enduring homes for their families, homes built to last and to endure the sometimes harsh climatic conditions of life on Inishark.

In addition to drains, houses on Inishark also contained another feature that would not have been easily visible to residents or visitors to the home: in most houses, builders often placed at least one large white quartz stone, laid above or at head height, in one or more of the gable walls (Fig. 4.11). Once the walls reached full height, builders applied a plaster-like covering to them, hiding these white stones, another hidden aspect of making a home on Inishark. Interestingly, we have found no evidence of these quartz stones in exposed gable walls in neighbouring Inishbofin. These stones raise an interesting quandary about house building on Inishark. Why did builders use these stones in gable walls while their nearest neighbours (who were also often kin) eschewed this architectural practice? Folklorist Tok Thompson describes Irish traditions surrounding white quartz stones which are often utilised in cursing or associated with the *sí*-folk. One story from County Donegal specifically instructed people to never use these stones in building a house or byre or to have them in a fire because they invited malevolence and bad luck into the home.[32]

We can offer no certain answers regarding why the Inishark islanders commonly incorporated white quartz stones into a gable wall within their houses. One potential theory to explain this architectural practice draws on the early medieval Christian tradition of people bringing water-worn white quartz pebbles to shrine complexes to deposit them on altars (*leachta*) as part of a pilgrimage. In excavating approximately 40 per cent of the Clochán Congleo shrine complex on the island's southeastern coastline, we found nearly 9,000 white quartz pebbles that pilgrims and penitents deposited when they visited. At the Clochán Leo shrine, located within the historic village, we discovered more than a thousand of these stones.[33] Ryan Lash has written about the maintenance and transformation of early medieval Christian sites on Inishark, and perhaps over the centuries islanders preserved a positive sense of attachment to white quartz.[34]

To construct such a home that could sustain and nurture generations of residents required experience, skill, and knowledge of masonry, topography, water management and thatching. Eric Carlson's reconstruction of a late nineteenth- and early twentieth-century Errislannan mainland house located south of Clifden illustrates how we believe these homes and kitchen gardens might generally have appeared to their inhabitants (Fig. 4.16). Carlson's drawing depicts inhabitants working in a garden located next to the thatch-roofed two-room house, with an office and stone fences behind the home. While this general setting helps us understand how the Inishark village's homes may have appeared, there are a few architectural differences that are important to note. Most early and mid-nineteenth-century houses on Inishark contained hearths without formal chimneys roughly centred along a gable wall.

Fig. 4.16: Reconstruction of a nineteenth-century home in Errislannan, County Galway (by artist Eric Carlson, CLIC Archives)

Second, this reconstruction does not depict the 'street', the raised stone walkway running along at least one of the longest sides of Inishark's homes.

While none of Inishark's residents owned the houses in which they lived until the turn of the twentieth century, they nevertheless invested time, labour and knowledge into building the best home possible for themselves and their families within the restrictions of time, available material resources and knowledge. Given the structural violence, poverty and oppression embedded within Britain's occupation of Ireland, these residences clearly evoke colonial struggles while testifying to the resiliency and success in overcoming such challenges. Many of these houses remain standing, and the original inhabitants' descendants continue to thrive, whether living in Inishbofin, Fountainhill, England, Australia or America. The year that the team excavated House 20, CLIC director Ian Kuijt stood next to the house and telephoned one of the family's descendants, who happened to be a graduate student at the University of Notre Dame, to describe what we found in his ancestors' home.

As archaeologists, we tend to focus on the houses themselves, but we must remember that a home on Inishark encompassed many facets of the island. Islanders made a living on the land and by the sea, combining farming, fishing and craftwork (especially weaving, knitting, sewing and other handwork) to sustain their families. Kitchen gardens allowed villagers to grow potatoes, onions and any other desired herbs or vegetables. One former islander described how they used to apply onion skins to wool as a form of brown dye. In the agricultural fields, islanders grew hay and oats for animal fodder. Families raised chickens, ducks, geese, sheep and cows for eggs, dairy products, wool and meat. Horses and donkeys were used to transport peat, gathered from peat bogs to the northeast of the mountain, back to homes for heat and fuel. Islanders gathered kelp from the seashore and dried it on racks near homes or used it as fertiliser for gardens, and they collected shellfish for themselves to eat and for sale.[35] Archaeological testing in two garden plots found more than a meter deep of enriched soil, with layers and patches of limpet shells deposited as fertiliser.[36] Most importantly, islanders plied the waters surrounding their island home, fishing for haddock, cod, ling, lobsters and crayfish.

We pay attention to how people moved across the island and surrounding seascape because it gives us a more nuanced understanding of what home meant to the islanders: not just their houses, offices and garden plots but the entire island. In Kieran Concannon's wonderful film *Bás Oileáin* (*Death of an Island*), George Murray powerfully says, 'Fountainhill, I've never called it home, really. I could never call it home. The first thing I used to do was go out outside there, looking at Shark. If I dreamt at night, it was always about Shark.' Theresa Lacey explained, 'Well, I was bred, born and reared there. There was food and water, and the nature is there. There is something about it. It lies deeply with me.'[37]

Within and outside the walls of these island homes, in kitchen gardens, fields, pastures, peat bogs, coastlines and on the sea, Inishark people's lives unfurled in daily tasks as they celebrated births, christenings, marriages and daily triumphs of nourishing one's family. These places also witnessed family strife, struggles to support one's family and pay rent to the landlord, and mourning associated with the deaths of loved ones and loss from emigration off the island to places far and near. Like dressers and delph, the architecture of these houses, the stone field walls and the wider land- and seascapes tell stories about life in Inishark's village. As archaeologists, we began with the built environment because it offered islanders an enduring stage for life's challenges and accomplishments, however small or large, where these stories emerged and coalesced. For our research, houses provided a defined space where we knew we could find the material footprints of islanders' lives. We think of the artefacts we recovered within and around these homes as both personal possessions and witnesses to these emergent stories. We now turn to the belongings inhabitants used to furnish their homes, overcome obstacles, and thrive.

Homemaking on Inishark, 1780–1960: furnishing a home, making a living

When Inishark islanders were forcibly moved from the island to the mainland on 20 October 1960, they carried as many belongings as possible down to the pier for loading onto *currachs* to be ferried to the larger boat, *The Lilly*, for transport to new houses in coastal Fountainhill, Claddaghduff.[38] Emptying these island homes as quickly and thoroughly as possible, villagers loaded tables, chairs, beds, mattresses, bedding, clothing, ceramics, musical instruments and at least one dresser for transport to their new homes (Figs 4.17 and 4.18). In *Bás Oileáin*, former islander Martin Murray describes how '[e]verybody was bringing down furniture, cups and saucers, teapots, pans'. Noel Gavin recounted that they also brought down cattle, yardbirds, dogs, donkeys and horses: he said it was like being at a fair.[39] Kate, whose father was born and raised on Inishark, described how her aunt, at that time a

Fig. 4.17: Inishark islanders carrying furniture and belongings down to the pier for transport to their new mainland homes, 20 October 1960

Fig. 4.18: (above left) Inishark islanders with a dresser for loading onto a *currach* for transport to Inishbofin and transshipment to Cleggan; (above right) Inishark islanders on *The Lilly* heading to their new mainland homes in Fountainhill, Claddaghduff; **Fig. 4.19**: (opposite top) Anthony Carey Stannus' painting *An Irish Interior* (1860s) depicts many of the humble objects of everyday life likely to have been found in Inishark's homes; **Fig. 4.20**: (opposite bottom) Frances Livesay's *By the Fireside, Co. Mayo* (1875) depicts many of the more perishable objects that do not survive in the archaeological record, including basketry, clothing, foodstuff, rushes and wood objects

young girl, hid her beloved cat in a basket for transport to the mainland, since cats were considered ill luck on boats.[40] To transform new houses into homes, the islanders brought as many belongings as they could, in turn transporting a small part of their Inishark homes with them to the mainland.

Most of our excavations uncovered older generations of homes than those evacuated by the last islanders on Inishark. Nineteenth- and early twentieth-century ceramic sherds were the most common artefacts recovered, the best-preserved type of possessions adorning these homes. In addition to the ceramic tableware and crockery, islanders' homes contained glass vessels; baskets; cutlery of wood, bone and metal; metal cooking pots and other containers; clothing and bedding; weaving equipment; furniture such as tables, chairs, stools, hanging dressers (shelves attached to walls), presses and beds; stored foodstuffs; and space for a family's animals during inclement weather. Even accounting for the painter's staging of the

Fig. 4.21: Sherds from House 20 excavations (context 132), including a brown transfer-printed rim (centre), three spongeware sherds with blue, brown, red and green decorations (right and bottom left), and a purple and brown machine-turned slipware body sherd

scene and the gaze of outsiders,[41] paintings by Anthony Carey Stannus (*An Irish Interior*, 1860s) and Frances Livesay (*By the Fireside, Co. Mayo*, 1875) depict many of the architectural features described above, like the pebble outer hearth surface and hard-packed floor, as well as many belongings necessary to everyday life (Figs 4.19 and 4.20).

Even without recourse to interviewing nineteenth- and early twentieth-century Inishark islanders about delph and furnishings, excavated belongings offer tremendous information about their owners. Ceramics, in particular, can provide dates and place of vessel manufacture, as well as function(s) (Fig. 4.21). In fact, in excavating houses on Inishark, our team encountered some pieces from the same suite of tableware my research assistants and I recorded in dressers and delph collections of Inishbofin, Inishturk, Clifden and Cashel. In this chapter, we will focus on the age and function of vessels, leaving the discussion of manufacturing origins and economic and social networks to follow in Chapter 5, where I will compare the ethnographic and archaeological assemblages.

Fig. 4.22: Ceramic vessel #1026, a teacup excavated from House 8. A sherd from the cup's rim is at the top of the photo, body sherds in the middle, and the base sherds below.

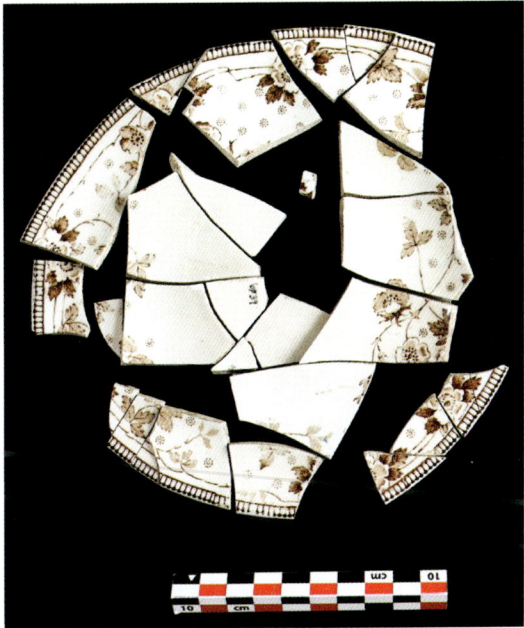

Fig. 4.23: Ceramic vessel #1185, a saucer excavated from House 8, in the process of joining sherds and reconstructing the vessel

All told, excavations in and around seven Inishark homes uncovered 4,800 ceramic sherds, ranging in date of manufacture from about 1780 to the 1950s. In order to make sense of the hundreds and thousands of excavated sherds we find in any site, archaeologists have developed a method to calculate the minimum number of vessels (MNV) required to create any assemblage of artefacts.[42] We examine and compare sherds from any excavation area to see if they might fit together – as if one were completing a puzzle whose pieces had been divided into different boxes and, in turn, many pieces went missing. We attempt to match and join similar-looking pieces by noting a sherd's thickness, its decoration on both interior and exterior sides, and the fabric (the combination of clay and temper) of a sherd's cross-section. We also closely examine rim sherds because these sherds can indicate the size of any vessel's opening (rim diameter), the percentage of that opening (how much of the rim survives), and the function of the vessel.

For instance, a rim sherd for a bowl has a more upright orientation and more concave shape than a plate rim, which comes from a vessel designed to lie flat. Figure 4.22 shows the remains of Vessel #1026, excavated from House 8. It is clear from the upright shape of the vessel's body, the thinness of the vessel walls, the shape of the nearly complete base, the stub from the broken and missing handle, and the thin finished edge of the rim (centre top) that this was a teacup. The stylistic combination of the green transfer-printed floral pattern and the spiralled fluting on the teacup, along with what we've learned about House 8 from the archival documents, suggests that it was made in the late nineteenth or early twentieth century.

For each excavated house, we calculated an MNV by grouping together numbers of unique and reconstructable vessels, including sherds or joinable sherds producing a complete profile of base, body and rim; distinguishable vessels with at least four joinable sherds; rim sherds with 20 per cent or greater diameter surviving; and base sherds with a maker's mark and with a fabric and surface treatments not matching any rim or joinable body sherds from the same category of vessel form and unique rim sherds (Fig. 4.23).

For example, the MNV for ceramic vessels in House 8 is 161, including 48 reconstructable vessels and 113 unique rim sherds. The entire excavated assemblage of 4,800 ceramic sherds from residential contexts on Inishark included 175 whole or reconstructable vessels and 451 unique rim sherds for a minimum total of at least 626 vessels (Table 4.2).

Vessel Form	House 8 #	House 8 %	House 57 #	House 57 %	House 9 and Space 105 #	House 9 and Space 105 %	House 14 #	House 14 %	House 20 #	House 20 %	House 28 #	House 28 %	House 78 #	House 78 %	ALL HOUSES #	ALL HOUSES %
Platters	8	5.0%	8	7.5%	18	11.0%	2	2.4%	2	5.7%	0	0.0%	5	7.0%	43	6.9%
Plates	56	34.8%	15	14.0%	44	27.0%	20	24.1%	6	17.1%	2	33.3%	19	26.8%	162	25.9%
Saucers	11	6.8%	11	10.3%	22	13.5%	3	3.6%	13	37.1%	0	0.0%	12	16.9%	72	11.5%
Teacups	28	17.4%	19	17.8%	8	4.9%	15	18.1%	4	11.4%	2	33.3%	7	9.9%	83	13.3%
Teapots	2	1.2%	7	6.5%	3	1.8%	4	4.8%	2	5.7%	0	0.0%	2	2.8%	20	3.2%
Mugs	11	6.8%	15	14.0%	17	10.4%	16	19.3%	3	8.6%	1	16.7%	6	8.5%	69	11.0%
Jugs and Milk Jugs	4	2.5%	6	5.6%	3	1.8%	2	2.4%	0	0.0%	0	0.0%	1	1.4%	16	2.6%
Bowls	28	17.4%	17	15.9%	30	18.4%	16	19.3%	4	11.4%	1	16.7%	16	22.5%	112	17.9%
Crockery Jars and Bowls	13	8.1%	8	7.5%	18	11.0%	5	6.0%	1	2.9%	0	0.0%	3	4.2%	48	7.7%
Eggcups	0	0.0%	1	0.9%	0	0.0%	0	0.0%	0	0.0%	0	0.0%	0	0.0%	1	0.2%
Total MNVs	161		107		163		83		35		6		71		626	

Table 4.2: Minimum Number of Vessel (MNV) counts for seven excavated houses on Inishark

Extensive investigations of Houses 8 and 57 offer a more detailed glimpse into the ceramic vessels owned by Inishark's inhabitants (Table 4.3). One of the first things to note is that the two houses contained all vessel types, with the exception of the eggcup recovered only in House 57. The reader will also see that the numbers of different vessel types, such as plates, teacups and bowls, can vary significantly. We believe that part of this variation arises from the specific life histories of each home: how long it was in use as a residence, if it had been used as a storage building or barn after the family moved out, and if people dismantled the home to recycle the stone for constructing another home or building.

Tracking the biographies of these structures is essential for archaeologists to interpret how the excavated objects arrived in these spaces and how they might have been used (or not) in these homes. For this reason, I will briefly describe the life histories of these two homes as best as we can reconstruct from the archaeological record, archival documents and oral histories. In this way, I hope to convey why our understanding and interpretations involve varying levels of certainty and ambiguity. I begin with House 57 because we understand the building's life history best, and then proceed to House 8.

Vessel Forms	House 8		House 57		Houses 8 and 57 Combined	
	#	%	#	%	#	%
Platters	8	5.0%	8	7.5%	16	6.0%
Plates	56	34.8%	15	14.0%	71	26.5%
Saucers	11	6.8%	11	10.3%	22	8.2%
Teacups	28	17.4%	19	17.8%	47	17.5%
Teapots	2	1.2%	7	6.5%	9	3.4%
Mugs	11	6.8%	15	14.0%	26	9.7%
Jugs and Milk Jugs	4	2.5%	6	5.6%	10	3.7%
Bowls	28	17.4%	17	15.9%	45	16.8%
Eggcups	0	0.0%	1	0.9%	1	7.8%
Crockery, Marmalade Jars and Other Stoneware Jars	13	8.1%	8	7.5%	21	0.4%
Total MNVs	161	100%	107	100%	268	100.0%

Table 4.3: Minimum Number of Vessel (MNV) counts for excavated Houses 8 and 57 on Inishark

Biography of House 57 and its associated belongings

House 57 was one of the westernmost houses in the village and appears on the 1838 Ordnance Survey map as a two-room house with paved streets along the exterior of its eastern and southern walls. Sometime between 1838 and 1898 (when it appears on the second edition of the Ordnance Survey map), occupants added at least two rooms – rendering this a four-room home for at least some period of time (Fig. 4.24). We are not sure exactly when these renovations took place in the mid-nineteenth century, or if they occurred at the same time or in separate events. Part of our uncertainty arises from two factors: (1) due to time and funding constraints, we were only able to excavate the original two rooms, and (2) many of the stones from Room 3, where we assume there was a street, were recycled for twentieth-century building projects (likely nearby House 1, constructed around 1920).

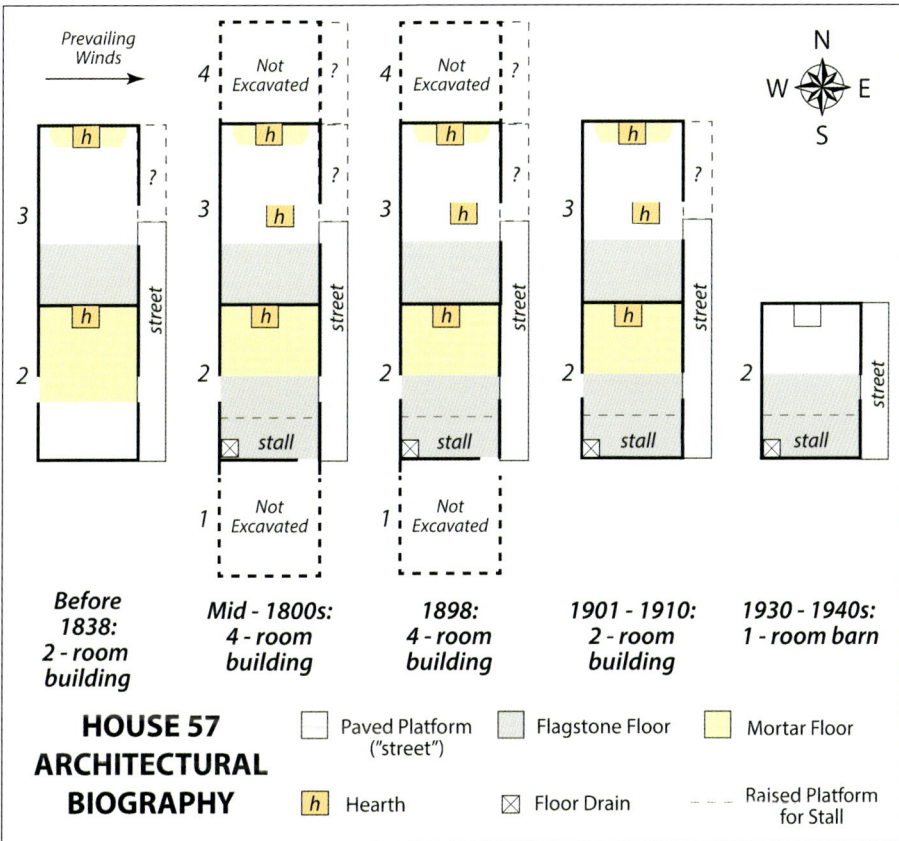

Fig. 4.24: Schematic architectural biography for House 57, Inishark

As one can see from the schematic plan, original Rooms 2 and 3 were constructed with hearths in the northern gable walls, and builders laid down a mortared floor throughout part of both rooms. Sometime in the mid-nineteenth century, occupants added flagstone flooring and a drain in the southern portion of Room 2, presumably for sheltering animals. It is not clear when exactly residents added a central hearth in Room 3, or when they added Rooms 1 and 4. However, the 1898 Ordnance Survey map shows a structure with these additions; therefore, it was sometime before the late nineteenth century. The roof was thatched, and occupants sank a series of stakes into the floors along the walls of the house as tie-downs for lashing the thatch securely.

The house and a series of three associated outbuildings (Buildings 80, 97 and 120) appear in the earliest 1855 Griffith's Valuation records and later editions as recently as 1941. A series of residents, represented only by the name of a male head-of-household, include John Murray (Jr?) from 1855 to 1862, James Holleran (1863–93), Thomas (Tom) Murray (1894–1904) and Thomas Cloonan (1910 until the construction of House 1). In the 1901 census, we believe that Thomas (Tom) Murray, his wife Anne, their two children Thomas and Mary and his two septuagenarian parents, Thomas and Margaret, lived in House 57. By the 1911 census, the Murrays had moved elsewhere, and Thomas Cloonan, his wife Jane and children Bridget, Mary, Julia, Patrick, John, Maggie, Ellen, Michael and Kate made House 57 into a

Fig. 4.25: Undergraduate student excavating *in situ* ceramic and glass vessels from Room 2 of House 57

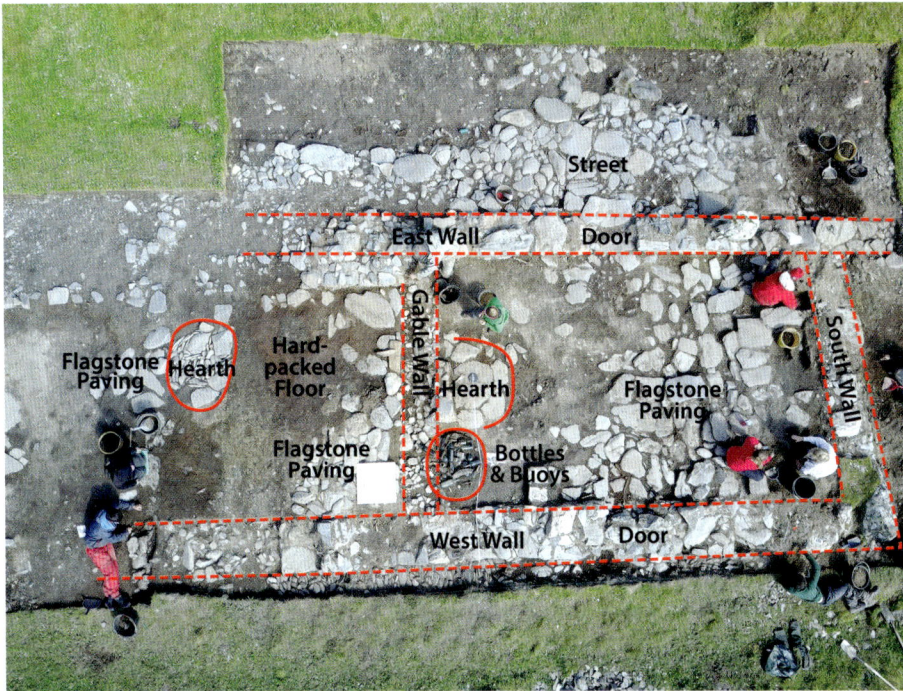

Fig. 4.26: View of excavations of House 57 from above

home. Interestingly, in both the 1901 and 1911 censuses, the recorders described the home as a two-room dwelling, and we remain unsure about when Rooms 1 and 4 were added and how long they were in use.

Oral histories offered by former Inishark residents described how the mid-twentieth-century residents of House 1, located to the east in the same plot of land, used House 57 as a barn to house animals and store equipment and some belongings in the early to mid-twentieth-century. Archaeologically, we found evidence for this most recent phase of the home's life history in a stake for tethering cattle still *in situ*, as well as a dense concentration of several complete ceramic and glass bottles and glass fishing buoys which had been stored in the northwestern corner of Room 2 (Figs 4.25 and 4.26). Additions to houses like this one, as well as the ability to move between houses, testify to islanders' resiliency and flexibility in establishing, maintaining and adapting homes to suit their needs.

All told, excavations of House 57 recovered the remains of a minimum of 107 ceramic vessels; eighty-one glass vessels; fragments of clothing and shoes; jewellery; buttons; clay pipe fragments; a porcelain crucifix base and remains of a metal

BELONGINGS FOUND INSIDE & AROUND HOUSE 57

Ceramic Vessels (MNV = 107)

Platters: 3, 3, 2

Plates: 3, 3, 3, 3, 3

Bowls: 3, 3, 3, 2, 3, 3

Saucers: 3, 3, 3, 2

Teacups: 3, 3, 3, 3, 3, 3, 1

Mugs: 3, 3, 3, 3, 3

Jugs or Milk Jugs: 3, 3

Teapots: 3, 3, 1

Marmalade Jars: 3, 3

Redware Crock: 1

Crock or Jar: 1

Eggcup

Glass Vessels (MNV = 81)

Food Jars: 3, 3, 3, 3, 3, 2

Wine or Champagne Bottles: 2

Medicine Bottles: 3, 3

Mineral Water Bottles: 1

Liquor or Beer Bottles: 1

+ 54 Vessels of Unidentified Function

Clay Pipes (MNV = 7)

3, 3, 1

Home & Kitchen Furnishings
1 Enameled Mug
1 Tin Mug
1 Fork (Head only)
1 Fork or Spoon Handle
1 Metal Cooking Pot
1 Copper Keg with Guinness Fitting
1 Brass Keyhole Plate
1 Copper Latch
1 Metal Knob
1 White Glass Doorknob
1 Padlock
2 Asbestos Roof Tiles

Personal Possessions
1 Child's Shoe
13 Buttons
1 Brooch
2 Rings
18 Glass Beads (for necklaces or rosaries?)
2 Metal Purse Clasps
1 Ceramic Crucifix Stand
1 Metal Crucifix

Tools & Equipment
7 Glass Buoys
1 Metal Pully (from Block & Tackle)
1 Wood Pully (from Block & Tackle)
Metal Fishing Weights
Metal Shop Weight
1 Scythe
1 Hammer Head
1 Crowbar (Fragment)
Numerous Metal Buckles, Hooks, Nails, Straps, Stakes, & Wire
2 Horse Shoes

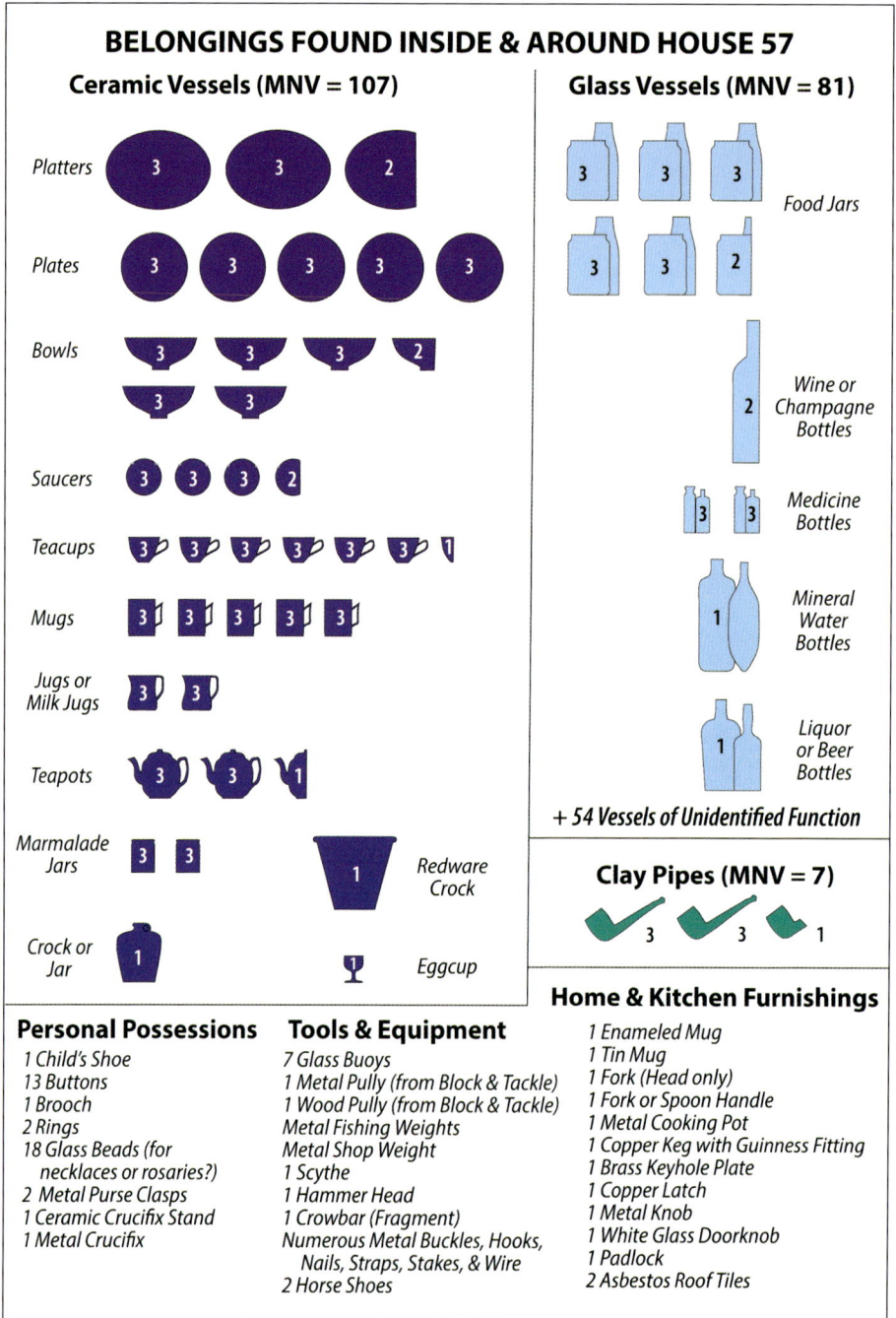

Fig. 4.27: Summary of belongings found inside and directly outside of House 57

crucifix; a wide range of metal tools for farming and building; home and kitchen furnishings; a wood block from a block and tackle; and seven glass buoys (Figs 4.27 – 4.37). The combination of artefact types reflects the house's life history, first as a home and then as a barn for sheltering animals and storing equipment and other possessions.

The ceramic vessels include a wide range of tableware and those used for storing and preparing foodstuffs (Figs 4.32 – 4.36). While many of House 57's ceramic vessels were undecorated and finished with a white glazed surface, others displayed brightly coloured spongeware designs or intricate transfer-printed and

Fig. 4.28: Child's shoe from House 57

Fig. 4.29: Ring (a) and metal crucifix (b) from House 57

hand-painted decorations. One can imagine how these items caught the light from the hearth or lamps, enhancing the enjoyment of a meal or tea break with their beauty. Two vessels from House 57 possessed identifiable maker's marks, including a transfer-printed plate with a blue floral pattern manufactured by John Mortlock Pottery in London around 1880 (Fig. 4.35)[43] and a stoneware marmalade jar made by Caledonian Pottery in Glasgow *c.* 1900–20 for the J.P. Hartley Jam Company operating out of London and Liverpool (Fig. 4.36).[44]

Fig. 4.30: (above) Metal fork (without handle) from House 57

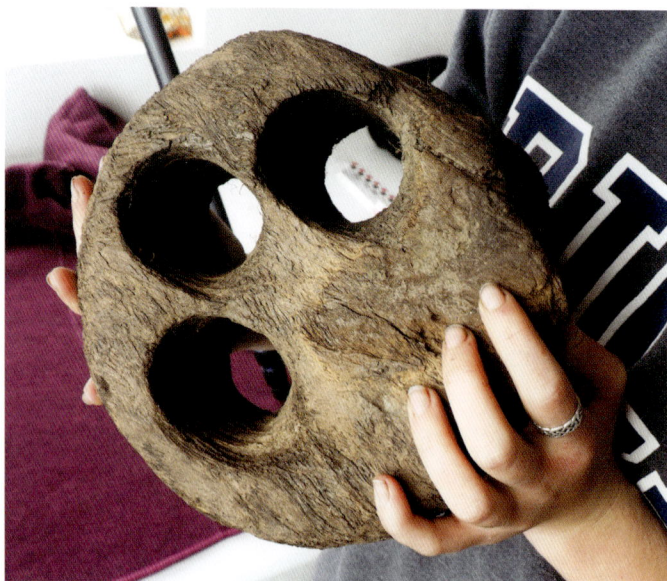

Fig. 4.31: (left) Wood pully from a block and tackle, found in House 57

Fig. 4.32:
(a) Transfer-printed teacup with imagery of a boat and bridge, vessel #1101;
(b) hand-painted mug, vessel #1091

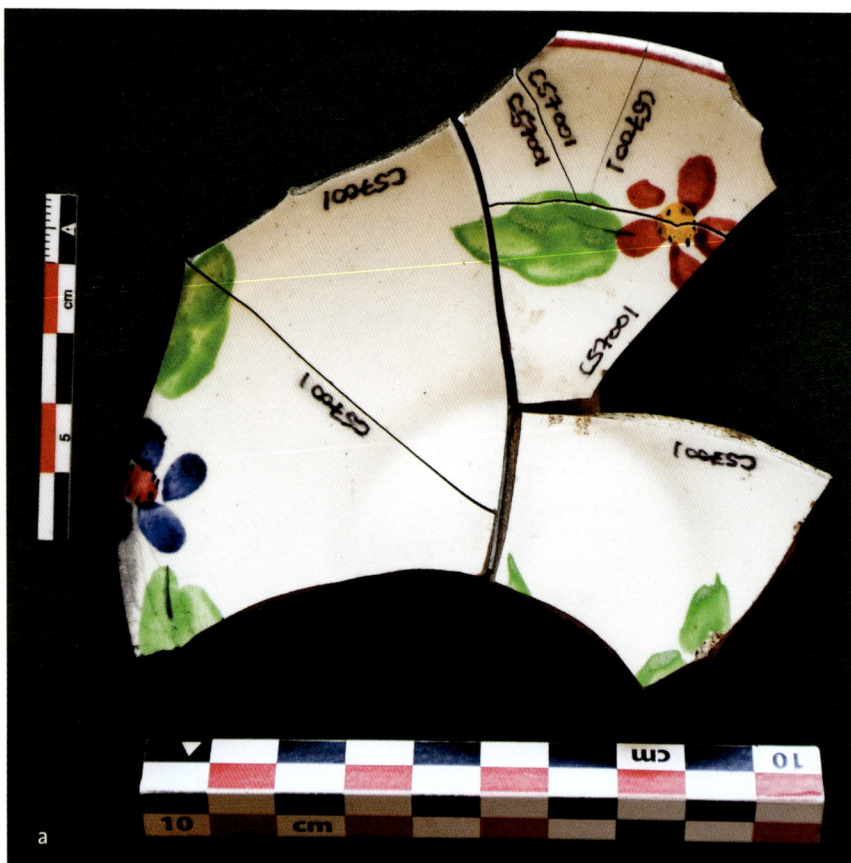

Fig. 4.33: (opposite page) House 57 ceramic vessels: (a) hand-painted saucer with floral motifs and a red band on rim, vessel #1088; (b) transfer-printed teacup with purple ribbon and shamrocks, vessel #1100 with interior surfaces on the left and exterior surfaces on the right

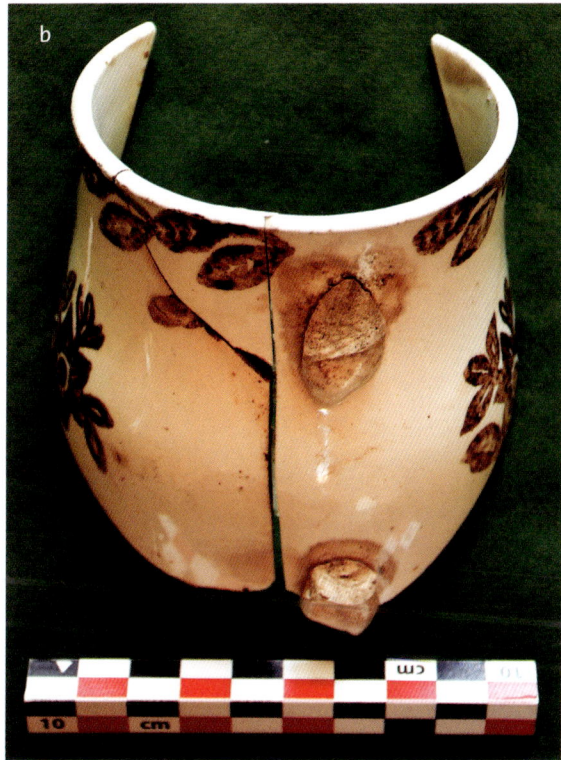

Fig. 4.34: (above and right) Two spongeware mugs from House 57, likely mid-nineteenth century: (a) vessel #1097; (b) vessel #1094

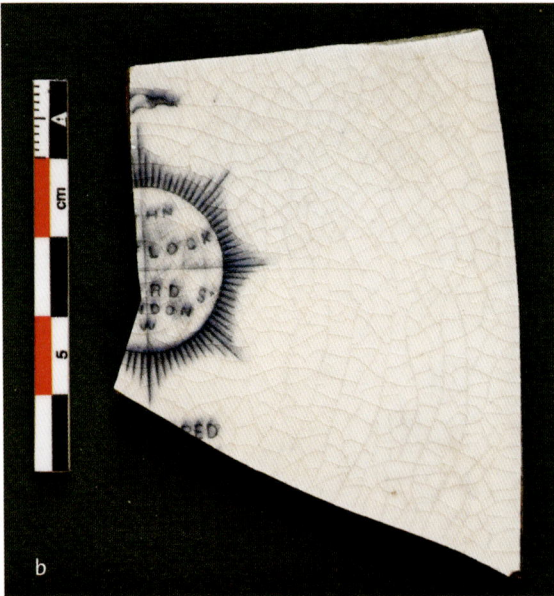

Fig. 4.35: (a) Plate made by John Mortlock Pottery in London, *c.* 1880, vessel #1093, House 57 and (b) its maker's mark

Fig. 4.36: Base and body of a stoneware marmalade jar made by Caledonian Pottery in Glasgow for the W.P. Hartley Jam Company, operating out of London and Liverpool, *c.* 1900–20, vessel #1124, House 57

House 57's glass vessels complement the ceramic assemblage, echoing the domestic nature of everyday items, including several jars that originally contained foodstuffs, like jam (which were then likely reused to store food and other materials), wine or champagne bottles, medicine bottles, one mineral water bottle and one beer or spirits bottle (Fig. 4.37).

Residents likely purchased food jars in shops located on Inishbofin or the mainland, either full of some foodstuff or empty for canning, and then reused the jars for preserves, storing foodstuffs used regularly for cooking, and sending lunches or snacks out with or to people working in the fields or on the sea. Eleven of House 57's seventeen glass jars were marked with an FMF icon (like the one pictured on this marmalade jar in Fig. 4.38), identifiable as vessels made for the Food Manufacturers Federation in the early twentieth century.[45]

House 57's iconic blue medicine bottles could have been acquired by visits to the doctor and nurses on Inishbofin, or to chemists on the mainland.[46] Islanders may have also purchased self-medicating products since a trip to the physician or chemist on the mainland would have required a great deal of effort, time and money. Three bottles marked with Successors to the California Fig Company would have contained a laxative when originally purchased, and two of these bottles contain marks that indicate the bottles were produced in the UK after 1917. Two

Fig. 4.37: (above) A variety of partially excavated glass vessels that would have contained medicines, alcoholic beverages and food found in House 57. Note glass buoys beginning to emerge: one just above the right side of the scale bar and below the remains of a leather strap in the right foreground, the other at the top centre nestled between an alcohol bottle on its right and a food jar on the left.

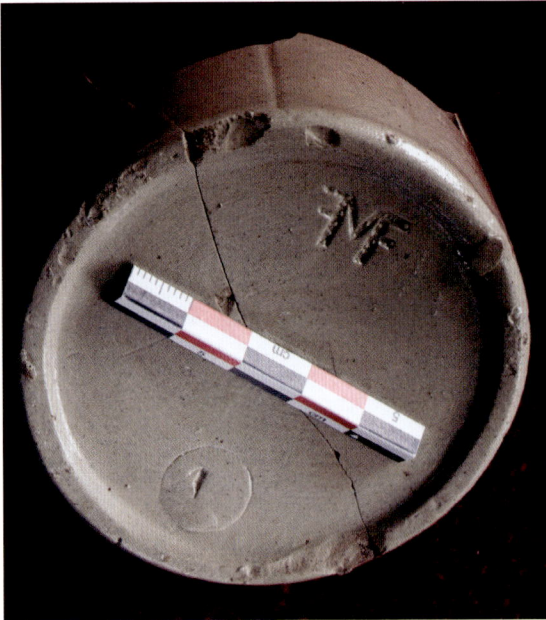

Fig. 4.38: (left) FMF icon on the bottom of a marmalade jar excavated in a unit near St Leo's Church, not associated with any single house structure (Unit 4, context 401)

bottles were embossed with 'ELLIMAN'S EMBROCATION' and (at least in the mid to late nineteenth century) contained a liniment for rheumatism and sore muscles produced in Slough, England.[47] Initially marketed for horses, the company expanded its customer base to include people and manufactured this product until 1936, when they changed its name. Finally, the one bottle designed to contain carbonised beverages, sometimes referred to collectively as mineral water, may have held liquids used as a remedy for upset stomachs and other common ailments.[48]

One of the fascinating yet challenging aspects of analysing glass bottles arises from the fact that they are easy to reuse, and thus we must take that recycling into account when considering a vessel's function as a storage or serving container. For instance, one of House 57's glass bottles that we would automatically classify as a wine or champagne bottle actually contained tar. One can imagine an islander treating the hull of a *currach* with tar stored in this bottle. Nevertheless, we can consider the original use of any jar or bottle as an important starting point for how it arrived into Inishark and for thinking about everyday tasks and their material footprints.

The extraordinary assemblage of residents' personal belongings, tools and home furnishings from House 57 represents a wide variety of daily activities and the material trappings of villagers' lives. The colourful ceramic vessels, gleaming glass bottles, and smaller items such as jewellery, purse clasps and a crucifix all testify to the beauty to be found in these humble possessions that surrounded residents in their home. We turn now to House 8, located four houses to the east of House 57 along the trackway towards the church and the village centre.

Biography of House 8 and its associated belongings

Like House 57, House 8 appears on both the Ordnance Survey 1838 and 1898 maps, meaning that builders constructed the two-room house sometime in the early nineteenth century (Figs 4.39 and 4.40). Situated under the lee of the mountain and oriented roughly north–south, the house contains extensive stone sub-floor drains to manage the water running off the hill behind it. From its initial construction, a back-to-back hearth in the gable wall separated its two rooms. As in House 57, we found stakes drilled into the floors along the interior walls for tying down the roof thatch, a well-made mortared floor, and an elevated platform on the far north of the building (likely for sleeping and storage). Unfortunately, much of the stone in the walls had been recycled for other building projects, and we could not

Fig. 4.39: View of excavations of House 8 in 2014. Note the southern gable wall of House 6 meeting the field wall running behind House 8 and seen above the head of the surveyor in the background.

determine if either (or both) Room 1 and 2 contained opposing doorways on the eastern and western walls, as we saw in Houses 6 and 57. Furthermore, we lack a certain understanding of when exactly occupants renovated the southern end of the building to create a small shed, although we hypothesise that this change occurred around the turn of the nineteenth to twentieth century.

House 8 appears in the valuation records together with two other houses on the same large plot of land: neighbouring House 16 (located to the south and also built sometime before 1838) and House 7 (adjacent to House 8 and built after 1838 but before the 1855 Griffith's Valuation). We can track the life history of House 7 until its abandonment in the early twentieth century relatively well through oral histories, census documents and valuation records. Of the two earlier Houses 8 and 16, one disappears from the valuation records sometime after 1895, although House 8 does appear on the 1898 Ordnance Survey map, albeit shortened to two rooms from its previous three. We know from a few of the belongings found within House 8 that date to after 1900 that the house was still standing at that point. If our reasoning is correct, then the house's valuation records began in 1860: Patrick (Richard) Davis was the head-of-household in House 8 from 1860 to 1876. In 1881, his widow Catherine Davis was listed as the head-of-household. By 1885, a different

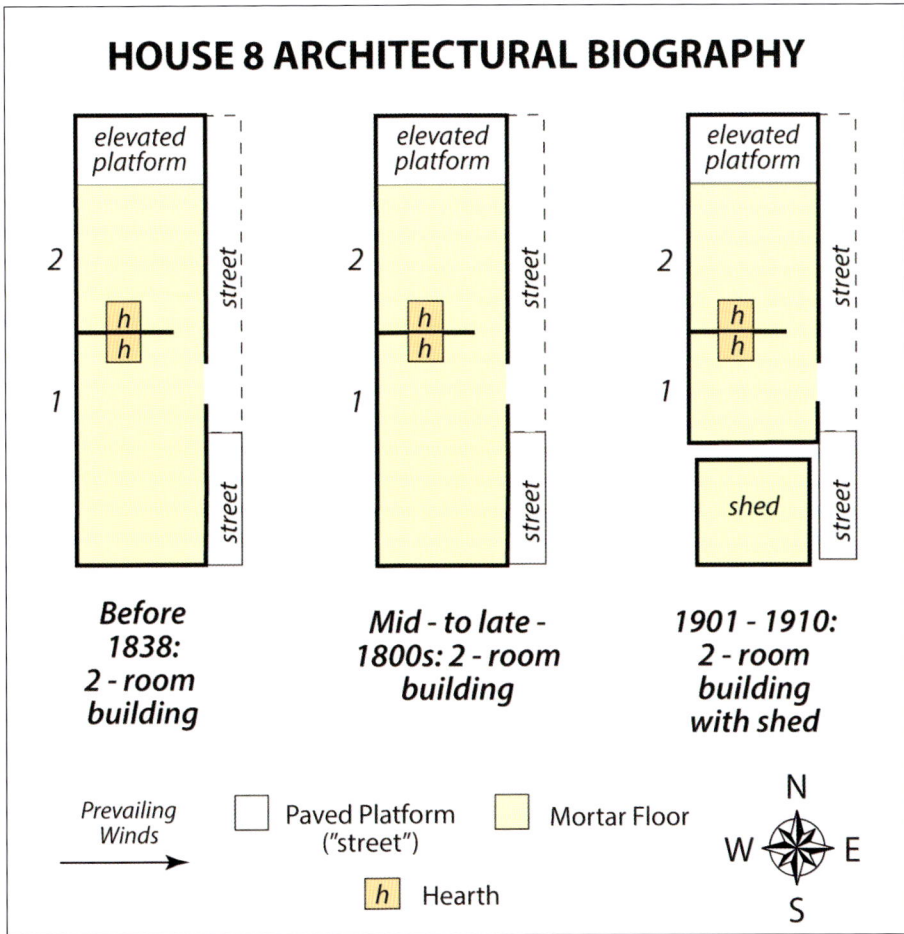

HOUSE 8 ARCHITECTURAL BIOGRAPHY

Before 1838: 2 - room building

Mid - to late - 1800s: 2 - room building

1901 - 1910: 2 - room building with shed

Prevailing Winds

Paved Platform ("street")

Mortar Floor

h   Hearth

N W E S

Fig. 4.40: Schematic architectural biography for House 8, Inishark

family had moved into the home: Michael Halloran was listed as the head-of-household from 1885 to 1893. In 1894, a new tenant was listed: Patrick King, who appeared in the 1904 valuation of this property. If our understanding of the chain of occupancy is correct, then seventy-year-old Patrick King resided in this home with his sixty-seven-year-old wife Jane and twenty-seven-year-old son Martin at the time of the 1901 census. Sometime between the 1904 and 1910 valuations, the Kings moved off the island or passed away, and the most recent occupant listed in the valuation records was John (Judy) Lavelle, who is described as living in the house but not working any land. In 1914, the valuation record noted that House 8 was 'down', likely collapsed, dismantled, or both, and uninhabitable.

Fig. 4.41: Undergraduate student checking her dustpan for small ceramic and glass sherds while excavating a concentration of complete or nearly complete glass bottles and ceramic vessels in House 8, visible in the foreground

The valuation records associated with House 8 exemplify the dynamic nature of residency in the village, with many families moving into and out of houses, often after the former residents transferred into another house, emigrated or died. Especially from the 1880s until 1921, valuation and census records show many villagers transferring families and belongings from one house to another. With the CDB's reforms, these types of transfers were nearly universal, unintentionally foreshadowing the island's abandonment in 1960. As people moved into a new-to-them house or built a new CDB-style house, they once again needed to make that house into a home by personalising the furnishings. Homemakers entered into a building's shell and transformed it into a home, employing their belongings (furniture, delph, tools and personal possessions) and contributing to a new set of memories and stories. The sticky qualities of these movable furnishings made them particularly powerful tools in villagers' homemaking efforts.

The changes in the tenants who resided in House 8 late in its life history contributed to an extraordinary and unusual archaeological record (Fig. 4.41). Excavators found a dense concentration of complete or nearly complete ceramic

BELONGINGS FOUND INSIDE & AROUND HOUSE 8

Ceramic Vessels (MNV = 161)

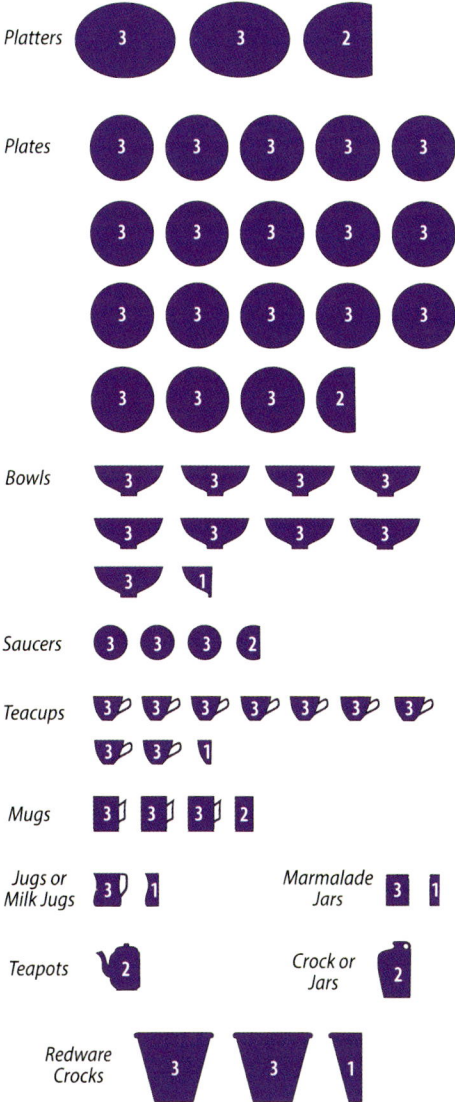

Platters — 3, 3, 2

Plates — 3, 3, 3, 3, 3 / 3, 3, 3, 3, 3 / 3, 3, 3, 3, 3 / 3, 3, 3, 2

Bowls — 3, 3, 3, 3 / 3, 3, 3, 3 / 3, 1

Saucers — 3, 3, 3, 2

Teacups — 3, 3, 3, 3, 3, 3, 3 / 3, 3, 1

Mugs — 3, 3, 3, 2

Jugs or Milk Jugs — 3, 1

Marmalade Jars — 3, 1

Teapots — 2

Crock or Jars — 2

Redware Crocks — 3, 3, 1

Glass Vessels (MNV = 49)

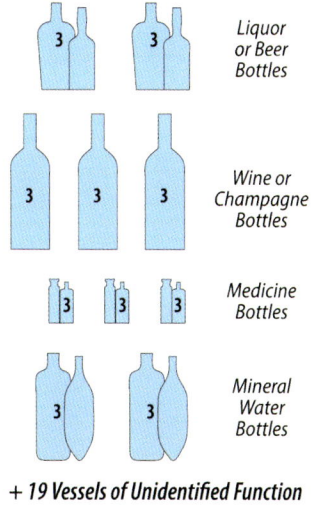

Liquor or Beer Bottles — 3, 3

Wine or Champagne Bottles — 3, 3, 3

Medicine Bottles — 3, 3, 3

Mineral Water Bottles — 3, 3

+ 19 Vessels of Unidentified Function

Clay Pipes (MNP = 19)

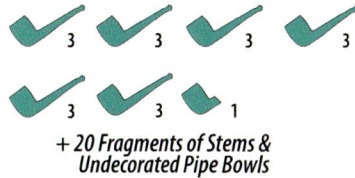

3, 3, 3, 3 / 3, 3, 1

+ 20 Fragments of Stems & Undecorated Pipe Bowls

Other Possessions

1 Pair of Spectacles
Fragments from 1 School Slate
4 coins: 1862 Half Penny (UK), shilling with unreadable date (UK), 1871 Penny (UK), & 1942 Penny (Irish)
1 Piece Unidentified Piece of Clothing
2-hole White Glass Button
1 Whetstone
1 Metal Pully (from Block & Tackle)
Several Corroded & Unidentifiable Metal Objects
1 Stone Weight

Fig. 4.42: Summary of belongings found within and around House 8 during excavation

vessels and glass bottles, including the largest ceramic MNV count of any excavated house (at least 161 pottery vessels; Fig. 4.42); at least forty-nine glass bottles and nineteen clay pipes; four coins; a pair of spectacles; two joinable fragments of a school slate with two sets of initials inscribed on them; a large fragment of a piece of clothing; a two-hole white glass button; a stone weight and a whetstone; and several metal objects including a metal pully from a block and tackle.

Similar to what we found in House 57, the residents of House 8 brightened the interior of their home with white, glazed ceramic vessels as well as brightly coloured vessels adorned with transfer-printed, spongeware and hand-painted designs. In terms of functional categories, excavations recovered examples of ceramic serving, storage and food preparation vessels (Figs 4.43 – 4.50). All of these vessels may have been functional, but they were also pleasing to the eye. Interestingly, we found a larger-than-expected number of serving vessels, particularly platters, plates, bowls and teacups, than we would normally see within a single household context. Several of these vessels had maker's marks, including one purple spongeware plate[49] and multiple jam jars[50] made in Scotland.

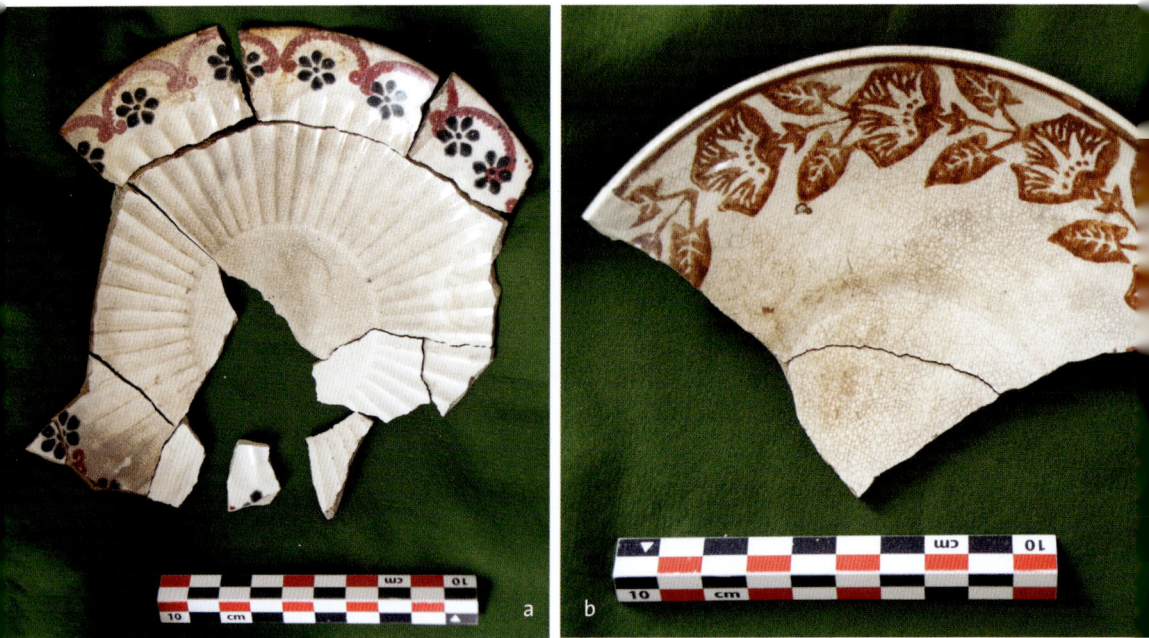

Fig. 4.43: House 8 saucers: (a) vessel #1006; (b) vessel #1008

Fig. 4.44: House 8 ceramic vessels: (a) plate (vessel #1182) with an 'Imperial, D M & Sons' stamped maker's mark on the base and produced by David Methven & Sons Pottery, Kirkcaldy, Scotland, *c.* 1870s; (b) transfer-printed platter (vessel #1019) with geometric design

Fig. 4.45: House 8 serving vessels: (a) spongeware plate (vessel #1181); (b) spongeware bowl (vessel #1193)

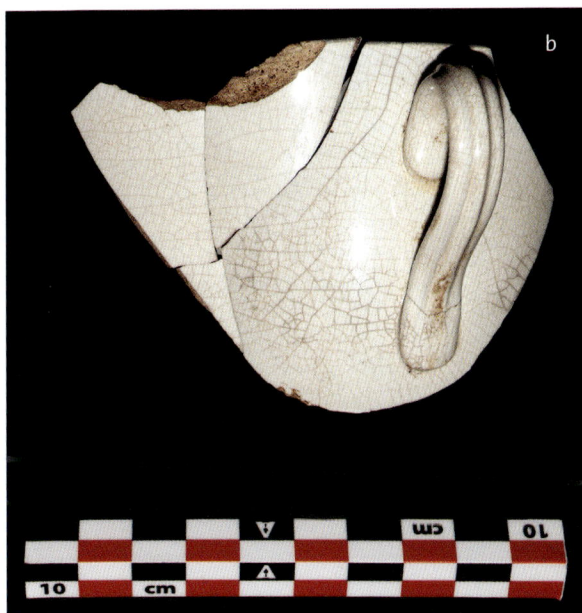

Fig. 4.46: House 8 teacups: (a) hand-painted teacup sherds from vessel #1191; (b) teacup handle, rim and body sherds from vessel #1027

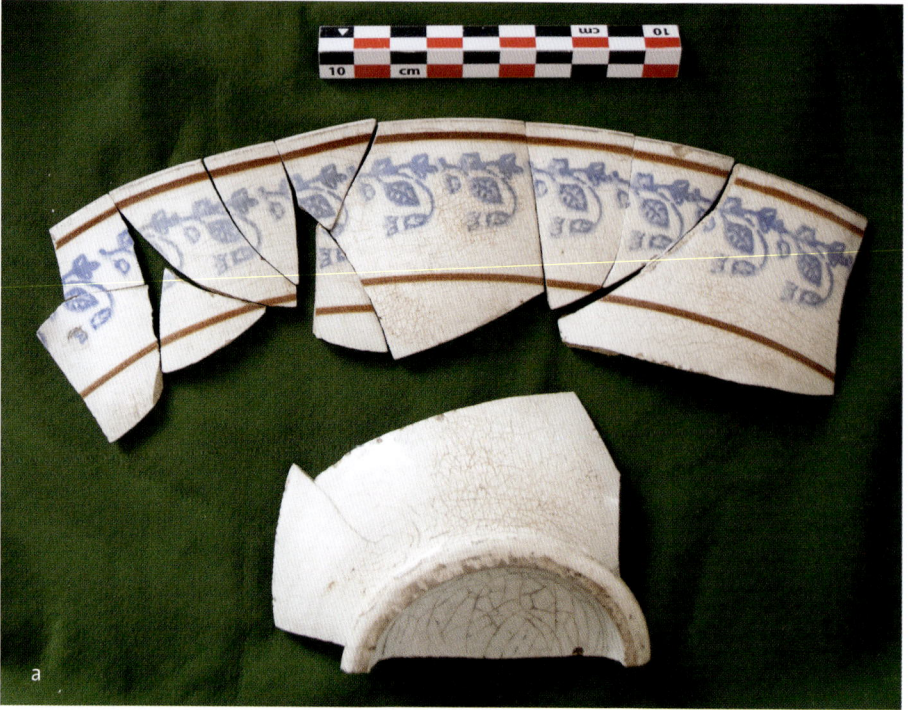

Fig. 4.47: House 8 serving vessels: (a) spongeware and banded bowl (vessel #1009); (b) spongeware mug (vessel #1004)

Fig. 4.48: (a) House 8 transfer-printed mug (vessel #1183) with Cattle pattern (top: exterior; centre: base; bottom: interior body); (b) matching example of mug from Delia's delph collection

Fig. 4.49: (a) House 8 marmalade jar #1017; (b) base with mark details: made by Caledonian Pottery, Glasgow, c. 1900–20, for H.P. Hartley Jam Company operating out of London and Liverpool

Fig. 4.50: House 8 crockery sherds: (a) black-glazed redware bowl rim with body sherds (context 6108); (b) cream-glazed redware crock and stoneware base fragment (context 6085c1)

House 8's assemblage of glass bottles also compares well with those found in House 57, especially the numerous mineral water bottles, blue medicine bottles and alcohol bottles (Figs 4.51–4.53). Together with the high number of pipes, we have proposed that many of these serving vessels and pipes may have been used at a wake, with the house left uninhabited shortly afterwards.[51]

Fig. 4.51: House 8 carbonised beverage bottles

Fig. 4.52: House 8 alcohol bottles

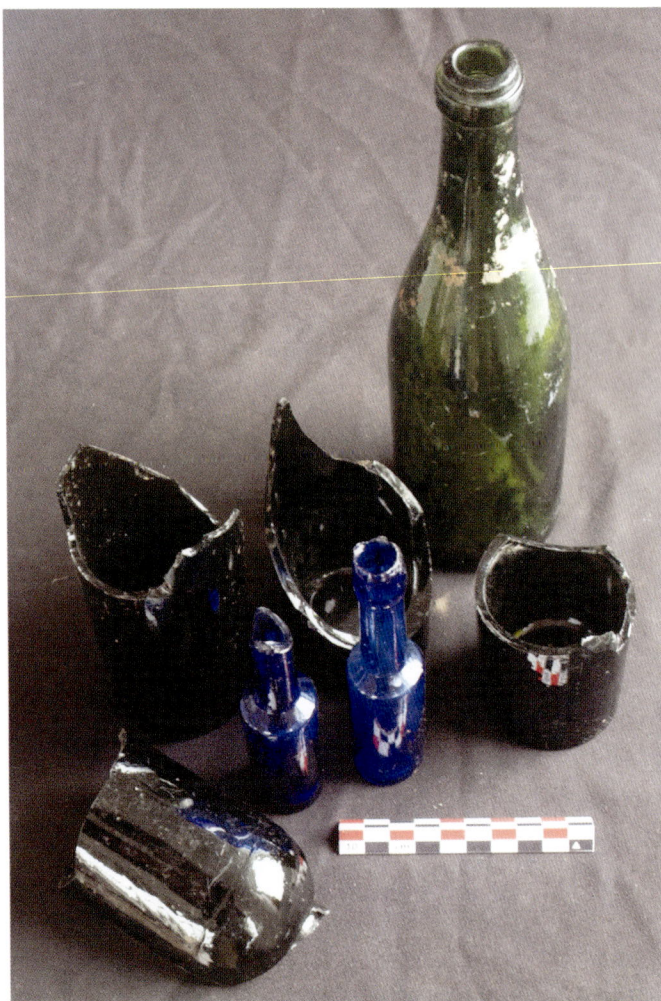

Fig. 4.53: Alcohol and carbonised beverage bottles found together in House 8 alongside two blue medicine bottles (context 6079-F3)

While House 8's ceramic and glass vessels relate easily to general categories of household furnishings, the coins, joinable fragments of a school slate, and spectacles resonate strongly as personal possessions to be treasured and certainly to be kept safe (Figs 4.54–4.57). Coins would have been hard-earned through the intense labour of one's body from fishing, farming, dairying, selling eggs, weaving or handwork (Fig. 4.54). The spectacles themselves speak to the ability to purchase this valuable item and the need to use them for reading and for other tasks requiring a keen eye, such as working as a seamstress, an occupation sometimes referenced in census records (Fig. 4.55).

Fig. 4.54: 1862 British halfpenny found on the floor of House 8

Fig. 4.55: Spectacles from House 8

The school slate fragments evoke the efforts of learning to read and write in the island's primary school, originally established sometime before 1855 when it first appears in the Griffith's Valuation record and its later incarnations in 1862 and 1898. The House 8 school slate fragments were inscribed with a set of initials. On one side, the older initials read 'FD' and suggest that it was possibly once used by a child in Patrick (Richard) Davis' household between 1860 and 1885 (Fig. 4.56). Before the initials were carved, someone carved neat, evenly spaced vertical lines onto this side of the slate, possibly to aid with writing and arithmetic exercises.

On the reverse side, someone carved the initials 'BH' twice (once on the far left and another time in the centre), possibly relating to a child residing in the home from 1885 to 1893, when Michael Halloran was listed as the tenant (Fig. 4.57). Only one vertical line was carved on this side, after the initials had been inscribed.

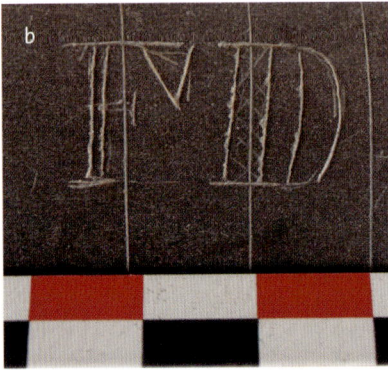

Fig. 4.56: (a) Joinable fragments from the school slate found in House 8 with (b) initials FD inscribed on one side

Fig. 4.57: (a) Joinable fragments from other side of the school slate found in House 8 with (b) initials BH inscribed twice on one side

Unfortunately, we have been unable to locate with absolute certainty the names of the children who lived in House 8 due to the lack of census records for this time period. One possible candidate for 'BH' was Bridget Halloran, born around 1880 on Inishark and who emigrated to Clinton, Massachusetts, to work in the mills in the early twentieth century. She is listed in the Clinton City Directory as living at 5 Richman Street with several other Inishark- and Inishbofin-born young women from 1901 to 1907, when these records indicate that she returned to Ireland.

Despite this large number of objects found within and directly around House 8, we could only identify two examples of matching items: six clay pipes manufactured by Hynes Pipe Factory in Galway (Fig. 4.58) and two saucers with hand-painted bands of red flanking alternating cut sponge red diamonds and blue flowers (Fig.

4.59). As archaeologists we are interested in matching items because it suggests that they might have been purchased together.[52] The pipes were likely purchased at a local shop on nearby Inishbofin or from one of the mainland shops in Cleggan, Clifden or Westport, where we know from oral histories and historical shop ledgers that Inishark islanders acquired goods. House 8's spongeware-decorated red and blue saucers represent one of the few cases where we found a match within a house beyond the common transfer-printed vessels decorated with more popular patterns, such as blue Willow or Asiatic Pheasant, that dominate the ceramic assemblages in all excavated houses.

The next chapter will focus on how Inishark and Inishbofin islanders acquired these belongings, particularly their ceramic vessels, and the fascinating networks of places, both near and far, we can see through the artefacts we encounter in the archaeological record and in people's dressers and delph collections. For now, we turn to consider the stories told by these recovered objects in Houses 8, 57, and the five others we excavated.

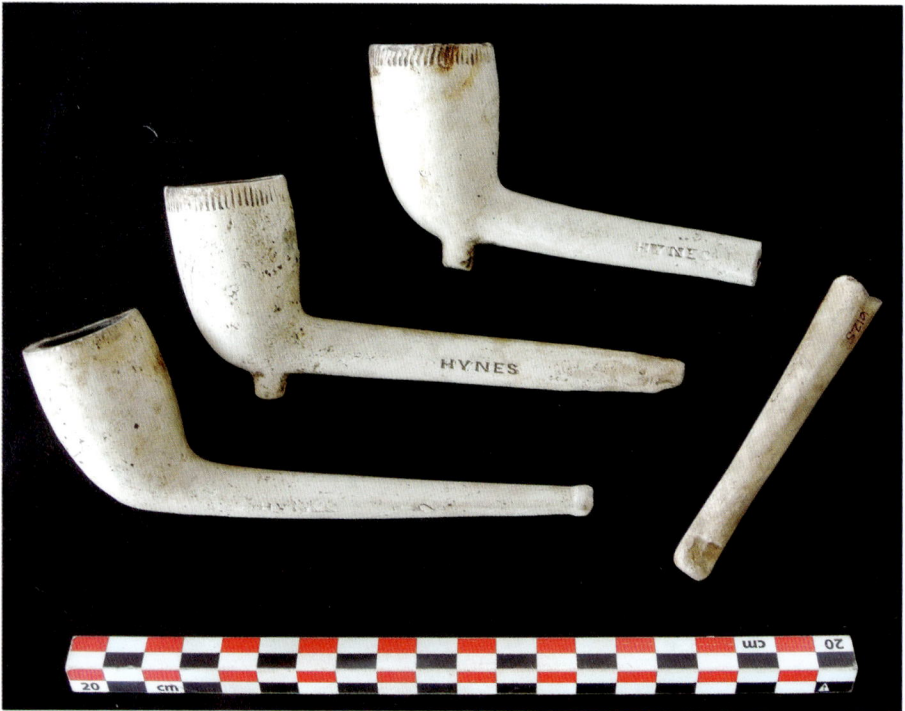

Fig. 4.58: House 8 pipes from Hynes of Galway

Fig. 4.59: House 8 saucers with matching decoration (but different sizes): (left) vessel #1015; (right) vessel #1016

Homemaking in Inishark's historic village

Houses 8 and 57 offer an excellent glimpse into how Inishark islanders creatively furnished and maintained their homes. Since ceramics are the best-preserved type of belonging, comparing the percentages of different forms within each home provides an interesting perspective (Fig. 4.60). Both houses contained the same suite of forms, except for the single eggcup we discovered in House 57. However, the relative proportions of different forms raise some interesting questions for us as archaeologists. We have already discussed the large numbers of plates, teacups, platters, bowls and pipes our team uncovered in House 8. However, when we compare the percentages of these forms in Houses 8 and 57, we see some other interesting differences. For instance, while we found the large number of teacups in House 8 intriguing, teacups appear just as frequently in House 57.

In contrast, mugs and jugs or milk jugs appear more than twice as often at House 57 than at House 8; teapots occur at more than four times the frequency in House 57. These differences may relate to the final life history events of each of the houses, but they also clearly speak to the inhabitants, each with individual senses of aesthetics and taste. Perhaps the inhabitants of House 57 had a special interest in acquiring jugs, as we saw in the dressers in Mary's house and the Doonmore Hotel. Alternatively, perhaps the residents in House 57 were renowned for their hospitality and tea service, as we saw in Michael's dressers and delph collection.

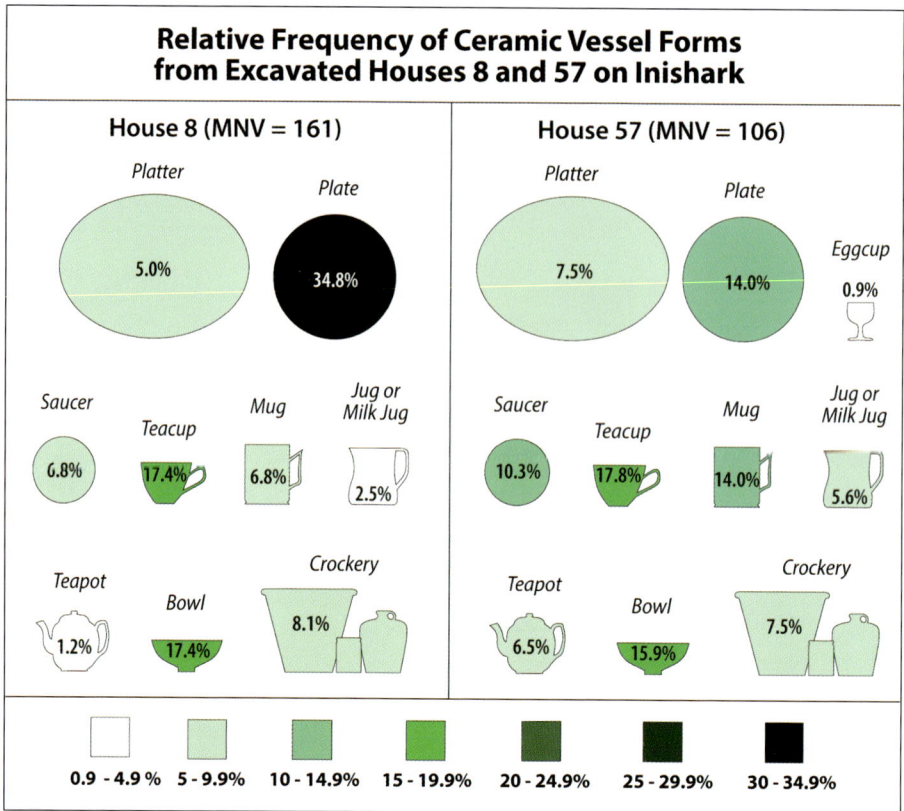

Relative Frequency of Ceramic Vessel Forms from Excavated Houses 8 and 57 on Inishark

House 8 (MNV = 161)

Platter 5.0%
Plate 34.8%
Saucer 6.8%
Teacup 17.4%
Mug 6.8%
Jug or Milk Jug 2.5%
Teapot 1.2%
Bowl 17.4%
Crockery 8.1%

House 57 (MNV = 106)

Platter 7.5%
Plate 14.0%
Eggcup 0.9%
Saucer 10.3%
Teacup 17.8%
Mug 14.0%
Jug or Milk Jug 5.6%
Teapot 6.5%
Bowl 15.9%
Crockery 7.5%

Legend: 0.9 - 4.9% 5 - 9.9% 10 - 14.9% 15 - 19.9% 20 - 24.9% 25 - 29.9% 30 - 34.9%

Fig. 4.60: Comparison of relative frequencies of ceramic forms in Houses 8 and 57

These relative frequencies offer insights into the popularity of forms acquired to furnish homes and the variation between household assemblages – hinting at the personalisation witnessed in dresser and delph collections. Depending upon the specific ages, occupations, involvement in migrant seasonal labour, and life histories, residents of these homes may have acquired different kinds of vessels throughout their lives. When we broaden the comparison to include the relative frequencies of ceramic vessel forms from the other excavated houses, we see a similar combination of familiar vessel forms present yet at different frequencies in each home (Fig. 4.61). Plates, teacups, mugs and bowls are found in all houses, although the frequencies differ as to how often they appear.

To explain variation, archaeologists must consider two main factors: the site formation processes (forces that influence the state of preservation and form that archaeologists find when they excavate, including human-induced and natural

Relative Frequency of Vessel Forms in Excavated Houses, Inishark (MNV = 626)

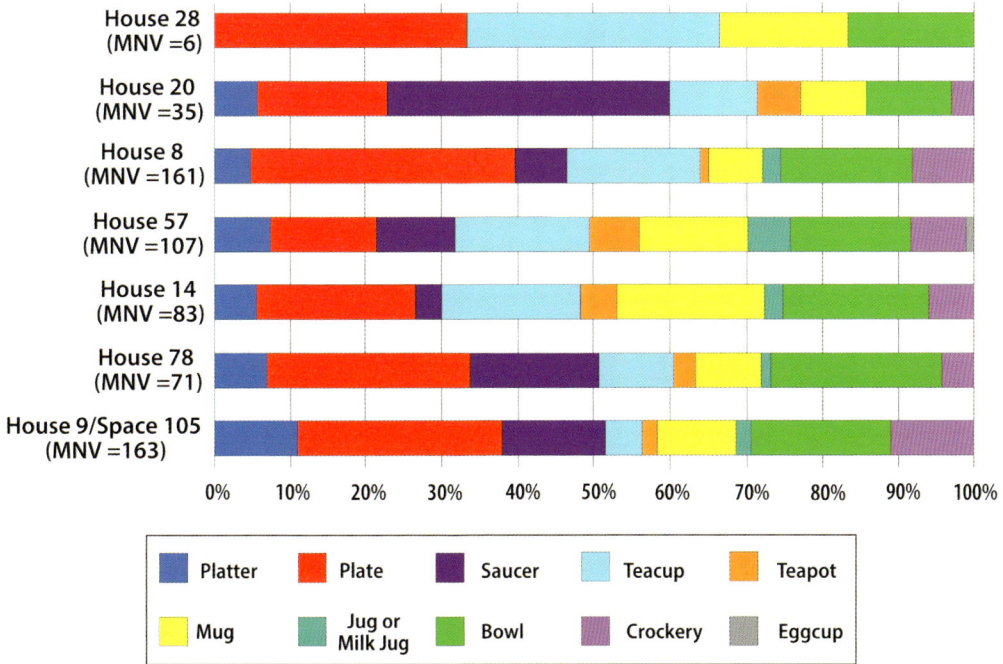

Fig. 4.61: Percentages of ceramic vessel forms present in the seven houses on Inishark excavated by the CLIC team, 2009–17

processes, like erosion and weathering) and how our own excavation methods might influence what we find. The differences we see in our comparison of the ceramics from these homes emerge not only from the varying life histories of the houses and their residents but also from the size of the area excavated at each house and how well the house was preserved. The amount we excavate largely influences the depth of our understanding and the number of questions we can ask and answer. In many ways, the more we can excavate, the greater the opportunity for asking and answering questions about the past. However, the desire to excavate more to learn more must be balanced with preservation: excavation necessitates the destruction of the sediments in which things are buried and often involves dismantling walls, floors and other features to understand how they were built. This paradox underlies all excavations, and therefore the decision to dig requires a thoughtful consideration of what may or may not be destroyed in the process.

For instance, we only excavated narrow trenches and small test units in Houses 14 and 20, both of which are well preserved with standing architecture. Our desire to preserve that standing architecture prevented us from excavating below floors, walls and other architectural features. Therefore, we possess a more limited understanding of Houses 14's and 20's life histories as well as a smaller sample of their artefacts. House 9 presents a slightly different set of constraints, with standing architecture next to an open field where we discovered the scanty remains of an earlier home extending below House 9 and some associated features near this building.[53] The very high MNV count for the combined House 9 and the earlier building and features is misleading in some ways because we have a poor understanding of the life histories of both homes because so little was excavated of both.

Several houses without standing architecture were excavated as fully as possible within typical time and funding constraints, including Houses 8, 57, 28 and 78. House 28 is located near the edge of the cliffs along the southern coastline of Inishark. Due to safety concerns, the entire house could not be uncovered. However, large portions of its two rooms were excavated, and the architectural preservation varied from relatively well-preserved to very poor. Unlike the later homes with hearths built against a gable wall, the hearth was located in the centre of the room. Builders also constructed the house as a semi-subterranean structure: one would have stepped down into the house, whose floor was constructed approximately fifty centimetres below the outside ground level. House 28 is the oldest house we excavated: it appears on the 1816 Bald map but was not featured on the 1838 or 1898 Ordnance Survey maps. The team uncovered only fifty-five ceramic sherds, with an MNV of only six vessels, and the ceramics themselves did not help us define the chronology of the building. We believe that House 28 was a relatively short-lived building, constructed sometime before 1816 and abandoned and dismantled before 1838. The low number of artefacts is likely associated with its short life history and its proximity to the sea, which offered an excellent and easy way to dispose of their trash – one of the most important sources for our understanding of daily life in any of these homes.

House 78, on the other hand, was better preserved and longer-lived than House 28. This two-room house with an adjacent turf rack or small outbuilding was located midway between the mountain at the village's northern end and the southern coastline. Due to its situation, farther downslope from the hill and orientation aligning it with the trackway, its builders constructed the most extensive series of below-floor drains our team has uncovered. Additionally, floors in the western and the central rooms were paved with flagstones, and there is some evidence that the eastern room may have been paved as well – it seems that the building materials of the northern wall and parts of the eastern room were recycled for a later building project (perhaps the CDB construction of walls flanking the road adjacent to the house). A hearth was located in the central room, built against the gable wall separating it from the western room, and there is evidence of a floor drain (similar to what we saw in House 57) in the corner of this room, likely where they stabled animals. The easternmost room was the least well-preserved and most poorly constructed; it does not show signs of having been incorporated into the house as a living space, suggesting that it may have been used as a turf-drying rack at least during its later life history. By the time it appeared on the 1898 Ordnance Survey map, it was recorded as a one-room house, with only the central room roofed and possibly inhabited.

Valuation records list House 78 as one of two houses on the land plot, sharing it with House 68 and outbuilding 102, all of which appear on the 1898 Ordnance Survey map. From 1855 to 1875, the valuation records list only one house on the plot of land with two successive residents: Patrick McGreale (house and land 1855–68) and Michael Lavelle (1869–75). In 1876, the records list two houses and different residents: Patrick (Bryan) Cloonan (1876–80, house and land) and Patrick King (1876–80, house and land). In 1881–4, Patrick King is listed as the head-of-household in both homes. In 1885–93, no one was listed as inhabiting either house, and the occupants holding land included Cyril Allies (the landlord), George Lacey and Michael Halloren (the king of Inishark). In 1894–5, only Cyril Allies was listed as the occupant of the land, but in 1904 Michael Cloonan was indicated as head-of-household for one of the houses, with Patrick King working the land. Michael Cloonan appears as head-of-household with house and land in the 1911–41 valuation records, but with a different plot number: it is not clear if the plot was renumbered (a common circumstance from approximately 1890 onwards) or if he had moved into a different house. Several questions arise from the valuation records: Which house was built first? Which house was lived in longer? Did Patrick Cloonan, Patrick King and Michael Cloonan live in House 68 or 78?

From this brief overview of the excavated homes, we hope it is clear that our understanding of house biographies and furnishings is always partial and dependent on multiple factors. Nevertheless, the combined material footprints of excavated ceramic and glass vessels and other personal possessions demonstrate that villagers used many of the same types of items to furnish homes. Moreover, they acquired and kept these furnishings and renovated and maintained homes over several generations, they made places, enlivening them with possessions that accumulated stories, histories and memories that a touch or glance could invoke, reminding people of senses of belonging and experiences, good and ill. The sticky and voiceful qualities of the delph, the furniture and the home itself imbued these places with a sense of history and heritage. Much like dressers' and delph's ability to connect with loved ones across time and space, the houses in the village and their contents contributed to the homemaking endeavours of the island's inhabitants.

Persevering through time: dwelling in homes

Endurance and durability combine in these structures to demonstrate how islanders transformed houses into homes, maintaining them for families and descendants. By juxtaposing what we learn about a home's architectural history and contents through excavation with evidence from oral histories, maps, valuation records, census information and oral histories, we can document the overall lifespans for the buildings we have investigated (Fig. 4.62). In all cases, these buildings were built to last, 'made to grow old', as we heard about dressers in the previous chapter. Even House 28, the shortest-lived of the village's early homes, housed one or more families for approximately twenty-five years. The home with the longest documented lifespan, House 20, appears in the oldest map of the village from 1816 and in the most recent valuation records from 1941. These houses were also designed to 'grow different' while growing old. Archaeologically, these buildings displayed a resiliency over many generations that allowed islanders to personalise them as people moved into and out of these homes, renovating them to accommodate growing or shrinking families.

As several Inishark islanders have recounted to us in oral history interviews, home was the island itself, encompassing the houses in which they lived, kitchen gardens, the seashore, pasturelands, peat bogs, wells, trackways, graveyard and church. Villagers constructed houses, stone field walls, turf racks, pathways, schools and sheds to last for generations, thereby making places for stories and memories to accrue. In the late nineteenth century, residents renovated St Leo's Church and made pilgrimages to the then-ancient medieval monuments still

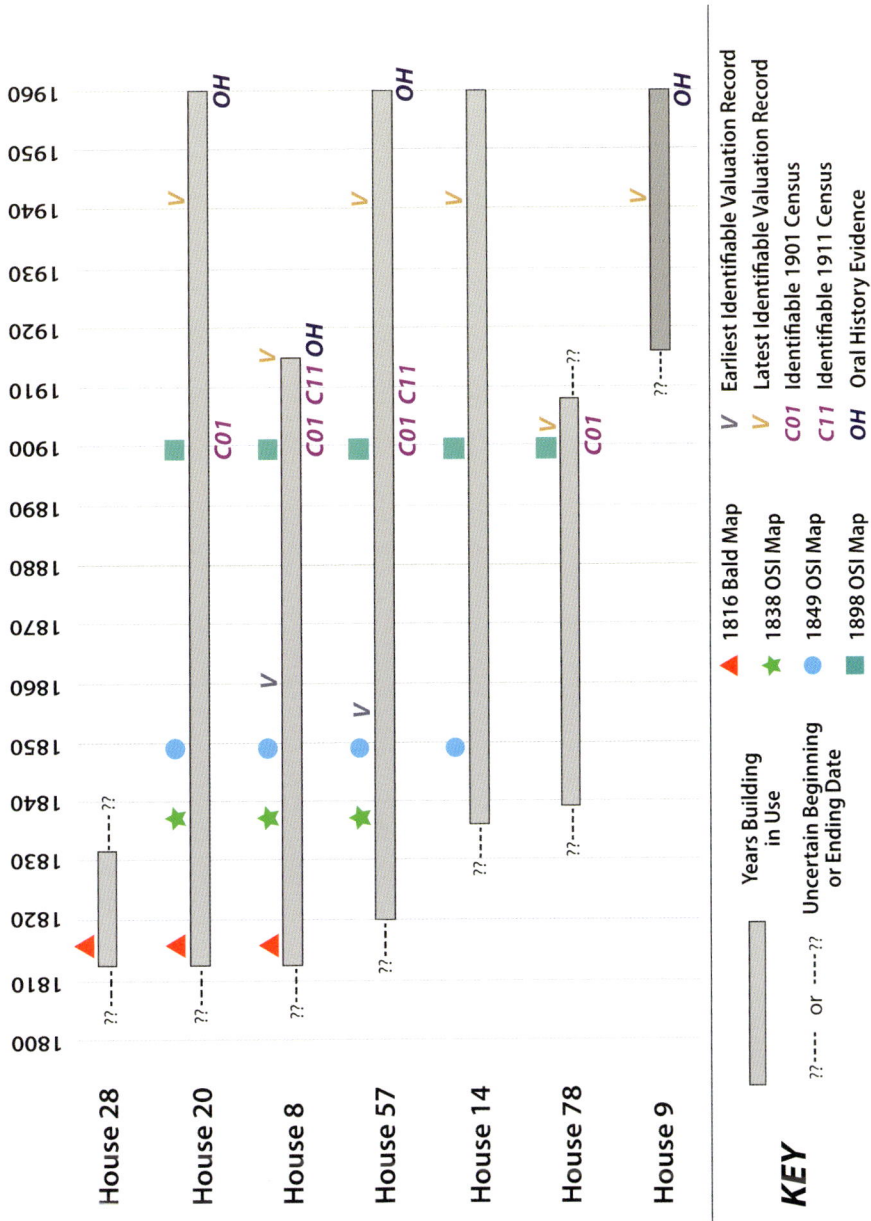

Fig. 4.62: Summary of house life histories, documentary sources and oral histories associated with each home

Fig. 4.63: Looking back at the village of Inishark after finishing CLIC's archaeological field season in 2014

visible within and around the village.[54] McLaughlin's 1942 folklore accounts speak of cake dances on Clochán Congleo without specifying it as an ancient medieval shrine, visits to the island's holy well, sleeping overnight in Clochán Leo, and making annual *turas* circuits on St Leo's Day on 11 April at Inishark's fourteen stations.[55] For these islanders, home was everyone, everything and every place on Inishark (Fig. 4.63).

In many ways, islanders' long-term efforts to make places meaningful (or meaningful places), whether as a convenient location to perform daily tasks or as an area imbued with histories and experiences (or likely both together), rendered the entire island as their home. In an oral history interview with Ellen, born and raised on Inishbofin and whose ancestors lived on Inishark, she describes why islands are special places:

> Island life is hard, but I wouldn't live anywhere else. The other side of it is great. It's a great place to grow up. It's a great place to raise children. The freedom. You can come and go anywhere you want to. There's no danger. But there's a bond, there's a bond that you don't get anywhere else. Islands should never be abandoned. They should never be given up on. They shouldn't. People who live on them shouldn't allow the outside world to give up on them. Certainly not like what happened here [Inishark] where they were allowed to be bullied off.[56]

Thus, making a home requires forging a bond between people and places. We believe that stories about people's experiences, recent or from long ago, act as one of the most important bonding agents, the glue, between islanders and their island homes.

Moreover, these stories powerfully transcend space and time and often reside in durable forms, like buildings, dressers, delph and glass vessels – those humble belongings in which reside such powerful memories and stories. The ability to travel through space and back in time while remembering stories of loved ones, as one might when holding a teacup brought as a gift during a visit by one's grandmother who long ago emigrated to America, represents a powerful element of homemaking. In the next chapter, I compare the archaeological ceramic and glass vessels with those we recorded in contemporary dressers and delph collections to explore how these possessions propel people back through time and across vast distances of the globe while simultaneously strengthening a sense of belonging, perseverance and home.

5

The Taste of Home: Delph, consumption and connections to the wider world

It happens in the present tense and it is, itself, a continuous present of active, dynamic movements, judgements and decisions … This bowl was made by someone I didn't know, in conditions that I can only imagine, for functions that I may have got wrong.

But the act of reimagining it by picking it up is an act of remaking.

Edmund de Waal, potter and author[1]

Dressers and delph make us remember and reflect upon our lives, our connections to other people and places, and our origins. The stories transport viewers through time, inviting us to imagine and remember people and places near and far in an act of mental hospitality, gathering and safely storing memories, histories and personal experiences. Potter Edmund de Waal describes this power to connect people to distant times and places in profoundly personal and personalised experiences: every time he picks up an old bowl, he remakes it by reimagining the stories it holds. As encounters with delph and dressers occur through time and with different people, these sticky belongings accumulate layers of history, which archaeologist Shannon Dawdy calls a patina.[2] In the case of dressers and delph, the age, origins, life history, associations with other furnishings, location within the home and the attached memories coalesce to create an especially potent homemaking tool. Like de Waal, every time we interact with them, in a brief glance, thoughtful gaze or careful handling, we reignite the belonging's past and reposition it in our present. We listen to the stories our possessions tell us, and we share these stories with others. Most of these stories grow out of specific places that people or these objects have visited, moved through, or remained in for varying amounts of time. Moreover, dressers- and delph-keepers choose which belongings to display or to place into storage and, therefore, decide which stories to tell openly and which to narrate more selectively.

Storytelling is an art in itself, an example of what anthropologists call expressive culture. Henry Glassie noted that the belongings people displayed in their dressers and throughout homes in Ballymenone should be understood as ornaments – as art – not mere useful items or knick-knacks:

> Judge the kitchen's ornaments on their inherent, particular merit and you will miss the point. Find them lacking as art, and all you have uncovered is an economic fact. These are not wealthy people, and if only rich people can own art, then art is reduced to commodity, and – to put it plainly – all is lost. No, what individual ornaments appear to be is the least significant thing about them. Their meaning lies less in the manifest content than in their magical capacity to bring events and human beings to life in the mind … The art of ornaments does not lie in them, as part of their fabric. They become art in mind and manipulation. They exist to clean and to order.[3]

Cleaning, ordering and ornamenting comprise fundamental placemaking behaviours that are key to homemaking, from the moment the foundation is laid through ongoing and everyday dwelling in a home. Whether we think of these sticky ideas as patina, social memories, biographies or works of art, dressers and delph carry these stories and associations. This chapter describes the fascinating evidence I found for these stories, especially those that connect people to other places and times. I begin by introducing the reader to five voiceful belongings to offer a sense of how we can begin to listen to the stories they recount.

Five sticky vessels
Heirlooms 1 and 2: Honor's and Thomas' historic jugs (Fig. 5.1)

Honor displays her family's two oldest pieces of delph, two jugs that hold silk flowers, on deep window wells in the family's renovated CDB cottage. The oldest, shown on the right, was given to her husband Thomas by his aunt who had emigrated to the United States many decades ago. This spongeware jug has a slightly scalloped

Fig. 5.1: Jugs from Honor's (right) and Thomas' (left) ancestors

body, moulded decoration on the lower portions that flows towards the base, and two bands of green geometric cut-sponge design encircling the vessel below the rim and below the handle. The maker's mark on its base is a transfer-printed heraldic lion and unicorn flanking a shield with the initials 'W.M. CO.' below, proclaiming its origin as the Willets Manufacturing Company in Trenton, NJ with a date of 1879–1885.[4]

The second jug was given to Honor by her uncle many decades ago. It is adorned with a decal decoration of two ponies grazing on its right-handed orientation and a small floral design on its opposite side. Mould-made decorations give the upper body of the vessel flourishes that embellish the handle, rim and spout. The jug lacks a maker's mark and prevents us from knowing exactly where it was manufactured. Honor recounted that in the 1920s and '30s, they used to purchase jam in jugs like this one, and she believes that the jug came to her family when one of her ancestors purchased jam from a shop.[5] In addition to jugs of jam, customers in general shops commonly purchased many everyday items, including dinner plates, teapots, sugar, soap, tins of food, dried fruits, flour, tea, bread, tobacco and bottles of fig syrup (likely similar to the bottles we found in House 57).

Honor's and Thomas' original old dresser had to be discarded, but they continue to display these two jugs in prominent positions in their home to be enjoyed every day. These two seemingly mundane jugs convey stories about emigration, loss, kinship and early twentieth- and late nineteenth-century markets. These heirlooms transport the viewer back in time and across oceans, evoking the Irish diaspora, the hopes of a new life in a new place, and the mourning of deceased kin.

Heirloom 3: Anne's flow blue bowl (Fig. 5.2)

Unlike Honor's and Thomas' vessels, which were gifted to them by relatives, Anne purchased this flow blue bowl in an Irish antiques market. The bowl's decorations mimic patterns typical of east Asian motifs and, therefore, fall under the broad decorative category of chinoiserie.[6] Flow blue refers to the technique in which the blue ink was allowed to escape the boundaries of the lines in the transfer sheet during firing.[7] The intense blues of this vessel's decorations draw the eye, contrasting with the creamy white body of the bowl. The interior scene features a stag and a doe surrounded by stylised flowering plants. The maker's mark on its base names the decorative pattern as Cashmere, manufactured by Ridgway & Morley between

Fig. 5.2: Exterior and interior decorations of Anne's bowl

Fig. 5.3: Maker's mark on base of Anne's bowl

1842 and 1845 (Fig. 5.3).[8] Anne's bowl has been broken and repaired and now graces a bookshelf in the living room where she and her family can enjoy it every day.

Anne's collection of delph is not large but demonstrates her discerning eye, sense of style and aesthetic preferences. As we documented her delph collection and dresser, she recounted how this bowl was the only piece of delph she brought with her after leaving her first career and moving to a new home more than two decades ago. This bowl speaks to her strength and resiliency to start her life over and move forward, crossing time and space and encompassing the deeply personal (Anne's life history, residency, and style in homemaking and decorative arts) and the global (regional and international production of industrialised ceramics in the nineteenth and twentieth centuries and current markets for collectors of these types of antiques).

Heirloom 4: Delia's glass IV bottle, kept by her daughter Bridget (Fig. 5.4)

Delia's daughter, Bridget, keeps her mother's IV vacuum glass bottle, manufactured by the Cutter Laboratories in Berkeley, California in the mid-twentieth century. The bottle's rubber stopper and inscribed volume marks speak to the history of intravenous medical therapies before the invention of plastic IV bags and tubing. Born on Inishturk, Delia worked in England as a nurse through the Second World War. She moved to Inishbofin after the war when she married a local man and served as a public health nurse on the island and elsewhere until her retirement in the 1980s. In sharing the bottle with us, Bridget clearly showed her appreciation for Delia's life's work as a public health nurse, helping inhabitants of Inishbofin and other western communities. A few years ago, I met a visiting musician on Inishbofin whom Delia had delivered in Athlone several decades ago. He had come to the island to play music, and the day I met him, he was setting off to pay his

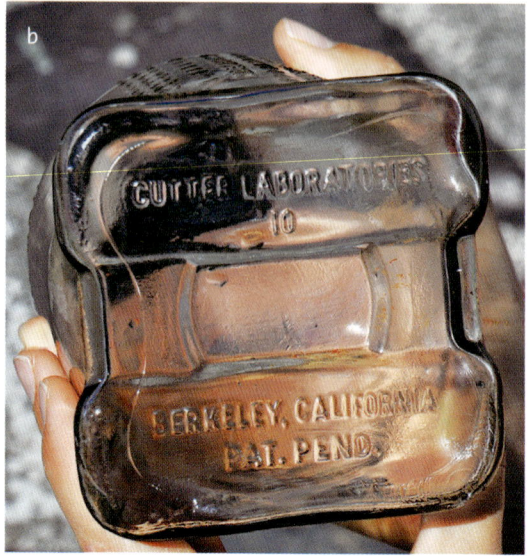

Fig. 5.4: (a) Delia's glass IV bottle with (b) mark patented and produced by Cutter Laboratories in Berkeley California in the 1940s

respects to Delia in her home. This bottle carries stories that are deeply personal and simultaneously expansive enough to speak to community histories, changing medical technologies, emigration to work in foreign countries, globalisation of manufacturing and exports throughout the twentieth century, and the Irish women and men who served in the British military during the Second World War and in their own communities for decades.

Heirloom 5: Mary's favourite plate (Fig. 5.5)

Mary's most cherished plate once belonged to her father, who was the craftsman who built her home's dresser and house shrine that grace the main room. She greets every day with this plate, thinking of her father as she eats her breakfast of toast and jam. The plate invites memories of her father and love for him, re-instilling his presence daily through her morning routine. The plate's manufacturing origins connect her home in Cashel with the urban manufacturing city of Stoke-on-Trent in Staffordshire, UK, referencing the global markets of high-quality ceramics in the mid-twentieth century. This plate's twin sits on her dresser, further emphasising her connections to her father, her house shrine (nestled next to the dresser), the history

Fig. 5.5: (a) Mary's favourite plate, decorated with the Broadway pattern and (b) produced by Foley Pottery in Staffordshire from 1948 to '63

of the family, and the resiliency of herself and her ancestors as they maintained this home for more than a century.

These five sticky belongings work to anchor the homes that they grace, transporting their owners across oceans and through more than a century of life in western Connemara with connections forged through kinship, employment, shopping and taste. Dressers and their contents, understood to be both art and heirlooms regardless of monetary value, tell poignant stories of the social, economic and political histories of people and home places. Dresser- and delph-keepers play primary roles in recounting these histories by carefully creating displays and choosing which stories they tell and which they keep silent. People craft stories and share memories by creatively displaying objects, and they stay current with changing styles and aesthetics in decorative arts and interior decoration.

In gathering these voiceful and sticky possessions for comparison and analysis, I found that together, they recount a history of life in these communities over the last two centuries, a history that both frames and enriches the homemaking process. This chapter describes the most prominent themes involving connections across space and through time and then considers the personalisation of dresser- and delph-keeping in telling important stories and homemaking. I start by considering linkages across space and describing how these belongings arrived in the archaeological and ethnographic homes of Inishark, Inishbofin, Inishturk, Clifden and Cashel.

Delph as pathways to the world: spatial linkages in present and past homes

In thinking about how delph and dressers offer material footprints linking homes to the broader world, I focus on two key queries: First, where were these items made? Next, by what pathways and events did they arrive in these homes? To answer these questions, I draw on ethnographic evidence from the contemporary homes I documented, archaeological evidence from the homes our team excavated, archival records, and oral histories we gathered in these communities over many years. As I noted earlier, the archaeological examples lack the specifics and vibrancy of people's voices, recollections and emotions that enrich the ethnographic, archival and oral historical evidence. Archaeological artefacts evoke possibilities of events and circumstances rather than more firmly grounded certainties of oral histories, with belongings' biographies encompassing manufacture, acquisition and use. Nevertheless, combining ethnographic and archaeological dressers and delph offers a wealth of information on how people in these communities forged linkages to the wider world through their homes, possessions and daily activities.

To answer the first question about origins, I start with dressers. As described in the third chapter, many of the older dressers were made by local craftspeople, who were long departed but still active in people's memories today. With no forests on the islands, the wood for these early dressers often came from salvaged beams that washed onto beaches.[9] In other cases, we do not know exactly where they were made or by whom. For instance, Andrew, one of the Doonmore Hotel's managers, told us that their dresser was made on the mainland over a century ago and brought to the island in the distant past, long before he was alive: he doesn't know where or by whom it was crafted, just that it has always been part of his family's life.

The more recently fashioned dressers, like George's or Peggy and William's, were purchased ready-made from mainland shops and transported to Inishbofin homes without any information concerning manufacturing location. We do not know the original sources of wood, nails, screws, glue, varnish, or paint used to make these pieces. On the other hand, Ellen knows the name of the craftsperson who made her dresser in the 1990s: Tony O'Toole, from Westport. Anne's 1989 dresser was purchased from a local Clifden shop, and she knew that it was one of the early dressers crafted by student woodworkers at what is now called the Atlantic Technological University campus of Letterfrack. While we do not know the name of the student(s) who made the dresser, they wrote the year of its making on the exterior of its backing boards.

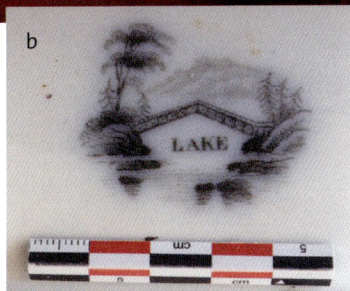

Fig. 5.6: (a) Platter displayed above the bar at the Doonmore Hotel with the (b) Lake pattern, made by G.L. Ashworth and Brothers Ltd of Hanley, Staffordshire, UK, 1862–84

The ceramic vessels, glass bottles and other belongings stored in dressers and presses present a more varied and complicated case for analysis. All but a very few ceramic objects were not made locally. While in recent years, George's kiln has produced vessels that appear in a few dressers, for the most part the vast majority of documented vessels were manufactured in other places, mostly England, Scotland and other parts of the Republic of Ireland. Out of the 1,596 vessels in the ethnographic study, only 145 featured maker's marks like the transfer-printed backstamp on this lovely nineteenth-century platter that sits above the bar in the Doonmore Hotel on Inishbofin (Fig. 5.6).

Of this assemblage, 138 marks allowed us to identify the country of origin, and we were able to date them by a combination of the marks, oral histories, style of decoration and form, and manufacturing technology (Table 5.1). In most cases, these vessels were unique within the dresser or delph collection, but there were several instances of matching vessels or even sets.[10]

I discovered several key trends in investigating patterns based on manufacturing origins, form, decoration and technology. First, participants in this study

Country of Manufacture	Dressers (n = 21)		Delph Collections (n = 9)		Total Marks	Total % Country of Origin
	No.	%	No.	%		
England	45	54.2%	40	64.5%	85	58.6%
Scotland	1	1.2%	8	12.9%	9	6.2%
Republic of Ireland	26	31.3%	5	8.1%	31	21.4%
Northern Ireland	0	0.0%	1	1.6%	1	0.7%
Japan	3	3.6%	0	0.0%	3	2.1%
China	1	1.2%	1	1.6%	2	1.4%
US	0	0.0%	2	3.2%	2	1.4%
Germany	1	1.2%	1	1.6%	2	1.4%
Czechoslovakia	1	1.2%	0	0.0%	1	0.7%
Finland	1	1.2%	0	0.0%	1	0.7%
Greece	0	0.0%	1	1.6%	1	0.7%
Unidentifiable	4	4.8%	3	4.8%	7	4.8%
TOTALS	83		62		145	

Table. 5.1: Maker's marks by country of origin on ceramic vessels (or matching sets of vessels) in ethnographic dresser and delph assemblages

possessed pottery from many different countries, from as far away as Japan and China, and as close as counties Galway, Cork or Wicklow (Figs 5.7 and 5.8). This span represents the global market in ceramics, especially the expanding scope of exchange that developed during the early twentieth century, linking Japan and China to Europe and North America. Second, vessel origins demonstrate clear shifts in manufacturing and distribution networks and styles through time, forming three chronological groups: 1840–1927, 1928–69 and 1970–2000s.

In the earliest period (1840–1927), most delph vessels were manufactured in

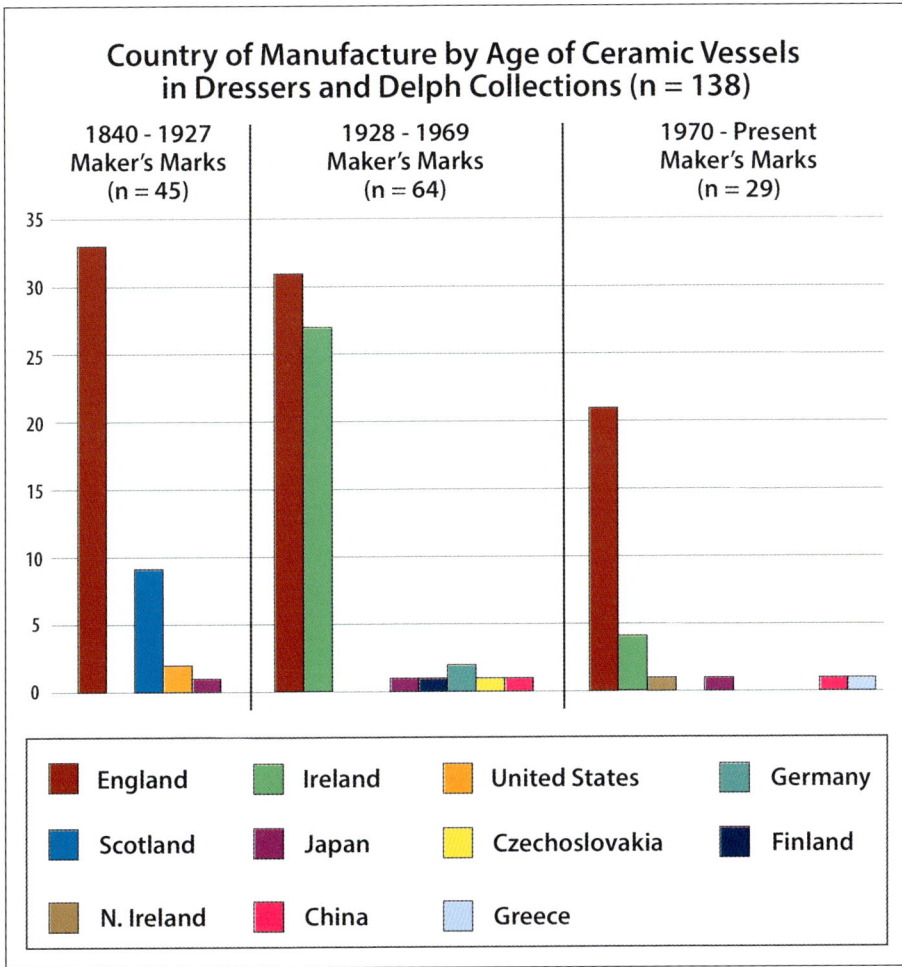

Fig. 5.7: Trends of manufacturing origins of ceramic vessels through time in ethnographic dresser and delph-only assemblages

English pottery factories. In fact, delph from England dominates the entire ethnographic assemblage, regardless of the time period: the majority of delph on dressers and in delph collections was manufactured in Staffordshire (Fig. 5.9). With the exception of two US-made vessels and a Japanese-made tea set, all of the earliest documented pottery was made in Scotland or England. Three vessels (Fig. 5.10) represent England's, especially Staffordshire's, heavy representation as a manufacturing origin in this study's delph, with vessels made by Ford & Sons,[11] Coalport Pottery[12] and Hollinshead & Kirkham.[13]

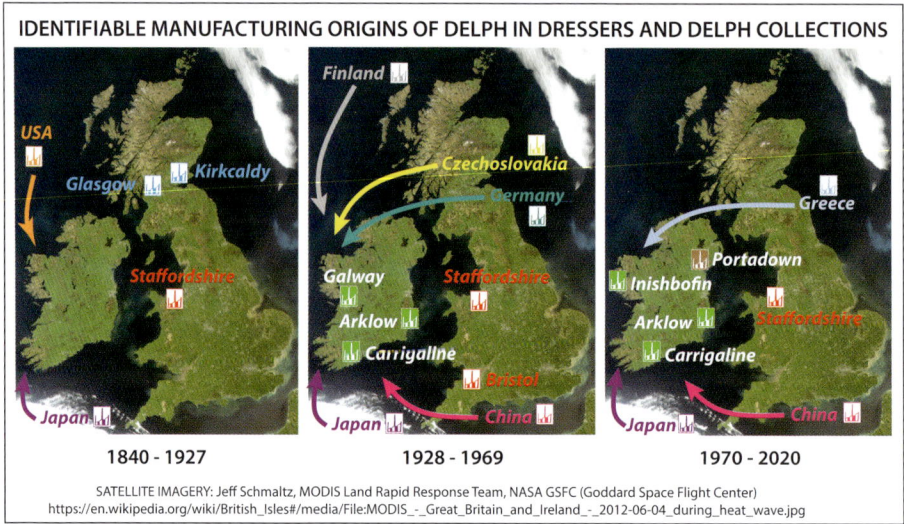

IDENTIFIABLE MANUFACTURING ORIGINS OF DELPH IN DRESSERS AND DELPH COLLECTIONS

1840 - 1927 | 1928 - 1969 | 1970 - 2020

SATELLITE IMAGERY: Jeff Schmaltz, MODIS Land Rapid Response Team, NASA GSFC (Goddard Space Flight Center)
https://en.wikipedia.org/wiki/British_Isles#/media/File:MODIS_-_Great_Britain_and_Ireland_-_2012-06-04_during_heat_wave.jpg

Fig. 5.8: Identifiable manufacturing origins of 138 ceramic vessels in dressers and delph collections

As noted earlier, participants often connected Scottish-made vessels to migrant labour practices, especially sending young people to work seasonally as domestics and agricultural labourers in Scotland. Transfer-print was the most common decoration technique, and the most common colours were brown, blue, red and green. Regardless of whether the vessels were made in England or Scotland, they offer testament to the active participation of members of these island and rural coastal communities in international exchange networks as discerning consumers.

The second phase of delph acquisition (1928–69) begins with the establishment of the first potteries in the south of Ireland, namely Carrigaline in 1928 and Arklow in 1934. Many people began to acquire Irish-made pottery; at the same time Ireland was establishing itself as a nation (Figs 5.11 and 5.12). Patrick's Carrigaline banded milk jug and Bridget's Garland Rose platter represent the marked change in manufacturing origins of pottery vessels in this study as a significant number of Irish-made vessels found their way into dressers and delph collections – though English potteries still supplied the majority of delph in this study made between 1928 and 1969, such as Michael's floral plate made by Barratt's of Staffordshire.[14] In addition to these English- and Irish-made vessels, participants possessed delph from a wider variety of countries, including China, Czechoslovakia, Finland, Germany and Japan. Transfer-printed vessels remained popular, especially the Willow pattern, but the scope of decorative techniques expanded to include decals, gilding, moulding and hand-painting.

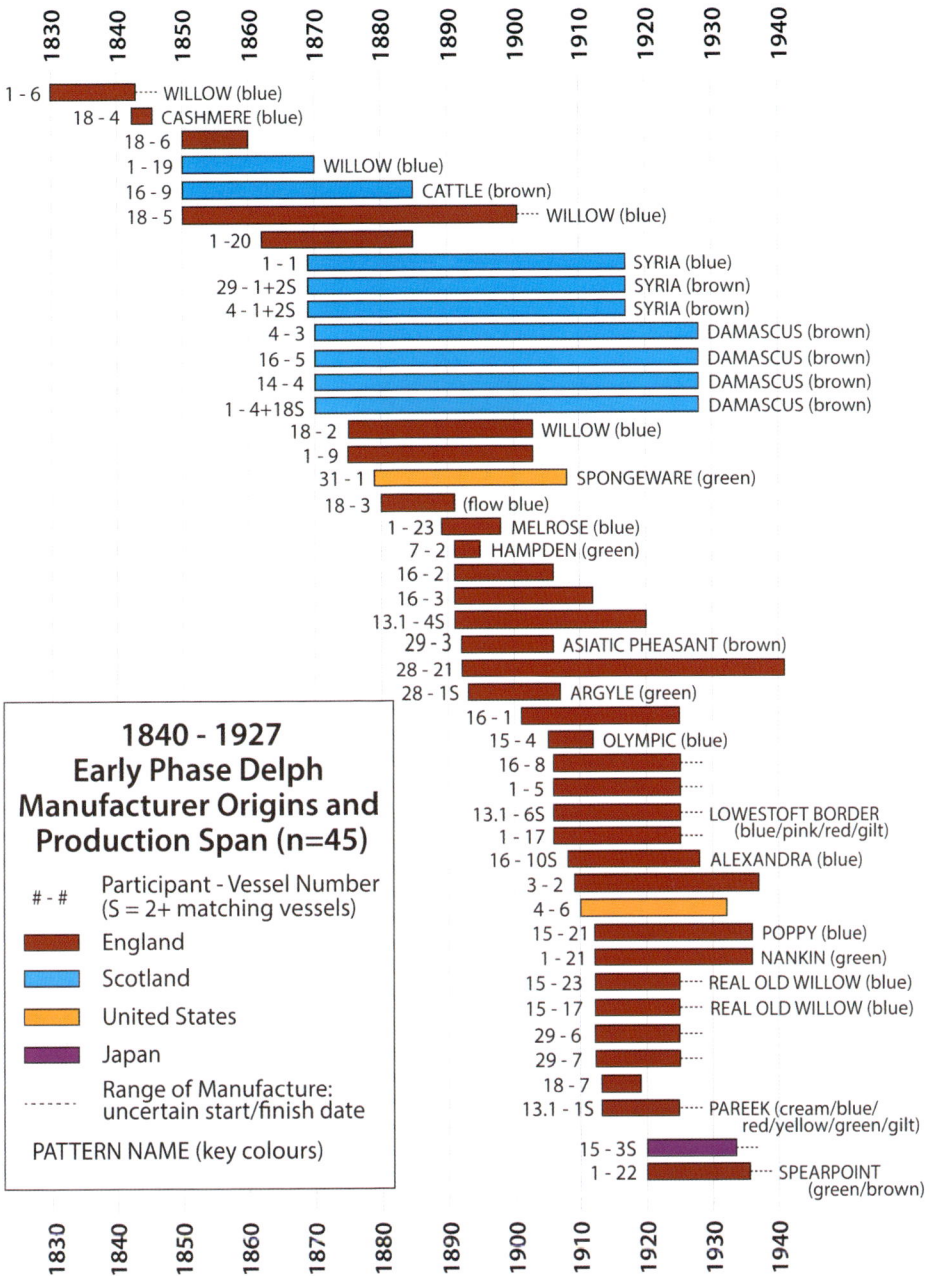

Timeline axis (top and bottom): 1830, 1840, 1850, 1860, 1870, 1880, 1890, 1900, 1910, 1920, 1930, 1940

Chart entries (Participant-Vessel Number — PATTERN NAME (key colours)):

- 1 - 6 — WILLOW (blue)
- 18 - 4 — CASHMERE (blue)
- 18 - 6
- 1 - 19 — WILLOW (blue)
- 16 - 9 — CATTLE (brown)
- 18 - 5 — WILLOW (blue)
- 1 -20
- 1 - 1 — SYRIA (blue)
- 29 - 1+2S — SYRIA (brown)
- 4 - 1+2S — SYRIA (brown)
- 4 - 3 — DAMASCUS (brown)
- 16 - 5 — DAMASCUS (brown)
- 14 - 4 — DAMASCUS (brown)
- 1 - 4+18S — DAMASCUS (brown)
- 18 - 2 — WILLOW (blue)
- 1 - 9
- 31 - 1 — SPONGEWARE (green)
- 18 - 3 — (flow blue)
- 1 - 23 — MELROSE (blue)
- 7 - 2 — HAMPDEN (green)
- 16 - 2
- 16 - 3
- 13.1 - 4S
- 29 - 3 — ASIATIC PHEASANT (brown)
- 28 - 21
- 28 - 1S — ARGYLE (green)
- 16 - 1
- 15 - 4 — OLYMPIC (blue)
- 16 - 8
- 1 - 5
- 13.1 - 6S — LOWESTOFT BORDER (blue/pink/red/gilt)
- 1 - 17
- 16 - 10S — ALEXANDRA (blue)
- 3 - 2
- 4 - 6
- 15 - 21 — POPPY (blue)
- 1 - 21 — NANKIN (green)
- 15 - 23 — REAL OLD WILLOW (blue)
- 15 - 17 — REAL OLD WILLOW (blue)
- 29 - 6
- 29 - 7
- 18 - 7
- 13.1 - 1S — PAREEK (cream/blue/red/yellow/green/gilt)
- 15 - 3S
- 1 - 22 — SPEARPOINT (green/brown)

Legend box:

**1840 - 1927
Early Phase Delph
Manufacturer Origins and
Production Span (n=45)**

- # — Participant - Vessel Number (S = 2+ matching vessels)

- England
- Scotland
- United States
- Japan

------ Range of Manufacture: uncertain start/finish date

PATTERN NAME (key colours)

Fig. 5.9: Graph showing the ages and manufacturing origins of forty-five ceramic vessels or sets of matching vessels with identifiable maker's marks in the earliest manufacturing period (1840–1927). Each entry represents a single or set of matching vessels with identifiable maker's marks that provide details of date range and manufacturing origins. When identifiable, entries include the name of specific decorative patterns, such as Willow or Asiatic Pheasant.

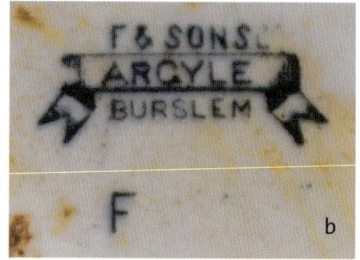

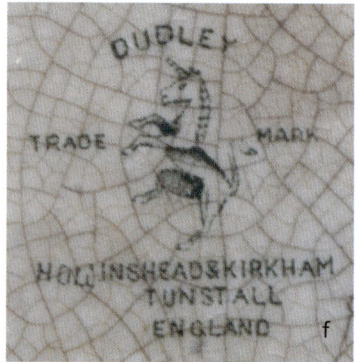

Fig. 5.10: Transfer-printed delph examples from England made before 1928: (a) Patrick's plate and (b) mark for Ford & Sons, Burslem, Staffordshire, UK, 1893–1907; (c) Catherine's teacup and saucer made by (d) Coalport Pottery, UK 1891–1920; (e) Delia's Dudley platter with (f) mark for Hollinshead & Kirkham, Tunstall, UK, 1900–24

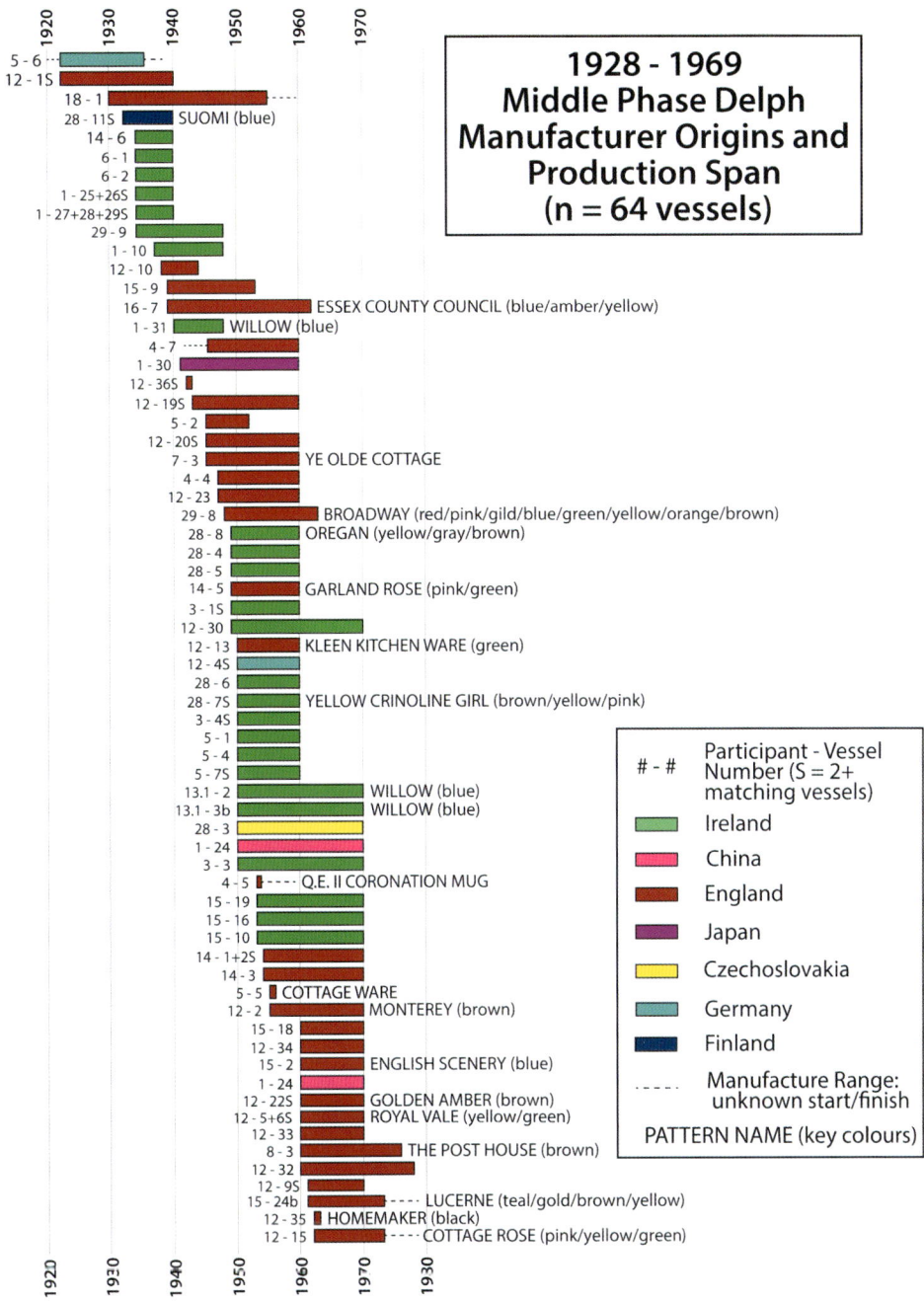

Fig. 5.11: Graph showing the ages and manufacturing origins of sixty-four ceramic vessels or sets of matching vessels with identifiable maker's marks in the middle manufacturing period (1927–69). Each entry represents a single or set of matching vessels with identifiable maker's marks that provide details of date range and manufacturing origins. When identifiable, entries include the name of specific decorative patterns, such as Cottage Rose or yellow crinoline girl.

Fig. 5.12: Delph manufactured from 1928 to
'69: (a) Patrick's banded milk jug with (b)
mark from Carrigaline, Ireland, 1930–40s;
(c) Michael's dinner plate made by (d)
Barratt's, Staffordshire, England, 1945–53;
(e) Bridget's Garland Rose platter from
(f) Arklow, Ireland, 1950–60s

The final and most recent phase coincides with the consolidation and frequent bankruptcies of many pottery factories from the 1970s onwards, as well as technological innovation associated with the widespread use of dishwashers and microwave ovens. Once again, English-made pottery dominates the assemblage and presumably the regional markets where people acquired their ceramics, such as Catherine's Finlandia teacup from Myott, Michael's small bowl from Staffordshire Tableware[15] and Penelope's Memory Lane plate from Churchill Pottery (Figs 5.13

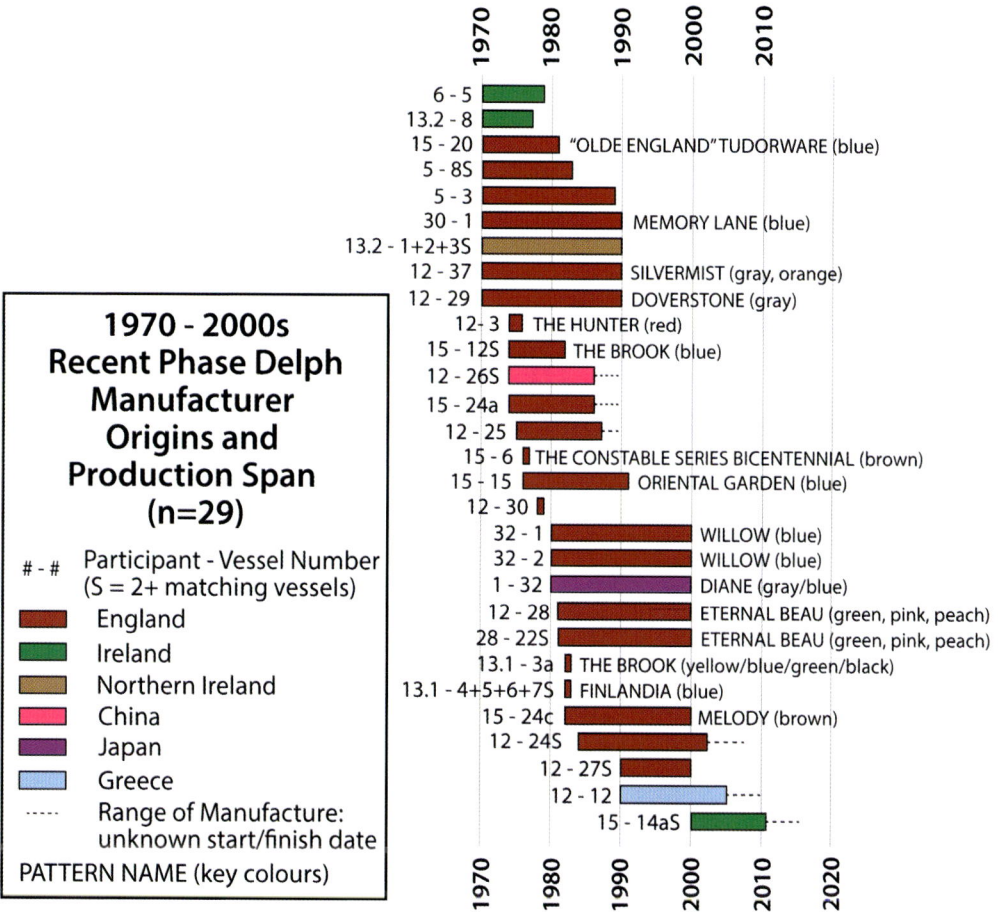

Fig. 5.13: Graph showing the ages and manufacturing origins of twenty-nine ceramic vessels or sets of matching vessels with identifiable maker's marks in the most recent manufacturing period (1970–2000s). Each entry represents a single or set of matching vessels with identifiable maker's marks that provide details of date range and manufacturing origins. When identifiable, entries include the name of specific decorative patterns, such as Willow or Eternal Beau.

Fig. 5.14: English transfer-printed delph produced after 1970: (a) Catherine's Finlandia teacup from (b) Myott Pottery, England, 1982 onwards (matching saucer and small bowl not pictured); (c) Michael's chequered bowl by (d) Staffordshire Tableware, England, 1990–2000; (e) Penelope's blue Willow plate from (f) Grindley Pottery, UK, 1970s onwards

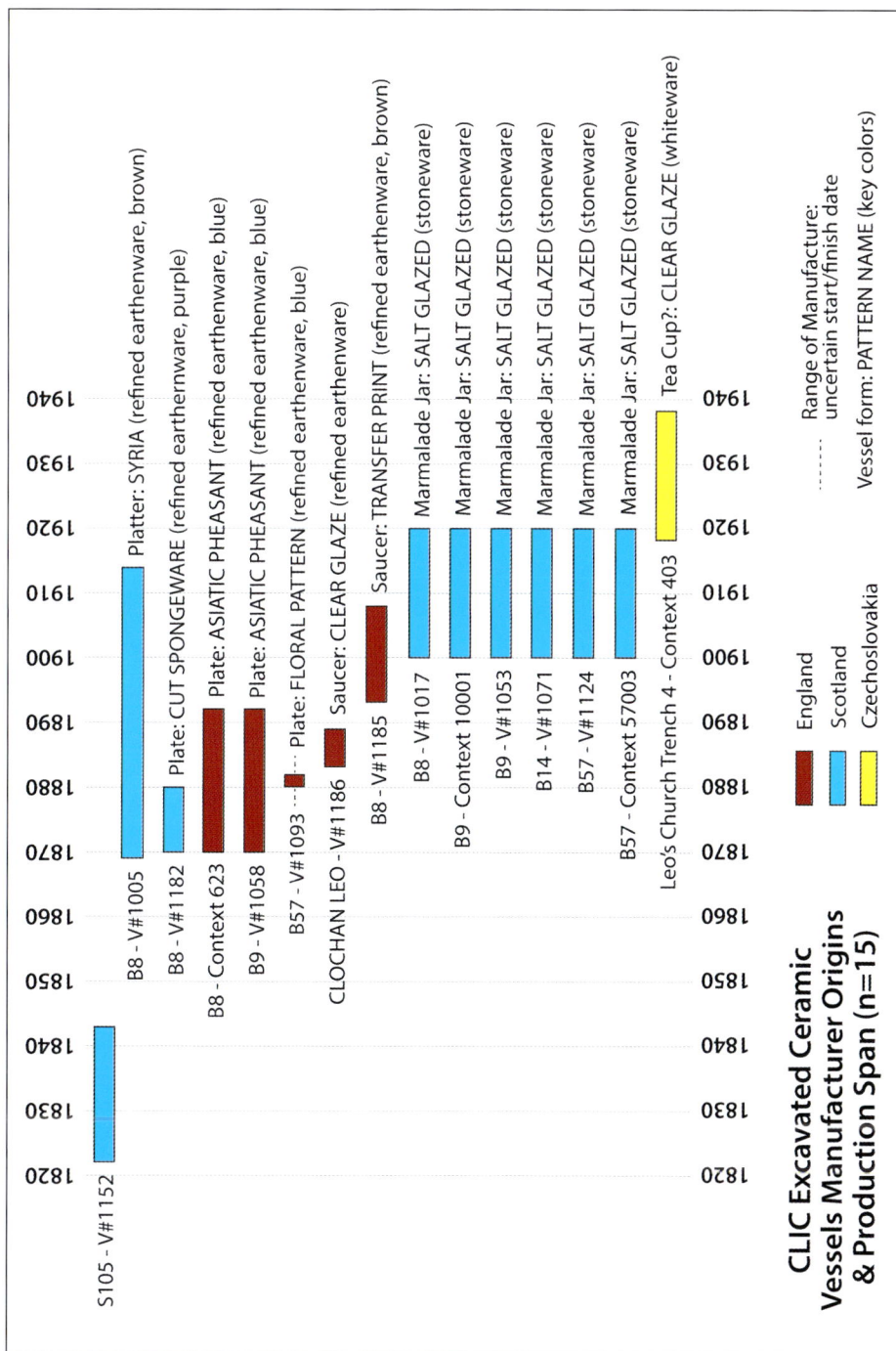

CLIC Excavated Ceramic Vessels Manufacturer Origins & Production Span (n=15)

S105 - V#1152

B8 - V#1005 — Platter: SYRIA (refined earthenware, brown)

B8 - V#1182 — Plate: CUT SPONGEWARE (refined earthenware, purple)

B8 - Context 623 — Plate: ASIATIC PHEASANT (refined earthenware, blue)

B9 - V#1058 — Plate: ASIATIC PHEASANT (refined earthenware, blue)

B57 - V#1093 — Plate: FLORAL PATTERN (refined earthenware, blue)

CLOCHAN LEO - V#1186 — Saucer: CLEAR GLAZE (refined earthenware)

B8 - V#1185 — Saucer: TRANSFER PRINT (refined earthenware, brown)

B8 - V#1017 — Marmalade Jar: SALT GLAZED (stoneware)

B9 - Context 10001 — Marmalade Jar: SALT GLAZED (stoneware)

B9 - V#1053 — Marmalade Jar: SALT GLAZED (stoneware)

B14 - V#1071 — Marmalade Jar: SALT GLAZED (stoneware)

B57 - V#1124 — Marmalade Jar: SALT GLAZED (stoneware)

B57 - Context 57003 — Marmalade Jar: SALT GLAZED (stoneware)

Leo's Church Trench 4 - Context 403 — Tea Cup?: CLEAR GLAZE (whiteware)

England
Scotland
Czechoslovakia

Range of Manufacture:
uncertain start/finish date

Vessel form: PATTERN NAME (key colors)

Fig. 5.15: Dates and manufacturing origins of nineteenth- and early twentieth-century ceramic vessels from excavations on Inishark

and 5.14).[16] With the exception of the few examples of hand-thrown and hand-decorated vessels, the vast majority were decorated with transfer-printed designs invoking nostalgia for bucolic past lifeways or floral designs.

The archaeological record from Inishark presents a fairly similar picture to the ethnographic delph from the earliest phase, although the date range for these ceramics begins and ends earlier. Of the 4,800 sherds we recovered in excavating seven houses, we calculated that it would have required at least 626 vessels to produce those sherds. Within this assemblage, we found only thirteen vessels with identifiable maker's marks, which allowed us to determine the place and date range of a vessel's manufacture (Fig. 5.15). Two other identifiable vessels were excavated in non-residential contexts: a saucer base with an identifiable mark indicating the manufacturer from a medieval shrine site, Clochán Leo, located in the historic village, and the base of a teacup made in Czechoslovakia in the early twentieth century. While the number of identifiable vessels is very small, especially in relation to the entire ceramic assemblage, they nevertheless provide important information about how Inishark villagers engaged in economic networks and furnished their homes.

The earliest maker's mark we found in archaeological contexts (and ethnographic ones as well) was on a small stoneware jar's lower body just above the base, where it was stamped with the words 'PRICE & SONS BRISTOL'. This company produced these jars from 1822 to 1843 in Bristol, UK.[17] The most recent vessels we excavated with maker's marks were a teacup from Czechoslovakia and six stoneware marmalade or jam jars, all of which were made by the same company – Caledonian Pottery – between 1900 and 1920, located in Glasgow and producing vessels for the British W.P. Hartley jam company.[18] Unlike the ethnographic assemblage, Scottish-based potteries dominate the archaeological examples due to the prevalence of durable marmalade jar bases with maker's marks. In considering the vessels found in excavations of Inishark homes (Houses 8, 9, 14 and 57), all of the identifiable maker's marks were manufactured from around 1870–1920, and the manufacturing origins compare well with the ethnographic assemblage (Fig. 5.16).

Manufacturing marks in dressers and delph collections and within archaeological contexts indicate where and roughly when a vessel was manufactured, but they cannot indicate with certainty the manner in which these items arrived in a place – in this case Inishbofin, Inishark, Inishturk, Clifden or Cashel – or how long they were used or when discarded. They offer a starting point in a belonging's life history and serve as material footprints of the pathways it travelled to reach these

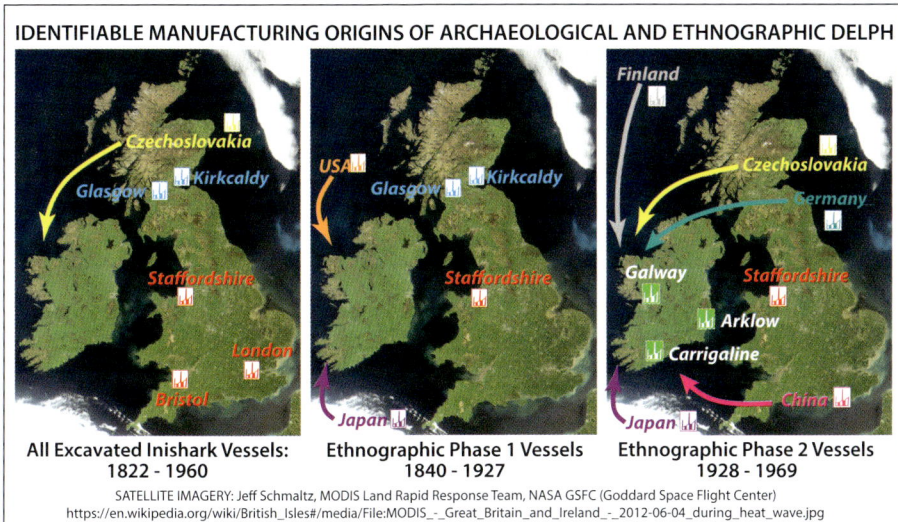

IDENTIFIABLE MANUFACTURING ORIGINS OF ARCHAEOLOGICAL AND ETHNOGRAPHIC DELPH

| All Excavated Inishark Vessels: 1822 - 1960 | Ethnographic Phase 1 Vessels 1840 - 1927 | Ethnographic Phase 2 Vessels 1928 - 1969 |

SATELLITE IMAGERY: Jeff Schmaltz, MODIS Land Rapid Response Team, NASA GSFC (Goddard Space Flight Center)
https://en.wikipedia.org/wiki/British_Isles#/media/File:MODIS_-_Great_Britain_and_Ireland_-_2012-06-04_during_heat_wave.jpg

Fig. 5.16: Comparison of manufacturing origins of ceramic vessels with maker's marks in the ethnographic (1840–1969) and archaeological (1820–1960) assemblages

communities. The next step requires us to evaluate oral, historical, ethnographic and documentary sources to consider how these objects arrived in these homes and by whose hands.

Delph, heritage and homemaking: delph stories bridging past and present

With stickiness and voicefulness, dressers and delph connect the past to the present through stories, especially ones that commemorate important events, experiences, places and people. Beyond the manufacturing origins of items, many times the specifics of their journey to these homes and businesses resonated strongly with the key memories or ideas attached to people's possessions: a gift from a returning kinswoman, a tourist souvenir commemorating a meaningful journey to someplace special, or the hard-earned gift that travelled back to a home in the hands of a revered ancestor who had worked so hard abroad as a seasonal migrant labourer.

Except for two Inishbofin-produced mugs, none of the ceramic and glass vessels I discuss in this book were manufactured in these communities. Each piece or set of pieces took specific journeys to arrive for display or safe storage in people's homes or businesses. As I noted earlier, the vast majority of these objects were made in

Fig. 5.17: (a) One of Patrick's five matching plates made in (b) Helsinki, Finland by the Arabia Pottery factory, 1932 to mid-1940s

England, Scotland and other parts of Ireland. In a few cases, delph manufactured in the United States, Germany, Czechoslovakia, Finland, Greece, China and Japan links these communities to far-distant places (Fig. 5.17). Patrick's set of five blue-banded dinner plates made by the Arabia Pottery factory in Helsinki offers a prime example of expanding mid-century ceramic markets.[19]

Many of these vessels, especially those made of glass, originally contained food products, including jams, mineral water, alcohol and medicines. These food and other consumable products, especially coffee, tea, tobacco and other foodstuffs, testify to islanders' participation in global economic markets. They give material testimony that clearly refutes the idea that people in these rural, western communities lacked access to material goods or the knowledge and discernment to be sophisticated consumers of not only glass and ceramic vessels but other products as well.

While analysing people's belongings through a biographical lens may seem to be a very idiosyncratic and narrow line of inquiry, the stories associated with these possessions offer fascinating microhistories of families, communities and the region. Through this research, I gained two key insights: (1) how inhabitants of these rural, western communities interacted with other parts of Ireland, Britain,

Europe and the rest of the world, and (2) how people's local consumption linked them to broader national and international economic networks and popular trends. Of the scores of stories we recorded about delph origins and associations, five themes of connections to nearby and distant places resonated most frequently: (1) shopping and acquiring goods within the region; (2) migrant labour and foreign employment; (3) heirlooms, emigration and gifts from kin; (4) gifts for key milestones in a person's life; and (5) travel, souvenirs and mementoes of journeys. Ultimately, these sticky and voiceful belongings instilled powerful memories and meanings into homes, contributed to placemaking, and acted as material footprints of a family's and community's histories.

Acquiring goods to furnish homes and nurture families

From a range of documentary and oral historical sources, we know that brick-and-mortar shops in villages and towns, supplemented by weekly open-air markets in larger towns, offered a wide range of goods to people living in rural communities in the late nineteenth and early to mid-twentieth centuries.[20] In particular, weekly markets in Clifden and Roundstone provided a relatively convenient source for people to purchase food and other supplies, and other country shops were scattered throughout the region. As part of this research, we recorded portions or all of several old shop ledgers in Westport, Clifden, Cleggan, Inishturk and Tullycross, as well as a fishing business ledger from Inishbofin. While we have only made preliminary analyses of a few of these ledgers, it is clear that people living in Inishbofin, Inishark, Inishturk, Cashel and Clifden furnished homes with goods acquired from shops or itinerant merchants in a variety of ways: purchased on credit or with cash, bartered with goods or labour, or gifted.

Many general shops, both large and small, provided a wide range of items for sale, including foodstuffs, house furnishings, farming tools and medicines (Fig. 5.18).[21] Other shops offered more specialised inventories, such as meat or clothing (including ready-made items, shoes, cloth and sewing supplies) (Fig. 5.19). All shops kept ledgers to track the date and types of goods sold and the amount paid or owed by each customer. In his painting *The Country Shop*, Jack B. Yeats depicts a shopkeeper with a ledger, surrounded by a wide variety of goods.

These shops also acted as local banking institutions by offering goods on credit to accommodate for the fluctuations in people's access to hard currency based

Fig. 5.18: *The Country Shop* by Jack B. Yeats (1912) depicts a shopkeeper with her day ledger.

on seasonal labour (e.g. fishing, farming or handwork). For example, the 1892 Congested Districts Board account noted that families whose livelihood relied heavily on fishing tended to run through savings around Christmas.[22] Depending on the time of the year and the customer, shopkeepers sold goods for cash, on credit or in exchange for labour or goods. For instance, a Clifden butcher recorded the transaction of a tailor exchanging a man's suit to pay off part of his debt in 1915. Inishbofin oral histories recount that islanders would exchange eggs and fish for tea, sugar, tobacco, and sometimes they would trade fish for flour.[23]

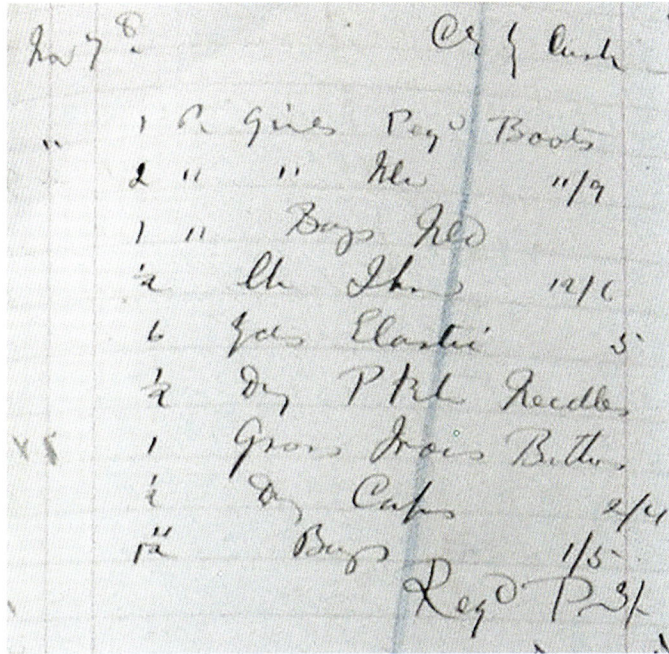

Fig. 5.19: Excerpt from a more specialised shop: purchases of clothing, boots, needles, elastic, buttons and caps from a Clifden clothing and clothing supplies shop on 7 November 1921 with the purchased goods to be sent to an Inishbofin customer by post (delivered to Cleggan and then to Inishbofin by boat)

Oral histories, Browne's early ethnography, the 1892 CDB reports and other archival documents recount that people on Inishark and Inishbofin earned money for shopping, primarily by farming, fishing, sewing, knitting and working as labourers. Islanders sold fish and shellfish destined for local and international markets (Fig. 5.20), livestock (primarily sheep, cattle and pigs), kelp (for fertiliser), eggs, butter, knitted goods and quilts.[24] In one oral historical account, an Inishbofin woman explained that women commonly sold eggs and butter to a Mrs King in Cleggan. King would send old tea chests, tea boxes and large shipping containers for matches to Inishbofin to collect the eggs and butter she would buy to sell in her own shop in Cleggan.[25] Typical for post-medieval excavations in Europe, we recovered only a handful of coins dating from the mid-nineteenth- and early twentieth-century homes we investigated. Inishbofin and Inishark tenants and later homeowners, who largely relied on fishing, farming and craftwork for their livelihoods, would have treasured these coins and made sure to keep them safe.

Oral histories tell us that all five of Inishbofin's villages hosted at least one shop during the late nineteenth and early twentieth centuries.[26] In 1893, Browne reported that '[t]here are three or four small shops [on Inishbofin], but only one has a regular counter, and it is also the only public house on the islands'.[27] That

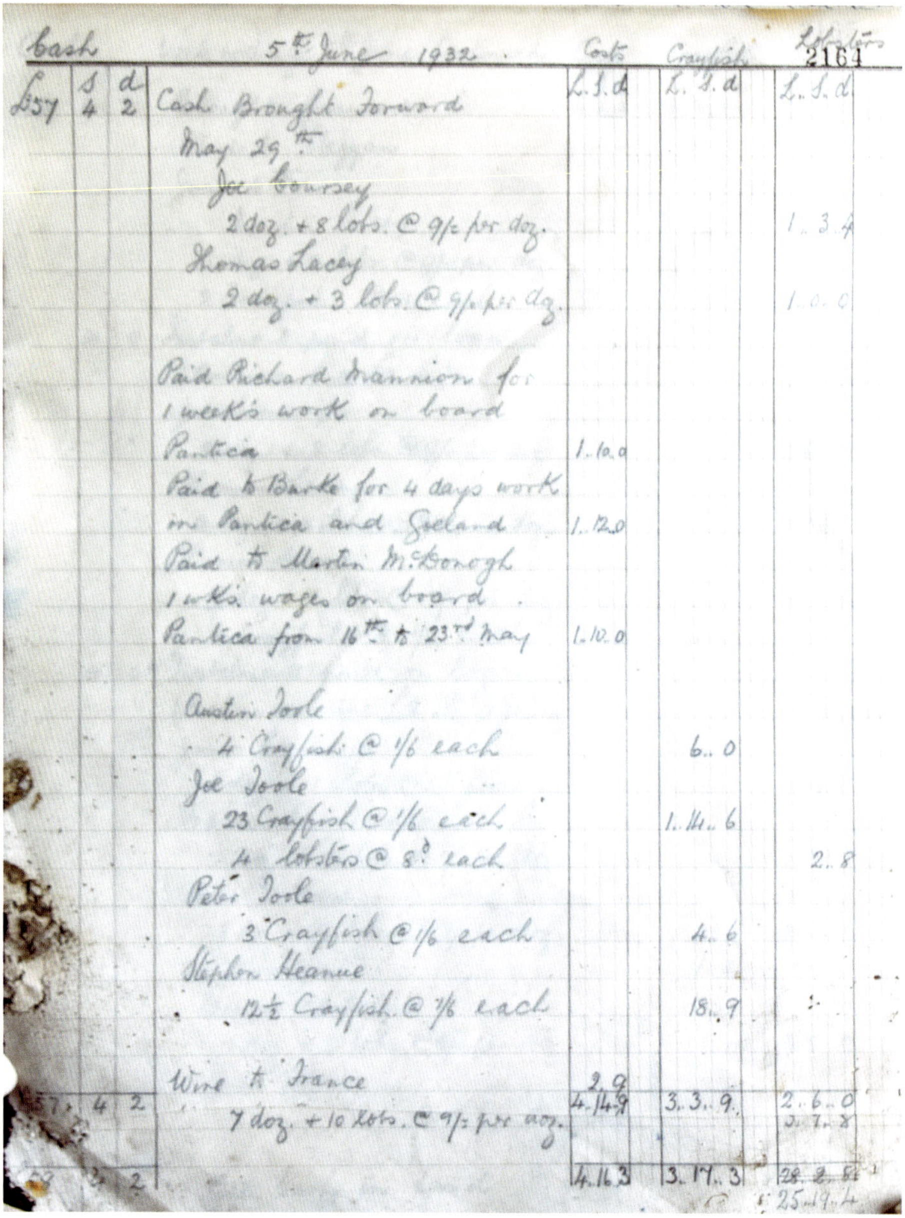

Cash			5th June 1932.	Costs	Crayfish	Lobsters 2161
£	s	d		£. s. d	£. s. d	£. s. d
£57	4	2	Cash Brought Forward			
			May 29th			
			Joe Coursey			
			2 doz. + 8 lobs. @ 9/2 per doz.			1. 3. 4
			Thomas Lacey			
			2 doz. + 3 lobs. @ 9/- per dz.			1. 0. 0
			Paid Richard Mannion for			
			1 week's work on board			
			Pantica	1. 10. 0		
			Paid to Burke for 4 days work			
			in Pantica and Ireland	1. 12. 0		
			Paid to Martin McDonogh			
			1 wk's wages on board			
			Pantica from 16th to 23rd May	1. 10. 0		
			Austin Toole			
			4 Crayfish @ 1/6 each		6.. 0	
			Joe Toole			
			23 Crayfish @ 1/6 each		1.. 14.. 6	
			4 lobsters @ 8d each			2.. 8
			Peter Toole			
			3 Crayfish @ 1/6 each		4.. 6	
			Stephen Heanue			
			12½ Crayfish @ 1/6 each		18.. 9	
			Wire to France	2. 9		
	4	2	7 doz. + 10 lobs. @ 9/- per doz.	4..14..7	3. 3. 9.	2. 6. 0
						3.. 7.. 8
		2		4..16.3	3. 17. 3	28. 2. ..
						£ 25..19..4

Fig. 5.20: Inishbofin fishing ledger from 1932, showing shellfish caught by Inishbofin and Inishark fishermen, who sold their catches to an intermediary based on the mainland who managed the transfer of shellfish to France. Note that the intermediary paid for catches by individual fishermen as well as for any labour provided by crewmen.

business is still in existence: The Beach – Days Bar and B&B, located at the old pier in the harbour. These island shopkeepers acquired goods to sell from mainland mercantile establishments. In recording early twentieth-century ledger entries, we found that at least two shopkeepers, Patrick Murray and Patrick Burke, owned boats and brought their supplies from a Westport general store (Fig. 5.21). Patrick Murray ran his shop in Westquarter, and this 1910 entry documents his purchase of bulk supplies of forty 224-pound bags of flour, five bags of sugar, one keg of baking soda, seven pounds of half-pound teabags, one half-stone of half-pound sugar bags, one half-stone of 3.5-pound sugar bags, one pound of black thread, one pound of white thread, one stone of bread, and twenty shovels. On Thursday, 25 November 1915, Cloonamore shopkeeper Patrick Lavelle travelled with Patrick Burke, who ran a Middlequarter shop, on Burke's boat to this Westport store to purchase supplies. Like Murray, they acquired a wide range of goods to sell locally on Inishbofin, including flour (Enterprise and W.W. brands), tea, sugar, tobacco, baking soda, alcohol, soap (Sunlight brand), matches, candles and other items.

Inhabitants of these communities purchased household goods in local shops as well as at establishments in villages and larger market towns like Clifden, Cleggan and Westport: ledgers from these communities list customers from both mainland and island communities, including Inishturk, Inishark and Inishbofin. One mainland general shop's ledgers from 1925 to 1935 document customers purchasing basic everyday foodstuffs and tobacco, and boxes of writing paper and envelopes, butter, blacking, cigarettes, clothing items, delph, medicine, pipes and thatching yarn. Late nineteenth- to early twentieth-century residents of these communities used all of the items listed in these varied ledgers as crucial tools in maintaining, furnishing and organising homes. Many of the glass jars and stoneware vessels we have documented in people's dressers ethnographically or recovered from Inishark's homes archaeologically originally held foodstuffs, medicines and alcohol acquired from these local and regional shops.

While purchased locally, the origins of these goods spanned the globe, connecting rural, western Irish people to global markets of foodstuffs, ceramic products and glass containers. The tea and coffee they drank, vessels containing these common beverages, tobacco consumed in pipes, and raisins baked into scones and breads: all of these mundane materials connected the west of Ireland to the rest of the world, even if many of her residents never journeyed far from their home communities. This combination of the ordinary and extraordinary with the

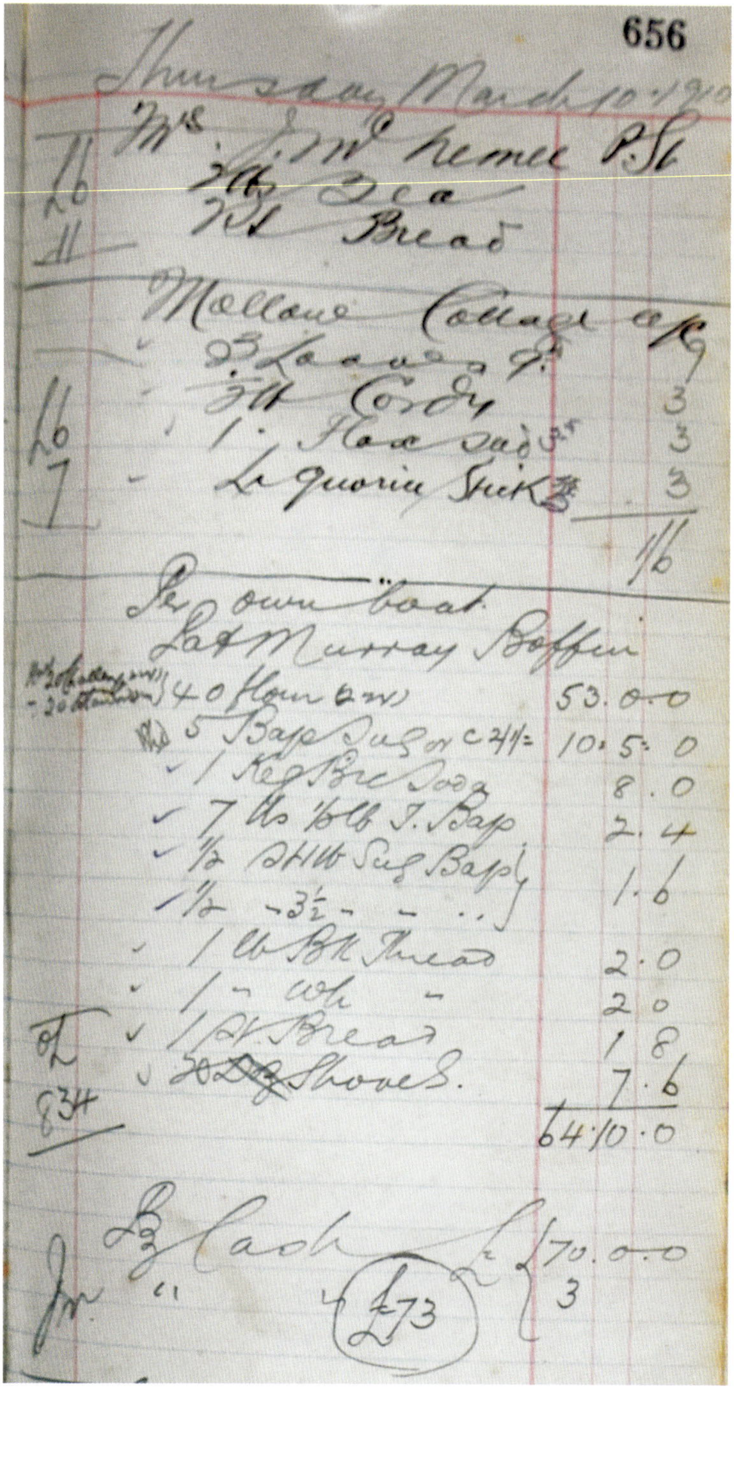

Thursday March 10. 1910

Mrs J. M² hemee P.Sk

16 ... ½b Zea
11 ... ¾l Bread

Mellow Cottage a/c
✓ ... ½ Loaves 9d
16 ... ¾b Cordy 3
7 ... 1. Floa oad 3d 3
... Liquorin Stick 3
                           1/6

Per own boat.
Pd Murray Boffin
40 Flour 6.w) 53.0.0
5 Bags Sugor c 2/1= ... 10.5.0
1 Keg Brc Soda 8.0
7 lbs ½.lb J. Bags 2.4
½ 3.Hb Sug Bags 1.6
½ ... 3½ ... .
1 W Blk Thread 2.0
1 ... wh 2.0
1 Pk Bread 1.8
... Shoves 7.6
                      64.10.0

834

By Cash £ 70.0.0
                    £3

£73

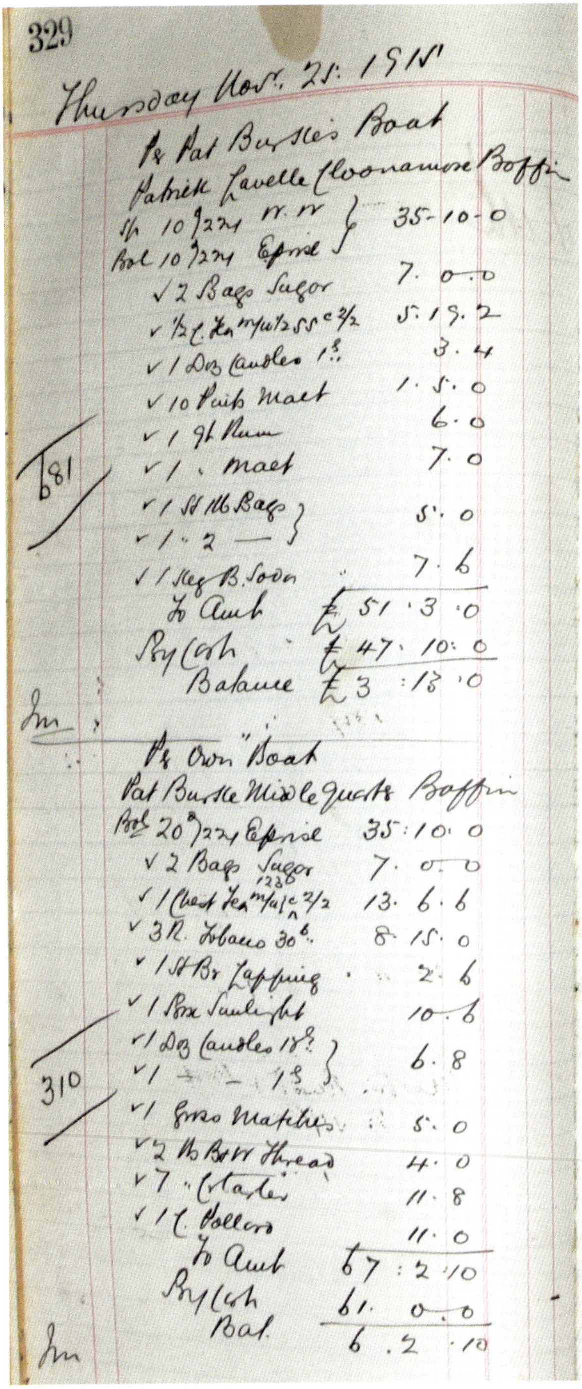

Fig. 5.21: Early twentieth-century ledger entries from a Westport general shop showing purchases by Pat Murray, Pat Burke and Patrick Lavelle, three Inishbofin shopkeepers who acquired stock in Westport: (opposite page) the bottom half of the page shows the 10 March 1910 entry for Pat Murray, who sailed to Westport and purchased goods, to have delivered to his boat at the port; (right) this ledger page from 25 November 1915 shows two orders of goods, one by Pat Burke and the other by Patrick Lavelle, to be delivered to Pat Burke's boat at the port

Fig. 5.22: The right side of George's dresser with the etched glass door open, displaying delph manufactured in England and purchased from shops in the mid-twentieth century

local and the non-local rendered all of these everyday belongings as sticky and particularly powerful – though often unremarked – tools of homemaking in these historic and contemporary homes.

As we all know from homewares shops today, shopping for home furnishings produced in far-flung places still plays a major role in homemaking. Many of the dressers and their contents testify to more recently purchased possessions that also connected these communities to regional, national and global markets and places. For instance, George's dresser was purchased in 1965 from a Clifden store, and its contents were overwhelmingly manufactured after 1950 and made in England (Fig. 5.22).

The oldest and most recent dressers and delph collections we recorded contain both older and more recently manufactured belongings, including Honora's dresser with its late twentieth-century delph[28] and Michael's mid-century delph[29] in his parlour's glass and mirror display cabinet (Figs 5.23 and 5.24). The bottom shelf of Margaret's and James' old dresser displays objects purchased in shops in Ireland

and the US after 1950, including a teapot, glass cooking casseroles, platters, a teapot and a jug (Fig. 5.25). Dresser- and delph-keepers update their collections and displays by purchasing old and new objects in antique shops, online stores and in regional homewares stores. Anne enjoys adding to her delph collection by finding just the right pieces of old delph to display in her home, like her British late nineteenth-century pedestalled bowl (Fig. 5.26).[30] These possessions link these rural communities to other places through global markets and manufacturing.

Fig. 5.23: (a) Honora's modern Willow pattern plate, made by (b) English Ironstone Tableware company, Staffordshire, UK, 1973–94

Fig. 5.24: (a) Michael's matching teacup, saucer and small plate from a larger set, manufactured by (b) Ridgway Potteries in the UK, 1955–64

Fig. 5.25: Bottom shelf of James' and Margaret's dresser with more recently purchased items

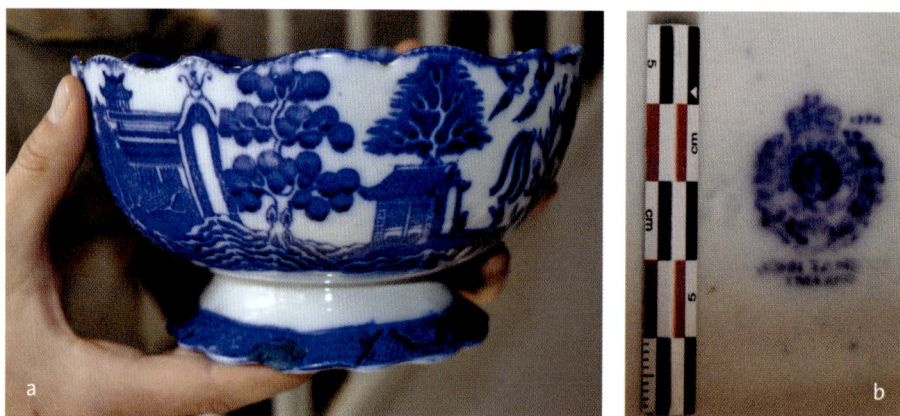

Fig. 5.26: (a) Anne's chinoiserie pedestalled bowl displayed in her home with (b) maker's mark from John Tam's Crown Pottery, 1875–1903, Longton, Staffordshire, UK

Migrant labour and foreign employment

Many of the documented belongings may also have travelled to these communities as gifts or mementoes acquired in Scotland or England by migrant labourers in the late nineteenth and early twentieth centuries, such as three Scottish-manufactured platters[31] from these time periods (Fig. 5.27).[32]

In the 1892 CDB annual report, Ruttledge-Fair noted that '[a]bout seventeen labourers proceed from Inishbofin Electoral Division to Scotland, remaining there about six months. They are said to earn £1 per week during this period'.[33] In speaking of George's three old Scottish platters, Nicholas and George recounted the stories of 'tattie

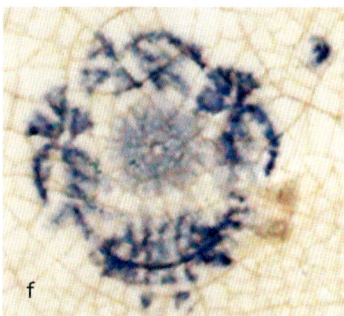

Fig. 5.27: Three Scottish-produced vessels from the Doonmore Hotel delph collection: (a) blue Willow platter made by (b) J. & M.P. Bell Co. Ltd, Glasgow, 1850–70; (c) Damascus platter made by (d) David Methven & Sons, Kirkcaldy, Scotland, 1870–1928; (e) Syria platter in blue with (f) mark from Britannia Pottery, Glasgow, 1855–96

Fig. 5.28: Spongeware vessels: (a) spongeware vessel from the Doonmore Hotel delph collection; (b) spongeware bowl (vessel #1007) excavated from Inishark House 8 in 2012

hoaking' in Scotland by their ancestors. We documented eight Scottish-made platters and one mug in other people's dresser and delph collections. We also excavated three Scottish vessels decorated with Syria and Damascus patterns matching several Scottish platters from people's delph collections, a reconstructable brown transfer-printed mug (Vessel#1183 in Fig. 4.48 matching Delia's 'cow mug' in Fig. 3.35), as well as six marmalade jars produced in Glasgow by Caledonian Pottery in the early twentieth century.

In addition to these Scottish-produced transfer-printed vessels, our excavations in House 8 recovered a plate with a purple geometric spongeware decoration and a maker's mark identifying it as manufactured by David Methven & Sons Pottery, Kirkcaldy, Scotland, *c*. 1870s (Fig. 4.45). Spongeware vessels were produced from about 1835 to 1935 primarily by Scottish, English and Dutch manufacturers for global distribution.[34] Many spongeware manufacturers did not place a maker's mark on these vessels, making it difficult to know the origins with absolute certainty. We believe that this study's ethnographic and archaeological delph lends strong support to Franc Myles' argument that unmarked spongeware vessels excavated on Inishark offer intriguing hints at seasonal labour connections with Scotland.[35] Migrant workers likely purchased a single bowl, teacup, saucer, mug, plate or platter to bring back home to their family after working in Scotland (Fig. 5.28). All seven excavated houses on Inishark and several delph and dresser collections contained spongeware vessels. With only one exception of the almost-matching saucers from House 8 (Fig. 4.59), all of the spongeware decorations were unique. Obtaining matching pieces did not seem to be necessary for gifting or collecting these mementoes of time away from home: the stories invoked would reinforce those connections when loved ones were absent for seasonal labour.

Heirlooms and gifts from kin

Dresser- and delph-keepers identified a vast number of belongings as heirlooms inherited or gifted from kin. These possessions keep those kin ties alive, symbolising connections to family members, living and deceased. Sociologist Helen Holmes names the transfer of belongings as 'passing on' and the symbolic phenomenon as 'material affinities', by which she means that

> … the material and sensory qualities of objects help to shape and construct
> kin ties, through memorializing, imagining, celebrating, 'reckoning' and

displaying kin ties, both biological and social, in and through time …
they are characters of these kin ties – the handed down dungarees, the
special crockery sets – holding a novel and special place in particular
family narratives. They are physically and imaginatively central to their
stories [of kinship].[36]

When family members pass on possessions, by gifting or through inheritance, they
can enhance the potency of kinship links within that family; Holmes argues that
this process is part of 'doing family'. When Delia passed away recently, Bridget
began distributing her large delph collection as heirlooms to family members.
She told me she dedicated much thought to choosing exactly the right vessel to
pass on to brothers, sisters, children, grandchildren, nieces, nephews, grandnieces
and grandnephews. The belongings themselves invite discussion of stories of this
person, that event or some place, highlighting the dynamic linkages between kin.
Archaeologist Siân Jones notes that furnishings like these offer powerful tools in
negotiating social, economic and political relationships, particularly when they
evoke linkages between the past and present.[37]

In a region where so many people departed to establish new lives in the United
States, Britain, Australia and elsewhere, 'doing family' by passing on heirlooms
helped to nurture kinship ties despite separation. Stories of emigration, the Irish
diaspora and the distance between kin featured frequently in conversations with
delph- and dresser-keepers, who identified specific pieces of delph gifted to them or
other family members by emigrant relatives who returned for visits (Fig. 5.29). Two
of Catherine's cups and saucers[38] were given to her by family members returning
from abroad to visit kin. The large number of tales we heard linking emigration
and hardship resonate strongly with memories of people's lives in rural, western
Connemara in the nineteenth and early twentieth centuries. As they struggled to
survive repeated famine years, colonial governance and oppression, revolution,
statehood, economic malaise and two world wars, many people left their homes
to forge new lives in other places.[39] Historian Kevin Kenny[40] notes that the vast
majority of Irish emigrants left home between 1841 and 1900, the period for which
our team has excavated several homes on Inishbofin and Inishark. The material
remains of these ancient houses and their contents testify to the challenges faced by
those islanders who resisted the pull of emigration and confronted the difficulties
in sustaining their lives and communities. Moreover, these excavated buildings, still

Fig. 5.29: Catherine's teacups and saucers, gifts to her from her grandmother who emigrated to the US on visits back home to Ireland: (a and b) made in England by Johnson Brothers, Staffordshire, 1913–1930s; (c and d) transfer-printed and hand-painted Lowestoft Border pattern, made by Booth's, 1906–1920s

containing the remains of ceramic serving vessels, crockery, metal cooking pots, glass bottles and personal items of adornment, speak poignantly to historical efforts to maintain island communities in western Ireland in the face of rural abandonment and emigration. Similarly, contemporary dresser and delph collections bear witness to more recent emigration of the latter half of the twentieth and beginning of the twenty-first centuries.

Historians often focus on the mobile half of the European emigration story by exploring immigrants' arrival, reception and efforts to embrace life in a new country.[41] Yet Eleanor Wilner's poem 'Emigration' about Charlotte Brontë and her friend Mary Taylor encourages us to remember the burdens and challenges faced by the people who remained at home. The poem opens:

> There are always, in each of us,
> these two: the one who stays,
> the one who goes away –
> Charlotte, who stayed in the rectory
> and helped her sisters die in England;
> Mary Taylor who went off to Australia
> and set up shop with a woman friend.
> 'Charlotte,' Mary said to her, 'you are all
> like potatoes growing in the dark.'
> And Charlotte got a plaque in Westminster
> Abbey; Mary we get a glimpse of
> for a moment, waving her kerchief
> on the packet boat, and disappearing.
> No pseudonym for her, and nothing
> left behind, no trace
> but a wide wake closing.[42]

Historically (and currently), the departure of fit, young people and older persons with decades of experience and expertise in working and living in rural Irish communities not only inflicted painful emotional tolls on those remaining but also required those who stayed to reorganise their lives to sustain the economic and social obligations. Delph and dressers tell stories of that wide wake closing painfully and remorselessly and testify to the tangible strategies of those resilient souls who remained despite the often-overwhelming adversities they faced amid the tumult of the nineteenth and twentieth centuries. The biographies of Inishark's and Inishbofin's excavated houses, as well as the jugs, plates, teacups and platters in dressers and delph collections in people's homes today, attest to the resiliency of those who stayed, who restructured daily lives and rebuilt their community and sense of self despite the frequent reminders of loss: the uninhabited house, the vacant chair at the kitchen table, the empty bed, the ill-kept grave, or the *currach* left on the beach. These simple, mundane objects demonstrate how people used everyday material culture in their homes to recraft lives and communities despite the difficulties and the frequent tangible reminders of enduring absences of loved ones.

Marking the passage of time: life milestones and gifts

Many dressers and delph collections contained gifts from important events in people's lives, what anthropologists often call rites of passage, an event or series of related events that transform a person from one status to another. As a category, rites of passage might include a ceremony (like a baptism) or accomplishments (like successfully learning to ride a bike or earning your licence to drive a car) that people experience throughout a lifetime. The first time you broke a bone, drank a beer, married, learned to read, became a parent or threw a birthday party for your one-year-old child all qualify as rites of passage. Delph- and dresser-keepers frequently display or keep objects linked to specific milestones in life, especially wedding gifts

Fig. 5.30: (a) Vessels from a Japanese tea set, made by (b) Moriyama Pottery, founded in 1911 in Morimachi, Japan, for the export market to Europe and the US, given as a wedding gift to Julia's grandparents for their wedding

Fig. 5.31: (a) Portion of the full dinner set given to Delia's mother-in-law as a wedding gift with (b) mark from Colclough & Company, 1908–28

given to parents, grandparents and themselves. Many of these gifts transport the viewer through space and back in time. For instance, Julia's grandparents received a Japanese tea set[43] in celebration of their wedding (Fig. 5.30). This set was crafted for the foreign export market in the 1920s and '30s, but the details of who gave them this set and how they acquired it have sadly been lost to time. For Julia, the key resonances touch upon her grandparents starting a life together with marriage.

Similarly, Bridget's paternal grandmother moved to Inishbofin in the early twentieth century from Lough Rea upon her marriage to a local man. Her wedding set[44] is almost entirely intact, missing only one teacup accidentally broken by a family member just before leaving home to become a nun (Fig. 5.31). In turn, her daughter-in-law, Delia, inherited this wedding set. In 2015, when we recorded this nearly complete set, Delia kept it safely stored in a press in a back hallway, and her daughter Bridget carefully and lovingly brought it out of storage for us to document, telling us stories associated with these objects.

Like many other old dressers, James' and Margaret's Inishturk dresser was crafted as a wedding gift to the young couple in the late nineteenth century. Today, it displays delph wedding gifts given to James and Margaret and to their parents (Fig. 3.3).

Fig. 5.32: Honora's glass and metal chicken vessel proudly displayed on her dresser on Inishturk. It was gifted to her on her twenty-first birthday by the original proprietress of the Doonmore Hotel on Inishbofin.

Fig. 5.33: Religious belongings and mementoes in Sarah's dresser: (a) Mary and Child of Prague statues; (b) plastic bottle of holy water from Lourdes

Fig. 5.34: Everyday belongings associated with dressers and delph collections: (a) a pocket watch, spectacles and an old lighter in Michael's house with a banded mug resting behind them; (b) Bedelia's very large blue medicine bottle, from which she frequently dispensed milk of magnesia to ailing Inishturk residents

Weddings are not the only rituals that find space on dressers and in delph collections. Birthday gifts and cards (Fig. 5.32), christening candles, memorial cards from funerals and devotional statues and bottles of holy water help to ground the home's inhabitants in connections across space and time (Fig. 5.33). Finally, many everyday items testify to quieter daily rituals, such as the first cup of tea or coffee in the morning or reading a newspaper or letters from friends and families (Fig. 5.34).

Travel, souvenirs and mementoes

Finally, dressers and delph collections contain belongings acquired while travelling abroad for a variety of reasons, including holiday trips, journeys to visit family members who live internationally, and religious pilgrimages. Two older dressers contained plastic bottles of holy water from the shrines at Knock and Lourdes. Michael displayed a souvenir glass milk jug from Rangeley Lakes, Maine (US) (Fig. 5.35a), while Julia's parents' dresser held a coffee cup and saucer from Crete, Greece (Fig. 5.35b). Similarly, the top shelf of Honora's dresser featured modern coffee mugs from Denmark and Zagreb, Croatia (Fig. 5.36). These items clearly connect people to different places by commemorating their journeys.

The ethnographic and archaeological delph in past and present homes give testament to the connections – economic, social, kinship, religious and political – linking these rural, western Irish communities to the rest of the

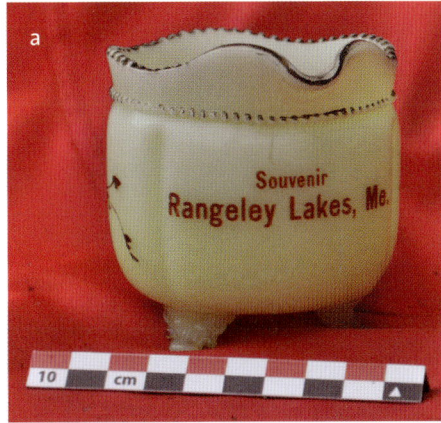

Fig. 5.35: Souvenir delph from (a) Michael's parlour and (b) Julia's parents' dresser

Fig. 5.36: Souvenir mugs from (a) Denmark and (b) Zagreb, Croatia in Honora's dresser

world. While these stories began with manufacturing origins, the stories of who, how, when and why these belongings arrived in specific homes offer fascinating insights into items that bridge between western Irish dresser- and delph-keepers and other places around the world. I learned that acquiring and keeping these possessions enhanced senses of kinship and placemaking in homes and allowed people to travel in their minds as they remembered specific places they had journeyed to, and to reconnect with loved ones who emigrated to other countries they might never physically visit.

Altogether, I recorded scores of belongings in both the archaeological and ethnographic assemblages that signal connections to distant places and times (Fig. 5.37). In this way, dressers and delph act like transportation devices, making and maintaining connections without the viewer ever needing to step outside the front door. More importantly, the ability of these sticky possessions to evoke memories and to bridge across time and space anchors homes, transforming a house into a place rich with meanings and memories.

The thoughtful deployment of these furnishings also holds power. How people select particular belongings, how and why they display or keep them safely hidden in presses, and the stories attached to them speak to the specific ways they seek to

Fig. 5.37: Dressers and delph as vehicles to transport people to different places and times

decorate and personalise their homes. In this next section, I will describe how we can see changing trends in technologies, styles and aesthetic preferences of dresser- and delph-keepers through time.

Discerning consumers and arbiters of taste: changing preferences of delph and dressers

In ornamenting homes with dressers and delph, people's decisions of what to acquire, gift, store and display changed over time. These shifts emerged from several practical factors, including technological developments in manufacturing, the range of products on offer, and variations in people's physical and financial access to these objects through regional and local markets. Beyond the logistical parameters of who had access to which items, the agency of consumers to make choices about which furnishings they owned or gifted involved a complex interplay between changing styles and fashions in decorative arts, personal life histories, and the notion of good (and bad) taste over the years.

Anthropologists rarely satisfy their curiosity by only answering the simple questions 'What did someone do?' and 'What is this thing?' We ultimately want to understand the 'Why?' underlying people's choices and behaviours. For instance, I ask the reader to consider two vessels. The first is a teacup excavated from House 57, catalogued as reconstructable vessel #1100 and decorated with a purple transfer-printed design of a ribbon and shamrocks below the rim on the vessel's interior and exterior surfaces, where someone's lips sipped tea or coffee from this teacup's depths (Fig. 5.38). Its base has been lost to time; thus, we will never know if it featured a maker's mark with which we could have determined its manufacturing origins. Who acquired this teacup, and when and how did it come into their hands and House 57? Did this teacup bring a smile to the owner's face when they used it? Was it passed on as a treasured heirloom or as an inherited everyday item that reminded the owner of a deceased relative, like Mary's breakfast plate? Did the purple colour or the shamrocks possess some special significance, or did the vessel

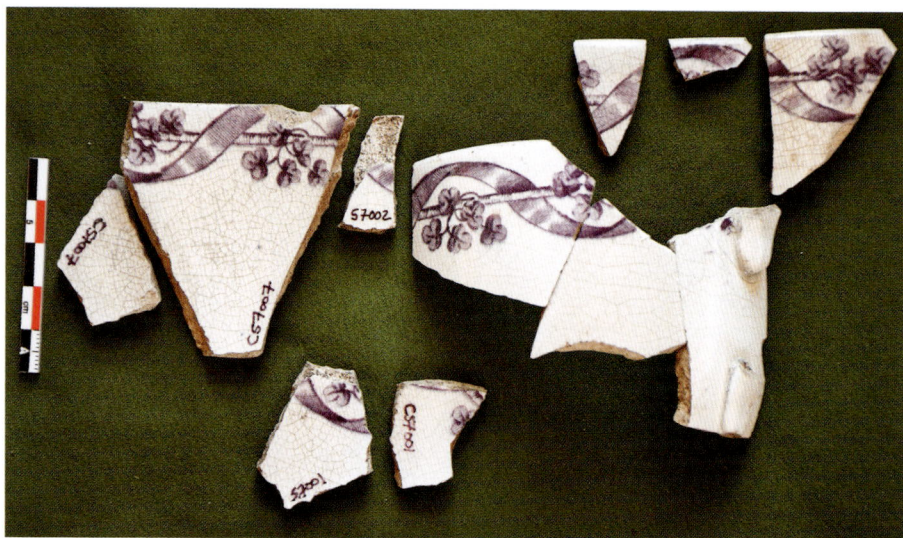

Fig. 5.38: Purple transfer-printed teacup from House 57 (vessel #1100)

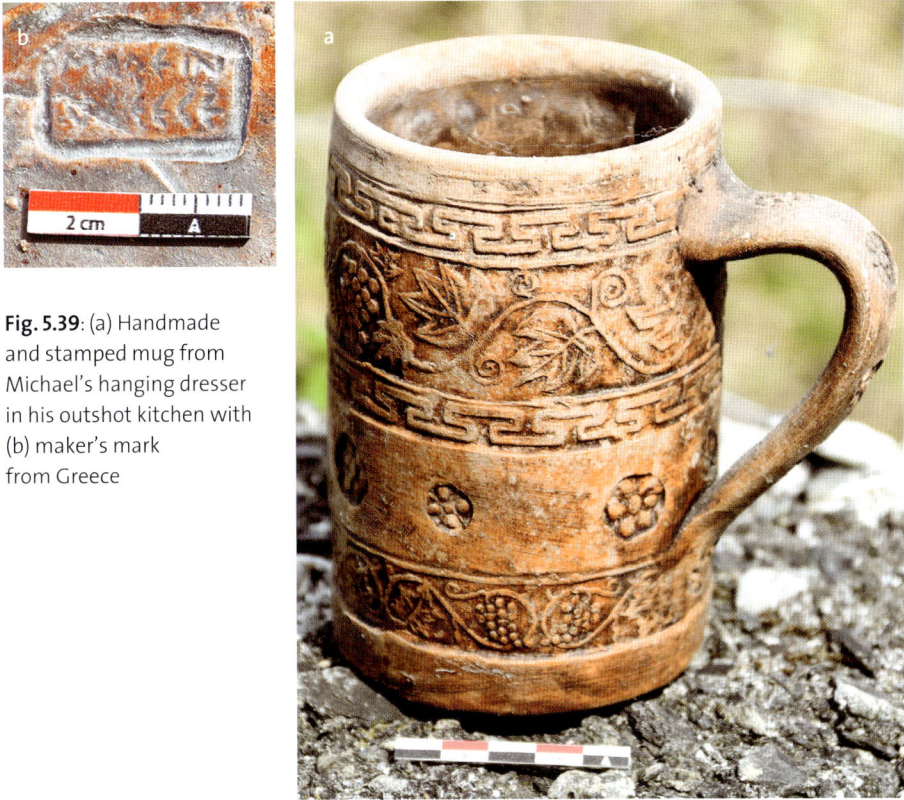

Fig. 5.39: (a) Handmade and stamped mug from Michael's hanging dresser in his outshot kitchen with (b) maker's mark from Greece

simply appeal to the owner's or gifter's sense of style and aesthetics, like Anne's flow blue vessels?

The second vessel is a handmade and hand-decorated earthenware mug, made in Greece in the late twentieth or early twenty-first century. It rested on Michael's hanging dresser in the kitchen (Fig. 5.39). One participant who was raised not far from Michael's house recounted that one of Michael's younger relatives married someone from Greece. They were not surprised by its presence in Michael's home, replete with scores of English-made delph. Michael passed away years before I began this study of dressers and delph; thus, I was never able to ask him about this mug and confirm its journey to Inishbofin through his kinship network. Within easy reach on the hanging dresser, I can imagine him sipping his morning coffee or tea from this vessel and considering his tasks for the day. Still, I must acknowledge that whatever my imagination offers to me, I will never know the specific details about how he acquired this mug or his attachments to it.

Even though we must accept a certain degree of ambiguity in our understanding of why people acquired, used and cherished these vessels, we can begin to explore some of these issues. In ethnographic interviews, I can simply ask what a dresser or vessel means to the owner and how they acquired it: they speak for the belonging, telling me associated stories and demonstrating its stickiness and voicefulness. Many times, however, these types of interviews are not possible, and we must step back and rely on less direct methods. In these cases, anthropologists work from the known to the less well-known by comparing what we learned from speaking with people to cases where we do not enjoy the privilege of working with such detailed information. We juxtapose our findings of the certain and less knowable, looking for similarities and differences. We can then begin to ask and build hypotheses to explain the patterns we find through this comparative process.

As a first step in exploring the 'why' behind these patterns, anthropologists often interrogate the ideas that people take for granted in life: the naturalised beliefs and behaviours that we generally never interrogate. Naturalisation occurs when people do not question why something is the way it is or why we think of some aspect of our lives in a particular way. People often say, 'It's natural to do X or Y.' Anthropologists challenge this taken-for-grantedness in everyday life. For instance, when people assume that women are more nurturing or emotionally engaged than men, they draw on naturalised and culturally constructed ideas about gender. Anthropologist Pierre Bourdieu devised a toolkit for analysing naturalised behaviours, especially those that surround notions of how people understand, discern and act on ideas about good and bad taste.[45] According to Bourdieu, taste expresses the valued or devalued ways people go about their lives. It emerges from people's decisions to follow or challenge unwritten rules or ideals that all cultural groups construct. As decision-makers, people can assess and decide whether to defy conventional notions of taste, rules and restrictions or conform on a case-by-case basis. In other words, as people make choices daily, they ultimately perform a mental calculus that resonates with a fundamental question: should I follow and live up to the naturalised ideals of behaviour in my society, or shall I push those boundaries and set new standards for good or bad taste?

To consider how people answer that question about their behaviour, such as in purchasing a particular piece of delph to give to a relative or in keeping or discarding a family heirloom, Bourdieu argued that good and bad taste carry elements of accountability with them. Taste always involves some element of judgement, such as weighing available options with known values. Taste is also always relational and contextual: people evaluate their and others' behaviours for how well or poorly they behaved in specific places and times. In certain contexts, acting in bad taste may be judged as ill-mannered or morally inept; displaying good taste may garner material or intangible rewards. This process necessarily engages a person's relationships with the wider world and other people.

With this combination of relationality and accountability, Bourdieu noted that people face consequences for acting in good or poor taste. There is always the risk of one's behaviour being assessed in a negative light. He suggested the notion of social capital to explain what can be lost or enhanced in this judgement process. Social capital often resonates simultaneously across three realms (cultural, economic and symbolic) that undergird how we value someone's good or bad taste and performance and reference the relationships people maintain in social networks. Cultural capital demonstrates possessing the knowledge to behave in a valued way: to be 'in-the-know', to make 'appropriate' choices, to be esteemed within a community, and to be associated with people with these qualities. For example, Inishbofin's parish records from the 1870s to 1890s list the heads-of-households for homes that hosted a station mass at Easter or Christmas during certain years. The honour of being chosen to host a station mass may have accrued cultural and symbolic capital, raising one's status within a village as a respectable family and home (Fig. 5.40).

Economic capital signals financial and physical access to objects, places or economic networks: to have the money or ability to be in certain places or possess certain things. In speaking with participants about ledgers and shopkeepers, people noted that shopkeepers maintained a higher level of economic capital in the community: they enjoyed access to many mundane and special goods and made decisions about offering or denying credit to customers and which goods to stock in their shops. Lastly, one gains symbolic capital, esteem and greater status when acting in good taste. For instance, Michael's household was renowned for its hospitality, especially in serving tea and coffee with all the accoutrements, formalities and graces. He possessed many different coffee and tea sets, demonstrating his ability to purchase multiple matching sets of ceramic vessels. The reverse correlate to good taste means that one risks the loss of economic, cultural and symbolic capital when one acts in poor taste.

Our homes and belongings offer tangible evidence of this complex calculus of assessing how we choose to conform to broader notions of good taste or when

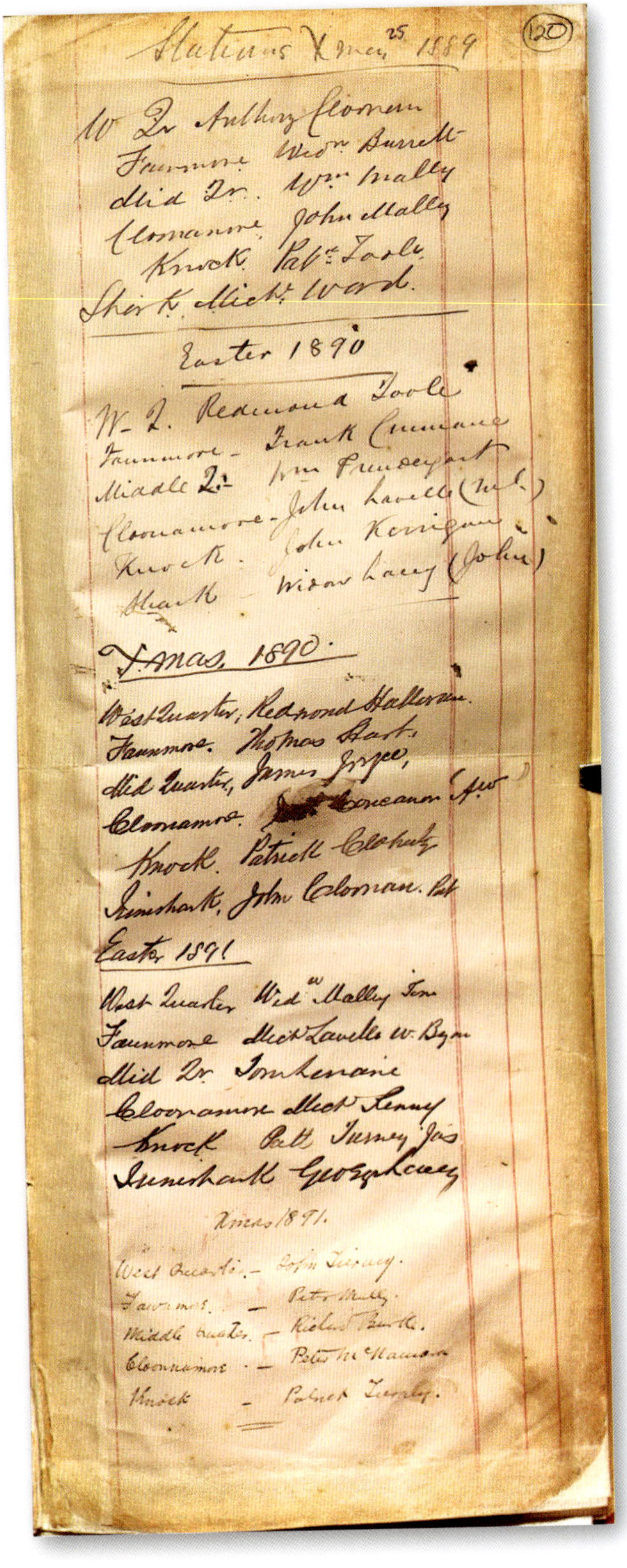

Fig. 5.40: Inishbofin parish records of Easter and Christmas station masses 1890–1 with transcription (opposite page)

Stations Xmas, 1889
WQr [Westquarter] Anthony Cloonan
Fawnmore William Barrett
Mid Qr [Middlequarter] William Mally
Cloonamore John Mally
Knock Pat^k [Patrick] Toole
Inishark Mich^l [Michael] Ward

Easter 1890
W.Q. [Westquarter] Redmond Toole
Fawnmore Frank Cunnane
Middle Qr. William Prendergast
Cloonamore John Lavelle (M^l [Michael])
Knock John Kerrigan
Inishark Widow Lacey (John)

Xmas 1890
Westquarter Redmond Halloran
Fawnmore Thomas Hart
Mid Quarter James Joyce
Cloonamore J[ohn?] Concannon (A^w [Andrew])
Knock Patrick Cloherty
Innishark John Cloonan Pat

Easter 1891
West Quarter Wid^w [Widow] Malley Tom
Fawnmore Mich^l [Michael] Lavelle w Bryan
Mid Qr [Middlequarter] Tom Lenane
Cloonamore Mich^l [Michael] Kenny
Knock Patt Tierney Jas [James]
Innishark George Lacey

Xmas 1891
West Quarter John Tierney
Fawnmore Peter Mally
Middle Quarter Richard Burke
Cloonamore Peter McNamara
Knock Patrick Tierney
[No listing for Inishark]

we decide to push the boundaries of those cultural frameworks. In the case of archaeological vessels and ethnographic dressers and delph, we can see how people negotiated the geographical and financial logistics of access to goods as they assessed current-to-them ideas about style and aesthetics. For instance, when we examine the types of decorative techniques present in the archaeological assemblage from Inishark's excavated houses, we can see that transfer-printed, spongeware and hand-painted vessels were the most popular types of decorated vessels in homes on the island (Fig. 5.41). People in all houses had access to these vessels and acquired them in shops, by barter or as gifts in order to brighten homes and display their good taste.

Interestingly, Houses 28 and 9 stand out with low variation in decorative techniques, and it is worthwhile to consider the 'Why?' behind this pattern. As usual,

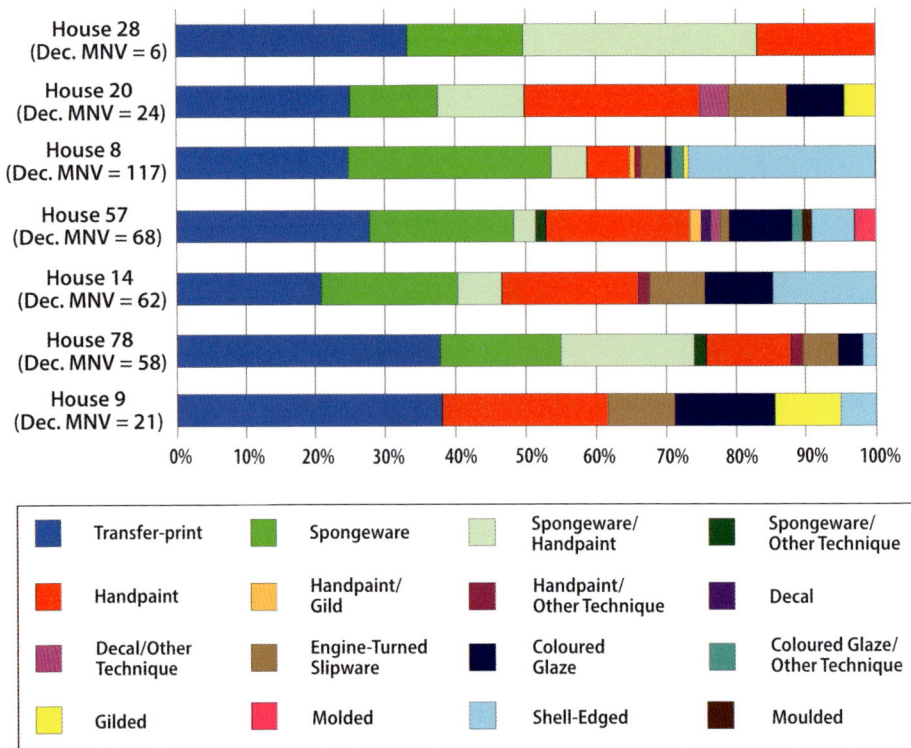

Fig. 5.41: Percentages of decoration techniques on the minimum number of decorated serving vessels from Inishark's excavated post-medieval houses (n=356 vessels; stoneware and crockery vessels not included)

the answer to most archaeological questions involves a good deal of uncertainty and complications. That said, House 28 presents a fairly clear situation: it was one of the earliest houses built (sometime before 1816), the earliest abandoned (sometime before 1838), and the least well-preserved. Perched near the edge of a cliff along the southern coastline of Inishark, this house has suffered the most from nearly two centuries of wind, rain and waves. The team recovered only fifty-five sherds: just over 1 per cent of the 4,800 sherds recovered in excavating the seven houses. Only six distinct vessels could be verified with the MNV calculation of that small number of sherds. With such a small sample size, it makes sense that only four decorative techniques are represented in House 28.

On the other side of the chronological equation, House 9 was the most recently constructed, and five important factors might help to explain why it contained fewer types of decorated vessels, especially spongeware, which was very common to other houses. First, House 9's life history offers some clues. It was built in the early twentieth century as part of the Congested Districts Board loans to islanders to purchase land and build homes. Spongeware vessels were produced from roughly 1835 to 1935, and House 9 was constructed at the tail end of this production span. We also must consider the site formation processes: how this house and its remains arrived at the point in 2016 when we began excavating it. The inhabitants might have taken most of the delph from the home when they departed the island in 1960 – thus leaving little for our archaeological team to find.

Third, the near-absence of spongeware in this count definitely emerges from how I calculated the house's minimum number of decorated vessels (MNDV). If I were to include body sherds in this count, spongeware as a distinct category would be present: the interior surface of seven body sherds of unknown forms were decorated with spongeware. In this case, the 'spongeware and other' category contains one vessel: a spongeware and hand-painted rim of a saucer.[46] Fourth, financial or geographical considerations might have prevented the inhabitants from acquiring these vessels. Finally, the residents may have preferred certain decorative motifs and techniques – especially transfer-print and hand-painted decorations. My hunch is that all of these possible explanations may have influenced the patterning we see but that the low overall MNV[47] for the house (MNV = 27) suggests that House 9's inhabitants took most of their delph with them to use in new homes after leaving Inishark in 1960.

The ethnographic research into dressers and delph provides the opportunity to ask living people why they or their relatives acquired, kept, displayed or discarded delph and dressers. As part of these conversations, people often remarked on preferences for certain kinds of dressers, delph and styles. As discussed earlier, styles in dresser decoration and forms changed over time, and dresser-makers kept current with the types of dressers they produced. Before the 1950s or 1960s, older dressers in this region were typically built with wide, vertical backing boards, sledge feet, plate rails, and cornices with crown moulding and were painted and decorated with carved pilasters, fascia boards and frames. Dressers made more recently often feature glass-fronted doors, feet that do not protrude out from the front of the press, and narrow, vertical backing boards. The differences do not arise from basic functional traits: these dressers all fulfil the need to store and display the same types of belongings. In fact, three old dressers on Inishbofin had been retrofitted with doors, stripped, and stained to give them a more modern feel and look – they still accomplish the same physical and symbolic work.

Michael's old dresser, built in the late nineteenth or early twentieth century, never had doors to enclose the upper shelves, but it sported sledge feet, plate rails, crown moulding and painted decoration (see Fig. 3.23). Honora's dresser, fashioned in 1999 by Mark, conforms to the more recent style of dressers, with narrow backing boards, originally a varnished (and now painted) surface, and non-protruding feet (see Fig. 3.17). However, he did not install doors on the upper shelves, and two features speak to the older style: the cornice is a traditional crown moulding, and he has carved a bead on the pilasters and the fascia board. Honora commissioned this dresser for her bed and breakfast, and to me it seems appropriate and apt to combine the older and newer styles in this context – it feels right for this space. In talking with dresser-owners, especially about older dressers, some recounted how they preferred the traditional, painted style; others felt that the dresser needed to maintain its paint scheme to make it feel 'right' and 'proper' to them. The entire notion of something being proper speaks powerfully about people's individualised senses of taste and of naturalised ideas about how a dresser should look.

I identified two key patterns by examining the possessions displayed on older and more recent dressers or in delph collections. First, the types of delph people acquired shifted through time, highlighting the developments in manufacturing technologies, distribution networks and major historical developments (like the establishment of the Republic of Ireland or the world wars). Second, people personalised collections and displays as part of homemaking, displaying individual aesthetic sensibilities and tastes. To provide a foundation for personalisation, I begin with the historical trends in delph collections and displays.

Historical trends in delph preferences in form, decoration and manufacturing origins

By comparing the vessels with maker's marks to unmarked ones, I found broad trends in the types of vessels and their decorations through time in the archaeological and ethnographic assemblages. In other words, I traced the changing preferences for delph decorations, forms and producers in these communities (Table 5.2; see also Figs 5.7 through 5.14). During the first period (1840–1927), the vast majority of English and Scottish vessels were decorated with transfer-printed and spongeware techniques. Mary's brown transfer-printed platter offers a fine example of the

Time Period	Origins of Most Frequent Producers	Most Frequent Decorative Motifs or Patterns	Most Frequent Vessel Forms Collected	Most Frequent Decorative Technique
Period 1: 1840–1927	England, Scotland	Blue Willow, Asiatic Pheasant, Syria, Damascus, various floral motifs, spongeware geometric and floral designs	Platters, dinner plates, small plates	Transfer-printed and spongeware
Period 2: 1928–69	Ireland, England	Roses and other floral motifs, blue willow	Jugs, small plates, teapots, saucers	Transfer-printed, hand-painted, gilded, decal
Period 3: 1970–2000s	England	Vintage British countryside scenes, floral motifs, blue willow	Plates, teapots, teacups, saucers, milk jugs	Transfer-printed

Table. 5.2: Summary of manufacturer origin by country, popular vessel forms, and most frequent decorative motifs and techniques through time

Fig. 5.42: Vessels from the early period in delph assemblages: (a) Mary's Asiatic Pheasant platter with (b) mark from Thomas Cone Ltd, UK, 1912–35; (c) Patrick's green Argyle pattern tureen, which was accompanied by five matching plates and a second tureen, (d) made by Ford & Sons in Burslem, Staffordshire, UK, 1893–1907

Fig. 5.43: Delph styles from period 2 (1928–69): (a) Michael's English-made plate with floral and gild decoration, made by (b) Alfred Meakin after 1945; (c) Catherine's Irish-made Willow pattern teacup with gilded rim and handle, made by (d) Arklow, 1949–1950s; (e) Patrick's Irish-made jug with the woman in the yellow dress (yellow crinoline girl), made by (f) Arklow, 1949–1960s

Asiatic Pheasant design,[48] which was very popular during this time (Fig. 5.42, top), along with Willow, Syria, Damascus, and other floral patterns predominantly in blue and brown. Other patterns and colours were also used in these early vessels, and Patrick's dresser contained two matching tureens (Fig. 5.42, bottom) and five plates of the Argyle pattern transfer-printed in green.[49]

The second period begins shortly after the Irish revolutionary period and alongside the establishment of the Irish Free State, represented in the delph assemblages by the early production of Irish-made pottery at Carrigaline and Arklow potteries. Of the fifty-eight vessels with identifiable maker's marks from this period, the majority were English- and Irish-made jugs, small plates, teapots, teacups and saucers. The most popular decorative techniques included transfer-prints, hand-painting, gild and decal, and gild often accompanying other decorations. Floral motifs, such as Michael's set of British plates which also featured gild, were increasingly popular. Blue Willow continued to appeal to consumers, like Catherine's Arklow teacup and saucer. Popular patterns on jugs included the yellow crinoline girl, India Tree, and floral motifs (Fig. 5.43).

The third period (1970 – current) witnessed a renewed popularity for English-made vessels, particularly those with transfer-printed motifs that displayed idealised visions of a bucolic British past (Fig. 5.44). With pattern names like The Hunter, The Post House, Memory Lane, The Constable and The Brook, these vessels featured nostalgic scenes of rural lifeways. Plates, teacups and saucers dominated the delph forms from this period. Many of the vessels with marks also note technological changes in production associated with the widespread use of dishwashers and microwaves.

These trends offer us a chronological framework for considering what types of vessels were produced and acquired by people in these rural communities over the years, as well as popular stylistic trends. However, I cannot use this chronology to predict which vessels are displayed in dressers of different ages: old dressers still in use today and newer dressers may contain very old and very recent vessels. Moreover, understanding the age of delph cannot answer the thornier questions about which types of vessels appear in dressers and delph assemblages today, why people collect or keep certain types of vessels, and how the aesthetic sensibilities and tastes of dresser- and delph-keepers influence how they use these items to create that feeling of home. Similarly, historical delph trends also cannot capture the powerful stories and personal attachments that make these items so important to their owners and

b

d

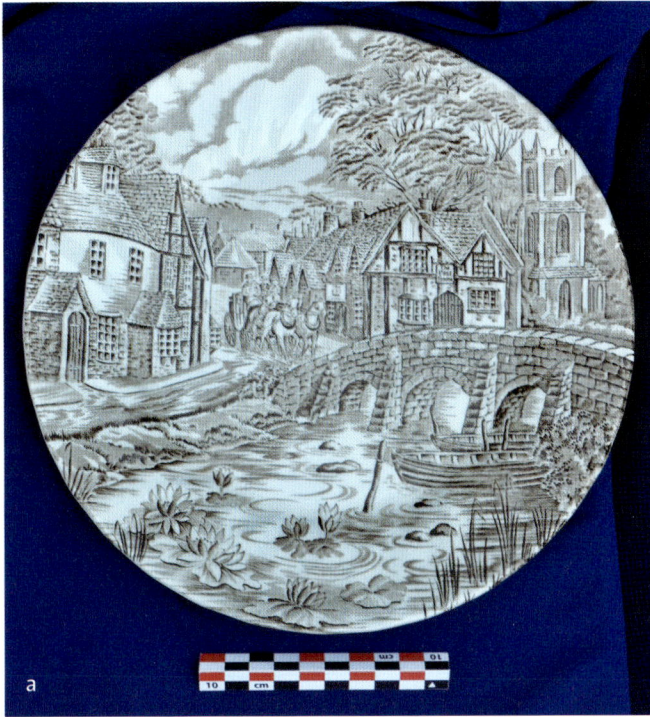

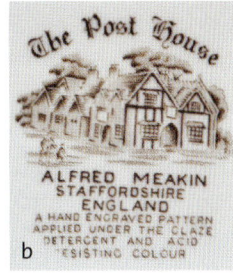

Fig. 5.44: Two English-made transfer-printed plates made after 1970: (a) Ellen's plate with The Post House design, made by (b) Alfred Meakin; (c) a plate from Julia's family with the Olde England design, made by (d) Royal Tudor Ware

caretakers. The different ways that dresser- and delph-keepers collect and display specific objects to craft a welcoming and anchoring presence in homes highlights the importance of personal histories and tastes in homemaking.

Personalisation and taste: producing a sense of home

The different ways people combine ceramic and glass vessels of varying ages, decorations, colours and forms in dressers and delph collections demonstrate the creativity and aesthetic sensibilities of delph- and dresser-keepers. Examining what people collect and display offers a good start for thinking about delph preferences and tastes. I found that dressers contain many more recent vessels than delph collections, both stored away or displayed in people's homes. This difference may arise from the fact that delph caretakers sometimes possess more delph than they can practically display in their home or business. Alternatively, they store the older delph, often heirlooms that they inherited or were gifted, safely tucked away for fear of breakage.

Second, delph in dressers destined for daily use often includes newer vessels, perhaps because of breakage events, but also may relate to the number of family members who use these vessels on a daily basis. For example, more recently assembled dressers holding belongings intended for daily use contain more mugs and small bowls but fewer teacups and saucers than those dressers assembled before 1970. Preferences for vessel forms shift according to fashion in ceramics and in combination with changing technologies to produce our foods (for instance, needing microwave-safe bowls and plates) and the types of foods we eat daily. Microwave- and dishwasher-safe bowls and mugs serve a family with more practicality than elegance on a daily basis, and many people today consume more hot and cold breakfast cereals, yoghurts and fresh fruit in small bowls than was fashionable and common in the past. Regardless of the age of delph or dressers, these possessions contribute towards homemaking processes, including placemaking and storytelling in both quiet and more obvious ways. In Michael's kitchen delph I found a plate decorated with the 'Homemaker' pattern, designed by Enid Seeley and made by Ridgway Potteries in the 1950s and '60s for sale in Woolworth stores (Fig. 5.45).[50] The mid-century design depicts key material components to furnishing a home: tables, cutlery, houseplants, food and kitchen implements. Each of the depicted furnishings acts as a symbol, index and icon: symbolising the necessary belongings

Fig. 5.45: (a) Michael's Homemaker plate; (b) the backstamp codes indicate its production in the second half ('2') of 1962 ('62')

to create a home, indexing ideals of homemaking and hospitality, and representing archetypal possessions immediately understandable to everyone. In this way, the Homemaker plate explicitly links the mundane, humble belongings, such as a plate, with popular ideals and values about what twentieth-century modern homes should embody.

Dresser and delph assemblages also differ in the presence of matching sets of vessels. Delph collections, especially those stored away safely, often contain more matching place settings, teacups, saucers, small plates and small bowls. Platters

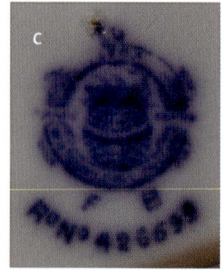

Fig. 5.46: Anne's flow blue tureen: (a) view from the side; (b) base interior and (c) maker's mark: W.H. Grindley & Company Ltd 1880–1914, Staffordshire UK; (d) lid exterior and (e) maker's mark on interior: Co-Operative Wholesale Society Ltd Staffordshire UK, 1911–20

Fig. 5.47: The contents of Michael's dresser in the main room of his uninhabited home

appear to be a preferred item for many delph-owners, although Delia's and the Doonmore Hotel delph assemblages contain the majority of these platters. Dressers contain many more jugs, and Mary and the Doonmore Hotel's dresser-keepers preferred to display these vessels prominently. Similarly, dinner and small plates, teapots, teacups and milk jugs were more often displayed in dressers than found in dresser collections.

People add or change vessels in dressers and delph collections over time. Decorative Arts scholar Moira Vincentelli argues that people who collect antiques, like delph, experience pleasure in learning about different forms and decorations and enjoy applying that body of knowledge when evaluating and purchasing items that fit their personal interests, style and taste.[51] For instance, Anne enjoys shopping for just the right vessel to display in her home and she prefers to purchase nineteenth-century or early twentieth-century vessels. She relishes the process of adding to her small collection of delph, which in 2015 contained several bowls, plates and three tureens. Anne's collection displays her discerning style and aesthetic preferences: it was clear that she prefers the colour blue on her vessels, especially flow blue (Fig. 5.46). Her blue tureen with gilded accents exemplifies her sense of aesthetics. Interestingly, this vessel presents a puzzle: the maker's marks on the lid and base do not match exactly, but the slight differences are only apparent with close inspection.[52]

While Anne prefers nineteenth-century vessels with blue decorations, other dresser- and delph-keepers gravitated towards an entirely different aesthetic. Michael's large delph collection and the dresser in the main room of his home contained mostly British-made vessels manufactured from the 1950s through the 1970s. Though the house had been uninhabited for years when I recorded his dressers and delph, the vessels stored in the glass-fronted dresser and cabinet were in pristine condition and displayed with an eye towards symmetry and neatness (Fig. 5.47). His matching German coffee set, manufactured in the 1950s or 1960s, stands out in his large collection for its resplendent colour (Fig. 5.48). Though Michael did possess a few older pieces of delph, his collection suggests that he enjoyed purchasing current-to-him pieces and sets of matching vessels.

In comparing Anne's and Michael's delph, it is clear that both were educated and sophisticated delph collectors in their own ways. Moreover, each display

Fig. 5.48: Teacup, saucer and coffeepot from Michael's German coffee set displayed in his parlour

demonstrated two different approaches to style and taste. Anne prefers old vessels and displays them singly and distributed throughout her living room, situated on walls, bookshelves or tables. Michael's house was bursting with delph, situated in three separate rooms within two dressers, on mantelpieces, hung on walls, and in display cases – almost always in groups. His vessels mainly dated to the middle of the twentieth century and gave me the sense of someone who appreciated new styles and decorative motifs. For instance, his four coffeepots differ from each other in decoration and shape (see Fig. 3.34 for his three other coffeepots). Purchasing and displaying exactly the right-for-you possession, such as a coffeepot or tureen, involves the purchaser discerning the details of the object's economic, cultural and symbolic capital. People enjoy adding belongings to their collections that signal a discerning sense of taste, an appreciation for family and heritage, and beautiful pieces that bring pleasure to the viewer.

Sociologist Ian Woodward suggests that certain possessions can embody a 'taste epiphany' when the combined economic, cultural and symbolic capital are further enhanced by the specific object biography and its associated stories.[53] Taste epiphanies are associated with pleasure in objects and the feeling of well-being associated with owning and engaging with those belongings. I believe that dresser and delph displays also offer opportunities for taste epiphanies. People gain pleasure from acquiring specific items, but taste epiphanies can also occur with handling, washing, using and arranging objects to assemble a display. In her study of Welsh dressers, Vincentelli notes that 'pleasure is an important factor, whether in the visual appeal of a display or, in this case, in the actual handling of china and the pleasure of arranging and rearranging'.[54]

With such a personal touch, it is not surprising that dresser and delph displays exhibit a great deal of variation in every aspect. For instance, in comparing vessel forms in Sarah's, Peggy's and William's, Betty's, and Catherine's rental cottage dressers, whose contents are destined for frequent use, only small bowls and mugs appear in each case (Fig. 5.49). Mugs tend to be the most consistent in frequency, but all vessel forms vary to lesser or greater degrees. Even greater variation of vessel forms exists for the eight dressers whose contents were rarely, if ever, used. These display-oriented dressers all contain platters, dinner plates and teacups, but the frequency of these forms differs in each dresser. In dressers with jugs and saucers, their presence also ranges from very high to very low. In particular, old jugs are either a preferred vessel form displayed often and prominently or are absent entirely.

Variation in Vessel Forms on Dressers for Display and Daily Use

VESSELS PRIMARILY FOR DISPLAY OR ENTERTAINING GUESTS

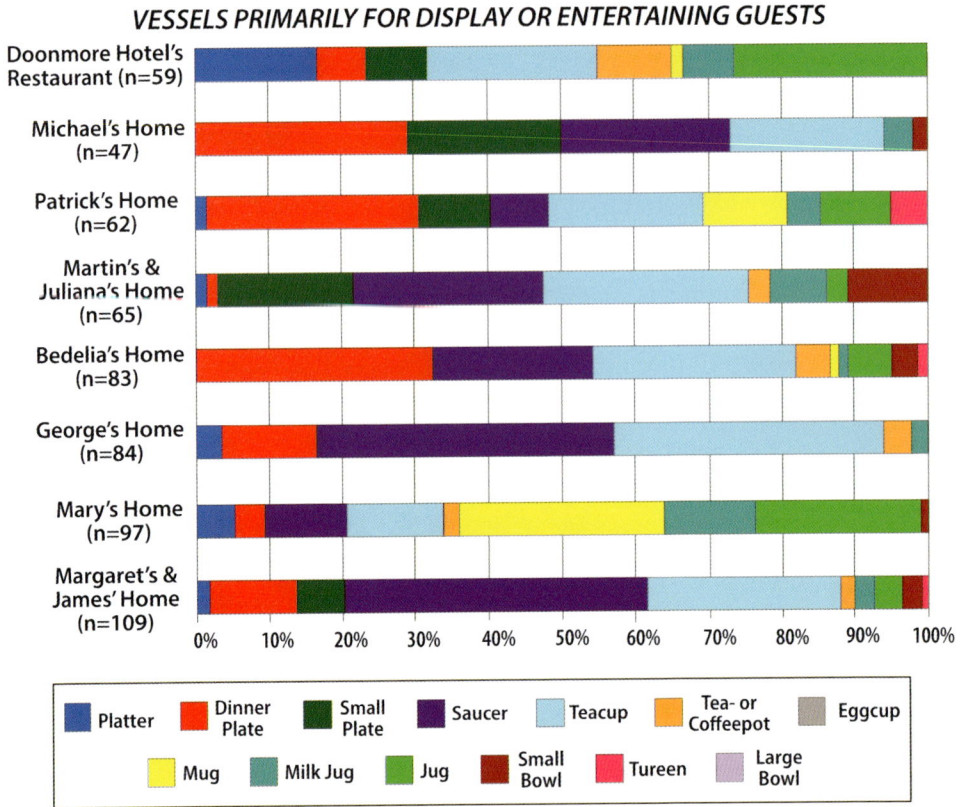

Legend:
- Platter
- Dinner Plate
- Small Plate
- Saucer
- Teacup
- Tea- or Coffeepot
- Eggcup
- Mug
- Milk Jug
- Jug
- Small Bowl
- Tureen
- Large Bowl

VESSELS PRIMARILY FOR DAILY USE

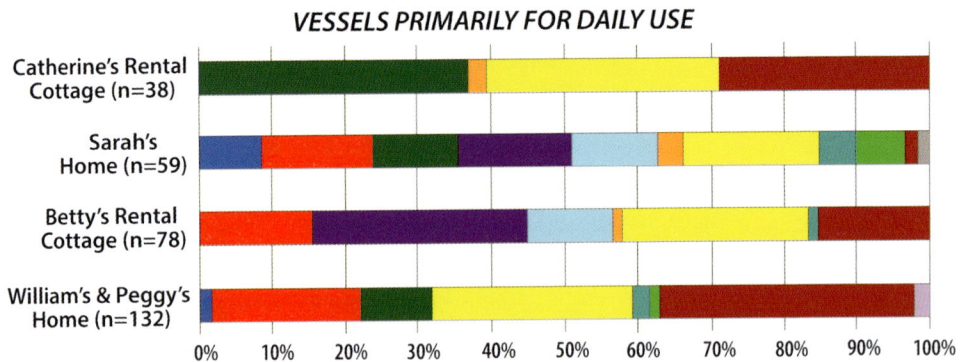

Fig. 5.49: Percentages of vessel forms in dressers whose contents are displayed but rarely used and in dressers whose contents are used daily

Fig. 5.50: Dresser designed with a bursting abundance approach, with every cubic centimetre filled with objects: second and third shelves of Mary's dresser

An equally crucial element to considering the tastes of dresser- and delph-keepers emerges from how they gathered together and displayed these objects. I found that dresser-keepers followed three basic approaches to arranging items for display: bursting abundance (Fig. 5.50), full but not overflowing (Fig. 5.51), and restrained elegance (Fig. 5.52). Regardless of the approach used by the dresser-keeper, all of these dressers are beautiful, enjoyable and bring a smile to my face. The number of belongings and how they are arranged in a dresser reference not only broadly held ideas about aesthetics but also how each person engages with those standards. In interviewing dresser- and delph-keepers, arranging delph displays involved many different components, including personal preferences for colour, designs and numbers, fears for the safety of specific pieces, and the desire to highlight pieces that are particularly sticky and voiceful.

Beyond the density of objects in any dresser or delph display, the arrangement often varied by how the possessions were grouped. Some dresser-keepers arranged matching sets of vessels on the same shelf, standing up plates in the rear to offer a backdrop to teacups, saucers, milk jugs and other items. Other dressers exhibited specific vessel forms, such as jugs, on shelves (Fig. 5.53). Teacups were often hung on hooks on shelf fronts, with matching saucers stacked below other teacups. Other people emphasised a particular colour scheme, while some maintained symmetry in dresser presentations. In a few cases, dresser-owners explained that the arrangement of pieces fulfilled a sense of taste and aesthetics while celebrating histories and stories attached to specific items on their dressers.

Fig. 5.51: Dressers designed to be full, but not overflowing: (top) Bedelia's dresser; (bottom) Penelope's dresser

The distinctive ways that people used dressers and arranged sticky belongings allowed them to not only exhibit good taste, creativity and aesthetic sensibilities but also to highlight the stories that speak most strongly for them about their homes, histories, current life and hopes for the future. Homemakers updated delph decorations over time, displaying new items as life experiences, sense of aesthetics, and taste changed as they grew, met new people, journeyed to new places and learned more about their histories. From the perspective of dressers, dresser-makers developed and maintained traditional local styles within each region in the study

Fig. 5.52: Dresser designed with elegant restraint and fewer pieces arranged artfully: Catherine's rental cottage dresser

Fig. 5.53: Dresser display grouping certain vessels by form, and with attention to symmetry and colour: second and third shelves of the Doonmore Hotel dresser on Inishbofin

area but also adapted to the needs of customers and to changing styles and tastes over time. In turn, delph-keepers also evaluated changing manufacturing technologies, decorative trends and forms as they acquired and exhibited or stored these objects. Dresser-makers and delph consumers both demonstrated awareness of regional and international styles and aesthetics.

While inhabitants of these western Connemara communities may have resided (and continue to do so) far from governmental and manufacturing centres, they nevertheless purchased and presented the same types of objects as those living closer to seats of political and economic power. In the past and present, participants in this project (including those who created the archaeological remains we have excavated on Inishark and Inishbofin) acquired possessions through the very same global economic networks. They evaluated popular regional trends to collect specific delph styles and forms to store and display at home, acting as arbiters of good taste in their own communities. Carpenters considered local tastes as they crafted dressers and other pieces of furniture, choosing to include or exclude stylistic elements such as sledge feet, glass door fronts, carved or dental moulding, and paint schemes or varnish.

By researching the life histories of dressers and delph and how they bridge time and space, dressers and delph elucidate the material footprints of social relations in western Connemara in three main arenas: local markets and integration with regional and international manufacturing and distribution networks; longstanding regional migrant and emigrant labour practices; and local and family histories of marriages, deaths, christenings, graduations, moves, pilgrimages, visits from relatives who have moved away, and other small and large happenings that enrich or challenge people throughout their lives. In all three realms, dressers and delph strongly invalidate the denigrating stereotypes of marginality, absence of cultural discernment, and impoverishment often applied to members of these communities in the past and present.

Moreover, these objects highlight that when people acquire goods, be they jam jugs, a new or new-to-them platter or a large piece of furniture like a dresser, they reinscribe that belonging with meanings as it moves through its life history. People infuse these furnishings with stories and values crucial to themselves and personalise their use, situated in a specific physical, historical and cultural context. As potter de Waal argues, in picking up that ceramic bowl or glass goblet, one remakes it, and one reimagines its place in the world. In using these possessions to homemake, each possession is absorbed into the home, helping to anchor it, whether it is displayed daily or only sees the light of day on special occasions. As ornaments, they not only order a house, they also beautify it.

This intensely personal aspect to dressers and delph in many ways enhances their potency as homemaking tools. These furnishings offer powerful ingredients for the homemaking recipe and act as the raw materials for the homemaker's creative efforts, allowing them to integrate a personal style with family heritage. This very personal connection means that for dresser-owners and delph collectors, these sticky and voiceful belongings are not just objects but an important part of their very personhood, helping them overcome the challenges of everyday life by offering centring points that strengthen a sense of self and fortitude to persevere through difficulties, including those at the personal scale and those emerging from region-wide social, economic, religious and political forces. Dressers and delph provide vehicles to connect people across space and time, but they also speak to the immediate present and the hoped-for future of the here-and-now. Moreover, the enduring presence of these furnishings in homes allows for change: change in personal histories and experiences, style and taste, and in the nature of one's home and sense of self. By glance, touch and thought in recalling associated stories, dressers and delph encompass the past, present and future while bridging the world through networks of kinship, labour, industry and beauty.

6

'Made to grow old': Dressers, heritage and the future of homemaking

*I used to cry me eyes out coming home from work in the evening.
I could see the sun setting, you know the big red sun setting. It was
setting over Inishark, over home. I said, 'I'm not having it out here
no longer. I'm going home.' Brother, was that not a nice thing to see,
coming in and looking out at that island in front of you.
I'm telling you, it chokes me even to think about it, it does.*

Jane, Fountainhill, 2012

Born on Inishark and married to an Inishark man, Jane asserted until her passing that she did not want to leave her home in October 1960 (Fig. 6.1). After their family was settled in Fountainhill, she helped her husband during the fishing season, often rowing with him in a *currach* thirteen kilometres out to High Island to set and collect the catch from pots. Those days on the water she came closer to her home, but never did she return there at day's end to put the kettle on and relax. She was not alone in missing a life on Inishark. Former resident George Lacey related in the film *Bás Oileáin* that when he dreamed, he was always on his island home.[1] We weave ourselves into homes, one moment, day, month, season and year at a time: the tapestry composed of the mundane rhythms of life with decorative embellishments arising from extraordinary moments of high emotion and great striving. People torn from home, for whatever reason, lose that anchoring foundation and must build a new set of experiences and histories to forge those connections and establish themselves in a new place.

Practising familiar tasks offers one particular avenue for maintaining a link with a former homeplace. In their film *Nets of Memory*, Ian Kuijt and William Donaruma

Fig. 6.1: Drone's-eye view of the village of Inishark

present the story of Festus O'Halloran, as recounted by his grandson and other descendants. Festus emigrated from Inishark in the late nineteenth century and settled down in the US in Clinton, Massachusetts, a mill town approximately fifty miles to the west of Boston and the sea.[2] In 1903, he married Bridget Davis, who had emigrated from Inishbofin to Clinton in 1900. At the time of the couple's wedding, marriage records listed him as a foundry operator and she as a weaver working in a local textile mill. Together, they raised a family and made a home in this small mill town far from the Atlantic Ocean. Both Bridget and Festus never returned to Inishark or Ireland, leaving island life in the past. Yet, in his free time, Festus continued to fashion fishing nets. Over his adult lifetime in Clinton, he made hundreds of fishing nets, hanging each finished one in his shed, never to be taken down or immersed in the salty ocean water so far from his and Bridget's home. Keeping that part of his island life alive may have helped him make a new home in a very different context.

Jane never needed to travel as far as Festus and Bridget to establish her new home in Claddaghduff. Some of Jane's children, grandchildren, grand-nieces and grand-nephews have absorbed aspects of her connection to her previous island life and home. Sixty years after she left Inishark, one of her sons is a talented carpenter and boatwright who makes and repairs *currachs* and fashions *currach* models in his workshop (Fig. 6.2), carrying on the tradition of his island ancestors though he lives on the mainland. Jane, Festus and Bridget all engaged in the key homemaking tasks of placemaking (Festus making nets and hanging them in his shed), dwelling (Jane making a new life on the mainland) and being resilient (building a foundation for a family's future as immigrants to the United States).

More recently, Ellen's son Richard emigrated from Inishbofin to the US about a decade ago. Despite living in places hours or even two long days of driving from the Atlantic Ocean, he began to build a *currach*, channelling all that he had learned from two of his older kinsmen who were renowned carpenters, boatwrights and boatmen: John Joe O'Toole of Inishturk and Martin of Inishbofin (Figs 6.3 and 6.4).

In explaining the connection between islanders, boats and homes, Richard said, 'You have the boats make the people, and the people make the boats.'[3] For him, his *currach* bridges the immense distance from his island home by inserting a small element of the everyday rhythms, sounds, smells, touch and sights of life on Inishbofin. His workshop and the *currach* remind him of his life there, grounding him in this new home far from his homeplace.

I believe that we might assert the same claim about homes: our homes make us, and we make our homes. As resilient creatures, humans can create new homes in different places, often bringing with them a little bit of the past to anchor their present and future. I certainly have done so, settled into the vast flatlands of the Upper Midwest with no scent of the sea or the cadences of southern accents surrounding me. I first left the US South when I travelled north for university in 1985. Whenever I return to the landscapes of my young adulthood, I feel at home with the sights, sounds, landscapes, accents, conversational patterns and familiar places. Our understanding of home encompasses the houses in which we reside(d), the surrounding topography and geography of places, and the sights, smells, sounds, languages, foods and rhythms of daily life. For good or ill, our past homes stick with us.

In fact, sometimes our senses of home in the present resonate strongly with our homes in the past. In resettling into a different house or flat, whether that place

Fig. 6.2: *Currach*-making as part of home: Jane's son in his workshop making a *currach* and *currach* models

Fig. 6.3: Richard and his *currach* in Auburn, Alabama

Fig. 6.4: Martin inspecting a *currach* he was painting on the beach below the Inishbofin House Hotel

be down the road or across the ocean, people bring sticky and voiceful belongings from their past to anchor their new homes. For instance, when Inishark islanders were forced to move to Fountainhill, they brought as many home furnishings, personal possessions and animals as possible. Documented by a British newspaper, we know that at least one dresser made that voyage to the mainland (Fig. 4.18a), transplanting a key element from an islander's original home into their new one.

Irish dressers and delph offer wonderful examples of sticky possessions that help transform a new residence into a home. Dressers appear in many Irish American homes as well. In talking with people about this research, especially those who are Irish American, they often recount stories of their parents' and grandparents' dressers and delph. Through his work as a curator for a Chicago-based private collector of Irish art, furniture and other crafts, Stephen has acquired two lovely old Irish dressers for his own home (Fig. 6.5). The smaller dresser had acquired a bit of fame during its lifetime. He found it in a Chicago antique shop whose owner had purchased it in a Dublin antique fair. As it sat outside on the footpath awaiting shipment, a photographer named Walter Pfeiffer asked the dealer if he could use the dresser for a shoot for a few days. The dresser became immortalised in a famous photograph often seen in postcards and posters celebrating Irish dressers. When Stephen entered the Chicago shop he noticed the famous poster and commented to the owner that he had seen this poster many times. The owner immediately asked if Stephen would like to see the actual dresser, which was for sale. Stephen purchased the dresser then and there, and keeps a copy of Pfeiffer's famous photograph on top of it.

This dresser's ornate carved pilasters, shoulders and cornice give it a very formal and ornate feel. Interestingly, the decorations on close inspection also speak to vernacular and rural motifs: small embellishments of carved seashells, carved arches on the doors that resonate with Moorish styles from rural southern dresser styles, and a compartment that he believes may have housed a hen on the left end of the press. Three or four generations of owners have modified it over time, adding drawers, new door and drawer pulls, and numerous sequences of paint schemes. His other dresser (Fig. 6.5b) had been stripped of paint sometime in the past, but the carved date of 1845, the fishtails, and the hearts on the fascia remain well preserved and clear. Stephen uses his dressers as ornaments in a room, holding family photographs and other meaningful objects. Both dressers and the contents tell stories about Stephen's family and history, resonating especially with his Irish American heritage.

Moreover, dressers and delph appear globally and adorn the homes of people with no Irish background at all. Often, these items are called by different names. In the US South, I grew up calling dressers 'hutches' or 'cabinets', and we referred to delph with the generalised word 'china', regardless of whether the vessels were actually made of refined earthenware, porcelain or bone china. Irrespective of location and time, each person creates their home, conducting a never-ending calculus of work-to-be-done: make a place, maintain that place and persevere in that place. Daily rhythms of life help us to weave ourselves into a place, both the residence in which we live as well as the community and landscapes surrounding our homes. In our day-to-day existence, we repeat many of the same movements and tasks: making coffee or tea in the morning, tending our gardens, walking our dogs, going to work or school, and preparing and eating meals. These experiences lend depth to our engagements with place, situating our memories of the past and our present experiences into a kind of dialogue that emerges from within our homes. Building up that foundation of memories and experiences helps many people to persevere through the challenges and to appreciate the victories and gifts life offers all of us over time.

This study's dresser- and delph-owners spoke of these furnishings as key elements in crafting a sense of welcome, generosity, beauty, order and hospitality in homes or businesses. These belongings offer a personalised palette that people can update as styles, family histories and personal tastes change over time. People can choose which sticky possessions to display and emphasise to highlight different stories and varying elements of their family, connections to other places and experiences, and broader community heritage. The very simplicity of dressers and delph, as both containers and objects to be displayed, renders them a flexibility that allows people to redesign tableaus and decorations as they choose. Dressers and delph combine constancy with creative innovation, growing old in homes and with owners and users to offer emotional and historical anchoring points to meet future trials and rejoice in welcome events and circumstances.

Inishark's archaeological evidence for homemaking gives further testament to a rich history of homemaking in these rural communities, beginning with building homes, acquiring or making possessions, and then living for several generations on the island. The delph and glass we documented through our archaeological research represent a small portion of the things that islanders actually owned. We can also consider other types of goods that surrounded Inishark's residents daily, especially those that do not survive well in the archaeological record: clothing, basketry and wood vessels. Belongings brightened homes with glazed white and decorated ceramics, glass vessels, and other furnishings that transformed houses into personalised homes, even if the government did not legally recognise their right of ownership. For more than a century, Inishark villagers lived as tenants

Fig. 6.5: Stephen's Irish dressers: (a) found in a Chicago antique shop; (opposite) (b) purchased from a Connecticut estate sale

b

under the sufferance of the landlords and land managers in houses they themselves built. These homes testify to the resiliency needed to survive more than a century in a system that established islanders as perpetually owing rather than owning and speaks to people's tenacity, cleverness and hope for a better future.

Homemaking, creative heritage and sustainable futures

It may seem overly optimistic to bestow such potency and relevancy to dressers and delph, but any sustainable future must be grounded in homes that encompass the residences in which people live as well as the landscape in which they dwell. Dressers and delph contribute to homemaking as tools to order people's lives, tell stories about the past and present and pave pathways to a future. Successful

Fig. 6.6: Drone's-eye view looking to the northwest over Inishbofin's Old Pier, Inishbofin House Hotel, The Beach and St Colman's Church (all in the foreground) with Middlequarter, Fawnmore and the Westquarter commonage spreading to the horizon

homemaking builds a future for people and their communities. As the old adage goes, you build a wall one stone at a time: in these communities, sustainable futures are built one home at a time.

For the western island communities of Inishbofin and Inishturk, whose residents must fight for governmental support for their ferry service, medical facilities, national schools and farming and fishing industries, homemaking and sustainability comprise an important element of the vibrant tourism sector (Fig. 6.6). Proprietors of hotels, restaurants, rental cottages and craft shops strive to make guests feel welcome, to feel at home. The Beach – Days Bar and B&B on Inishbofin features a mural with the motto: 'Arrive as visitors … leave as Friends'. Inside the pub, the proprietor displays old crockery vessels above the bar, and Julia's old dresser graces the side room. Approximately one mile to the west, the Doonmore Hotel's dining room is adorned with delph and the family's old dresser (Figure 6.7). A sense of history and island heritage surrounds diners seated as they enjoy a meal; the Galley Restaurant's dresser similarly exudes heritage and welcome to its diners.

In his dissertation research, Ryan Lash examined how Inishbofin islanders have

Fig. 6.7: Breakfast in the Doonmore Hotel dining room

skilfully harnessed their heritage to attract tourists over the years. He argues that heritage is a creative and ongoing endeavour and that islanders are well aware of the complexity of such a concept:

> Islanders know the affordances of their archaeological heritage. They understand how the scenic, seemingly archaic landscape and monumental ruins draw in visitors, and they understand how rather ordinary objects keep alive more intimate family histories and maintain a distinctive identity for their community. They also know that heritage is not confined to objects in the landscape. Heritage also includes the embodied knowledge generated from engaging with those objects in the landscape. Heritage is also the know-how to recite a tale connected to a house, to knit a pattern from memory, to bake brown bread, to recognize the best landing places

and paths across the water depending on the height of the tide, to navigate an advantageous path through commonage while gathering sheep, and to anticipate when to slow your vehicle when approaching sharp bends or blind intersections along the island's narrow roads …[4]

I strongly agree with his conceptualisation of heritage: it encompasses both tangible resources, like old homes converted into rental cottages often furnished with dressers and delph, and intangible ones, such as the knowledge of how to craft a dresser or a delph display and to tell the stories attached to these belongings. Inishbofin's tourism industry relies largely on repeat guests, many of whom today enjoyed holidays on the island as children and now share that joy with their own growing families. Lash argues that these returning tourists are drawn back to the island by a feeling of belonging and attachment to this community. They feel a connection to the island based on the experiences of enjoying the food, music, scenery and sense of islander heritage. Dressers and delph feature prominently in placemaking efforts to welcome visitors into restaurants, hotels, rental cottages, beds and breakfasts and the planned Offshore Islands Museum (an expanded Inishbofin Heritage Museum, founded and directed by local historian Marie Coyne). Many islanders have decorated homes with these furnishings: they are not just for show for the tourists. Moreover, it does not escape me that the word 'belonging' here involves two powerful concepts: the feeling of attachment to some place or community, and the possessions that help us to form those attachments to places.

Inishturk islanders likewise have forged a similar connection with tourists, welcoming return guests over many decades into this community (Fig. 6.8). Dressers and delph also feature in the crafting of that welcoming feeling, that sense of home and belonging (Fig. 6.9). In Honora's bed and breakfast dining room, one's eye is drawn to her fine dresser, made by Mark over twenty years ago. Throughout the kitchen of Celia's bed and breakfast, she displays delph on the tops of the upper press cabinets or on a high shelf. In the community centre, some photographs of residents in their homes include dressers in the background.

Yet, some people do not keep old dressers and delph. Despite their sticky qualities, or perhaps especially because of the associated stories and memories, some people discard these possessions. In 2019, Catherine rang me to let me know that someone had abandoned a dresser from a house that was being renovated in Inishbofin's Rusheen village (Fig. 6.10). I found the dresser lying in a generous

Fig. 6.8: View looking eastwards towards the main harbour of Inishturk from the road leading to the community centre

patch of nettles and leaning against an uninhabited structure overlooking Rusheen's beautiful beach. It was an old dresser, most recently painted in a bright blue and white paint scheme.

That day, it was in a sad state and rotting in several places. I imagine that at one time, someone loved this old dresser (Fig. 6.11). The fascia board sported carved decorations, a similar decorative technique to that used on Stephen's 1845 dresser in his Chicago home. The press contained two drawers and one central door, but the panels on the doors did not show any evidence of decorative carving; perhaps the original paint scheme embellished these flat plains. The backing boards behind the open shelving were narrow, and a plain cornice capped the top, which was painted white. Doors had enclosed the upper shelves, but those doors were not in evidence

Fig. 6.9: Inishturk dresser and delph in bed and breakfasts: (opposite page) Honora's dresser in the dining room; (right) Celia's delph displayed above the kitchen sink in view of bed and breakfast guests

that day. As I was not dressed for wading into the nettles, close inspection to glean clues about its life history was not possible. I could not discern if the framing for the doors had been added as a renovation or if the craftsperson had originally built the dresser with the doors. It appeared that someone retrofitted this dresser in the mid-twentieth century with doors, likely removing the shoulders flanking the worktop and replacing the sides and cornice to make the dresser slightly wider. At a guess, I would estimate that this dresser started its life in the early to mid-twentieth century and was carefully maintained and updated until the last decade or so when its presence graced an uninhabited cottage.

Sometimes, dressers are not the only old belongings to be discarded. More than

Fig. 6.10: Discarded dresser in the east end of Inishbofin

Fig. 6.11: A closer view of the discarded dresser

one participant shared a story about an entire delph collection that was purposefully broken into pieces and discarded in a large pit on a property after the owner passed away. I learned that the distribution of the delph would have caused a tremendous amount of strife in the family, and they chose to avoid the disruption. Although many archaeologists might cringe at such a circumstance, I understand why people might decide that the past is better left buried if it threatens the future.

Despite these examples, the arts and antiques industry in Ireland recently found reason for hope emerging from growing concerns with climate change and concerns for sustainability. In 2019, the Irish Antique Dealers Association (IADA) sought VAT-free status as a green industry.[5] McElhatton reported that the IADA positioned themselves as 'the original recyclers', quoting the organisation's president Paul Brereton, because their industry produces a very low carbon footprint as it does not involve a modern manufacturing process. In a more recent *Irish Times* article, Denise O'Connor reports that increased purchasing of antique furniture reflects growing concern for climate change and sustainability.[6] She relates that many customers are increasingly frustrated with possessions that are manufactured to make it difficult, if not impossible, to repair. They prefer to purchase furniture and other belongings that are designed to last for years if not decades. She also notes that people interested in sustainability appreciate the low carbon footprint of antiques and that purchasing vintage furniture and other goods supports local craftspeople who make a living repairing and refurbishing these antique objects.

Tony Donoghue's Sundance-award-winning short animated 2012 film *Irish Folk Furniture*[7] and Claudia Kinmonth's renowned second edition of her *Irish Country Furniture and Furnishings 1700–2000*[8] both testify to a significant and ongoing enthusiasm for older, hand-crafted furniture and delph. Michael Fortune's research efforts to collect Irish folklore (including a dresser documentation project and his dresser calendars)[9] has found a popular audience on Facebook, with 89,000 people following his page (Fig. 6.12). Likewise, the Facebook group Arklow Pottery connects roughly 2,000 enthusiasts of the pottery, whether they be collectors and/or former employees of the company.[10] Similarly, the Irish Vernacular Furniture Facebook group features postings for roughly 5,900 enthusiasts and often includes postings about dressers.[11] Many people in Ireland and beyond nurture a devotion to these sticky items.

Growing concerns around climate change, and the consequent desire for sustainability and low carbon footprints, combine with an appreciation for these belongings that were 'made to grow old', like the dressers and delph documented in

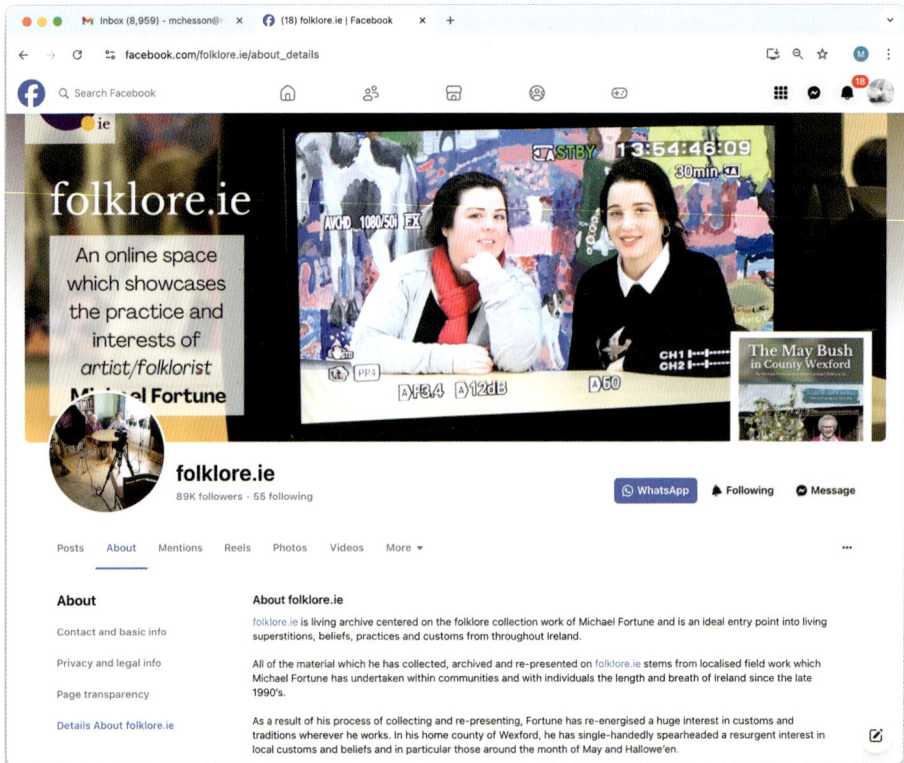

Fig. 6.12: Screenshot of a portion of Michael Fortune's Facebook page, with 89,000 followers

this project. In rural communities like Inishbofin, Inishturk, Cashel and Clifden, many people utilise these heritage possessions as key tools in homemaking for themselves or in crafting a homey feel for their businesses. Homes require grounding histories, like the stories often told by sticky and voiceful dressers and delph, in order to mature and support future generations. I believe that these furnishings act as testaments to the promise for those future generations, offering meaningful narratives of kinship and friendship between people near and far, tangible proof of the resiliency of ancestors, and enduring outlets for the creative display of people's histories and discerning senses of taste.

Homemaking's deep prehistoric past continues to resonate in today's serious challenges to sustaining our communities and homes. The alarming global crises of climate change, armed conflicts, massive forced migrations, poverty, and rising inequality of access to basic human necessities like clean water, food, shelter and safety threaten many of our fundamental ideals of what a home should be – safe, enduring and nurturing. In such a way, I believe that individual homemaking at a local level offers a platform for confronting the dire consequences of decades of unsustainable decisions. In furnishing our homes with old dressers and delph, in creating a welcoming place to nourish our families, and in recognising the resiliency of our ancestors and their knowledge of living with renewable resources, we help create a more sustainable future for ourselves and our descendants. It inspires me to see how, in these western communities of Connemara, people are crafting futures one dresser, piece of delph and home at a time (Fig. 6.13).

Fig. 6.13: Detail of jugs on the Doonmore Hotel's dresser, including a blue transfer-printed Melrose pattern vessel, produced by Barkers and Kent Ltd in Staffordshire, England (1889–98; Godden mark 264, 266; Kowalsky and Kowalsky mark B177, B180)

Notes

Chapter 1
An Anthropology of Homemaking in Western Ireland

1   Robyn Rowland, 'Unbroken Stone in a Stubborn Sea: Epic of Inishbofin', in *Line of Drift* (Inverin, County Galway: Doire Press, 2015), pp. 49–54.

2   Alison Blunt and Robyn Dowling, *Home* (London: Routledge, 2006); Akiko Busch, *Geography of Home: Writings on where we live* (New York: Princeton Architectural Press, 1999), particularly chapters on the kitchen, dining room and living room; Padraic Colum's poems 'The Fire Bringer' and 'Old Woman of the Roads', in *Wild Earth* (Dublin: Maunsel & Co., 1907, pp. 7–8 and 15 respectively); Irene Cieraad (ed.), *At Home: An anthropology of domestic space* (Syracuse, NY: Syracuse University Press, 2006), especially her introductory chapter and the following chapters: Moira Munro and Ruth Madigan, 'Negotiating Space in the Family Home', pp. 107–17, Paul J.J. Pennartz, 'Home: The experience of atmosphere', pp. 95–106, and Elizabeth Shove, 'Constructing Home: A crossroads of choices', pp. 130–43; Judith Flanders, *The Making of Home: The 500-year story of how houses became our homes* (New York: St Martin's Press, 2015); the second chapter of 'Home (Landscape of the Heart)', in J. Douglas Porteous and Sandra E. Smith, *Domicide: The global destruction of home* (Montreal: McGill-Queen's University Press, 2001); Annette Carruthers (ed.), *The Scottish Home* (Edinburgh: National Museums of Scotland, 1996), especially her chapter on the kitchen, as well as the following chapters: Ian Gow, 'The Dining Room', pp. 125–54, and Naomi Tarrant, 'The Bedroom', pp. 181–202; James Deetz, *In Small Things Forgotten* (New York: Anchor Books, 1996); Nicola Frost and Tom Selwyn (eds), *Travelling Towards Home: Mobilities and homemaking* (New York: Berghahn, 2018); bell hooks, 'The Politics of Radical Black Subjectivity', in *Yearning: Race, gender, and cultural politics* (Boston: South End Press, 1990), pp. 15–22; Rachel Hurdley, *Home, Materiality, Memory, and Belonging: Keeping culture* (Basingstoke, Hampshire: Palgrave Macmillan, 2013); Adrienne Rich, 'Natural Resources', in *The Dream of a Common Language: Poems 1974–1977* (New York: W.W. Norton & Company, 1978), pp. 60–7; Warsan Shire's poem 'Home', in *Bless the Daughter Raised by a Voice in Her Head* (London: Chatto & Windus, 2022), pp. 24–5; Barbara Smith, *Home Girls: A Black feminist anthology* (Boston: Kitchen Table Press, 1983); and Poetry Ireland's Writing Home project led by poet Colm Keegan, https://www.creativeireland.gov.ie/en/event/poetry-ireland/; https://www.youtube.com/watch?v=icPvlAplHH8.

3   Archaeological photographs of belongings and buildings always include a scale bar. In this case, the scale bar on Michael's mantel is 40 cm long. In most photographs of ceramic vessels and other possessions, the scale bars are 5, 10 or 20 cm long, with occasional 2-cm-long scale bars for maker's marks. In photographs of surveyed buildings and excavated features, scale bars are generally larger: 1 metre long for buildings and 30 or 40 cm long for larger features.

4 Nicholas Wolff, 'At Home in Prehistory: Critical approaches to the built environment in the south Italian Bronze Age', unpublished PhD thesis, Boston University, 2014, p. 6.

5 Henry Glassie, *Passing the Time in Ballymenone* (Philadelphia: University of Pennsylvania Press, 1982), p. 342.

6 Cartographer and author Tim Robinson's books on Connemara beautifully capture the paradox of home, simultaneously intimate and expansive, and interwoven with geological, ecological and social histories and lived experiences of being and becoming in specific places: *Connemara: Listening to the wind* (Dublin: Penguin Ireland, 2006), *Connemara: The last pool of darkness* (Dublin: Penguin Ireland, 2008), and *Connemara: A little Gaelic kingdom* (Dublin: Penguin Ireland, 2011).

7 Three anthropologists have greatly influenced my own approach to homemaking, landscapes and interlinked scales of analysis: Henry Glassie, *Passing the Time in Ballymenone* and *Vernacular Architecture* (Bloomington, IN: Indiana University Press, 2000); Julia Hendon, *Houses in a Landscape: Memory and everyday life in Mesoamerica* (Durham, NC: Duke University Press, 2010); and Peter Whitridge, 'Landscapes, Houses, Bodies, Things: "Place" and the archaeology of Inuit imaginaries', *Journal of Archaeological Method and Theory*, vol. 11, no. 2, 2004, pp. 213–50.

8 Ireland and much of Europe separate archaeology into a separate discipline. I was trained in North America, where archaeology is often subsumed under the discipline of anthropology. Thus, I learned archaeological methodologies and theoretical approaches with a strong grounding in anthropological thought: my research employs both archaeology and anthropology.

9 These three practices are exhaustively discussed and demonstrated by many other archaeologists, including Nicholas (Tico) Wolff's dissertation on homemaking in the southern Italian Bronze Age: 'At Home in Prehistory'; Annelise E. Morris, '"We all lived in that house together": Persistence as resistance on an Illinois farmstead, 1845 to present', unpublished PhD dissertation, University of California, Berkeley, 2015.

10 Several other scholars' work has greatly influenced my own research, including Keith Basso, *Wisdom Sits in Places: Landscape and language among the western Apache* (Albuquerque, NM: University of New Mexico Press, 1996); Whitney L. Battle-Baptiste, *Black Feminist Archaeology* (Walnut Creek, CA: Left Coast Press, 2011); Pierre Bourdieu, 'The Berber House, or the World Reversed', *Social Science Information*, vol. 9, 1970, pp. 151–70; Ray Cashman, 'Critical Nostalgia and Material Culture in Northern Ireland', *Journal of American Folklore*, vol. 119, no. 472, 2006, pp. 137–60; Maria Franklin and Nedra Lee, 'Revitalizing Tradition and Instigating Change: Foodways at the Ransom and Sarah Williams Farmstead, *c.* 1871–1905', *Journal of African Diaspora Archaeology and Heritage*, vol. 8, no. 3, 2019, pp. 202–25; Laurie Wilkie, *The Archaeology of Mothering: An African-American midwife's tale* (New York: Routledge, 2003) and *Creating Freedom: Material culture and African-American identity at Oakley Plantation, Louisiana, 1845–1950* (Baton Rouge, LA: Louisiana State University Press, 2000).

11 Franklin and Lee, 'Revitalizing Tradition'; Morris, '"We all lived in that house together"'.

12 Delft (eighteenth-century tin-glazed earthenware, whose production used a specific set of technologies and materials) is not the same type of object as delph (a term commonly

used for everyday ceramic tablewares and crockery). See Peter Francis, *Irish Delftware: An illustrated history* (London: Johnathan Horne Publications, 2000), p. 7.

13 All of these topics have been expertly covered elsewhere. The most recent and comprehensive overview of rural Irish home furnishings is to be found in Claudia Kinmonth's exhaustive overview, *Irish Country Furniture and Furnishings 1700–2000* (Cork: Cork University Press, 2020). For discussions of mythologising the west of Ireland, see Justin Carville, 'Visible Others: Photography and romantic ethnography in Ireland', in Maria McGarrity and Claire A. Culleton (eds), *Irish Modernism and the Global Primitive* (New York: Palgrave Macmillan, 2009), pp. 93–114; Marguérite Corporaal, 'Traveling Cabins: The popularity of Irish local-color fiction in early nineteenth-century Europe', in Marguérite Corporaal and Christina Moran (eds), *Traveling Irishness in the Long Nineteenth Century* (Cham, Switzerland: Palgrave Macmillan, 2017), pp. 103–18; Luke Gibbons, 'Synge, Country and Western: The myth of the west in Irish and American culture', in Luke Gibbons (ed.), *Transformations in Irish Culture* (Cork: Cork University Press, 1996), pp. 23–35; Elizabeth Gilmartin, '"Magnificent Words and Gestures": Defining the primitive in Synge's *The Aran Islands*', in Maria McGarrity and Claire A. Culleton (eds), *Irish Modernism and the Global Primitive* (New York: Palgrave Macmillan, 2009), pp. 63–76; Diarmuid Ó Giolláin, *Locating Irish Folklore: Tradition, modernity, identity* (Cork: Cork University Press, 2000).

14 Indigenous scholars and researchers working with and for First Nation and Native American peoples in the United States and Canada persuasively argue that archaeologists must acknowledge that artefacts we find and document were not simply objects: they were someone's belongings. In studying people's dressers, delph and other possessions, this argument resonates profoundly. No one with whom I spoke ever talked about their delph or dressers as 'objects' or 'artefacts'; these things were always framed as family heirlooms, prized possessions or things that spoke about themselves and their family on a personal level. See Sean P. Connaughton, Genevieve Hill, Jesse Morin, Cory Frank, Nancy Green and David McGee, 'Tidal Belongings: First Nations-driven archaeology to preserve a large wooden fish trap panel recovered from the Comox Harbour Intertidal Fish Trap Complex in British Columbia', *Canadian Journal of Archaeology*, vol. 46, 2022, pp. 16–51; Sara L. Gonzalez, Ian Krietzler and Briece Edwards, 'Imagining Indigenous and Archaeological Futures: Building capacity with the confederated tribes of Grande Ronde', *Archaeologies*, vol. 14, 2018, pp. 85–114; and David M. Schaepe, Bill Angelbeck, David Snook and John R. Welch, 'Archaeology as Therapy: Connecting belongings, knowledge, time, place, and well-being', *Current Anthropology*, vol. 58, no. 4, 2017, pp. 502–33.

15 Sara Ahmed, 'Happy Objects', in Melissa Gregg and Gregory J. Seigworth (eds), *The Affect Theory Reader* (Durham, NC: Duke University Press, 2010), pp. 29–51; Jeanne E. Arnold, Anthony P. Graesch, Enzo Ragazzini and Elinor Ochs, *Life at Home in the Twenty-First Century: 32 families open their doors* (Los Angeles: Cotsen Institute, University of California, Los Angeles, 2012); Peter Jackson, 'Commodity Cultures: The traffic in things', *Transactions of the Institute of British Geographers*, vol. 24, no. 1, 1999, pp. 95–108; Barbara Kirshenblatt-Gimlet, 'Authoring Lives', *Journal of Folklore Research*, vol. 26, no. 2, 1989, pp. 123–49; Igor Kopytoff, 'The Cultural Biography of Things', in Arjun Apaddurai (ed.), *The Social Life of Things: Commodities in cultural perspective* (Cambridge: Cambridge University

Press, 1986), pp. 64–91; Lynn Meskell, *Archaeologies of Materiality* (Malden, MA: Blackwell Publishing, 2005); Daniel Miller, *Materiality* (Durham, NC: Duke University Press, 2005); Ian Woodward, 'Domestic Objects and Taste Epiphany: A resource for consumption methodology', *Journal of Material Culture*, vol. 6, no. 2, 2001, pp. 115–36.

16 Susan Kus, 'In the Midst of Moving Waters: Material, metaphor, and feminist archaeology', in Pamela L. Geller and Miranda K. Stockett (eds), *Feminist Anthropology: Past, present, and future* (Philadelphia: University of Pennsylvania Press, 2006), pp. 105–14, at p. 114.

17 Kenneth M. George, 'No Ethics Without Things', *Journal of Religious Ethics*, vol. 44, no. 1, 2016, pp. 51–67.

18 John Robb, 'Material Culture, Landscapes of Action, and Emergent Causation: A new model for the origins of the European Neolithic', *Current Anthropology*, vol. 54, no. 6, 2013, pp. 657–83.

19 Webb Keane, 'Semiotics and the Social Analysis of Material Things', *Language and Communication*, vol. 23, 2003, pp. 409–25; see also Rosemary A. Joyce's interview with Keane in Rosemary A. Joyce, '"What Eludes Speech": A dialogue with Webb Kean', *Journal of Social Archaeology*, vol. 11, no. 2, 2011, pp. 158–70; more recently, archaeologist Annalise Morris deftly uses Keane's approach in the study of her family's homeplace in her PhD thesis: Morris, '"We all lived in that house together"'.

20 Ahmed, 'Happy Objects' (emphasis in original); see also Miller, *Materiality*.

21 Siân Jones, 'Negotiating Objects and Authentic Selves: Beyond the deconstruction of authenticity', *Journal of Material Culture*, vol. 15, no. 2, 2010, pp. 181–203, at p. 189.

22 Jane Webster, Louise Tolson and Richard Carlton, 'The Artifact as Interviewer: Experimenting with oral history at the Ovenstone miners' cottages site, Northumberland', *Historical Archaeology*, vol. 48, 2014, pp. 11–29.

23 There exists an ongoing scholarly debate surrounding the original translation of Inis Airc with no current consensus of the name's meaning. Archaeologist Ryan Lash (personal communication, 2024) instructed me to look at Inishark's entry in the Placenames Database of Ireland (https://www.logainm.ie/en/18237). Lash notes that Fiachra Mac Gabhann prefers the personal name version (Arc's Island): pp. 708–62 in Fiachra Mac Gabhann, 'Aguisín: Logainmneacha Inis Airc', in *Logainmneacha Mhaigh Eo 2: Barúntacht Mhuraisce* (Baile Átha Cliath: Coiscéim, 2014). The local folklore and oral history volume *Inishbofin Through Time and Tide* suggests 'theories ranging from "Island of Lovers" (John O'Donovan citing the opinion of his Bofin informant, John Moran), to "Island of the Sea Monster". It is likely that the island takes its name from somebody name Earc. This man's name occurs frequently in ancient Irish history and Mythology': Kieran Concannon (ed.), *Inishbofin Through Time and Tide* (Inishbofin: Inishbofin Development Company, printed in Athlone: Temple Printing Company, 1997). Lash also called my attention to the name of Sherkin Island in Cork, which comes from Inis Arcáin, with Arcáin as a diminutive form of Arc/Earc. Arcáin in this case is interpreted as an early form of orcán, meaning piglet (https://www.logainm.ie/en/13016). He suggests that Island of the Piglet aligns well with the names of neighbouring islands: island of the White Cow (Inishbofin), Island of the Ox (Davillaun) and Island of the Boar (Inishturk). To learn more about the history of Inishark, readers can watch a lecture by Lash given in 2021 on his archaeological and

ethnographic research conducted on Inishark and Inishbofin: https://www.youtube.com/watch?v=cH6kxoIqN_I&t=7s.

24 Susan Kus, 'Archaeology as Anthropology: Much ado about something after all?', *Journal of Archaeological Method and Theory*, vol. 4, nos. 3–4, 1997, pp. 199–213.

25 Ibid., p. 207.

26 More recently, archaeologists have considered senses and emotions of past peoples: Karen Dempsey and Jitske Jasperse, 'Multisensorial Musings on Miniature Matters', *Das Mittelalter*, vol. 25, no. 2, 2020, pp. 249–70; Jeffrey B. Fleisher and Neil Norman (eds), *The Archaeology of Anxiety: The materiality of anxiousness, worry, and fear* (New York: Springer, 2016); Yiannis Hamilakis, *Archaeology of the Senses: Human experience, memory, and affect* (Cambridge: Cambridge University Press, 2014); Robin Skeates, *An Archaeology of the Senses: Prehistoric Malta* (Oxford: Oxford University Press, 2010); Robin Skeates and Jo Day (eds), *The Routledge Handbook of Sensory Archaeology* (London: Routledge, 2019); Sarah Tarlow, 'Emotion in Archaeology', *Current Anthropology*, vol. 41, no. 5, 2000, pp. 713–46 and 'The Archaeology of Emotion and Affect', *Annual Review of Anthropology*, vol. 41, 2012, pp. 169–85.

27 For a discussion of personalisation, taste and material culture, see Kirshenblatt-Gimlet, 'Authoring Lives'; Woodward, 'Taste Epiphanies'; and Hurdley, *Home, Materiality, Memory, and Belonging*.

28 Keane, 'Semiotics and Social Analysis of Material Things'.

29 See Keane in Joyce, '"What Eludes Speech"'.

30 Archaeologist Roberta Gilchrist argues that anthropologists must consider the full life course of people and their lived experiences: Roberta Gilchrist, *Medieval Life: Archaeology and the life course* (Woodbridge, UK: Boydell Press, 2012).

31 bell hooks, *Yearning: Race, gender, and cultural politics* (Boston: South End Press, 1991) and Smith, *Home Girls*. For more recent archaeological perspectives, see Battle-Baptiste, *Black Feminist Archaeology* and '"In This Here Place": Interpreting enslaved homeplaces', in Akinwumi Ogundiran and Toyin Falola (eds), *Archaeology of Atlantic Africa and the African Diaspora* (Bloomington, IN: Indiana University Press, 2007), pp. 233–48; Maria Franklin, 'A Black-Feminist-Inspired Archaeology?', *Journal of Social Archaeology*, vol. 1, 2001, pp. 108–25; Maria Franklin and Nedra Lee, 'African American Descendants, Community Outreach, and the Ransom and Sarah Williams Farmstead Project', *Journal of Community Archaeology & Heritage*, vol. 7, no. 2, 2020, pp. 135–48; Morris, '"We all lived in that house together"'; Wilkie, *Archaeology of Mothering* and *Creating Freedom*.

Irish ethnographer Donna Birdwell-Pheasant utilises a slightly different concept, called The Home 'Place', in Irish rural contexts where she characterises houses with multi-generational histories that represent, physically and metaphorically, the residential history and heritage of a family: Donna Birdwell-Pheasant, 'The Home "Place": Center and periphery in Irish house and family systems', in Donna Birdwell-Pheasant and Denise Lawrence-Zúniga (eds), *House Life: Space, place and family in Europe* (Oxford: Berg, 1999), pp. 105–29.

32 Glassie, *Vernacular Architecture*, p. 17.

33 Henry Glassie, *Folk Housing in Middle Virginia* (Knoxville, TN: University of Tennessee

Press, 1975); see also Alan Gailey, *Rural Houses of the North of Ireland* (Edinburgh: John Donald Publishers, 1984) and Caoimhín Ó Danachair, 'The Combined Byre-and-Dwelling in Ireland', *Folk Life*, vol. 2, no. 1, 1964, pp. 58–75; Rachel McKenna, *Traditional Architecture in Offaly: History, materials and furniture 1800 to present day* (Tullamore, County Offaly: Offaly County Council, 2022).

34   Arnold, Graesch, Ragazzini and Ochs, *Life at Home*.

35   Anthropologist Pierre Bourdieu developed an anthropological toolkit for investigating the cultural construction of taste – good, bad or otherwise – and how people learn to discern and value different styles, fashions and behaviours: Pierre Bourdieu, *Distinction: A social critique of the judgement of taste*, translated by R. Nice (London: Routledge & Kegan Paul, 1984); Pierre Bourdieu, 'The Forms of Capital', in John G. Richardson (ed.), *Handbook of Theory and Research for the Sociology of Education* (Westport, CT: Greenwood Press, 1986), pp. 241–58. Chapter 5 will engage specifically with Bourdieu's model for taste.

36   For a broad selection of ethnographic and archaeological approaches to homes and houses, see Janet Carston and Stephen Hugh-Jones (eds), *About the House: Lévi-Strauss and beyond* (Cambridge: Cambridge University Press, 1995); Karen Dempsey, 'Home Is Where the Heart(h) Is?', *Archaeology Ireland*, vol. 34, no. 1, 2020, pp. 49–51; James J. Fox (ed.), *Inside Austronesian Houses: Perspectives on domestic designs for living* (Canberra: Australian National University, 1993); Lee Horne, *Village Spaces: Settlement and society in northeastern Iran* (Washington, DC: Smithsonian Institute Press, 1994); Audrey Horning, *In the Shadow of Ragged Mountain: Historical archaeology of Nicholson, Corbin, and Weakley Hollows* (Luray, VA: Shenandoah National Park Association Inc., 2004); Rosemary A. Joyce and Susan D. Gillespie (eds), *Beyond Kinship: Social and material reproduction in house societies* (Philadelphia: University of Pennsylvania Press, 2000); Ron G. Knapp and Kai-Yin Lo (eds), *House, Home, Family: Living and being Chinese* (Honolulu: University of Hawaii Press, 2005); Carol Kramer, *Village Ethnoarchaeology: Rural Iran in archaeological perspective* (New York: Academic Press, 1982); Charles E. Orser, Jr (ed.), *Unearthing Hidden Ireland: Historical archaeology in Ballykilcline, County Roscommon* (Bray: Wordwell, 2006); Bradley J. Parker and Catherine P. Foster (eds), *New Perspectives on Household Archaeology* (Winona Lake, IN: Eisenbrauns, 2012); Roxana Waterson, *The Living House: An anthropology of architecture in Southeast Asia* (Kuala Lumpur: Oxford University Press, 1990).

37   For examples, see Birdwell-Pheasant, 'The Home "Place"'; Robin Fox, *The Tory Islanders: A people of the Celtic fringe* (Notre Dame, IN: University of Notre Dame Press, 1995), Glassie, *Passing the Time*; Gailey, *Rural Houses of the North of Ireland*, pp. 15–26; Kevin Danaher, *The Hearth and Stool and All! Irish rural households* (Dublin: Mercier Press, 1985); Kinmonth, *Irish Country Furniture and Furnishings 1700–2000*; Caoimhin Ó Danachair, 'Traditional Forms of the Dwelling House in Ireland', *Journal of the Royal Society of Antiquaries of Ireland*, vol. 102, no. 1, 1972, pp. 77–96; Barry O'Reilly, 'Hearth and Home: The vernacular house in Ireland from 1800', *Proceedings of the Royal Irish Academy*, vol. 111C, 2011, pp. 193–215; Clive Symmons and Seamus Harkin, *The Disappearing Irish Cottage: A case-study of north Donegal* (Bray: Wordwell, 2004); and Jane Walsh, 'The Social Organisation of an Island Community in Western Ireland: Clare Island, County Mayo', unpublished PhD thesis, University of Edinburgh, 1958.

38   Mark Gardiner, 'Folklore's Timeless Past, Ireland's Present Past, and the Perception of Rural Houses in Early Historic Ireland', *International Journal of Historical Archaeology*, vol. 15, no. 4, 2011, pp. 707–24.

39   For recent archaeological approaches to contemporary refugee homemaking efforts, see Ángela María Arbeláez Arbeláez and Edward Mulholland, 'Interrupted Journeys: Drawings by refugees at the Kara Tepe camp, Lesvos, Greece', *Journal of Contemporary Archaeology*, vol. 3, 2016, pp. 233–44; Beverly Butler and Fatima al-Nammari, '"We Palestinian Refugees" – Heritage Rites and/as the Clothing of Bare Life: Reconfiguring paradox, obligation, and imperative in Palestinian refugee camps in Jordan', *Journal of Contemporary Archaeology*, vol. 3, 2016, pp. 147–59; Rui Gomes Coelho, 'The Garden of Refugees', *Journal of Contemporary Archaeology*, vol. 3, 2016, pp. 261–70; and Kostis Kourelis, 'If Place Remotely Matters: Camped in Greece's contingent countryside', *Journal of Contemporary Archaeology*, vol. 3, 2016, pp. 215–27. Archaeologists have also examined how unhoused people strive to create homes: Ann Danis, 'Home(less) Place and Home-Making at the Albany Bulb', in Elena Sesma and Evan Taylor (eds), *Contemporary Archaeologies in Old Places: Material politics between past and future*, Archaeological Papers of the American Anthropological Association, vol. 33, 2020, pp. 106–21; Larry J. Zimmerman and Jessica Welch, 'Displaced and Barely Visible: Archaeology and the material culture of homelessness', *Historical Archaeology*, vol. 45, no. 1, 2011, pp. 67–85.

40   For descriptions of form and construction of a crannóg, see Christina Fredengren, *Crannógs* (Bray: Wordwell, 2002); Aidan O'Sullivan, Finbar McCormick, Thomas R. Kerr and Lorcan Harney, *Early Medieval Ireland AD 400–1100: The evidence from archaeological excavations* (Dublin: Royal Irish Academy Publications, 2014), pp. 46–138.

41   https://www.craggaunowen.ie/.

42   Eoin Grogan, 'Excavations at Mooghaun South 1995, Interim Report', in *Discovery Programme Reports no. 5* (Dublin: The Discovery Programme, 1999), pp. 125–30, at pp. 128–9.

43   Illustration by artist David Hill, Fig. 23 in Eoin Grogan, *Mooghaun* (Dublin: The Discovery Programme, 1999).

44   These types of enclosure sites have traditionally been referred to as ring forts. More recently, archaeologists use names that more clearly define the nature of their construction: *rath* for an earthworks enclosure and *cashel* or *caher* for a stone enclosure. For an overview of early medieval enclosure sites (AD 400–1000), see O'Sullivan, McCormick, Kerr and Harney, *Early Medieval Ireland*, pp. 46–138.

45   Christopher J. Lynn, 'Reconstruction of an Eighth-Century House Based on the Evidence from Deer Park Farms', in Christopher J. Lynn and Jackie A. McDowell, *Deer Park Farms: The excavation of a raised rath in the Glenarm Valley, Co. Antrim*, Northern Ireland Archaeological Monographs 9 (Belfast: Northern Ireland Environmental Agency and The Stationery Office, 2011), pp. 594–602.

46   http://www.myucdblog.com/experimenting-with-archaeology/; Lynn and McDowell, *Deer Park Farms*; Michael Potterton (ed.), *Moynagh Lough Studies 1* (Dublin: Four Courts Press, 2025).

47   Aidan O'Sullivan and Tríona Nicholl, 'Early Medieval Settlement Enclosures in Ireland:

Dwellings, daily life, and social identity', *Proceedings of the Royal Irish Academy. Section C: Archaeology, Celtic Studies, History, Linguistics, Literature*, vol. 111C, special issue: Domestic life in Ireland, 2011, pp. 59–90, see pp. 61–3.

48   O'Sullivan and Nicholl, 'Early Medieval Settlement Enclosures', pp. 80–1.

49   Eugene Costello, *Transhumance and the Making of Ireland's Uplands, 1550–1900* (Woodbridge: Boydell & Brewer, 2020); Wes Forsythe, 'The Measure and Materiality of Improvement in Ireland', *International Journal of Historical Archaeology*, vol 17, no. 1, 2013, pp. 72–93 and 'On the Edge of Improvement: Rathlin Island and the modern world', *International Journal of Historical Archaeology*, vol. 11, no. 3, 2007, pp. 221–40; Audrey Horning, 'Materiality and Mutable Landscapes: Rethinking seasonality and marginality in rural Ireland', *International Journal of Historical Archaeology*, vol. 11, 2007, pp. 358–78 and 'Minding the Gaps: Exploring the intersection of political economy, colonial ideologies, and cultural practice in early modern Ireland', *Post-Medieval Archaeology*, vol. 52, no. 1, 2018, pp. 4–20; Audrey Horning, Colm Donnelly, Ruairí Ó Baoill and Paul Logue (eds), *The Post-Medieval Archaeology of Ireland: 1550–1850* (Bray: Wordwell, 2007); Colin Rynne, *Industrial Ireland 1750–1930: An archaeology* (Cork: The Collins Press, 2006); Rachel Tracey, 'Ulster Plantation Towns: An archaeology of rhetoric and reality', in Brendan Scott (ed.), *Society and Administration in the Ulster Plantation Towns, 1610–89* (Dublin: Four Courts Press, 2019), pp. 6–19; and David A. Whelan and Tadhg O'Keeffe, 'The House of Ussher: Histories and heritages of improvement, conspicuous consumption, and eviction on an early nineteenth-century Irish estate', *International Journal of Historical Archaeology*, vol. 18, no. 4, 2014, pp. 700–25. Historical, ethnographic and folkloric treatments of villages, housing and homes in the recent past abound. For previously uncited sources, see Jim Gilligan, *Graziers and Grasslands: Portrait of a rural Meath community 1854–1914*, Maynooth Studies in Local History, vol. 72 (Portland: Irish Academic Press, 1998); Henry Glassie, *The Stars of Ballymenone* (Bloomington, IN: Indiana University Press, 2006); Anne O'Dowd, 'Women in Rural Ireland in the Nineteenth and Early Twentieth Centuries: How the daughters, wives and sisters of small farmers and landless labourers fared', *Rural History*, vol. 5, no. 2, 1994, pp. 171–83; and Ellen Rowley, 'Housing in Ireland, 1740–2016', in Eugenio F. Biagini and Mary E. Daly (eds), *The Cambridge Social History of Modern Ireland* (Cambridge: Cambridge University Press, 2017), pp. 212–32.

50   See also Stephen A. Brighton and Andrew J. Webster, 'Of Hearth and Home: The material biography of an Irish cabin', *Post-Medieval Archaeology*, vol. 57, no. 1, 2023, pp. 125–42. Richard Clutterbuck, 'Wretched beyond Description: The excavation of a cottier's cabin in Cookstown, Co. Meath', *Seanda*, no. 1, 2006, pp. 46–7; Shannon Dunn, '"Little More than a Winter Home": An historical archaeology of Irish seasonal migration at Slievemore, Achill Island', unpublished PhD thesis, Syracuse University, 2008; Theresa McDonald, 'The Deserted Village, Slievemore, Achill Island, County Mayo, Ireland', *International Journal of Historical Archaeology*, vol. 2, no. 2, 1998, pp. 73–112; Charles E. Orser Jr, 'Three Nineteenth-Century House Sites in Rural Ireland', *Post-Medieval Archaeology*, vol. 44, no. 1, 2010, pp. 81–104 and 'Of Dishes and Drains: An archaeological perspective on Irish rural life in the

Famine era', *New Hibernia Review*, vol. 1, no. 1, 1997, pp. 120–35.

51 Tómas Ó Criomthain, *The Islander*, transl. Gary Bannister and David Sowby (Dublin: Gill & Macmillan, 2012 [1929]); Muiris Ó Súilleabháin, *Twenty Years A-Growing*, transl. Moya Llewellyn Davies and George Thompson (Oxford: Oxford University Press, 1983 [1933]); and Peig Sayers, *Peig: The autobiography of Peig Sayers of the Great Blasket Island* (Dublin: Talbot Press, 1974).

52 Glassie, *Vernacular Architecture*, p. 48.

53 See Kinmonth, *Irish Country Furniture and Furnishings* for a comprehensive and richly illustrated discussion of rural home furnishings and houses in Ireland. See also Bernard J. Cotton, 'Irish Vernacular Furniture', *Regional Furniture*, vol. 3, 1989, pp. 1–28; Alan Gailey, 'Kitchen Furniture', *Ulster Folklife*, vol. 12, 1966, pp. 18–34; Claudia Kinmonth, *Irish Rural Interiors in Art* (New Haven, CT: Yale University Press, 2006); Vera Kreilkamp (ed.), *Rural Ireland: The inside story* (Chicago: University of Chicago Press, 2012); Harold Mytum, 'Domesticity and the Dresser: An archaeological perspective from rural nineteenth-century Pembrokeshire', in James Symonds (ed.), *Table Settings: The material culture and social context of dining, AD 1700–1900* (Oxford: Oxbow, 2010), pp. 87–98; Gabriel Olive, 'Dressers in the West Country', *Regional Furniture*, vol. 3, 1989, pp. 40–51; Moira Vincentelli, 'Artefact and Identity: The Welsh dresser as domestic display and cultural symbol', in *Our Sisters' Land: The changing identity of women in Wales* (Cardiff: University of Wales Press, 1994), pp. 228–41; Jane Webster, 'Resisting Traditions: Ceramics, identity, and consumer choice in the Outer Hebrides from 1800 to present', *International Journal of Historical Archaeology*, vol. 3, no. 1, 1999, pp. 53–73.

54 Glassie, *Passing the Time*, p. 394.

55 The term 'uninhabited' indexes a crucial distinction here. While houses in these communities, even those in ruins, may not be inhabited, they are never abandoned. People own these houses and believe that these buildings simply await attention in order to become homes again.

56 See Jackson, 'Commodity Culture'.

57 Thomas J. Westropp, 'Clare Island Survey: History and archaeology', *Proceedings of the Royal Irish Academy*, vol. 31, section 2 (Dublin: Hodges, Figgis & Co., 1911), pp. 45–52

Chapter 2
Dressers, Delph and Homemaking in Western Connemara

1 Interview for film *Nets of Memory* / Líonta na Cuimhne, Ian Kuijt and William Donaruma (directors) (Walkabout Productions, 2019).

2 Rowland, 'Unbroken Stone'.

3 This section offers only a small taste of each of these communities based on my engagement with that community throughout this research project. For detailed treatments of Inishbofin and Inishark's history and heritage, please see: Concannon (ed.), *Inishbofin Through Time and Tide*; Kieran Concannon (director), *Inis Airc: Bás Oileáin* (TG4, 2007); Peter J. Corrigan, 'Memories of Inishark', in James Morrissey (ed.), *Inishbofin and Inishark,*

Connemara (Dublin: Crannóg Books, 2012), pp. 143–8; Marie Coyne, *St Colman's Abbey and Cemetery, Inishbofin* (Inishbofin: Inishbofin Development Company, 2008); Thomas W. Freeman, 'Inishbofin: An Atlantic island', *Economic Geography*, vol. 34, 1958, pp. 202–9; Michael Gibbons and Jim Higgins, 'Three Western Islands', *Archaeology Ireland*, vol. 7, no. 2, 1993, pp. 20–3; Jim Higgins and Michael Gibbons. 'Missing Artwork: A lost early Christian cross-decorated monument from Inishark (Inis Airc), Co. Galway', in Jim Higgins (ed.), *Recent Explorations and Discoveries in Irish Heritage* (Galway: Crow's Rock, 2017), pp. 70–4; Brian MacLaughlin, 'Material Concerning the Surviving Antiquities of Inish Airc (Inishark)', National Folklore Collection, University College Dublin, vol. 839, 1942; James Morrissey (ed.), *Inishbofin and Inishark, Connemara* (Dublin: Crannóg Books, 2012); Michael O'Connell and Edel Ní Ghráinne, with contributions by Michael Gibbons, 'Inishbofin: Palaeoecology', in Peter Coxon and Michael O'Connell (eds), *Clare Island and Inishbofin, Field Guide No. 17* (Dublin: Irish Association for Quaternary Studies, 1994), pp. 61–101; Paul Walsh, 'Cromwell's Barrack: A Commonwealth garrison fort on Inishbofin, Co. Galway', *Journal of the Galway Archaeological and Historical Society*, vol. 42, 1989, pp. 30–71. For a history of Clifden, see Kathleen Villiers-Tuthill, *Beyond the Twelve Bens: A history of Clifden and district 1860–1923* (Athlone: Connemara Girl Publications, 1997) and *A Colony of Strangers: The founding and early history of Clifden* (Athlone: Connemara Girl Publications, 2012). For more regional treatments of western Connemara, including Cashel, see Robinson's Connemara trilogy: *Listening to the Wind, The Last Pool of Darkness* and *A Little Gaelic Kingdom*.

4   Beyond the references cited above, see also Nathan Goodale, Madeleine Bassett, David G. Bailey, Ryan Lash and Ian Kuijt, 'Early Medieval Seascapes in Western Ireland and the Geochemistry of Ecclesiastical Cross Stones', *Journal of Archaeological Science: Reports*, vol. 19, June 2018, pp. 894–902; Ian Kuijt, Ryan Lash, William Donaruma, Katie Shakour and Tommy Burke, *Island Places, Island Lives: Exploring Inishbofin and Inishark heritage, Co. Galway, Ireland* (Bray: Wordwell, 2015); Colin P. Quinn, Ian Kuijt, Nathan Goodale and John Ó Néill, 'Along the Margins? The later Bronze Age seascapes of western Ireland', *European Journal of Archaeology*, vol. 22, no. 1, 2019, pp. 44–66; Katherine E. Shakour, 'From Colonial Legacy to Difficult Heritage: Responding to and remembering *An Gorta Mór*, Ireland's Great Hunger', unpublished PhD thesis, University of South Florida, 2020.

5   Ryan Lash, 'Enchantments of Stone: Confronting other-than-human agency in Irish pilgrimage practices', *Journal of Social Archaeology*, vol. 18, no. 3, 2018, pp. 284–305; 'Pebbles and *Peregrinatio*: The taskscape of medieval devotion on Inishark Island, Ireland', *Medieval Archaeology*, vol. 62, no. 1, 2018, pp. 83–104; 'Island Taskscapes: Heritage, ritual, and sustainability of Inishark and Inishbofin, Ireland', unpublished PhD thesis, Department of Anthropology, Northwestern University, 2019; and *Island Endurance: Creative heritage on Inishark and Inishbofin* (Indianapolis: Indiana University Press, 2025); Ryan Lash, Ian Kuijt, Elise Alonzi, Meredith S. Chesson and Tommy Burke, '"Differing in Status, but One in Spirit": Sacred space and social diversity at island monasteries in Connemara, Ireland', *Antiquity*, vol. 92, no. 362, 2018, pp. 437–55.

6   The word *turas* means 'journey' or 'pilgrimage' and is associated with processions and rituals practised at stations (like medieval shrines) on saints' feasts days in Ireland. Lash,

'Enchantments of Stone'; Lash et al., '"Differing in Status, but One in Spirit"'; Ryan Lash, Meredith S. Chesson, Elise Alonzi, Ian Kuijt, Terry O'Hagan, John Ó Néill and Tommy Burke, 'Sensational Ensembles: Picnicking and pilgrimage on Inishark island, Co. Galway, Ireland 1650–1960', *Current Anthropology*, vol. 64, no. 4, 2023, pp. 380–409.

7   Concannon, *Inishbofin Through Time and Tide*; Walsh 'Cromwell's Barrack'.

8   The 2022 census listed Inishbofin's residents as numbering 184 people: https://data.cso.ie/.

9   Ian Kuijt, Meagan Conway, Katie Shakour, Casey McNeill and Claire Brown, 'Vectors of Improvement: The material footprint of nineteenth- through twentieth-century Irish national policy, Inishark, County Galway, Ireland', *International Journal of Historical Archaeology*, vol. 19, no. 1, 2015, pp. 122–58, see p. 133.

10 Ibid.; Wes Forsythe, 'The Measure and Materiality of Improvement' and 'On the Edge of Improvement'.

11 *Irish Times*, 'Relief for Innishboffin', 27 March 1886.

12 Fred H. Aalen, 'Public Housing in Ireland, 1880–1921', *Planning Perspectives*, vol. 2, 1987, pp. 175–93; Seán Beattie, *Donegal in Transition: The impact of the Congested Districts Board* (Newbridge: Irish Academic Press, 2013); John Crowley, William Smyth and Mike Murphy, *Atlas of the Great Irish Famine* (Cork: Cork University Press, 2012); Timothy W. Guinnane and Ronald I. Miller, 'The Limits to Land Reform: The Land Acts in Ireland, 1870–1909', *Economic Development and Culture Change*, vol. 45, no. 3, 1997, pp. 591–612; John P. Huttman, 'The Impact of Land Reform on Agricultural Production in Ireland', *Agricultural History*, vol. 46, no. 3, 1972, pp. 353–68; *Irish Times*, 'Relief for Innishboffin'; William L. Micks, *An Account of the Constitution, Administration and Dissolution of the Congested Districts Board for Ireland from 1891 to 1923* (Dublin: Eason & Son, 1925); Robert Ruttledge-Fair, 'Annual Report of the Congested Districts Board for the Clifden and Carna Regions', published in James Morrissey (ed.), *On the Verge of Want: A unique insight into living conditions along Ireland's western seaboard in the late nineteenth century* (Dublin: Crannóg Books, 2001).

13 Kuijt et al., 'Vectors of Improvement', p. 126.

14 For other recent publications by the CLIC team, see Nicholas Ames, 'Traversing the Hearth: Navigating the structures of nineteenth century Irish migrations', unpublished PhD thesis, University of Notre Dame, 2021; Meagan Conway, 'A Choice to Engage: Selective marginality and dynamic households on the eighteenth- to nineteenth-century Irish coast', unpublished PhD thesis, University of South Carolina, 2019; Lauren Couey, 'A Shifting Island Landscape: Changes in land use and daily life in the nineteenth- and twentieth-century village of Inishark, Co. Galway, Ireland', unpublished MA thesis, University of Denver, 2018; Ian Kuijt, Meredith S. Chesson, Sara Morrow, Diarmuid Ó Giolláin and Ryan Lash, 'Dying the Good Death and Materialized Mourning: Nineteenth and twentieth century coastal Ireland', *International Journal of Historic Archaeology*, vol. 25, 2021, pp. 333–74; Lash et al., 'Sensational Ensembles'; Franc Myles, 'In Small Things Remembered: The sponge decorated ceramics from Inishark, Galway. With apologies to Jim Deetz', blogpost, 28 June 2013, https://wastedonarchaeology.wordpress.com/2013/06/28/in-small-things-remembered-the-sponge-decorated-ceramics-from-inishark-galway/; and Katherine Shakour, Ian Kuijt and Tommy Burke, 'Different Roles, Diverse Goals: Understanding

stakeholder and archaeologists positions in community-based projects', *Archaeologies*, vol. 15, no. 3, 2019, pp. 372–99.

15 Concannon, *Inishbofin Through Time and Tide*; Conway, 'A Choice to Engage'; Couey, 'A Shifting Island Landscape'; Coyne, *St Colman's*; Higgins and Gibbons, 'Missing Artwork'; Gibbons and Higgins, 'Three Western Islands'; Goodale et al., 'Early Medieval Seascapes'; Kuijt et al., 'Vectors of Improvement'; Kuijt et al., 'Dying the Good Death'; Kuijt et al., *Island Places, Island Lives*; Lash, *Island Endurance*, 'Enchantments of Stone', 'Pebbles and Peregrenatio'; Lash et al., '"Differing in Spirit"'; Lash et al., 'Sensational Ensembles'; Quinn et al., 'Along the Margins?'; Shakour, 'From Colonial Legacy to Difficult Heritage'.

16 Concannon, *Bás Oileáin*.

17 Priest on Inishbofin 1884–6, http://www.stcolmans-inishbofin.ie/; and Inishbofin parish records in National Library of Ireland (available through Ancestry.com).

18 Charles R. Browne, in 'The Ethnography of Inishbofin and Inishshark, County Galway', *Proceedings of the Royal Irish Academy (1889–1901)*, vol. 3, 1893, pp. 317–70, recounts a brief explanation of the position from Myles Joyce, at that time the national school teacher for Inishbofin: 'The title of king is not hereditary in the island. There is at present a man removed something beyond his neighbours in the way of education and position, who is, *par excellence*, the king; and to whom all persons who want any information about the island or its history must apply' (p. 350). For a more extensive discussion of the position of king on Inishark, see Lash, 'Island Taskscapes', pp. 341–2.

19 In studying the 1901 and 1911 census records for Inishark, we found that it was common for many of the older men and women of the village to be described as 'cannot read or write' by the census takers. Some of the names of the signatories of this letter appear in the 1901 records, and of those, several are characterised as illiterate. However, many other men and women of the same generation are listed as being able to read and write, so it is clear that this skill was learned by many growing up in the late nineteenth century on Inishark. Historians and historical archaeologists have learned that census records abound with inaccuracies, particularly in descriptions of an individual's age, name spelling, occupation and education. For example, listed ages on Inishark, Inishbofin and Inishturk's 1901 and 1911 census records can vary widely, with someone ageing only three years over a ten-year interval or as many as twenty years. In her study of African American midwife Lucretia Perryman, Laurie Wilkie argues that discrepancies in census records may have emerged from people representing themselves in a way to benefit themselves – they worked the system to gain stature and status in whatever way fit their personal context and situation: Wilkie, *Archaeology of Mothering*, p. 124.

20 Kuijt et al., 'Vectors of Improvement', p. 153.

21 Concannon, *Inishbofin Through Time and Tide*; Concannon, *Bás Oileáin*.

22 Concannon, *Bás Oileáin*.

23 Westropp, 'Clare Island Survey: History and archaeology', pp. 50–1; Charles R. Browne, 'The Ethnography of Clare Island and Inishturk, Co. Mayo', *Proceedings of the Royal Irish Academy*, vol. 5, 1898–1900, pp. 40–72.

24 Kathleen Villiers-Tuthill, *Alexander Nimmo and the Western District* (Athlone: Connemara Girl Publications, 2006); see also https://www.con-telegraph.ie/2024/01/06/local-history–

1823-report-on-proposed-harbour-on-mayos-inishturk/.

25   Concannon, *Inishbofin Through Time and Tide*, pp. 63–4.

26   Ivor Hamrock, 'The Famine in Mayo 1845–1850', https://www.mayo.ie/library/local-history/historical-events/the-great-famine; https://www.mayo.ie/getmedia/f7ba7bd8-7354-4353-8877-30d0e3dac099/The-Famine-in-Mayo-1845-1850-Mayo-County-Library-Exhibition2.pdf.

27   Originally published as a series of letters in *The Times*, they were eventually collated and published in a monograph: Finlay Dun, *Landlords and Tenants in Ireland* (London: Longmans, Green & Co., 1881).

28   Alexander Turner, 'TurkFest: Ireland's little festival with a big heart – a photo essay', *The Guardian*, 21 August 2019, https://www.theguardian.com/travel/2019/aug/21/inishturk-turkfest-ireland-festival-photo-essay.

29   Villiers-Tuthill, *A Colony of Strangers*.

30   Claudia Kinmonth, 'Irish Vernacular Furniture: Inventories and illustrations in interdisciplinary methodology,' *Regional Furniture*, vol. 10, 1996, pp. 1–26.

31   Jackson, 'Commodity Cultures', p. 104.

32   This approach falls under the umbrella of engaged anthropology, sometimes called community-based participatory research. See Sonya Atalay, *Community-Based Archaeology: Research with, by, and for indigenous and local communities* (Berkeley, CA: University of California Press, 2012) and 'Can Archaeology Help Decolonize the Way Institutions Think? How community-based research is transforming the archaeology training toolbox and helping to transform institutions', *Archaeologies*, vol. 15, no. 3, 2019, pp. 514–35; Sonya Atalay and Alexandra McCleary, *The Community-Based PhD: Complexities and triumphs of conducting CBPR* (Tucson, AZ: The University of Arizona Press, 2022); Jeff Oliver, Jackson Armstrong, Elizabeth Curtis, Neil Curtis and Jo Vergunst, 'Exploring Co-production in Community Heritage Research: Reflections from the Bennachie Landscapes Project', *Journal of Community Archaeology & Heritage*, vol. 9, no. 3, 2022, pp. 196–215; Uzma Rizvi, 'Community-based and Participatory Praxis as Decolonizing Archaeological Methods and the Betrayal of New Research', in Kisha Supernant, Jane Baxter, Natasha Lyons and Sonya Atalay (eds), *Archaeologies of the Heart* (New York: Springer Publishing, 2020), pp. 83–96.

33   All academic disciplines grow and change, and anthropology is no exception. For example, ethnographers working more recently offer perspectives on how ethnography in Ireland was transforming itself to grow beyond its foundation: Thomas M. Wilson, 'From Clare to the Common Market: Perspectives of Irish ethnography', *Anthropological Quarterly*, vol. 57, no. 1, 1984, pp. 1–15; Thomas M. Wilson (ed.), *The Anthropology of Ireland* (Oxford: Berg Publishers, 2006); and Bridget Edwards, 'How the West Was Wondered: County Clare and directions in Irish ethnography', *Folklore Forum*, vol. 27, no. 2, 1996, pp. 65–78. Like many other scholars, I found some of the most troubling studies to be by Conrad M. Arensberg, *The Irish Countryman: An anthropological study* (London: Macmillan & Co., 1937); Conrad M. Arensberg and Solon T. Kimball, *Family and Community in Ireland*, 2nd edn (Cambridge, MA: Harvard University Press, 1968); Hugh Brody, *Inishkillane: Change and decline in the west of Ireland* (Harmondsworth: Penguin, 1973); Browne, 'The Ethnography of Inishbofin and Inishshark'; John C. Messenger, *Inis Beag: Isle of Ireland* (New York: Holt, Rinehart & Winston, 1969); John C. Messenger, *Inis Beag*

Revisited: The anthropologist as observant participator (Salem, WI: Salem Publishing, 1983); and Nancy Scheper-Hughes, *Saints, Scholars and Schizophrenics: Mental illness in rural Ireland* (Berkeley, CA: University of California Press, 1979).

34   Michael Viney, 'The Yank in the Corner: Why the ethics of anthropology are a worry for rural Ireland', *Irish Times*, 6 August 1983, p. 9. For an overview of the history of folklore and ethnography in Ireland, see Diarmuid Ó Giolláin, *Locating Irish Folklore* and *Exotic Dreams in the Science of the Volksgeist: Towards a global history of European folklore stories* (Helsinki: The Kalevala Society, 2022).

35   Henry Glassie is an excellent example of an ethnographer who consistently interacts with participants in a respectful, honourable and ethical manner: see his *Passing the Time* and *The Stars of Ballymenone*. Other recent ethnographies that demonstrate how the discipline has changed include Claire J. Brown, 'A Pony World – Hoofed Commodities: Breeding capital and culture through human–horse relations in the west of Ireland', unpublished PhD thesis, Binghamton University, State University of New York, 2019; and Adam Kaul, *Turning the Tune: Traditional music, tourism, and social change in an Irish village* (New York: Berghahn Books, 2012).

36   For more information about the Belmont Principles, see https://www.hhs.gov/ohrp/regulations-and-policy/belmont-report/index.html.

37   I delved into the 1901 and 1911 Inishbofin, Inishark and Inishturk censuses, nineteenth- and twentieth-century valuation records, and late nineteenth-century Inishbofin parish records for names to use as pseudonyms for the project's participants who wished to remain anonymous. The reader will note that as a rule no participants were photographed facing the camera for this research, nor were the outsides of their homes, which might be easily recognisable. I acknowledge that despite my best efforts to use pseudonyms and photographs without people's faces and homes, local community members will easily be able to identify themselves and their neighbours through photographs and descriptions of dressers and delph.

38   We did not record the wood(s) used to make dressers because we could not systematically document this information for all twenty-one dressers. Most were heavily painted, and their owners themselves did not know what wood was used. Similarly, the composition of the paints, stains and varnishes were unknown to all but the one dresser-maker we interviewed, and he only knew the details because he had built two of the documented dressers.

39   Anthropologists call this method of gathering participants for research 'snowball sampling'.

40   Clifford Geertz, 'Deep Hanging Out', *New York Times Review of Books*, 22 October 1998, pp. 69–72.

41   Vessel form identifications: (A) Julia's Poppy pattern platter; (B) Julia's transfer-printed plate; (C) Honor's and Thomas' spongeware jug; (D) Anne's chinoiserie small bowl; (E) Catherine's Lowestoft Border pattern teacup and saucer; (F) Celia's banded milk jug; (G) Michael's banded mug; (H) Patrick's Argyle pattern tureen; (I) Doonmore Hotel's Rockingham Ware teapot; (J) Patrick's small stoneware jar; (K) Sarah's black-glazed redware crock basin or bowl, approximately 45 cm tall.

42   After completing the initial analysis of the archaeological assemblage, I added eggcups to

this list, though their numbers were very low. Unfortunately, I do not have an appropriate photograph of a complete eggcup from the archaeological or ethnographic assemblages, and combined with such low numbers, have not included the category in Figure 2.21.

43   While I photographed and noted features of dressers in museums and heritage centres, like the Inishbofin Heritage Museum & Gift Shop, I did not record counts of vessels and vessel types on these dressers and delph collections since they had been removed from their original contexts.

44   The results of post-medieval archaeological research on Inishark will be detailed in Chapter 4.

45   The term 'descendant community' was first coined in the 1990s by biological anthropologist Dr Michael Blakey. He led a research term investigating the lives of enslaved Africans and African Americans in seventeenth- and eighteenth-century New York City after a large cemetery had been uncovered during the construction of a governmental building in Manhattan. For excellent overviews of that project, see Michael L. Blakey, 'African Burial Project: Paradigm for cooperation?', *Museum International*, vol. 62, nos 1–2, 2010), pp. 61–8, and his recent article 'Under the Blinding Light of Race', *Current Anthropology*, *vol.* 61, supplement 22, 2020, pp. S183–97; see also the project's public volume *The New York African Burial Ground: Unearthing the African presence in colonial New York*, vol. 5 (Washington, DC: Howard University Press, 2009).

46   For a history of the Ordnance Survey, see Stiofán Ó Cadhla, *Civilising Ireland – Ordnance Survey 1824–1842: Ethnography, cartography, translation* (Dublin: Irish Academic Press, 2007).

47   Francis McGee, *The Archives of the Valuation of Ireland, 1830–1865* (Dublin: Four Courts Press, 2018).

48   Additionally, the surnames of people often were recorded with different spellings for the same person and over generations (Murry/Murray, Lacy/Lacey, Halloran/Holleran, Hildebrand/Hildebrande, and Magreal/MacGreal/McGreal/McGrail/McGreale), a practice that adds to the complexity.

49   http://www.census.nationalarchives.ie/search/.

50   For a more global perspective on public-facing archaeological research, see recent case studies from Irish archaeology (Audrey Horning, 'Collaborators and Conflict: Archaeology and peacebuilding in Northern Ireland', *Archaeologies*, vol. 15, no. 3, 2019, pp. 444–65; Shakour et al., 'Different Roles, Diverse Goals'), Canada (Laura Kelvin, Emma Gilheany, Nicholas Flowers, Denver Edmunds, Mackenzie Frieda, Claire Igloliorte, Halle Lucy and John Piercy, 'Strength-Based Approaches to Involving Inuit Youth in Archaeological Research', *Canadian Journal of Archaeology*, vol. 44, 2020, pp. 83–104; Schaepe et al., 'Archaeology as Therapy'), Israel (Raphael Greenberg, 'Wedded to Privilege? Archaeology, academic capital, and critical public engagement', *Archaeologies*, vol. 15, no. 3, 2019, pp. 481–95), Italy (Meredith S. Chesson, Isaac I.T. Ullah, Giovanni Iiriti, Hamish Forbes, Paula K. Lazrus, Nicholas Ames, Yesenia Garcia, Sarah Benchekroun, John Robb, Nicholas P.S. Wolff and Maria Olimpia Squillaci, 'Archaeology as Intellectual Service: Engaged archaeology in San Pasquale Valley, Calabria, Italy', *Archaeologies*, vol. 15, no. 3, 2019, pp. 422–43), the Philippines (Stephen Acabado and Marlon Martin, 'Decolonizing the Past,

Empowering the Future: Community-led heritage conservation in Ifugao, Philippines', *Journal of Community Archaeology & Heritage*, vol. 7, no. 3, 2020, pp. 171–86), the United States (Atalay, 'Can Archaeology Help Decolonize the Way Institutions Think?'; Bonnie J. Clark, 'Collaborative Archaeology as Heritage Process', *Archaeologies*, vol. 15, no. 3, 2019, pp. 466–80; Alexandra Jones, 'Archaeology for a New Generation: Exploring education and intersectionality', *Archaeologies: Journal of the World Archaeological Congress*, vol. 18, no. 1, 2022, pp. 287–309; Stephen A. Mrozowski and D. Rae Gould, 'Building Histories That Have Futures: The benefits of collaborative research', *Archaeologies*, vol. 15, no. 3, 2019, pp. 400–21; Katherine Sebastian Dring, Stephen W. Silliman, Nathasha Gambrell, Shianne Sebastian and Ralph Sebastian Sidberry, 'Authoring and Authority in Eastern Pequot Community Heritage and Archaeology', *Archaeologies*, vol. 15, no. 3, 2019, pp. 352–70), Zimbabwe (Innocent Pikirayi, Plan Shenjere-Nyabezi and Munyaradzi Elton Sagiya, 'Landscape, History and Power: The Zimbabwe culture and the Nambya state, northwestern Zimbabwe', *Journal of Community Archaeology & Heritage*, vol. 9, no. 3, 2022, pp. 175–9), and a synthetic discussion by Alison Wylie, 'Crossing a Threshold: Collaborative Archaeology in Global Dialogue', *Archaeologies*, vol. 15, no. 3, 2019, pp. 570–87.

Chapter 3
'Round the house and mind the dresser': The lives of dressers

1   https://www.merriam-webster.com/dictionary/vernacular for a general definition geared towards language; for architecture, see Glassie, *Vernacular Architecture* and Cotton, 'Irish Vernacular Furniture'.
2   Cotton, 'Irish Vernacular Furniture', pp. 2–3.
3   Ryan Lash alerted me to two recently composed reels with the very same name of 'Around the House and Mind the Dresser', recorded in 2005 by Danú on *When All Is Said and Done* (Shanachie, 2005) and in 2004 by The Dunne Family on *Legacy* (The Dunne Family, 2004); see also https://www.irishtune.info/tune/4561/.
4   Glassie, *Passing the Time in Ballymenone*, p. 364.
5   Rachael Ritchie, 'Arklow Back Stamps', unpublished manuscript provided by the author, 2024.
6   Steve Birks manages an extraordinary website that provides historical information on major potteries that operated in Stoke-on-Trent: http://thepotteries.org/index.html. I identified many of the marks identified in this study by using this resource: http://thepotteries.org/mark/b/ABC.html.
7   Kinmonth, *Irish Country Furniture and Furnishings*. In the Dresser Project study, glass-fronted dressers generally dated from the 1960s onwards; for a similarly later date, see Dabeo Rynne, 'Furniture Making in County Clare: The O'Halloran Brothers', *Regional Furniture*, vol. 8, 1994, pp. 87–9.
8   Arnold A. Kowalsky and Dorothy E. Kowalsky, *Encyclopedia of Marks: On American, English, and European earthenware, ironstone, and stoneware, 1780–1980* (Atglen, PA: Schiffer Publishing, 1990), p. 155 (mark B595); Geoffrey A. Godden, *Encyclopaedia of British Pottery*

and Porcelain Marks (New York: Crown Publishers, 1964), p. 157 (mark 965).

9   Kowalsky and Kowalsky, *Encyclopedia of Marks*, p. 284 (mark B1692); Godden, *Encyclopaedia of British Pottery and Porcelain Marks*, p. 433 (mark 2651).

10   See Dunn, '"Little More than a Winter Home"'; Myles, 'In Small Things Remembered'; Anne O'Dowd, *Spalpeens and Tattie Hokers: History and folklore of the Irish migratory agricultural worker in Ireland and Britain* (Blackrock, County Dublin: Irish Academic Press, 1991); Cormac Ó Gráda, 'Seasonal Migration and Post-Famine Adjustment in the West of Ireland', *Studia Hibernia*, no. 13, 1973, pp. 48–76; Peadar O'Donnell, 'Achill, Arranmore and Kirkintilloch, Dealing with the Question of Migratory Labourers', *Ireland To-day*, vol. 2, no. 10, 1937, pp. 45–50.

11   http://www.thepotteries.org/allpotters/888.htm.

12   Godden, *Encyclopaedia*, p. 640 (mark 3964).

13   Kowalsky and Kowalsky, *Encyclopedia of Marks*, p. 246 (mark B1369).

14   Kirshenblatt-Gimlet, 'Authoring Lives'.

15   Glassie, *Passing the Time*, p. 369.

16   Cotton, 'Irish Vernacular Furniture', p. 7.

17   Concannon's compilation of folklore, history and ethnography for Inishbofin offers a short description of boatwrights, who were often also carpenters who made dressers, tables, chairs, wardrobes and other pieces of furniture for Inishbofin homes: Concannon (ed.), *Inishbofin Through Time and Tide*, pp. 111–12.

18   Formally known as the Galway-Mayo Institute of Technology.

19   While fewer people learn the craft of furniture making, the Letterfrack campus of the Atlantic Technological University (https://cc.careersportal.ie/colleges/college.php?client_id=183&college_id=79) hosts a well-respected programme in furniture design and technology.

20   Roughly a third of the dresser-keepers in this calendar are men; see Michael Fortune's *The Irish Dresser – 2021 Calendar* (https://thedresserproject.ie), with a foreword 'Behind the Dresser Door'. Produced in collaboration with the Folklore Department of University College Cork, the National Museum of Ireland – Country Life and https://www.facebook.com/folklore.ie, a Facebook page managed by Fortune.

21   Pauline Garvey, *Unpacking Ikea: Swedish design for the purchasing masses* (London: Routledge, 2018).

22   The National Archives of Britain offers a helpful web page detailing how to read registration marks: https://www.nationalarchives.gov.uk/help-with-your-research/research-guides/registered-designs-1839-1991/#appendix-1-diamond-mark-month-codes.

23   For an enlightening discussion of how we understand the idea of 'use' that expands beyond the simple functional definition, see Sara Ahmed's recent book which explores the history of how people attached the notion of usefulness to happiness and wellbeing: Sara Ahmed, *What's the Use? On the uses of use* (Durham, NC: Duke University Press, 2019).

24   Kinmonth, *Irish Country Furniture*, pp. 179–239.

25   We recorded a total of 1,232 vessels on 21 dressers but have excluded the single gravy boat on the Doonmore dresser from the analysis because it is unique and has no comparative examples in the ethnographic or archaeological vessel assemblages.

26 Eggcups were interesting because they appeared in ceramic, glass and metal forms on three dressers. Most of the vessels in dressers and delph appear only as ceramic pieces. This study only includes the small number of ceramic examples found on Penelope's dresser.

27 Dresden: Kowalsky and Kowalsky, *Encyclopedia of Marks*, p. 259 (mark B1464B); Flow blue: Kowalsky and Kowalsky, *Encyclopedia of Marks*, p. 289 (mark B1751).

28 Sadler Kleen Kitchen: Godden, *Encyclopaedia*, p. 560 (mark 3437).

29 Godden, *Encyclopaedia*, p. 125 (mark 760); Kowalsky and Kowalsky, *Encyclopedia of Marks*, p. 138 (mark B451).

30 Godden, *Encyclopaedia*, pp. 85–7; http://www.thepotteries.org/allpotters/137.htm.

31 Glassie, *Passing the Time in Ballymenone*, pp. 363–4.

32 Golden Amber set: Godden, *Encyclopaedia*, pp. 538–9; http://www.thepotteries.org/allpotters/854a.htm; Celia's platter: Kowalsky and Kowalsky, *Encyclopedia of Marks*, p. 295 (mark B1811); Michael's hand-painted plate: http://thepotteries.org/allpotters/753a.htm; Bedelia's Arklow jugs: Dating from Rachael Ritchie, personal communication and https://arklowpottery.ie/arklow-back-stamps/; Celia's Cottageware teapot: Godden, *Encyclopaedia*, p. 514 (mark 3164); Doonmore Hotel blue Willow plate: Rachael Ritchie, personal communication, 2023.

33 See Rebecca Leach's article about people's relationships with ceramic delph: 'The Turnover Club: Locality and identity in the practice of turning over ceramic ware', *International Journal of Heritage Studies*, vol. 22, no. 6, 2016, pp. 482–94.

34 Michael's lovely old dresser was located in an outshot kitchen, but the vast majority of delph in this room was located in the sink or on counters. It was not clear which vessels belonged on the dresser, in the press, on the hanging dressers or elsewhere in the house, and therefore I excluded it from this part of the analysis.

35 Jean Lave and Etienne Wenger, *Situated Learning: Legitimate peripheral participation* (Cambridge: Cambridge University Press, 1991); Jean Lave, *Apprenticeship in Critical Ethnographic Practice* (Chicago: University of Chicago Press, 2011).

Chapter 4
Homemaking on Inishark: Enduring houses, delph and everyday life, *c.* 1780–1960

1 Ian Kuijt directed excavations on Inishark and leads the CLIC team; thus, I have asked him to be a co-author of this chapter, along with Meagan McDonald, Katherine Shakour, Nicholas Ames, Tommy Burke and Rachel Tracey, all of whom contributed enormously to the excavation and analysis of historic houses on Inishark and their contents, particularly Houses 8, 28, 57 and 78. Archaeology is a team endeavour, and the evidence I present here has been gathered, analysed and interpreted by a group of team members, including (in alphabetical order) Elise Alonzi, Catriona Baldwin, Jillian Brems, Claire Brown, Eugene Costello, Lauren Couey, William Donaruma, Nathan Goodale, Larry Lane, Ryan Lash, Philip Lettieri, Alessandro Martellaro, Linda Martellaro, Sara Morrow, Franc Myles, Alyssa Naumann, Terry O'Hagen, John Ó Néill, Colin Quinn, Casey Seal, Rachel Tracey, and a

talented group of volunteer staff members who participated as field school students over the years.

2   Rich, 'Natural Resources'.

3   Publications of the CLIC team's post-medieval research include: Ames, 'Navigating the Hearth'; Conway, 'A Choice to Engage'; Couey, 'A Shifting Island Landscape'; Kuijt and Donaruma, *Nets of Memory*; Kuijt et al., 'Vectors of Improvement'; Kuijt et al., 'Dying the Good Death'; Kuijt et al., *Island Places, Island Lives*; Kuijt et al., 'Vectors of Improvement'; Lash, *Island Endurance*; Lash et al., 'Sensational Ensembles'; Shakour, 'From Colonial Legacy to Difficult Heritage'.

4   Reconstructable vessels are those that are partially or even nearly complete, and therefore archaeologists are more easily able to identify their form, decoration and functions.

5   Colum, 'The Fire Bringer'.

6   Gailey, *Rural Houses of the North of Ireland*, pp. 142–8; Ó Danachair, 'The Combined Byre-and-Dwelling in Ireland' and 'Traditional Forms of the Dwelling House in Ireland'; and O'Reilly, 'Hearth and Home'.

7   Audrey Horning, personal communication, 2021.

8   See https://nationalarchives.ie/help-with-research/research-guides/valuation-office-records/.

9   Gailey, *Rural Houses of the North of Ireland*, pp. 229–32.

10   Ibid., p. 7.

11   Ibid., pp. 140–71; Ó Danachair, 'The Combined Byre-and-Dwelling in Ireland'; Symmons and Harkin, *The Disappearing Irish Cottage*.

12   Gailey, *Rural Houses of the North of Ireland*, pp. 211–17; Danaher, *The Hearth and Stool and All!*, pp. 34–45; Ó Danachair, 'The Combined Byre-and-Dwelling in Ireland'.

13   Glassie, *Passing the Time*, p. 342.

14   Kinmonth, *Irish Country Furniture*, pp. 1–51, offers a thorough overview of furnishing rural homes in Ireland.

15   Browne, 'The Ethnography of Inishbofin and Inishshark, County Galway', p. 355.

16   Danaher, *The Hearth and Stool and All!*, p. 72; Gailey, *Rural Houses of the North of Ireland*, pp. 62–5.

17   Browne, 'The Ethnography of Inishbofin and Inishshark, County Galway', p. 355.

18   For comparative examples, see Gailey, *Rural Houses of the North of Ireland*, pp. 142–51.

19   Many Hallorans (and Hollerans) are listed as head-of-household for this plot and home until 1904, after which the Coursey family takes residence sometime before the 1910 valuation survey and the 1911 census.

20   Gailey, *Rural Houses of the North of Ireland*, pp. 100–3.

21   Ibid., 94–106.

22   Ibid., pp. 259: Gailey defines a scraw as the 'turf under thatch on a roof'.

23   Ibid. Gailey defines a scollop as a 'rod of hazel, osier, briar, or other pliable wood, sharpened at both ends, for pinning down thatch material to the scraw in thatching a roof'.

24   Anne O'Dowd, *Straw, Hay, and Rushes in Irish Folk Tradition* (Dublin: Irish Academic Press and National Museum of Ireland, 2015), p. 415. She notes that rye was grown for thatch in the west, while wheat, flax and oat straws were grown in other areas, with the specific crop changing according to shifts in local economies.

25 Gailey, *Rural Houses of the North of Ireland*, pp. 125–7.

26 Colum, 'An Old Woman of the Roads', in *Wild Earth* (Dublin: Maunsel & Co., 1907), pp. 7–8.

27 Compare Kinmonth, *Irish Country Furniture*, pp. 397–408 to Danaher, *The Hearth and Stool and All!*, p. 39. Danaher describes 'clevvies' as hanging dressers, differing from Kinmonth, and perhaps conflating clevy racks over the mantelpieces with hanging dressers or freestanding dressers with slots to place spits instead of plate rails.

28 'Browne, 'The Ethnography of Inishbofin and Inishshark'; for a general overview see Gailey, *Rural Houses of the North of Ireland*, pp. 114–22.

29 Kuijt et al., 'Vectors of Improvement', pp. 146–7.

30 Browne, 'The Ethnography of Inishbofin and Inishshark', p. 355.

31 Conway, 'A Choice to Engage', pp. 289–309.

32 Tok Thompson, '*Clocha Geala/Clocha Uaisle*: White quartz in Irish tradition', *Béaloideas*, vol. 73, 2005, pp. 111–33.

33 Lash, 'Pebbles and *Peregrinatio*'.

34 Lash, 'Island Taskscapes'; for a specific example of how Inishark islanders cultivated connections with their heritage sites, see Lash, *Island Endurance*, and Lash et al., 'Sensational Ensembles'.

35 Interview with Jane and Anthony, 22 June 2009 on Inishark, County Galway.

36 In Kieran Concannon's film *Bás Oileáin*, Martin Murray noted that the ground in Fountainhill to where they were moved had very poor land. His father wanted to establish a garden to sow potatoes but could find no land: everything was rock. Murray said that it broke his father's heart.

37 Ibid.

38 Interview with Jane and Anthony, 22 June 2009 on Inishark, County Galway.

39 Concannon, *Bás Oileáin*.

40 Conversation with Inishark descendant Kate (2019, personal communication).

41 Angela Bourke offers a cogent discussion of how many of these rural interior paintings were created. She notes that painters would travel to rural villages and pay local inhabitants to pose for these paintings in their homes during a time when many were struggling to feed families and avoid eviction from those homes: Angela Bourke, 'Inner Lives: Creativity and survival in Irish rural life', in Vera Kreilkamp (ed.), *Rural Ireland: The inside story* (produced by McMullen Museum of Art, Boston College; Chicago: University of Chicago Press, 2012), pp. 41–6.

42 For approaches to MNV calculations, see Clive Orton, Paul Tyers and Alan Vince, *Pottery in Archaeology (Cambridge Manuals in Archaeology)* (Cambridge: Cambridge University Press, 1993); Barbara L. Voss and Rebecca Allen, 'Guide to Ceramic MNV Calculation: Qualitative and quantitative analysis', Society for Historical Archaeology, *Technical Briefs in Historical Archaeology*, vol. 5, 2010, pp. 1–99.

43 Godden, *Encyclopaedia*, p. 452 (mark 2787).

44 Chris Jarrett, Morag Cross and Alistair Robertson, 'Containers and Teapots', in Alasdair Brooks (ed.), *The Importance of British Material Culture to Historical Archaeologies of the Nineteenth Century* (Lincoln, NE: University of Nevada Press; London: Society for

Historical Archaeology, 2015), pp. 69–106.

45 Dating based on the comment by Jeremy Kemp on 27 August 2017 on the website https://glassbottlemarks.com/bottlemarks-3/: 'The FVF mark is actually FMF, and stands for Food Manufacturers Federation. Established (I think) around 1913, it changed it's [*sic*] name to the Food and Drink Federation in the 1960s. The mark turns up commonly on the bases of both glass and stoneware jars, especially around the 1920s – 40s.'

46 Concannon, *Inishbofin Through Time and Tide*, p. 103.

47 See these websites for information on this product and company: https://www.gracesguide.co.uk/Elliman,SonsandCo; http://www.sloughhistoryonline.org.uk/assetarena/text/pdf/sl/sl/sl-sl-web2729elliman-d-00-000.pdf; https://mhc.andornot.com/en/permalink/artefact8188.

48 Historical archaeologists have discussed the use of soda water in medicinal capacities, including: Michael C. Bonasera and Leslie Raymer, 'Good for What Ails You: Medicinal use at five points', *Historical Archaeology*, vol. 35, no. 3, 2001, pp. 49–66; Meredith B. Linn, 'Irish Immigrant Healing Magic in Nineteenth-Century New York City', *Historical Archaeology*, vol. 48, no. 3, 2014, pp. 144–65.

49 Kowalsky and Kowalsky, *Encyclopedia of Marks*, p. 284 (mark B1695).

50 Jarrett et al., 'Containers and Teapots'.

51 For a full discussion of this idea, see Kuijt et al., 'Dying the Good Death'.

52 It should be noted that white, undecorated ceramics by their nature 'match' with each other, but they do not allow archaeologists to determine if any sets of decorated vessels were purchased with the intention of creating a set.

53 We called this area Outdoor Space 105, because we did not excavate enough to gain a clear sense of the architectural life history of this earlier building and its surrounding features, including the remnants of a corn kiln.

54 Lash et al., 'Sensational Ensembles'.

55 MacLaughlin, 'Material Concerning the Surviving Antiquities of Inish Airc (Inishark)'; see also Lash, 'Island Taskscapes'.

56 Kuijt and Donaruma, *Nets of Memory* / Líonta na Cuimhne.

Chapter 5
The Taste of Home: Delph, consumption and connections to the wider world

1 Edmund de Waal, *The White Road: Journey into an obsession* (London: Chatto & Windus, 2015).

2 Shannon Lee Dawdy, *Patina: A profane archaeology* (Chicago: University of Chicago Press, 2016).

3 Glassie, *Passing the Time*, pp. 369–70.

4 https://potteriesoftrentonsociety.org/research/records/excelsior-pottery/; http://www.trenton history. org/Made/Marks.html; Edwin Atlee Barber, *Marks of American Potters* (Philadelphia: Patterson & White, 1904).

5 Danaher, *The Hearth and Stool and All!*, p. 39.

6 Gillian Neale, *Miller's Encyclopedia of British Transfer-Printed Pottery Patterns, 1790–1930*

(London: Octopus Publishing Group, 2005), pp. 73–86.

7   Ibid., p. 135.

8   Kowalsky and Kowalsky, *Encyclopedia of Marks*, pp. 317–18 (mark 1989); Godden, *Encyclopaedia*, p. 536 (mark 3278a).

9   Oral history interview with Thomas, 5 July 2019; Claudia Kinmonth, *Irish Country Furniture*, pp. 21–4.

10 For the quantitative analysis, I counted matched vessels or sets of vessels as single entries. For instance, the entire wedding set of Delia's mother counted as a single instance of an early twentieth-century vessel made in England.

11 Kowalsky and Kowalsky, *Encyclopedia of Marks*, p. 195 (marks B960 and B961); Godden, *Encyclopaedia*, p. 253 (mark 1585).

12 Godden, *Encyclopaedia*, p. 157 (mark 959).

13 Kowalsky and Kowalsky, *Encyclopedia of Marks*, p. 238 (mark B1307); Godden, *Encyclopaedia*, p. 332 (mark 2073).

14 http://thepotteries.org/allpotters/68.htm.

15 https://en.wikipedia.org/wiki/StaffordshireTableware.

16 https://www.churchill1795.com/about-us.

17 See Hampshire Cultural Trust webpage, with links to collections: https://collections. hampshireculture.org.uk/topic/nineteenth-century-utilitarian-stoneware.

18 Jarrett et al., 'Containers and Teapots'.

19 Arabia Pottery Company, https://arabia.fi/eng/about-arabia/our-history.

20 Browne, 'The Ethnography of Inishbofin and Inishshark'; Concannon, *Inishbofin Through Time and Tide*; Robert Ruttledge-Fair, 'Annual Report of the Congested Districts Board for the Clifden and Carna Regions', section 8, p. 152; Kathleen Villiers-Tuthill, *Beyond the Twelve Bens*.

21 Margaret Chambers, '"Serving My Time": A picture from behind the counter in pre-war Ireland', *Béaloideas*, vol. 69, 2001, pp. 5–39.

22 Rutledge-Fair, 'Annual CDB Report 1892', section 24, p. 154; for comparative cases of island shops, see Fox, *The Tory Islanders*, p. 27; Walsh, 'Clare Island', pp. 66–71.

23 Concannon, *Inishbofin Through Time and Tide*, p. 104.

24 Browne, 'The Ethnography of Inishbofin and Inishshark', p. 351; Concannon, *Inishbofin Through Time and Tide*, p. 99; Rutledge-Fair, 'Annual CDB Report 1892', section 24, p. 154.

25 Concannon, *Inishbofin Through Time and Tide*, p. 99.

26 Ibid., pp. 103–7.

27 Browne, 'The Ethnography of Inishbofin and Inishshark', p. 351.

28 http://www.thepotteries.org/allpotters/390c.htm.

29 Kowalsky and Kowalsky, *Encyclopedia of Marks*, p. 317; Godden, *Encyclopaedia*, p. 537 (mark 3291).

30 Kowalsky and Kowalsky, *Encyclopedia of Marks*, p. 349 (mark B2276).

31 Blue Willow platter: Godden, *Encyclopaedia*, p. 66 (mark 318); Kowalsky and Kowalsky, *Encyclopedia of Marks*, p. 109 (mark B216); Damascus platter: Godden, *Encyclopaedia*, p. 433 (mark 2651); Kowalsky and Kowalsky, *Encyclopedia of Marks*, p. 284 (mark B1692); Syria platter: Godden, *Encyclopaedia*, p. 433 (mark 2651); Kowalsky and Kowalsky, *Encyclopedia of Marks*,

p. 284 (mark B1692) and South Lancashire Leisure and Culture, 'Museums', http://www. sllcmuseumscollections.co.uk/search.do?view=detail&page=1&id=135935&db=object.

32   See the story of Róise Rua for an excellent autobiography that offers rich accounts of Irish migrant labourers working in Scotland during the late nineteenth and early twentieth centuries: Pádraig Ua Cnáimhsí, *Róise Rua: An island memoir*, translated by J.J. Keaveny (Blackrock, County Dublin: Mercier Press, 2009).

33   Rutledge-Fair, 'Annual CDB Report 1892', section 21.

34   Henry E. Kelly, Arnold A. Kowalsky and Dorothy E. Kowalsky, *Spongeware 1835–1935: Makers, marks, and patterns* (Altglen, PA: Schiffer Publishing, 2001), pp. 8–10.

35   Myles, 'In Small Things Remembered'.

36   Helen Holmes, 'Material Affinities: "Doing" family through the practices of passing on', *Sociology*, vol. 53, no. 1, 2019, pp. 174–91, see pp. 187–8.

37   Jones, 'Negotiating Objects'; For an earlier and still relevant archaeological approach to heirlooms, see Katina T. Lillois, 'Objects of Memory: The ethnography and archaeology of heirlooms', *Journal of Archaeological Method and Theory*, vol. 6, 1999, pp. 235–62.

38   Pareek cup and saucer: Kowalsky and Kowalsky, *Encyclopedia of Marks*, p. 246 (mark B1368); Godden, *Encyclopaedia*, p. 356 (mark 2178); Lowestoft Border cup and saucer: Kowalsky and Kowalsky, *Encyclopedia of Marks*, p. 119 (mark B291); Godden, *Encyclopaedia*, p. 87 (mark 453)

39   Aalen et al., *Atlas of Rural Ireland*; Malcolm Campbell, *Ireland's New Worlds: Immigrants, politics, and society in the United States and Australia, 1815–1922* (Madison, WI: University of Wisconsin Press, 2008); Crowley et al., *Atlas of the Great Irish Famine*; Guinnane, *The Vanishing Irish*; Kevin Kenny, 'Irish Emigration, 1845–1900', in Thomas Bartlett (ed.), *The Cambridge History of Ireland* (Cambridge: Cambridge University Press, 2018), pp. 666–87; Donald M. MacRaild, *The Irish Diaspora in Britain, 1750–1939*, 2nd edn (New York: St Martin's Press, 2011).

40   Kenny, 'Irish Emigration', p. 666.

41   Heaven Crawley and Dimitris Skleparis, 'Refugees, Migrants, Neither, Both: Categorial fetishism and the politics of bounding in Europe's "migration crisis"', *Journal of Ethnic and Migration Studies*, vol. 44, no. 1, 2018, pp. 48–64; Irving Howe, *World of Our Fathers: The journey of east European Jews to America and the life they found and made*, 30th anniversary edn (New York: Open Road Media, 2017); Matthew F. Jacobson, *Whiteness of a Different Color: European immigrants and the alchemy of race* (Cambridge, MA: Harvard University Press, 1998); Susan F. Martin, *A Nation of Immigrants* (Cambridge: Cambridge University Press, 2011); Blanca Sánchez-Alonso, 'Those Who Left and Those Who Stayed Behind: Explaining emigration from the regions of Spain, 1880–1914', *The Journal of Economic History*, vol. 60, no. 3, 2000, pp. 730–55.

42   Eleanor Wilner, 'Emigration', in *Shekhinah* (Chicago: University of Chicago Press, 1984), pp. 3–4.

43   http://www.gotheborg.com/marks/twentiethcenturyjapan.shtml; http:/ modernjapanesepottery marks.blogspot.com/2014/09/made-in-japan.html.

44   Godden, *Encyclopaedia*, p. 161 (mark 986).

45   Bourdieu, *Distinction* and 'The Forms of Capital'.

46   This category encompasses a variety of combinations, including hand-painted rims whose decorative techniques also include gilding, coloured (not clear) glaze, engine-turned slipware, or a moulded body.

47   House 9 was situated over an older, poorly preserved nineteenth-century home whose building materials were likely recycled in later construction events. During excavation, this earlier occupational phase was named 'Space 105', and the calculations for the overall MNV and the MNDV for House 9 do not include vessels from this earlier time period.

48   Godden, *Encyclopaedia*, p. 165 (mark 1024).

49   Godden, *Encyclopaedia*, p. 253 (mark 1585); Kowalsky and Kowalsky, *Encyclopedia of Marks*, p. 195 (mark B960).

50   Simon Moss, *Homemaker: A 1950s design classic* (Moffat, Dumfriesshire, Scotland: Cameron Books, 1997). The backstamp on this plate indicates its production in the second half ('2' to the left of 'UNDERGLAZE') of 1962 ('62' to the right of 'UNDERGLAZE': Ibid., p. 51).

51   Vincentelli 1994, p. 239; see also Leach, 'The Turnover Club'.

52   Base maker's mark: Kowalsky and Kowalsky, *Encyclopedia of Marks*, p. 215 (mark B1127); lid maker's mark: http://www.thepotteries.org/allpotters/300.htm; see also Kowalsky and Kowalsky, *Encyclopedia of Marks*, p.154 (mark B584).

53   Woodward, 'Taste Epiphany'.

54   Vincentelli, 'Artefact and Identity', p. 240.

Chapter 6
'Made to grow old': Dressers, heritage and the future of homemaking

1   Concannon, *Inishbofin Through Time and Tide*.

2   Kuijt and Donaruma, *Nets of Memory*.

3   Ibid.

4   Lash, 'Island Taskscapes', p. 400.

5   Noelle McElhatton, 'Irish Dealers Pitch Environmental Credentials to Win VAT-free Status Ahead of Brexit', *Antiques Trade Gazette*, 17 September 2019, https://www.antiquestradegazette.com/news/2019/irish-dealers-pitch-environmental-credentials-to-win-vat-free-status-ahead-of-brexit/.

6   Denise O'Connor, 'Sort It: Antique sales on the rise as buyers seek out sustainable items', *Irish Times*, 5 March 2021, https://www.irishtimes.com/life-and-style/homes-and-property/interiors/sort-it-antique-sales-on-the-rise-as-buyers-seek-out-sustainable-items-1.4499251.

7   Tony Donoghue, *Irish Folk Furniture*, Mayfly Films, produced by Cathal Black, 2012.

8   Kinmonth, *Irish Country Furniture*.

9   https://folklore.ie/.

10   https://www.facebook.com/groups/732407180176034.

11   https://www.facebook.com/groups/irishfurniture.

Bibliography

Archival Sources

Ancestry.com, https://www.ancestry.com/

County Mayo Library archives, https://www.mayo.ie/library/local-history

Dublin City Library archives, https://www.dublincity.ie/residential/libraries/find-library/dublin-city-library-and-archive

Logainm.ie (placename database of Ireland), https://www.logainm.ie/en/

National Archives of Britain, 'How to look for records of intellectual property: registered designs 1839–1991', https://www.nationalarchives.gov.uk/help-with-your-research/research-guides/registered-designs-1839-1991

National Archives of Ireland (valuation records, census records), https://www.nationalarchives.ie/

National Library of Ireland (Catholic parish registries), https://registers.nli.ie/

Published Works

Aalen, Frederick H.A., Kevin Whelan and Matthew Stout, *Atlas of Rural Ireland*, 2nd edn (Cork: Cork University Press, 2011)

Acabado, Stephen and Marlon Martin, 'Decolonizing the Past, Empowering the Future: Community-led heritage conservation in Ifugao, Philippines', *Journal of Community Archaeology & Heritage*, vol. 7, no. 3, 2020, pp. 171–86

Ahmed, Sara, 'Happy Objects', in Melissa Gregg and Gregory J. Seigworth (eds), *The Affect Theory Reader* (Durham, NC: Duke University Press, 2010), pp. 29–51

———, *What's the Use? On the uses of use* (Durham, NC: Duke University Press, 2019)

Ames, Nicholas, 'Traversing the Hearth: Navigating the structures of nineteenth century Irish migrations', unpublished PhD thesis, University of Notre Dame, 2021

Anon., *Irish Times*, 'Relief for Innishboffin', 27 March 1886

Arabia Pottery Company, 'Our History' (website), https://arabia.fi/eng/about-arabia/our-history

Arbeláez Arbeláez, Ángela María and Edward Mulholland, 'Interrupted Journeys: Drawings by refugees at the Kara Tepe camp, Lesvos, Greece', *Journal of Contemporary Archaeology*, vol. 3, 2016, pp. 233–44

Arensberg, Conrad M., *The Irish Countryman: An anthropological study* (London: Macmillan & Co., 1937)

Arensberg, Conrad M. and Solon T. Kimball, *Family and Community in Ireland*, 2nd edn (Cambridge, MA: Harvard University Press, 1968)

Arnold, Jeanne E., Anthony P. Graesch, Enzo Ragazzini and Elinor Ochs, *Life at Home in the Twenty-First Century: 32 families open their doors* (Los Angeles, CA: Cotsen Institute, University of California, Los Angeles, 2012)

Atalay, Sonya, *Community-Based Archaeology: Research with, by and for indigenous and local communities* (Berkeley, CA: University of California Press, 2012)

———, 'Can Archaeology Help Decolonize the Way Institutions Think? How community-based research is transforming the archaeology training toolbox and helping to transform institutions', *Archaeologies*, vol. 15, no. 3, 2019, pp. 514–35

Atalay, Sonya and Alexandra McCleary, *The Community-Based PhD: Complexities and triumphs of conducting CBPR* (Tucson, AZ: The University of Arizona Press, 2022)

Barber, Edwin Atlee, *Marks of American Potters* (Philadelphia: Patterson & White, 1904)

Basso, Keith, *Wisdom Sits in Places: Landscape and language among the western Apache* (Albuquerque, NM: University of New Mexico Press, 1996)

Battle-Baptiste, Whitney L. '"In This Here Place": Interpreting enslaved homeplaces', in Akinwumi Ogundiran and Toyin Falola (eds), *Archaeology of Atlantic Africa and the African Diaspora* (Bloomington, IN: Indiana University Press, 2007), pp. 233–48

———, *Black Feminist Archaeology* (Walnut Creek, CA: Left Coast Press, 2011)

Beattie, Seán, *Donegal in Transition: The impact of the Congested Districts Board* (Newbridge: Irish Academic Press, 2013)

Birdwell-Pheasant, Donna, 'The Home "Place": Center and periphery in Irish house and family systems', in Donna Birdwell-Pheasant and Denise Lawrence-Zúniga (eds), *House Life: Space, place and family in Europe* (Oxford: Berg, 1999), pp. 105–29

Birks, Steve, 'The Local History of Stoke-on-Trent, England', http://thepotteries.org/index.html

Blakey, Michael L., 'African Burial Project: Paradigm for cooperation?', *Museum International*, vol. 62, nos 1–2, 2010, pp. 61–8

————, 'Under the Blinding Light of Race', *Current Anthropology*, vol. 61, supplement 22, 2020, pp. S183–97

Blunt, Alison and Robyn Dowling, *Home* (London: Routledge, 2006)

Bonasera, Michael C. and Leslie Raymer, 'Good for What Ails You: Medicinal use at five points', *Historical Archaeology*, vol. 35, no. 3, 2001, pp. 49–66

Bourdieu, Pierre, 'The Berber House, or the World Reversed', *Social Science Information*, vol. 9, 1970, pp. 151–70

————, *Distinction: A social critique of the judgement of taste*, translated by Richard Nice (London: Routledge & Kegan Paul, 1984)

————, 'The Forms of Capital', in John G. Richardson (ed.), *Handbook of Theory and Research for the Sociology of Education* (Westport, CT: Greenwood Press, 1986), pp. 241–58

Bourke, Angela, 'Inner Lives: Creativity and survival in Irish rural life', in Vera Kreilkamp (ed.), *Rural Ireland: The inside story* (Chicago: University of Chicago Press, 2012), pp. 41–6

Brighton, Stephen A. and Andrew J. Webster, 'Of Hearth and Home: The material biography of an Irish cabin', *Post-Medieval Archaeology*, vol. 57, no. 1, 2023, pp. 125–42

Brody, Hugh, *Inishkillane: Change and decline in the west of Ireland* (Harmondsworth: Penguin, 1973)

Brown, Claire J., 'A Pony World – Hoofed Commodities: Breeding capital and culture through human–horse relations in the west of Ireland', unpublished PhD thesis, Binghamton University, State University of New York, 2019

Browne, Charles R., 'The Ethnography of Inishbofin and Inishshark, County Galway', *Proceedings of the Royal Irish Academy (1889–1901)*, vol. 3, 1893, pp. 317–70

Busch, Akiko, *Geography of Home: Writings on where we live* (New York: Princeton Architectural Press, 1999)

Butler, Beverly and Fatima al-Nammari, '"We Palestinian Refugees" – Heritage Rites and/as the Clothing of Bare Life: Reconfiguring paradox, obligation and imperative in Palestinian refugee camps in Jordan', *Journal of Contemporary Archaeology*, vol. 3, 2016, pp. 147–59

Campbell, Malcolm, *Ireland's New Worlds: Immigrants, politics and society in the United States and Australia, 1815–1922* (Madison, WI: University of Wisconsin Press, 2008)

Carruthers, Annette (ed.), *The Scottish Home* (Edinburgh: National Museums of Scotland, 1996)

Carston, Janet and Stephen Hugh-Jones (eds), *About the House: Lévi-Strauss and beyond* (Cambridge: Cambridge University Press, 1995)

Carville, Justin, 'Visible Others: Photography and romantic ethnography in Ireland', in Maria McGarrity and Claire A. Culleton (eds), *Irish Modernism and the Global Primitive* (New York: Palgrave Macmillan, 2009), pp. 93–114

Cashman, Ray, 'Critical Nostalgia and Material Culture in Northern Ireland', *Journal of American Folklore*, vol. 119, no. 472, 2006, pp. 137–60

Chambers, Margaret, '"Serving My Time": A picture from behind the counter in pre-war Ireland', *Béaloideas*, vol. 69, 2001, pp. 5–39

Chesson, Meredith S., Isaac I.T. Ullah, Giovanni Iiriti, Hamish Forbes, Paula K. Lazrus, Nicholas Ames, Yesenia Garcia, Sarah Benchekroun, John Robb, Nicholas P.S. Wolff and Maria Olimpia Squillaci, 'Archaeology as Intellectual Service: Engaged archaeology in San Pasquale Valley, Calabria, Italy', *Archaeologies*, vol. 15, no. 3, 2019, pp. 422–43

Churchill Pottery, https://www.churchill1795.com/about-us

Cieraad, Irene (ed.), *At Home: An anthropology of domestic space* (Syracuse, NY: Syracuse University Press, 2006)

Clark, Bonnie J., 'Collaborative Archaeology as Heritage Process', *Archaeologies*, vol. 15, no. 3, 2019, pp. 466–80

Clutterbuck, Richard, 'Wretched beyond Description: The excavation of a cottier's cabin in Cookstown, Co. Meath', *Seanda*, no. 1, 2006, pp. 46–7

Coelho, Rui Gomes, 'The Garden of Refugees', *Journal of Contemporary Archaeology*, vol. 3, 2016, pp. 261–70

Colum, Padraic, 'Old Woman of the Roads', in *Wild Earth* (Dublin: Maunsel & Co., 1907), p. 15

———, 'The Fire Bringer', in *Wild Earth* (Dublin: Maunsel & Co., 1907), pp. 7–8

Concannon, Kieran (ed.), *Inishbofin Through Time and Tide* (Inishbofin: Inishbofin Development Company; printed in Athlone: Temple Printing Company, 1997)

——— (director), *Inis Airc: Bás oileáin* (TG4, 2007)

Connaughton, Sean P., Genevieve Hill, Jesse Morin, Cory Frank, Nancy Green and David McGee, 'Tidal Belongings: First nations-driven archaeology to preserve a large wooden fish trap panel recovered from the Comox Harbour Intertidal Fish Trap Complex in British Columbia', *Canadian Journal of Archaeology*, no.

46, 2022, pp. 16–51

Conway, Meagan, 'A Choice to Engage: Selective marginality and dynamic households on the eighteenth- to nineteenth-century Irish coast', unpublished PhD thesis, University of South Carolina, 2019

Corporaal, Marguérite, 'Traveling Cabins: The popularity of Irish local-color fiction in early nineteenth-century Europe', in Marguérite Corporaal and Christina Moran (eds), *Traveling Irishness in the Long Nineteenth Century* (Cham, Switzerland: Palgrave Macmillan, 2017), pp. 103–18

Corrigan, Peter J., 'Memories of Inishark', in James Morrissey (ed.), *Inishbofin and Inishark, Connemara* (Dublin: Crannóg Books, 2012), pp. 143–8

Costello, Eugene, *Transhumance and the Making of Ireland's Uplands, 1550–1900* (Woodbridge: Boydell & Brewer, 2020)

Cotton, Bernard J., 'Irish Vernacular Furniture', *Regional Furniture*, vol. 3, 1989, pp. 1–28

Couey, Lauren, 'A Shifting Island Landscape: Changes in land use and daily life in the nineteenth- and twentieth-century village of Inishark, Co. Galway, Ireland', unpublished MA thesis, University of Denver, 2018

Coyne, Marie, *St Colman's Abbey and Cemetery, Inishbofin* (Inishbofin: Inishbofin Development Company, 2008)

Crawley, Heaven and Dimitris Skleparis, 'Refugees, Migrants, Neither, Both: Categorial fetishism and the politics of bounding in Europe's "migration crisis"', *Journal of Ethnic and Migration Studies*, vol. 44, no. 1, 2018, pp. 48–64

Crowley, John, William J. Smyth and Mike Murphy (eds), *Atlas of the Great Irish Famine* (Cork: Cork University Press, 2012)

Danaher, Kevin, *The Hearth and Stool and All! Irish rural households* (Dublin: Mercier Press, 1985)

Danis, Ann, 'Home(less) Place and Home-Making at the Albany Bulb', in Elena Sesma and Evan Taylor (eds), *Contemporary Archaeologies in Old Places: Material politics between past and future*, Archaeological Papers of the American Anthropological Association, vol. 33, 2020, pp. 106- 21

Danú, 'Around the House and Mind the Dresser', on *When All Is Said and Done* (Shanachie, 2005)

Dawdy, Shannon Lee, *Patina: A profane archaeology* (Chicago: University of Chicago Press, 2016)

Deetz, James, *In Small Things Forgotten* (New York: Anchor Books, 1996)

Dempsey, Karen, 'Home Is Where the Heart(h) Is?', *Archaeology Ireland*, vol. 34, no. 1, 2020, pp. 49–51

Dempsey, Karen and Jitske Jasperse, 'Multisensorial Musings on Miniature Matters', *Das Mittelalter*, vol. 25, no. 2, 2020, pp. 249–70

de Waal, Edmund, *The White Road: Journey into an obsession* (London: Chatto & Windus, 2015)

Donoghue, Anthony, Irish Vernacular Furniture Facebook page, https://www.facebook.com/groups/irishfurniture

———, *Irish Folk Furniture* (Mayfly Films, produced by Cathal Black, 2012)

Dring, Katherine Sebastian, Stephen W. Silliman, Nathasha Gambrell, Shianne Sebastian and Ralph Sebastian Sidberry, 'Authoring and Authority in Eastern Pequot Community Heritage and Archaeology', *Archaeologies*, vol. 15, no. 3, 2019, pp. 352–70

Dun, Finlay, *Landlords and Tenants in Ireland* (London: Longmans, Green & Co., 1881)

Dunn, Shannon, '"Little More than a Winter Home": An historical archaeology of Irish seasonal migration at Slievemore, Achill Island', unpublished PhD thesis, Syracuse University, 2008

Dunne Family, The, 'Around the House and Mind the Dresser', on *Legacy* (The Dunne Family, 2004)

Edwards, Bridget, 'How the West Was Wondered: County Clare and directions in Irish ethnography', *Folklore Forum*, vol. 27, no. 2, 1996, pp. 65–78

Flanders, Judith, *The Making of Home: The 500-year story of how houses became our homes* (New York: St Martin's Press, 2015)

Fleisher, Jeffrey B. and Neil Norman (eds), *The Archaeology of Anxiety: The materiality of anxiousness, worry and fear* (New York: Springer, 2016)

Forsythe, Wes, 'On the Edge of Improvement: Rathlin Island and the modern world', *International Journal of Historical Archaeology*, vol. 11, no. 3, 2007, pp. 221–40

———, 'The Measure and Materiality of Improvement in Ireland', *International Journal of Historical Archaeology*, vol 17, no. 1, 2013, pp. 72–93

Fortune, Michael, *The Irish Dresser – 2021 Calendar*, https://thedresserproject.ie

———, Folklore.ie Facebook page', https://www.facebook.com/folklore.ie

Fox, James J. (ed.), *Inside Austronesian Houses: Perspectives on domestic designs for living* (Canberra: Australian National University, 1993)

Fox, Robin, *The Tory Islanders: A people of the Celtic fringe* (Notre Dame, IN: University of Notre Dame Press, 1995)

Francis, Peter, *Irish Delftware: An illustrated history* (London: Johnathan Horne Publications, 2000), p. 7.

Franklin, Maria, 'A Black-Feminist-Inspired Archaeology?', *Journal of Social Archaeology*, vol. 1, 2001, pp. 108–25

Franklin, Maria and Nedra Lee, 'Revitalizing Tradition and Instigating Change: Foodways at the Ransom and Sarah Williams Farmstead, *c.* 1871–1905', *Journal of African Diaspora Archaeology and Heritage*, vol. 8, no. 3, 2019, pp. 202–25

———, 'African American Descendants, Community Outreach, and the Ransom and Sarah Williams Farmstead Project', *Journal of Community Archaeology & Heritage*, vol. 7, no. 2, 2020, pp. 135–48

Fredengren, Christina, *Crannógs* (Bray: Wordwell, 2002)

Freeman, Thomas W., 'Inishbofin: An Atlantic island', *Economic Geography*, vol. 34, 1958, pp. 202–9

Frost, Nicola and Tom Selwyn (eds), *Travelling Towards Home: Mobilities and homemaking* (New York: Berghahn, 2018)

Gailey, Alan, 'Kitchen Furniture', *Ulster Folklife*, vol. 12, 1966, pp. 18–34

———, *Rural Houses of the North of Ireland* (Edinburgh: John Donald Publishers, 1984)

Gardiner, Mark, 'Folklore's Timeless Past, Ireland's Present Past, and the Perception of Rural Houses in Early Historic Ireland', *International Journal of Historical Archaeology*, vol. 15, no. 4, 2011, pp. 707–24

Garvey, Pauline, *Unpacking Ikea: Swedish design for the purchasing masses* (London: Routledge, 2018)

Geertz, Clifford, 'Deep Hanging Out', *New York Times Review of Books*, 22 October 1998, pp. 69–72

George, Kenneth M., 'No Ethics Without Things', *Journal of Religious Ethics*, vol. 44, no. 1, 2016, pp. 51–67

Gibbons, Luke, 'Synge, Country and Western: The myth of the west in Irish and American culture', in Luke Gibbons (ed.), *Transformations in Irish Culture* (Cork: Cork University Press, 1996). pp. 69–72

Gibbons, Michael and Jim Higgins, 'Three Western Islands', *Archaeology Ireland*, vol. 7, no. 2, 1993, pp. 20–3

Gilchrist, Roberta, *Medieval Life: Archaeology and the life course* (Woodbridge,

UK: Boydell Press, 2012)

Gilligan, Jim, *Graziers and Grasslands: Portrait of a rural Meath community 1854–1914*, Maynooth Studies in Local History, vol. 72 (Portland: Irish Academic Press, 1998)

Gilmartin, Elizabeth, '"Magnificent Words and Gestures": Defining the primitive in Synge's *The Aran Islands*', in Maria McGarrity and Claire A. Culleton (eds), *Irish Modernism and the Global Primitive* (New York: Palgrave Macmillan, 2009), pp. 63–76

Glassie, Henry, *Folk Housing in Middle Virginia* (Knoxville, TN: University of Tennessee Press, 1975)

———, *Passing the Time in Ballymenone* (Philadelphia: University of Pennsylvania Press, 1982)

———, *Vernacular Architecture* (Bloomington, IN: Indiana University Press, 2000)

———, *The Stars of Ballymenone* (Bloomington, IN: Indiana University Press, 2006)

Godden, Geoffrey A., *Encyclopaedia of British Pottery and Porcelain Marks* (New York: Crown Publishers, 1964)

Gonzalez, Sara L., Ian Krietzler and Briece Edwards, 'Imagining Indigenous and Archaeological Futures: Building capacity with the confederated tribes of Grande Ronde', *Archaeologies*, vol. 14, 2018, pp. 85–114

Goodale, Nathan, Madeleine Bassett, David G. Bailey, Ryan Lash and Ian Kuijt, 'Early Medieval Seascapes in Western Ireland and the Geochemistry of Ecclesiastical Cross Stones', *Journal of Archaeological Science: Reports*, vol. 19, June 2018, pp. 894–902

Gow, Ian, 'The Dining Room', in A. Carruthers (ed.), *The Scottish Home* (Edinburgh: National Museums of Scotland, 1996), pp. 125–54

Grace's Guide to British Industrial History, 'Elliman, Sons and Co', https://www.gracesguide.co.uk/Elliman,SonsandCo

Greenberg, Raphael, 'Wedded to Privilege? Archaeology, academic capital and critical public engagement', *Archaeologies*, vol. 15, no. 3, 2019, pp. 481–95

Grogan, Eoin, 'Excavations at Mooghaun South 1995, Interim Report', in *Discovery Programme Reports no. 5* (Dublin: The Discovery Programme, 1999), pp. 125–30

———, *Mooghaun* (Dublin: The Discovery Programme, 1999)

Guinnane, Timothy W., *The Vanishing Irish: Households, migration, and the rural economy in Ireland, 1850–1914* (Princeton, NJ: Princeton University Press, 1997)

Hamilakis, Yiannis, *Archaeology of the Senses: Human experience, memory, and affect* (Cambridge: Cambridge University Press, 2014)

Hampshire Cultural Trust, 'Nineteenth Utilitarian Stoneware', https://collections.hampshireculture.org.uk/topic/nineteenth-century-utilitarian-stoneware

Hamrock, Ivor, 'The Famine in Mayo 1845–1850', https://www.mayo.ie/getmedia/f7ba7bd8-7354-4353-8877-30d0e3dac099/The-Famine-in-Mayo-1845-1850-Mayo-County-Library-Exhibition_2.pdf; https://www.mayo.ie/library/local-history/historical-events/the-great-famine

Hendon, Julia, *Houses in a Landscape: Memory and everyday life in Mesoamerica* (Durham, NC: Duke University Press, 2010)

Higgins, Jim and Michael Gibbons, 'Missing Artwork: A lost early Christian cross-decorated monument from Inishark (Inis Airc), Co. Galway', in Jim Higgins (ed.), *Recent Explorations and Discoveries in Irish Heritage* (Galway: Crow's Rock, 2017), pp. 70–4

Holmes, Helen, 'Material Affinities: "Doing" family through the practices of passing on', *Sociology*, vol. 53, no. 1, 2019, pp. 174–91

hooks, bell, 'The Politics of Radical Black Subjectivity', in *Yearning: Race, gender, and cultural politics* (Boston: South End Press, 1990), pp. 15–22

———, *Yearning: Race, gender, and cultural politics* (Boston: South End Press, 1990)

Horne, Lee, *Village Spaces: Settlement and society in northeastern Iran* (Washington, DC: Smithsonian Institute Press, 1994)

Horning, Audrey, *In the Shadow of Ragged Mountain: Historical archaeology of Nicholson, Corbin, and Weakley Hollows* (Luray, VA: Shenandoah National Park Association Inc., 2004)

———, 'Materiality and Mutable Landscapes: Rethinking seasonality and marginality in rural Ireland', *International Journal of Historical Archaeology*, vol. 11, 2007, pp. 358–78

———, 'Minding the Gaps: Exploring the intersection of political economy, colonial ideologies and cultural practice in early modern Ireland', *Post-Medieval Archaeology*, vol. 52, no. 1, 2018, pp. 4–20

———, 'Collaborators and Conflict: Archaeology and peacebuilding in Northern Ireland', *Archaeologies*, vol. 15, no. 3, 2019, pp. 444–65

Horning, Audrey, Colm Donnelly, Ruairí Ó Baoill and Paul Logue (eds), *The Post-Medieval Archaeology of Ireland: 1550–1850* (Bray: Wordwell, 2007)

Howard University, *The New York African Burial Ground: Unearthing the African presence in colonial New York*, vol. 5 (Washington, DC: Howard University Press, 2009)

Howe, Irving, *World of Our Fathers: The journey of east European Jews to America and the life they found and made*, 30th anniversary edition (New York: Open Road Media, 2017)

Hurdley, Rachel, *Home, Materiality, Memory and Belonging: Keeping culture* (Basingstoke, Hampshire: Palgrave Macmillan, 2013)

Huttman, John P., 'The Impact of Land Reform on Agricultural Production in Ireland', *Agricultural History*, vol. 46, no. 3, 1972, pp. 353 68

Jackson, Peter, 'Commodity Cultures: The traffic in things', *Transactions of the Institute of British Geographers*, vol. 24, no. 1, 1999, pp. 95–108

Jacobson, Matthew F., *Whiteness of a Different Color: European immigrants and the alchemy of race* (Cambridge, MA: Harvard University Press, 1998)

Jarrett, Chris, Morag Cross and Alistair Robertson, 'Containers and Teapots', in Alasdair Brooks (ed.), *The Importance of British Material Culture to Historical Archaeologies of the Nineteenth Century* (Lincoln, NE: University of Nevada Press; and London: Society for Historical Archaeology, 2015), pp. 69–106

Jones, Alexandra, 'Archaeology for a New Generation: Exploring education and intersectionality', *Archaeologies: Journal of the World Archaeological Congress*, vol. 18, no. 1, 2022, pp. 287–309

Jones, Siân, 'Negotiating Objects and Authentic Selves: Beyond the deconstruction of authenticity', *Journal of Material Culture*, vol. 15, no. 2, 2010, pp. 181–203

Joyce, Rosemary A., '"What Eludes Speech": A dialogue with Webb Kean', *Journal of Social Archaeology*, vol. 11, no. 2, 2011, pp. 158–70

Joyce, Rosemary A. and Susan D. Gillespie (eds), *Beyond Kinship: Social and material reproduction in house societies* (Philadelphia: University of Pennsylvania Press, 2000)

Kaul, Adam, *Turning the Tune: Traditional music, tourism, and social change in an Irish village* (New York: Berghahn Books, 2012)

Keane, Webb, 'Semiotics and the Social Analysis of Material Things', *Language and Communication*, vol. 23, 2003, pp. 409–25

Kelly, Henry E., Arnold A. Kowalsky and Dorothy E. Kowalsky, *Spongeware 1835–1935: Makers, marks, and patterns* (Altglen, PA: Schiffer Publishing, 2001)

Kelvin, Laura, Emma Gilheany, Nicholas Flowers, Denver Edmunds, Mackenzie Frieda, Claire Igloliorte, Halle Lucy and John Piercy, 'Strength-Based

Approaches to Involving Inuit Youth in Archaeological Research', *Canadian Journal of Archaeology*, vol. 44, 2020, pp. 83–104

Kemp, Jeremy, 'Comment', 27 August 2017 on the website 'Glass Bottle Marks', https://glassbottlemarks.com/bottlemarks-3/

Kenny, Kevin, 'Irish Emigration, 1845–1900', in Thomas Bartlett (ed.), *The Cambridge History of Ireland* (Cambridge: Cambridge University Press, 2018), pp. 666–87

Kinmonth, Claudia, 'Irish Vernacular Furniture: Inventories and illustrations in interdisciplinary methodology', *Regional Furniture*, vol. 10, 1996, pp. 1–26

———, *Irish Rural Interiors in Art* (New Haven, CT: Yale University Press, 2006)

———, *Irish Country Furniture and Furnishings 1700–2000* (Cork: Cork University Press, 2020)

Kirshenblatt-Gimlet, Barbara, 'Authoring Lives', *Journal of Folklore Research*, vol. 26, no. 2, 1989, pp. 123–49

Knapp, Ron G. and Kai-Yin Lo (eds), *House, Home, Family: Living and being Chinese* (Honolulu: University of Hawaii Press, 2005)

Kopytoff, Igor, 'The Cultural Biography of Things', in Arjun Apaddurai (ed.), *The Social Life of Things: Commodities in cultural perspective* (Cambridge: Cambridge University Press, 1986), pp. 64–91

Kourelis, Kostis, 'If Place Remotely Matters: Camped in Greece's contingent countryside', *Journal of Contemporary Archaeology*, vol. 3, 2016, pp. 215–27

Kowalsky, Arnold A. and Dorothy E. Kowalsky, *Encyclopedia of Marks: On American, English, and European earthenware, ironstone, and stoneware, 1780–1980* (Atglen, PA: Schiffer Publishing, 1990)

Kramer, Carol, *Village Ethnoarchaeology: Rural Iran in archaeological perspective* (New York: Academic Press, 1982)

Kreilkamp, Vera (ed.), *Rural Ireland: The inside story* (Chicago: University of Chicago Press, 2012)

Kuijt, Ian, Meagan Conway, Katie Shakour, Casey McNeill and Claire Brown, 'Vectors of Improvement: The material footprint of nineteenth-through twentieth-century Irish national policy, Inishark, County Galway, Ireland', *International Journal of Historical Archaeology*, vol. 19, no. 1, 2015, pp. 122–58

Kuijt, Ian, Meredith S. Chesson, Sara Morrow, Diarmuid Ó Giolláin and Ryan Lash, 'Dying the Good Death and Materialized Mourning: Nineteenth and twentieth century coastal Ireland', *International Journal of Historic Archaeology*, vol. 25, 2021, pp. 333–74

Kuijt, Ian and William Donaruma (directors), *Nets of Memory / Líonta na Cuimhne* (Walkabout Productions, 2019)

Kuijt, Ian, Ryan Lash, William Donaruma, Katie Shakour and Tommy Burke, *Island Places, Island Lives: Exploring Inishbofin and Inishark heritage, Co. Galway, Ireland* (Bray: Wordwell, 2015)

Kus, Susan, 'Archaeology as Anthropology: Much ado about something after all?', *Journal of Archaeological Method and Theory*, vol. 4, nos 3–4, 1997, pp. 199–213

——, 'In the Midst of Moving Waters: Material, metaphor, and feminist archaeology', in Pamela L. Geller and Miranda K. Stockett (eds), *Feminist Anthropology: Past, present, and future* (Philadelphia: University of Pennsylvania Press, 2006), pp. 105–14

Lash, Ryan, 'Enchantments of Stone: Confronting other-than-human agency in Irish pilgrimage practices', *Journal of Social Archaeology*, vol. 18, no. 3, 2018, pp. 284–305

——, 'Pebbles and *Peregrinatio*: The taskscape of medieval devotion on Inishark island, Ireland', *Medieval Archaeology*, vol. 62, no. 1, 2018, pp. 83–104

——, 'Island Taskscapes: Heritage, ritual, and sustainability on Inishark and Inishbofin, Ireland', unpublished PhD thesis, Department of Anthropology, Northwestern University, 2019

——, *Island Endurance: Creative heritage on Inishark and Inishbofin* (Indianapolis: Indiana University Press, 2025)

Lash, Ryan, Ian Kuijt, Elise Alonzi, Meredith S. Chesson and Tommy Burke, '"Differing in Status, but One in Spirit": Sacred space and social diversity at island monasteries in Connemara, Ireland', *Antiquity*, vol. 92, no. 362, 2018, pp. 437–55

Lash, Ryan, Meredith S. Chesson, Elise Alonzi, Ian Kuijt, Terry O'Hagan, John Ó Néill and Tommy Burke, 'Sensational Ensembles: Picnicking and pilgrimage on Inishark island, Co. Galway, Ireland 1650–1960', *Current Anthropology*, vol. 64, no. 4, August 2023, pp. 380–409

Lave, Jean, *Apprenticeship in Critical Ethnographic Practice* (Chicago: University of Chicago Press, 2011)

Lave, Jean and Etienne Wenger, *Situated Learning: Legitimate peripheral participation* (Cambridge: Cambridge University Press, 1991)

Leach, Rebecca, 'The Turnover Club: Locality and identity in the practice of turning over ceramic ware', *International Journal of Heritage Studies*, vol. 22, no.

6, 2016, pp. 482–94

Lillois, Katina T., 'Objects of Memory: The ethnography and archaeology of heirlooms', *Journal of Archaeological Method and Theory*, vol. 6, 1999, pp. 235–62

Linn, Meredith B., 'Irish Immigrant Healing Magic in Nineteenth-Century New York City', *Historical Archaeology*, vol. 48, no. 3, 2014, pp. 144–65

Lynn, Christopher J., 'Reconstruction of an Eighth-Century House Based on the Evidence from Deer Park Farms', in Christopher J. Lynn and Jackie A. McDowell, *Deer Park Farms: The excavation of a raised rath in the Glenarm Valley, Co. Antrim*, Northern Ireland Archaeological Monographs 9 (Belfast: Northern Ireland Environmental Agency and The Stationery Office, 2011), pp. 594–602

Lynn, Christopher J. and Jackie A. McDowell, *Deer Park Farms: The excavation of a raised rath in the Glenarm Valley, County Antrim*. Northern Ireland Archaeological Monographs 9 (Belfast: Northern Ireland Environmental Agency and The Stationery Office, 2011)

Mac Gabhann, Fiachra, 'Aguisín: Logainmneacha Inis Airc', in *Logainmneacha Mhaigh Eo 2: Barúntacht Mhuraisce* (Baile Átha Cliath: Coiscéim, 2014)

MacLaughlin, Brian, 'Material Concerning the Surviving Antiquities of Inish Airc (Inishark)', National Folklore Collection, University College Dublin, vol. 839, 1942

MacRaild, Donald M., *The Irish Diaspora in Britain, 1750–1939*, 2nd edn (New York: St Martin's Press, 2011)

Martin, Susan F., *A Nation of Immigrants* (Cambridge: Cambridge University Press, 2011)

McDonald, Theresa, 'The Deserted Village, Slievemore, Achill Island, County Mayo, Ireland', *International Journal of Historical Archaeology*, vol. 2, no. 2, 1998, pp. 73–112

McElhatton, Noelle, 'Irish Dealers Pitch Environmental Credentials to Win VAT-Free Status Ahead of Brexit', *Antiques Trade Gazette*, 17 September 2019, https://www.antiquestradegazette.com/news/2019/irish-dealers-pitch-environmental-credentials-to-win-vat-free-status-ahead-of-brexit/

McGee, Francis, *The Archives of the Valuation of Ireland, 1830–65* (Dublin: Four Courts Press, 2018)

McKenna, Rachel, *Traditional Architecture in Offaly: History, materials and furniture, 1800 to present day* (Tullamore, County Offaly: Offaly County Council, 2022)

Meskell, Lynn, *Archaeologies of Materiality* (Malden, MA: Blackwell Publishing, 2005)

Messenger, John C., *Inis Beag: Isle of Ireland* (New York: Holt, Rinehart & Winston, 1969)

————, *Inis Beag Revisited: The anthropologist as observant participator* (Salem, WI: Sheffield, 1989)

Micks, William L., *An Account of the Constitution, Administration and Dissolution of the Congested Districts Board for Ireland from 1891 to 1923* (Dublin: Eason & Son, 1925)

Miller, Daniel, *Materiality* (Durham, NC: Duke University Press, 2005)

Morris, Annelise E., '"We all lived in that house together": Persistence as resistance on an Illinois farmstead, 1845 to present', unpublished PhD thesis, University of California, Berkeley, 2015

Morrissey, James (ed.), *On the Verge of Want: A unique insight into living conditions along Ireland's western seaboard in the late nineteenth century* (Dublin: Crannóg Books, 2001)

———— (ed.), *Inishbofin and Inishark, Connemara* (Dublin: Crannóg Books, 2012)

Moss, Simon, *Homemaker: A 1950s design classic* (Moffat, Dumfriesshire, Scotland: Cameron Books, 1997)

Mrozowski, Stephen A. and D. Rae Gould, 'Building Histories That Have Futures: The benefits of collaborative research', *Archaeologies*, vol. 15, no. 3, 2019, pp. 400–21

Munro, Moira and Ruth Madigan, 'Negotiating Space in the Family Home', in Irene Cieraad (ed.), *At Home: An anthropology of domestic space* (Syracuse, NY: Syracuse University Press, 2006), pp. 107–17

Museum of Health Care at Kingston, 'Research Collection Catalogue: Accession number 1981.8.2', https://mhc.andornot.net/en/permalink/artifact8188

Myles, Franc, 'In Small Things Remembered: The sponge decorated ceramics from Inishark, Galway. With apologies to Jim Deetz', blogpost 28 June 2013, https://wastedonarchaeology.wordpress.com/2013/06/28/in-small-things-remembered-the-sponge-decorated-ceramics-from-inishark-galway/

Mytum, Harold, 'Domesticity and the Dresser: An archaeological perspective from rural nineteenth-century Pembrokeshire', in James Symonds (ed.), *Table Settings: The material culture and social context of dining, AD 1700–1900* (Oxford: Oxbow, 2010), pp. 87–98

Neale, Gillian, *Miller's Encyclopedia of British Transfer-Printed Pottery Patterns, 1790–1930* (London: Octopus Publishing Group, 2005)

Ó Cadhla, Stiofán, *Civilising Ireland – Ordnance Survey 1824–1842: Ethnography, cartography, translation* (Dublin: Irish Academic Press, 2007)

O'Connell, Michael and Edel Ní Ghráinne, with contributions by Michael Gibbons, 'Inishbofin: Palaeoecology', in Peter Coxon and Michael O'Connell (eds), *Clare Island and Inishbofin, Field Guide No. 17* (Dublin: Irish Association for Quaternary Studies, 1994), pp. 61–101

O'Connor, Denise, 'Sort It: Antique sales on the rise as buyers seek out sustainable items', *Irish Times*, 5 March 2021, https://www.irishtimes.com/life-and-style/homes-and-property/interiors/sort-it-antique-sales-on-the-rise-as-buyers-seek-out-sustainable-items-1.4499251

Ó Criomhthain, Tómas, *The Islander*, transl. Gary Bannister and David Sowby (Dublin: Gill & Macmillan, 2012 [1929])

Ó Danachair, Caoimhín, 'The Combined Byre-and-Dwelling in Ireland', *Folk Life*, vol. 2, no. 1, 1964, pp. 58–75

———, 'Traditional Forms of the Dwelling House in Ireland', *Journal of the Royal Society of Antiquaries of Ireland*, vol. 102, no. 1, 1972, pp. 77–96

O'Donnell, Peadar, 'Achill, Arranmore and Kirkintilloch, Dealing with the Question of Migratory Labourers', *Ireland To-day*, vol. 2, no. 10, 1937, pp. 45–50

O'Dowd, Anne, *Spalpeens and Tattie Hokers: History and folklore of the Irish migratory agricultural worker in Ireland and Britain* (Blackrock, County Dublin: Irish Academic Press, 1991)

———, 'Women in Rural Ireland in the Nineteenth and early Twentieth Centuries: How the daughters, wives and sisters of small farmers and landless labourers fared', *Rural History*, vol. 5, no. 2, 1994, pp. 171–83

———, *Straw, Hay, and Rushes in Irish Folk Tradition* (Dublin: Irish Academic Press and National Museum of Ireland, 2015)

Ó Giolláin, Diarmuid, *Locating Irish Folklore: Tradition, modernity, identity* (Cork: Cork University Press, 2000)

———, *Exotic Dreams in the Science of the Volksgeist: Towards a global history of European folklore stories* (Helsinki: The Kalevala Society, 2022)

Ó Gráda, Cormac, 'Seasonal Migration and Post-Famine Adjustment in the West of Ireland', *Studia Hibernia*, no. 13, 1973, pp. 48–76

Olive, Gabriel, 'Dressers in the West Country', *Regional Furniture*, vol. 3, 1989, pp.

40–51

Oliver, Jeff, Jackson Armstrong, Elizabeth Curtis, Neil Curtis and Jo Vergunst, 'Exploring Co-production in Community Heritage Research: Reflections from the Bennachie Landscapes Project', *Journal of Community Archaeology & Heritage*, vol. 9, no. 3, 2022, pp. 196–215

Orser, Charles E. Jr, 'Of Dishes and Drains: An archaeological perspective on Irish rural life in the Famine era', *New Hibernia Review*, vol. 1, no. 1, 1997, pp. 120–35

——— (ed.), *Unearthing Hidden Ireland: Historical archaeology in Ballykilcline, County Roscommon* (Bray: Wordwell, 2006)

———, 'Three Nineteenth-Century House Sites in Rural Ireland', *Post-Medieval Archaeology*, vol. 44, no. 1, 2010, pp. 81–104

Orton, Clive, Paul Tyers and Alan Vince, *Pottery in Archaeology (Cambridge Manuals in Archaeology)* (Cambridge: Cambridge University Press, 1993)

O'Reilly, Barry, 'Hearth and Home: The vernacular house in Ireland from 1800', *Proceedings of the Royal Irish Academy*, vol. 111C, 2011, pp. 193–215

Ó Súilleabháin, Muiris, *Twenty Years A-Growing*, transl. Moya Llewellyn Davies and George Thompson (Oxford: Oxford University Press, 1983 [1933])

O'Sullivan, Aidan and Tríona Nicholl, 'Early Medieval Settlement Enclosures in Ireland: Dwellings, daily life, and social identity', *Proceedings of the Royal Irish Academy, Section C: Archaeology, Celtic Studies, History, Linguistics, Literature*, vol. 111C, special issue: Domestic Life in Ireland, 2011, pp. 59–90

O'Sullivan, Aidan, Finbar McCormick, Thomas R. Kerr and Lorcan Harney, *Early Medieval Ireland AD 400–1100: The evidence from archaeological excavations* (Dublin: Royal Irish Academy Publications, 2014), pp. 46–138

Parker, Bradley J. and Catherine P. Foster (eds), *New Perspectives on Household Archaeology* (Winona Lake, IN: Eisenbrauns, 2012)

Pennartz, Paul J.J., 'Home: The experience of atmosphere', in Irene Cieraad (ed.), *At Home: An anthropology of domestic space* (Syracuse, NY: Syracuse University Press, 2006), pp. 95–106

Pikirayi, Innocent, Plan Shenjere-Nyabezi and Munyaradzi Elton Sagiya, 'Landscape, History and Power: The Zimbabwe culture and the Nambya state, northwestern Zimbabwe', *Journal of Community Archaeology & Heritage*, vol. 9, no. 3, 2022, pp. 175–95

Poetry Ireland's Writing Home project led by poet Colm Keegan, https://www.

creativeireland.gov.ie/en/event/poetry-ireland; https://www.youtube.com/
watch?v=icPvlAplHH8)

Porteous, J. Douglas and Sandra E. Smith, *Domicide: The global destruction of home*
(Montreal: McGill-Queen's University Press, 2001)

Potteries of Trenton Society, https://potteriesoftrentonsociety.org/

Potterton, Michael (ed.), *Moynagh Lough Studies 1* (Dublin: Four Courts Press,
2025)

Quinn, Colin P., Ian Kuijt, Nathan Goodale and John Ó Néill, 'Along the
Margins? The later Bronze Age seascapes of western Ireland', *European Journal
of Archaeology*, vol. 22, no. 1, 2019, pp. 44–66

Rich, Adrienne, 'Natural Resources', *The Dream of a Common Language: Poems
1974–1977* (New York: W.W. Norton & Company, 1978), pp. 60–7

Ritchie, Rachael, 'Arklow Back Stamps', unpublished manuscript provided by the
author, 2024

Rizvi, Uzma, 'Community-based and Participatory Praxis as Decolonizing
Archaeological Methods and the Betrayal of New Research', in Kisha Supernant,
Jane Baxter, Natasha Lyons and Sonya Atalay (eds), *Archaeologies of the Heart*
(New York: Springer Publishing, 2020), pp. 83–96

Robb, John, 'Material Culture, Landscapes of Action, and Emergent Causation:
A new model for the origins of the European Neolithic', *Current Anthropology*,
vol. 54, no. 6, 2013, pp. 657–83

Robinson, Tim, *Connemara: Listening to the wind* (Dublin: Penguin Ireland, 2006)
———, *Connemara: The last pool of darkness* (Dublin: Penguin Ireland, 2008)
———, *Connemara: A little Gaelic kingdom* (Dublin: Penguin Ireland, 2011)

Rowland, Robyn 'Unbroken Stone in a Stubborn Sea: Epic of Inishbofin', in *Line
of Drift* (Inverin, County Galway: Doire Press, 2015), pp. 49–54

Rowley, Ellen, 'Housing in Ireland, 1740–2016', in Eugenio F. Biagini and
Mary E. Daly (eds), *The Cambridge Social History of Modern Ireland*
(Cambridge: Cambridge University Press, 2017), pp. 212–32

Ruttledge-Fair, Robert, 'Annual Report of the Congested Districts Board for the
Clifden and Carna Regions', in James Morrissey (ed.), *On the Verge of Want: A
unique insight into living conditions along Ireland's western seaboard in the late
nineteenth century* (Dublin: Crannóg Books, 2001)

Rynne, Colin, *Industrial Ireland 1750–1930: An archaeology* (Cork: The Collins Press,
2006)

Rynne, Dabeo, 'Furniture Making in County Clare: The O'Halloran brothers', *Regional Furniture*, vol. 8, 1994, pp. 87–9

Sánchez-Alonso, Blanca, 'Those Who Left and Those Who Stayed Behind: Explaining emigration from the regions of Spain, 1880–1914', *The Journal of Economic History*, vol. 60, no. 3, 2000, pp. 730–55

Sayers, Peig, *Peig: The autobiography of Peig Sayers of the Great Blasket Island* (Dublin: Talbot Press, 1974)

Schaepe, David M., Bill Angelbeck, David Snook and John R. Welch, 'Archaeology as Therapy: Connecting belongings, knowledge, time, place, and well-being', *Current Anthropology*, vol. 58, no. 4, 2017, pp. 502–33

Scheper-Hughes, Nancy, *Saints, Scholars, and Schizophrenics: Mental illness in rural Ireland* (Berkeley, CA: University of California Press, 1979)

Shakour, Katherine E., 'From Colonial Legacy to Difficult Heritage: Responding to and remembering *An Gorta Mór*, Ireland's Great Hunger', unpublished PhD thesis, University of South Florida, 2020

Shakour, Katherine, Ian Kuijt and Tommy Burke, 'Different Roles, Diverse Goals: Understanding stakeholder and archaeologists positions in community-based projects', *Archaeologies*, vol. 15, no. 3, 2019, pp. 372–99

Shire, Warsan, 'Home', in *Bless the Daughter Raised by a Voice in Her Head* (London: Chatto & Windus, 2022), pp. 24–5

Shove, Elizabeth, 'Constructing Home: A crossroads of choices', in Irene Cieraad (ed.), *At Home: An anthropology of domestic space* (Syracuse, NY: Syracuse University Press, 2006), pp. 130–43

Skeates, Robin, *An Archaeology of the Senses: Prehistoric Malta* (Oxford: Oxford University Press, 2010)

Skeates, Robin and Jo Day (eds), *The Routledge Handbook of Sensory Archaeology* (London: Routledge, 2019)

Slough History Online, 'Smoke, Steam and (Computer) Chips: Elliman, Sons & Co.', http://www.sloughhistoryonline.org.uk/asset_arena/text/pdf/sl/sl/sl-sl-web2729_elliman-d-oo-ooo.pdf

Smith, Barbara, *Home Girls: A Black feminist anthology* (Boston: Kitchen Table Press, 1983)

South Lancashire Leisure and Culture, 'Museums', http://www.sllcmuseumscollections. co.uk/search.do?view=detail&page=1&id=135935&db=object

Symmons, Clive and Seamus Harkin, *The Disappearing Irish Cottage: A case-study of north Donegal* (Bray: Wordwell, 2004)

Tarlow, Sarah, 'Emotion in Archaeology', *Current Anthropology*, vol. 41, no. 5, 2000, pp. 713–46

———, 'The Archaeology of Emotion and Affect', *Annual Review of Anthropology*, vol. 41, 2012, pp. 169–85

Tarrant, Naomi, 'The Bedroom', in Anne Carruthers (ed.), *The Scottish Home* (Edinburgh: National Museums of Scotland, 1996), pp. 181–202

Thompson, Tok, '*Clocha Geala/Clocha Uaisle*: White quartz in Irish tradition', *Béaloideas*, vol. 73, 2005, pp. 111–33

Tracey, Rachel, 'Ulster Plantation Towns: An archaeology of rhetoric and reality', in Brendan Scott (ed.), *Society and Administration in the Ulster Plantation Towns, 1610–89* (Dublin: Four Courts Press, 2019), pp. 6–19

Turner, Alexander, 'TurkFest: Ireland's little festival with a big heart – a photo essay', *The Guardian*, 21 August 2019, https://www.theguardian.com/travel/2019/aug/21/inishturk-turkfest-ireland-festival-photo-essay

Ua Cnáimhsí, Pádraig, *Róise Rua: An island memoir*, translated by J.J. Keaveny (Blackrock, County Dublin: Mercier Press, 2009)

Villiers-Tuthill, Kathleen, *Beyond the Twelve Bens: A history of Clifden and district 1860–1923*, 3rd edn (Athlone: Connemara Girl Publications, 2006)

———, *A Colony of Strangers: The founding and early history of Clifden* (Athlone: Connemara Girl Publications, 2012)

Vincentelli, Moira, 'Artefact and Identity: The Welsh dresser as domestic display and cultural symbol', in Jane Aaron, Teresa Rees, Sandra Betts and Moira Vincentelli (eds), *Our Sisters' Land: The changing identity of women in Wales* (Cardiff: University of Wales Press, 1994), pp. 228–41

Viney, Michael, 'The Yank in the Corner: Why the ethics of anthropology are a worry for rural Ireland', *Irish Times*, 6 August 1983, p. 9

Voss, Barbara L. and Rebecca Allen, 'Guide to Ceramic MNV Calculation: Qualitative and quantitative analysis', Society for Historical Archaeology, *Technical Briefs in Historical Archaeology*, vol. 5, 2010, pp. 1–99

Walsh, Jane, 'The Social Organisation of an Island Community in Western Ireland: Clare Island, County Mayo', unpublished PhD thesis, University of Edinburgh, 1958

Walsh, Paul, 'Cromwell's Barrack: A Commonwealth garrison fort on Inishbofin,

Co. Galway', *Journal of the Galway Archaeological and Historical Society*, vol. 42, 1989, pp. 30–71

Waterson, Roxana, *The Living House: An anthropology of architecture in Southeast Asia* (Kuala Lumpur: Oxford University Press, 1990)

Webster, Jane, 'Resisting Traditions: Ceramics, identity, and consumer choice in the Outer Hebrides from 1800 to present', *International Journal of Historical Archaeology*, vol. 3, no. 1, 1999, pp. 53–73

Webster, Jane, Louise Tolson and Richard Carlton, 'The Artifact as Interviewer: Experimenting with oral history at the Ovenstone miners' cottages site, Northumberland', *Historical Archaeology*, vol. 48, 2014, pp. 11–29

Westropp, Thomas J, 'Clare Island Survey: History and archaeology', *Proceedings of the Royal Irish Academy*, vol. 31, section 2 (Dublin: Hodges, Figgis & Co., 1911), pp. 45–52

Whelan, David A. and Tadhg O'Keeffe, 'The House of Ussher: Histories and heritages of improvement, conspicuous consumption, and eviction on an early nineteenth-century Irish estate', *International Journal of Historical Archaeology*, vol. 18, no. 4, 2014, pp. 700–25

Whitridge, Peter, 'Landscapes, Houses, Bodies, Things: "Place" and the archaeology of Inuit imaginaries', *Journal of Archaeological Method and Theory*, vol. 11, no. 2, 2004, pp. 213–50

Wilkie, Laurie, *Creating Freedom: Material culture and African-American identity at Oakley Plantation, Louisiana, 1845–1950* (Baton Rouge: Louisiana State University Press, 2000)

———, *The Archaeology of Mothering: An African-American midwife's tale* (New York: Routledge, 2003)

Wilner, Eleanor, 'Emigration', in *Shekhinah* (Chicago: University of Chicago Press, 1984), pp. 3–4

Wilson, Thomas M., 'From Clare to the Common Market: Perspectives of Irish ethnography', *Anthropological Quarterly*, vol. 57, no. 1, 1984, pp. 1–15

——— (ed.), *The Anthropology of Ireland* (Oxford: Berg, 2006)

Wolff, Nicholas, 'At Home in Prehistory: Critical approaches to the built environment in the south Italian Bronze Age', unpublished PhD thesis, Boston University, 2014

Woodward, Ian, 'Domestic Objects and Taste Epiphany: A resource for consumption methodology', *Journal of Material Culture*, vol. 6, no. 2, 2001, pp. 115–36

Wylie, Alison, 'Crossing a Threshold: Collaborative archaeology in global dialogue', *Archaeologies*, vol. 15, no. 3, 2019, pp. 570–87

Zimmerman, Larry J. and Jessica Welch, 'Displaced and Barely Visible: Archaeology and the material culture of homelessness', *Historical Archaeology*, vol. 45, no. 1, 2011, pp. 67–85

Index

Illustrations are indicated by page numbers in bold.

Ahmed, Sara, 7–8
Alfred Meakin Pottery, **295**
Allies, Cyril, 46, 53–5, 233
Allies, Thomas, 46
Ancestry.com, 83–5
anchor points, 4, 32, 34, 112, 160, 173
Anne, Clifden
    bowls, 242–3, **242–3**, 269, **270**, 301
    dresser, 60, 119, **120**, 246
    heirloom objects, 242–3, **242–3**
    plates, **141**, 301
    tureens, **300**, 301–2
Arabia Pottery, Helsinki, **260**, 260
Argyle pattern, **294**, 296
Arklow Pottery, **31**, 33, 99, **101**, **102**, 103, **149**, 250,
    295, 296, 327
art
    children's artworks, 8
    decorative arts, 62, 243
    historical, 30
    wall art, **16**, 17
asbestos roofs, 181
Asiatic Pheasant pattern, 228, 293–6, **294**
Atlantic Technological University, 119, 246
autobiographies, 29

Baker, John, 85
Bald map, 232
Baldwin, Catriona, **78**
Balfour, Arthur, 48
Ballybeg Island, 57
baptism records, 43, **44**, 81, 83–5, **85**, 86
Barratt's Pottery, Staffordshire, 250
bartering, 262
Bás Oileáin (2007), 190, **191**, 311
Battle-Baptiste, Whitney, 13
Beach restaurant, Inishbofin, 128, **130**, 265, 320
bed and breakfasts, 41, 60, 115, 131–3, 146, 158–9, 292,
    320, 322, **324–5**
Bedelia, Inishturk
    dresser, 114–15, **116**, 151, **152**, **306**
    jugs, **149**
    plates, 151, **152**

    teacups and saucers, 151, **152**
beds, 95, 108
Belmont Principles, 64–5, 87
belonging, 15, 163, 322
Betty, Inishturk: dresser, **133**, 158, 303
Bingham, George Charles, earl of Lucan, 56–9
Black feminist theory, 13
Blasket Islands, 29
boat-building, 34, 100, 115, **118**, 313, **314–15**
Booth's Pottery, 146, **147**, **275**
bottles
    beer or spirits bottles, 209, 222, **223**
    ceramic bottles, 201
    glass bottles, 176–8, **178**, 201, 209–11, **210**, 216,
        222, **223–4**, 243–4, **244**, **280**
    IV bottles, 243–4, **244**
    medicine bottles, 209–11, 222, **224**, **280**
    mineral water bottles, 209, 211, 222, **223–4**
    wine or champagne bottles, 209, 211, 222, **223**
Bourdieu, Pierre, 286–7
bowls
    Anne, Clifden, 242–3, **242–3**, 269, **270**, 301
    Celia, Inishturk, 146
    ceramic sherds from, 197–8, **218**, **220**, **222**,
        229–31
    for daily use, 304
    for display, 303–4
    flow blue decoration, 242, **242**
    James and Margaret, Inishturk, 99–100, **101**, 155
    John Tam's Crown Pottery, **270**
    frequency of occurrence in collections, 138–40,
        140, 145–6
    glass bowls, 99, 155
    Mary, Cashel, 155
    Michael, Inishbofin, 255, **256**
    occurrence in archival dressers, 139, 150, **151**, 152,
        153
    occurrence in dresser-less delph collections, **158**
    occurrence in post-1980 dressers, 139, **151**, **156**,
        157–8, 298
    Ridgway Potteries, 242–3, **242–3**
    Staffordshire Tableware, 255, **256**
    sugar bowls, 8, **10**

whiteware, 99–100, **101**
William and Peggy, Inishbofin, **145**, 145
see also dinner sets
Brereton, Paul, 327
Bridget, Inishbofin: platters, 250, **254**
Britannia Pottery, Glasgow, **271**
Broadhurst Pottery, Staffordshire, 99
Bronze Age, 23–4, 42, 50
Brown, George John, marquis of Sligo, 46, 57
Browne, Charles, 56, 179, 185, 186, 263
building materials, 15, 17, 18, 20, 23, 172–3, 176, 233
Burke, Michael, 113, **114**
Burke, Patrick, 265
Burke, Peter, 113
Burke, Tommy, **49**, 97, 176
Burke, Willie, 113
butter, 263
buttons, 201, 216
By the Fireside, Co. Mayo (Livesay), **193**, 194
byres, **21**, 173, 179, 188

Caher Island, 43, 57
Caledonian Pottery, Glasgow, 204, **209**, **221**, 258, 273
Campellfield Pottery, Glasgow, **144**
candlesticks, 146
Carrigaline Pottery, **31**, 33, 250, **254**, 296
Carrollton, Ohio, 111
Carlson, Eric, 188
Carlton, Richard, 8
carpentry, 29, 34, 100, 113–19, 308
Cashel, Co. Galway, 32–3, 41, 61, 66, 124, 261
cashels, 20, **23**, 23–6, **25**
casserole dishes, 99, 100, 269
Catherine, Inishbofin
    heirloom objects, 274, **275**
    rental cottage dresser, **133**, **157**, 158, 159, 303, **307**
    restaurant dresser, 114–15, **117**, 133, **134**
    teacups and saucers, **252**, 255, **256**, 274, **275**, **295**, 296
    vases, 159
cattle, 42, 173, 175, 176–9, 183, 190, 191, 201, 263
Celia, Inishturk
    bowls, 146
    dresser, 114–15, **117**, **119**, 145–6, 322, **325**
    mugs, 145
    platters, **148**
    teapots, **149**
cemeteries, 42, **43**
census records, 36, **80**, 81, 83, **84**, 167, 200–1, 213–14
Centre for Experimental Archaeology, UCD, 27
ceramic bottles, 201

ceramic sherds
    from bowls, 197–8, **218**, **220**, **222**, 229–31
    from eggcups, 197–8, 229–31
    House 8, **195**, 196–8, 214–16, **216–22**, 228–31, **229**
    House 9, 197, 231, 232, 290–1
    House 14, 197, 231, 232
    House 20, **194**, 197, 231, 232
    House 28, 197, 231, 232, 290–1
    House 57, 197, 198, 201–4, **205–9**, 229–31, 284, **284**
    House 78, 197, 231, 232–3
    from jars, 197–8, 204, **209**, **210**, **221**
    from jugs, 197–8, 229–31
    manufacturing origins, 258
    from milk jugs, 197–8, 229–31
    minimum number of vessels to create, 196, 201–2, 216, 258, 291
    from mugs, 197–8, **205**, **207**, **220–1**, 229–31
    quantity found, 79, 166, 196
    from plates, 197–8, 204, **208**, **217–18**, 229–31
    from platters, 108, 197–8, **217**, 229–31
    rim sherds, 196
    from teacups and saucers, **195**, 197–8, **205–6**, **216**, **219**, 227–8, **229**, 229–31, 284, **284**
    from teapots, 197–8, 229–31
chairs, 4, 32, 95
chicken vessels, **149**, 155, **279**
chickens, 175, 179, 190
Child of Prague statues, **279**
children's artwork, 8
children's games, 123–4
children's medals and trophies, 8, 124, 146
chimneys, 183, **184**, 185–6
China, 248, 250, 260
christening candles, 124, 146, 280
churches, 42, **43**, 49
Churchill Pottery, 255
Claddaghduff, Co. Galway, 313
Clanricarde barracks, Inishbofin, 44
Clare Island survey, 56
clay pipes, 111, 146, 201–2, 216, 222, 227–8, **228**
cleaning, 17, 32, 34, 69, 100, 121, 240
Cleggan, Co. Galway, 45, 49, 61, 87, 228, 261, 263, 265
Clifden, Co. Galway, **60**, 60–1, 81, 87, 107, 108, 112, 188, 228, 246, 261, 265, 268
climate change, 91, 327–8
Clochán Congleo shrine, Inishark, 188, 236
Clochán Leo shrine, Inishark, **78**, 188, 236, 258
Cloonamore, Inishbofin, 46, 49, 265
Cloonan, Michael, 233

Cloonan, Patrick, 85, 233
Cloonan, Thomas, 83, 200
Cloonan family, 83, **84**, 172, 200–1
clothing, 201, 216
Coalport Pottery, Staffordshire, 249, **252**
coffeepots
    frequency of occurrence in collections, 144
    Michael, Inishbofin, **143**, 144, 302, **302**, 303
    Myott Pottery, **143**
    Sadler Pottery, **143**
coins, 216, 224, **225**, 263
Coldridge, Edward, 46
Colleran, Martin, 54
colonialism, 189
Colum, Padraic, 167–8, 183
comfort, 14, 32
communities of practice, 152–3
community, 4, 11, 17, 33–4, 92, 113, 173
community histories, 41, 97, 160, 244
Concannon, Kieran, 79, 190
Congested Districts Board (CDB), 48–9, 55, 57, 214,
    262, 263, 270, 291
construction techniques, 17, 19–20, 26–8, 172–3, 176,
    179, 187–8
consumption, 34–5, 37, 261
contemporary archaeology, 62
cookie jars, 146, 155
cornices, **73**, 99, 105, 115, 128, 292, 323, 325
Cotton, Bernard, 96, 113
Country Shop, The (Yeats), 261, **262**
Courcey family, 168, 172
court records, 81
Coyne, Marie, 49, 322
craftwork, 189–90, 224, 262, 263
Craggaunowen Castle and Crannóg Park, **19**, 20,
    24–6, **25**
crannógs, **19**, 20
credit, 261–2
Crete, 281
Crimean War, 43
Croatia, 281
Cromwellian barracks, Inishbofin, 44, **44**
Crowley, Erin, **78**
crucifixes, 146, 201–3, **203**
cultural capital, 287, 303
Cultural Landscape of the Irish Coast (CLIC)
    project, 20, 50, 60, 76–9, 91–2, 166, 183, 189
currachs, 99, 115, **118**, 168, 178, 191, 311, 313, **314–15**
cutlery, 131, 145, 192, **204**
Cutter Laboratories, California, 243
Czechoslovakia, 250, 258, 260

Damascus pattern, 108, **271**, 273
D'Arcy, John, 60
David Methven & Sons Pottery, Kirkcaldy, 108, **217**,
    271, 273
Davis, Bridget, 85, 312–13
Davis, Catherine, 212
Davis, Patrick, 212, 226
Davis family, 172, 212, 226
Dawdy, Shannon, 239
de Waal, Edmund, 239, 308
decal decoration, **102**, 241, 250, 296
decorative arts, 62, 243
Deer Park Farms, Co. Antrim, **26**, 27
Delia, Inishbofin
    dinner sets, **278**
    glass bottles, 243–4, **244**
    heirloom objects, 243–4, **244**
    mugs, **144**, 145, 273
    platters, 142, **142**, **252**, 301
    tureen, 146, **147**
Denmark, 281
descendant communities, 79, 92, 165, 172, 189
dinner sets
    Broadhurst Pottery, Staffordshire, 99
    Delia, Inishbofin, **278**
    James and Margaret, Inishturk, 99, 103, 155
    rose pattern, 99
    wedding sets, 99, 103, 155, **278**
    whiteware, 99
    see also bowls; plates; teacups and saucers
dishwasher-safe items, 255, 296, 298
distribution networks, 34, 248, 308
dogs, 175, 179, 191
Don Bosco's Castle, Inishbofin, 44
Donaruma, Bill, 79, 311–12
donkeys, 179, 183, 190, 191
Donogue, Tony, 327
Doonmore Hotel, Inishbofin
    bar, 121, **122**
    dresser, 121, **126–7**, 126–7, 246, **307**, 320, **321**
    dresser-less delph collection, 121, **122**, 133–4
    jugs, **126–7**, 127, **149**, 229, 301
    milk jugs, 73, **272**
    plates, **149**
    platters, 121, **122**, **126–7**, 127, **247**, **271**, 301
drains, 173, 179, 187, 200, 211, 233
ducks, 179, 190
Dun, Finlay, 58–9
dwelling, 4, 13–14, 18–19, 29, 240, 313

earthen floors, 173, 182
economic capital, 287, 303

eggcups, 139–40, **151**, 197, 198, 229–31
eggs, 224, 262, 263
Elizabeth II, 111
Ellen, Inishbofin
    children's artworks, 8
    children's medals and trophies, 8, 124
    dresser, 8–11, **9**, 124, 246
    family photographs, 8, 9, 11, 124
    glass chicken vessel, **149**
    heirloom objects, 8–11, **10**
    kitchen, 11
    milk jug and sugar bowl, 8, **10**
    plates, **297**
    pocketknife, 9, **10**
    teapot, 9, **10**
emergent properties, 103, 135
emigration, 34, 55, 82, 91, 100, 111, 135, 160, 190, 227,
    240, 243–4, 261, 274–6, 312–13
English Ironstone Tableware company, **269**
Eternal Beau pattern, **31**, 33
ethnoarchaeology, 26, 61–2
evictions, 58, 59
experimental archaeology, 26–8
eye-wash vessels, 8, **10**

Facebook, 327, **328**
family histories, 34, 37, 41, 80, 97, 99, 124, 160, 308
family photographs, 8, 9, 11, 97, 103, 124, 155
famine, 48, 91
farming, 42, 48, 49, 55, 169–70, 188–9, 224, 263, 320
fascia boards, **73**, 99, 113, 115, 128, 292, 316, 323
Fawnmore, Inishbofin, 46, 49
feminist theory, 13
ferry services, 49, 59, 320
fertiliser, 190, 263
festivals, 50, 59, 60
field systems, 42
Finland, 250, 260
fishing, 48, 49, 91, 189–90, 224, 261, 262, 263, 311, 320
fishing ledgers, 87, 261, **264**
flagstone floors, 173, 182–3, 200, 233
flooring, 173, 182–3, 200, 211, 233
flow blue decoration, 242, **242**, **300**, 301–2
Foley Pottery, Staffordshire, **245**
folklore, 15, 36, 62, 81, 165, 188, 327
Food Manufacturers Federation, 209
Ford & Sons Pottery, Staffordshire, 249, **252**, **294**
Fortune, Michael, 124, 327
Fountainhill, Co. Galway, 55, 79, 189, 191, 311, 315
Franklin, Maria, 13

G. L. Ashworth and Brothers Pottery, Staffordshire,
    247
Gailey, Alan, 172–3, 182
Galley Restaurant, Inishbofin, 114–15, 133, 320
gardens, 57, 82, 172, 173, 188, 190
Gardiner, Mark, 18
Gavin, Noel, 191
geese, 175, 179, 190
gender roles, 29, 34, 100
generosity, 15, 32, 34, 97, 105, 115, 121, 142, 153, 317
George, Inishbofin
    dresser, 104–11, **105–6**, 112, 118, 121, 246, **268**, 268
    hearth, 104
    heirloom objects, 107–8, 112
    jugs, 107
    mugs, **109**, 111
    plates, 106, **109**, **110**, 111
    platters, 106, **107**, 108, 270–3
    statues, 106–7
    teacups and saucers, 106, 107, 111, 112
    teapot, 107, **109**, 111
George, Kenneth, 6
Germany, 99, 155, 250, 260
gilding, 107, 250, **295**, 296
Glasgow, 108, 144, 204, 258, 271, 273
glass bottles, 176–8, **178**, 201, 209–11, **210**, 216, 222,
    223–4, 243–4, **244**, **280**
glass bowls, 99, 155
glass buoys, 155, 201, 203, **210**
glass doors, 104–5, **105**, 128, 129, **136**, **268**, 292, 308
glass jars, 209
glass sherds, 166
Glassie, Henry, 2–4, 14–15, 17, 30, 32, 98, 113, 147–50,
    173, 240
gravy boats, 138
grazing, 55, 56–7, 178
Greece, 260, 281, 285
Griffith, Richard, 83
Griffith's Valuation, 56–7, 59, 83, 170–2, 200, 212
Grindley Pottery, **256**

Halloran, Bridget, 227
Halloran, Michael, 54–5, 213, 226, 233
Halloran/Holleran family, 158, 172, 179, 226–7
Hampden pattern, **148**
hand-painted decoration, 100, 111, **137**, 155, 204, **205**,
    207, 216, **219**, 250, 290, 296
hanging dressers, 33, **129**, 192, 285
Hartley Jam Company, 204, 221, 258
healthcare, 49, 59, 320
hearths
    as anchor points, 4, 32, 173–4

back-to-back hearths, 173, 183–5, **185**, 211
    for cooking, 32, 173–4, 183
    Craggaunowen Castle and Crannóg Park, **19**, 24, **25**
    Deer Park Farms, 27
    exterior hearths, **19**, 24, **25**
    George, Inishbofin, 104
    for heating, 32, 173–4, 183
    Inishark historic village, 173–4, 183–6, **185**, 200, 211, 232, 233
    James and Margaret, Inishturk, 99, 103
    Michael, Inishbofin, 1, **3**
    Mooghaun Fort, 23
    paired with dressers, 32, 95
    Patrick, Cashel, **30**
    Sarah, Inishbofin, **96**, 99
    as symbols of welcome, 32
heirloom objects
    Anne, Clifden, 242–3, **242–3**
    Catherine, Inishbofin, 274
    Delia, Inishbofin, 243–4, **244**
    Ellen, Inishbofin, 8–11, **10**
    George, Inishbofin, 107–8, 112
    Honor and Thomas, Inishbofin, 240–2, **241**
    James and Margaret, Inishturk, 99–100, **101**, 112, 155
    Mary, Cashel, **72**, 155, 244–5, **245**
    Oona, USA, 135, **137**
    responsibility to keep, 119–21
    symbolic of kinship ties, 273–4
heritage, 11, 33, 34, 37, 39, 41, 50, 97, 103, 113, 121, 124, 155, 160, 163, 320–2
High Island, 43, 311
Hildebrande, Henry, 46, 56–7
historic village, Inishark, 50, **50**, 77, 163–237, **165**, **166, 236, 312**
    House 1, 199, 200, 201
    House 2, 176, **177**
    House 6, 168–9, **169**, 179–**80**, 179–87, 182, 184, 186–7, 212
    House 7, 212
    House 8, **76, 78, 164**, 166–7, 173, **174**, 181, 183–5, **185, 195**, 196–8, 211–31, **212–29**, 273
    House 9, 166, 197, 231, 232, 290–1
    House 14, 166, 231, 232
    House 16, 212
    House 20, 166, 176, **177**, 189, **194**, 197, 231, 232, 234
    House 28, 166, 197, 231, 232, 234, 290–1
    House 57, 83, 166, **166**, 167, 179, 183, 197–211, **199–210**, 229–31, 233, 284, **284**
    House 68, 233
    House 78, 166, 179, 183, 185, 187, 197, 231, 232–3
Holleran, Ellen, 172, 179
Holleran, James, 200
Holleran, Mary, 85
Holleran, Thomas, 85
Holleran/Halloran family, 158, 172, 179, 226
Hollinshead & Kirkham Pottery, Staffordshire, 249
Holmes, Helen, 273–4
holy water, 124, 146, 178, **279**, 280, 281
holy wells, 42, 236
homelessness, 18
Honor and Thomas, Inishbofin
    heirloom objects, 240–2, **241**
    jugs, 142, 240–2, **241**
Honora, Inishturk
    chicken vessel, **279**
    dresser, 115, **119**, 124–6, **125**, 268, 292, 322, **324**
    mugs, 281, **282**
    plates, **269**
hooks, bell, 13
Horning, Audrey, 169
horses, 179, 183, 190, 191
hospitality, 11, 15, 32, 34, 41, 97, 105, 115, 121, 132–3, 142–4, 153, 160, 163, 287, 317
hotels, 36, 41, 60, 121, 131, 132–3, 320
house orientation, 169, 173, 187, 211, 232
house shrines, **72**, 95, 244
hut circles, 42, 50

iconic objects, 7, 13, 298–9
identity, 12, 33, 41
indexical objects, 7, 12, 298–9
industrialisation, 34
interviews, 63, 66, 79, 286, 291–2, 305
Inishark
    baptism records, 85
    census records, 83, **84**, 167, 200–1, 213–14
    evacuation, 55, **191–2**, 191–2, 214, 311–13, 315
    excavations, 20, 32, 36, 50, **56**, **76–8**, 76–9, 108, 163–237, **166, 200–1, 212, 214, 258**, 273, 274, 290–1, 317–18
    farming, 169–70, 189–90
    field systems, 50
    fishing, 189–90
    gardens, 82, 172, 173, 190
    grazing, 55, 178
    harbour, 55
    historic village *see* historic village, Inishark
    history, 42–3, 46–8, 50–5, 163–237
    hut circles, 50
    kelp, 190

king, 54–5, 233
land ownership, 46–8, 55, 169–70, 189
maps, **46**, **81–2**, 82–3, 168, 199, 200, 211, 212, 232, 233
marriage records, 85, 87–8
Martello tower, 56
medieval church, 56
offices (outbuildings), 83, 172, 200
oral histories, 36, 79, 164–8, 172, 179, 182, 201, 228, 234–6
pier, 50–5
prehistoric houses, 56
St Leo's church, 234
school, 185, 226
shrines, 50, **78**, 188, 236, 258
valuation records, 48, 55, 167, 170–2, 179, 200, 212–14, 233
wildlife, 55
Inishbofin
archaeological excavations, 20, **21**, 108, 274
baptism records, 43, **44**, 83–5, **85**, 86
cemetery, **43**
census records, **80**
Clanricarde barracks, 44
Cloonamore, 46, 49, 265
community centre, 49
Cromwellian barracks, 44, **44**
Don Bosco's Castle, 44
farming, 49, 320
Fawnmore, 46, 49
ferry service, 49, 320
festivals, 50
fishing, 48, 49, 261, 320
harbour, **40**, **45**
healthcare, 49, 320
heritage museum, 49, 322
history, 42–9
kelp, 48
Knock, 46
land ownership, 46–8
maps, **46**
marriage records, 85, 87–8, **89**
medieval church, **43**
Middlequarter, 46, 49, 85, 265
music, 49
oral histories, 43, 262–5
pier, **40**, **320**
the Poirtíns houses, 20, **21**, 179
population size, 45
restaurants, 49, 114–15, 128, 133, 320
Rusheen, 49, **104**, 322–5
St Colman's church, 49, 83–5, **320**

school, 49, 320
shops, 49, 228, 263–5
tourism, 49–50, 320–2
tourist accommodation, 49, 320–2
valuation records, 46, **47**, 48
Westquarter, 46, 49, 85, 265
Inishbofin House Hotel, 46, **320**
Inishdalla, 57
Inishturk
community centre, 59, 99, 322
ferry service, 59, 320
festivals, 59
gardens, 57
grazing, 56–7
harbour, **57**, **59**
healthcare, 59, 320
history, 42–3, 56–9
land ownership, 56–9
maps, **58**
population size, 59
St Columba's church, 59
school, 59, 320
shop, 59, 87, 261
sports pitch, 59
tourism, 59, 320, 322
tourist accommodation, 59, 115, 146, 320, 322
valuation records, 57
Irish Antique Dealers Association (IADA), 327
Irish Cabin, Spinning (Bradley), **175**
Irish Folk Furniture (2012), 327
Irish Interior, An (Stannus), **193**, 194
Irish Times, 48, 63, 327
Irish Vernacular Furniture Facebook Group, 327
Iron Age, 23–4

J. & M.P. Bell Pottery, Glasgow, **271**
Jackson, Peter, 63
James and Margaret, Inishturk
bowls, 99–100, **101**, 155
casserole dishes, 99, 100, 269
dinner sets, 99, 103, 155
dresser, 97–9, **98**, **100**, 101–4, 112–13, 131, 153–7, **154**, 268–9, **270**, 278
family photographs, 97, 103, 155
hearth, 99, 103
heirloom objects, 99–100, **101**, 112, 155
jugs, 100, **102**, 269
kitchen, 103
mugs, 100, 103
plates, 99, **101**
platters, 100, 103, 269
renovations, 103

teacups and saucers, 99, 100
teapots, 100, 155, 269
visits to ancestors' home on Inishark, 99, 168
Japan, 248, 249, 250, 260
jars
    Caledonian Pottery, 204, **209**, **221**, 258, 273
    ceramic sherds from, 197–8, 204, **209**, **210**, **221**
    cookie jars, 146, 155
    crockery jars, 73, **74**, 197–8
    glass jars, 209
    marmalade jars, 198, 204, **209**, **210**, **221**, 258,
        273
    stoneware jars, 73, 204, **209**, 258
jewellery, 201, **203**
John Mortlock Pottery, London, 204, **208**
John Paul II, 100
John Tam's Crown Pottery, Staffordshire, **270**
Johnson Brothers Pottery, Staffordshire, **109**, 111, **275**
Jones, Siân, 8, 274
jugs
    Arklow Pottery, **31**, 33, **102**, **149**, **295**
    Bedelia, Inishturk, **149**
    ceramic sherds from, 197–8, 229–31
    for daily use, 303–4
    for display, 303–4
    Doonmore Hotel, Inishbofin, **126–7**, 127, **149**,
        229, 301
    frequency of occurrence in collections, 139, **140**,
        142
    George, Inishbofin, 107
    Honor and Thomas, Inishbofin, 142, 240–2, **241**
    jam purchased in, 242
    James and Margaret, Inishturk, 100, **102**, 269
    Mary, Cashel, 155, 229, 301
    occurrence in archival dressers, 139, 150, **151**, 152,
        153
    occurrence in dresser-less delph collections, **158**
    occurrence in post-1980 dressers, 139, **151**, **156**
    Oona, USA, **137**
    Patrick, Cashel, **31**, 33, **295**
    Willets Manufacturing Company, 241
    see also milk jugs
Julia, Inishbofin
    dresser, 113, **114**, 128, **130**
    plates, **297**
    tea set, **277**, 278
    teacups and saucers, 281, **281**

kelp, 48, 190, 263
Kenny, Kevin, 274
King, Patrick, 213, 233
Kinmouth, Claudia, 61, 104–5, 138, 175, 183, 327

kinship networks, 34, 59, 99, 112–13, 160
Kirkcaldy, 108, 217, 271, 273
knitting, 175, 190, 263
Knock, Co. Mayo, 124, 281
Knock, Inishbofin, 46
Kuijt, Ian, 20, **76**, **122**, 189, 311–12
Kus, Susan, 6, 11–12

labour, 4, 15, 17, 20, 23–4, 28, 34, 108, 111, 181, 189,
    230, 250, 261–3, 270–3, 308
Lacey, George, 233, 311
Lacey, John, 85
Lacey, Theresa, 190
Lac(e)y family, 172
land ownership, 46–8, 55, 56–9, 169–70, 189
Lash, Ryan, 188, 320–2
Lavelle, Bridget, 85
Lavelle, John, 213
Lavelle, Michael, 233
Lavelle, Patrick, 265
Lavelle, Penelope, 85
Lavelle family, 172, 213
Lee, Nedra, 13
Letterfrack, Co. Galway, 118–19, 246
life milestones, 17, 99, 121, 124, 146, 160, 261, 277–80
loft spaces, 176, 180–1
Lourdes, 124, 281
lustreware, 8, 155
Lynn, Christopher, 27
Lyons, Liam, 99

McDonald, Meagan, **77**, **78**
McDonnell, James, 57
McDowell, Jackie, 27
McElhatton, Noelle, 327
McGreale, Patrick, 233
McHale, Patrick, 100
mantelpieces, **3**, 173, 183, 185
maps
    Bald map, 232
    Inishark, **46**, **81–2**, 82–3, 168, 199, 200, 211, 212,
        232
    Inishbofin, **46**
    Inishturk, **58**
    Ordnance Survey maps, 81, **81–2**, 82–3, 168, 199,
        200, 211, 212, 232, 233
markets, 261
marmalade jars, 198, 204, **209**, **210**, **221**, 258, 273
marriage records, 81, 85, 87–8, **89**, 312
Martello towers, 56
Martin and Juliana
    christening candle, 124

dresser, 124, 128, 131, **132**
holy water, 124
Mary, Cashel
    bowls, 155
    chicken vessels, 155
    dresser, **123**, 124, 131, 153–7, **154**, **305**
    family photographs, 155
    glass buoys, 155
    heirloom objects, **72**, 155, 244–5, **245**
    house shrine, **72**, 244
    jugs, 155, 229, 301
    memorial cards, 155
    milk jugs, 155
    mugs, 155
    plates, 142, 155, 244–5, **245**
    platters, 155, 293–6, **294**
    taxidermy display, **72**
    teacups and saucers, 155
    teapots, 155
    vases, 155
matching items, 227–8, 248, 299–301, 305
medicine bottles, 209–11, 222, **224**, **280**
medieval period, 20–9, 42–3, 50, 176, 188
memorial cards, 146, 155, 280
Michael, Inishbofin
    bowls, 255, **256**
    coffeepots, **143**, 144, 302, **302**, 303
    delph display in glass cabinet, **134**, 268
    dresser, **129**, 285, 292, **301**, 302
    hanging dresser, **129**, 285
    hearth, 1, **3**
    milk jugs, 281, **281**
    mugs, **144**, 145, **148**, **285**, 285
    plates, **148**, 250, **254**, **295**, 296, 298–9, **299**
    teacups and saucers, **269**
    teapots, 144
microwave-safe items, 255, 296, 298
Middlequarter, Inishbofin, 46, 49, 85, 265
migrant labour, 34, 108, 111, 230, 250, 261, 270–3, 308
military barracks, 44, **44**
milk jugs
    Carrigaline pottery, **31**, 33, 250, **254**
    ceramic sherds from, 197–8, 229–31
    for daily use, 303–4
    for display, 303–4
    Doonmore Hotel, Inishbofin, 73, **272**
    Ellen, Inishbofin, 8, **10**
    frequency of occurrence in collections, 138–40,
        140
    Mary, Cashel, 155
    Michael, Inishbofin, 281, **281**
    occurrence in archival dressers, 139, 150–2, **151**, **153**

    occurrence in dresser-less delph collections, **158**
    occurrence in post-1980 dressers, 139, **151**, **156**
    Patrick, Cashel, **31**, 33, 250, **254**
    see also jugs
Minton Pottery, **141**
monastic communities, 42–3, 50
Mooghaun Fort, Co. Clare, **22–4**, 23–4
Moriyama Pottery, **277**
Morley Ware, **148**
Morris, Annalise, 13
Moynagh Lough, Co. Meath, 27
mugs
    Campellfield Pottery, **144**
    Celia, Inishturk, 145
    ceramic sherds from, 197–8, **205**, **207**, **220–1**,
        229–31
    commemorative mugs, 100, 103, **109**, 111
    for daily use, 303–4
    Delia, Inishbofin, **144**, 145, 273
    for display, 303–4
    frequency of occurrence in collections, 138–9,
        140, 144–6
    George, Inishbofin, **109**, 111
    Honora, Inishturk, 281, **282**
    James and Margaret, Inishturk, 100, 103
    Mary, Cashel, 155
    Michael, Inishbofin, **144**, 145, **148**, **285**, 285
    occurrence in archival dressers, 139, 150, **151**, **153**
    occurrence in dresser-less delph collections, **158**
    occurrence in post-1980 dressers, 139, **151**, **156**,
        157–8, 298
    Ridgway Potteries, **148**
    souvenir mugs, 281, **282**
    Wade Pottery, **109**, 111
    William and Peggy, Inishbofin, **145**, 145
Murray, George, 190
Murray, John, 200
Murray, Martin, 191
Murray, Mary, 85, 172
Murray, Patrick, 85, 265
Murray, Thomas, 200
Murray family, 172, 200
Museum of Country Life, 61, 115
music, 30, 49, 59, 97
Myles, Franc, 108, 273
Myott Pottery, **143**, 255, **256**

Napoleonic Wars, 56
National Archives of Ireland, 83
National Centre for Excellence in Furniture Design
    and Technology, 118–19
naturalised beliefs, 286, 292

Navan Centre, Armagh, 27
Neolithic period, 7
Nets of Memory (2019), 311–12
New Wharf Pottery, **148**
Newman, Thomas H., 46
niches, 176, **177**
Nicholl, Tríona, 28–9

O'Boyle, Fr. John, 83
O'Connor, Denise, 327
O'Dowd, Anne, 181
Office of Public Works, 55
offices (outbuildings), 83, 172, 188, 200
Offshore Islands Museum, 322
O'Halloran, Festus, 312–13
Omey Island, 43
Oona, USA
    dresser, 135, **136**
    heirloom objects, 135, **137**
    jugs, **137**
    platters, **137**
oral histories, 36, 61, 79, 164–8, 172, 179, 182, 201,
        228, 234–6, 262–5
Ordnance Survey, 56, 81, **81–2**, 82–3, 168, 199, 200,
        211, 212, 232, 233
ornaments, 106–7, 146, 240
O'Sullivan, Aidan, 28–9
O'Toole, John Joe, 114–15, **118**, 145–6, 246, 313
O'Toole, Tony, 8

painted dressers, 35, 69, 97–9, 115, 119, 124, 128–30,
        157, 292, 308, 316
Palmer, Sir William, 46
parish records, 43, **44**, 81, 83–5
participant observation, 63, 66
Patrick, Cashel
    dresser, **30–1**, 32–3
    hanging dresser, 33
    hearth, **30**, 32–3
    jugs, **31**, 33, **295**
    kitchen, **30**, **62**
    milk jugs, **31**, 33, 250, **254**
    plates, **31**, 33, **252**, **260**, 260
    press, **30**
    settle, **30**, 33
    tureen, **31**, 33, **294**, 296
peat, 182, 190
Penelope, Inishbofin
    dresser, **133**, **158**, **306**
    plates, 255, **256**
Pfeiffer, Walter, 316
pilasters, **73**, 99, 113, 128, 292, 316

pilgrimages, 42–3, 124, 160, 188, 234–6, 281, 306
placemaking, 4, 13–14, 18–20, 23, 26, 29, 128, 160,
        165, 167, 240, 298, 313
plate rails, **73**, 108, 115, **117**, 128, 155, 292
plates
    Alfred Meakin Pottery, **295**, **297**
    Anne, Clifden, **141**, 301
    Arabia Pottery, **260**, 260
    Arklow Pottery, 99, **101**
    Barratt's Pottery, 250, **254**
    Bedelia, Inishturk, 151, **152**
    ceramic sherds from, 197–8, 204, **208**, **217–18**,
        229–31
    Churchill Pottery, 255
    for daily use, 303–4
    David Methven & Sons Pottery, **217**
    for display, 303–4
    Doonmore Hotel, Inishbofin, **149**
    Ellen, Inishbofin, **297**
    English Ironstone Tableware company, **269**
    Eternal Beau pattern, **31**, 33
    Foley Pottery, **245**
    Ford & Sons Pottery, **252**
    frequency of occurrence in collections, 138–42,
        140
    George, Inishbofin, 106, **109**, **110**, 111
    Grindley Pottery, **256**
    Honora, Inishturk, **269**
    James and Margaret, Inishturk, 99, **101**
    John Mortlock Pottery, 204, **208**
    Johnson Brothers Pottery, **109**, 111
    Julia, Inishbofin, **297**
    Mary, Cashel, 142, 155, 244–5, **245**
    Michael, Inishbofin, **148**, 250, **254**, **295**, 296,
        298–9, **299**
    Minton Pottery, **141**
    Morley Ware, **148**
    occurrence in archival dressers, 139, 150–2, **151**,
        153
    occurrence in dresser-less delph collections, **158**,
        159
    occurrence in post-1980 dressers, 139, **151**, **156**,
        157–8
    Patrick, Cashel, **31**, 33, **252**, **260**, 260
    Penelope, Inishbofin, 255, **256**
    Ridgway Potteries, 298–9, **299**
    rose pattern, **101**, **109**, 111
    Royal Tudor Ware, **297**
    W. H. Lockitt Pottery, 141
    whiteware, 99
    William and Peggy, Inishbofin, **145**
    Willow pattern, **110**, 111, **149**, **256**, **269**

see also dinner sets

platters
    Arklow Pottery, 250, **254**
    Asiatic Pheasant pattern, 293–6, **294**
    Bridget, Inishbofin, 250, **254**
    Brittania Pottery, **271**
    Celia, Inishturk, **148**
    ceramic sherds from, 108, 197–8, **217**, 229–31
    for daily use, 303–4
    Damascus pattern, 108, **271**
    David Methven & Sons Pottery, 108, **271**
    Delia, Inishbofin, 142, **142**, **252**, 301
    for display, 303–4
    Doonmore Hotel, Inishbofin, 121, **122**, **126–7**,
        127, **247**, **271**, 301
    frequency of occurrence in collections, 139, **140**,
        142
    G. L. Ashworth and Brothers Pottery, **247**
    George, Inishbofin, 106, **107**, 108, 270–3
    Hampden pattern, **148**
    Hollinshead & Kirkham Pottery, **252**
    James and Margaret, Inishturk, 100, 103, 269
    Mary, Cashel, 155, 293–6, **294**
    New Wharf Pottery, **148**
    occurrence in archival dressers, 139, 150, **151**, 152,
        153
    occurrence in dresser-less delph collections, **158**,
        159
    occurrence in post-1980 dressers, 139, **151**, **156**
    Oona, USA, **137**
    Robert Cochran & Sons Pottery, 108
    Syria pattern, **107**, 108, **271**
    Thomas Cone Pottery, **294**
    Willow pattern, 107, **271**
pocketknives, 9, **10**
Poirtíns, the, Inishbofin, 20, **21**, 179
post-medieval period, 29, 43, 50, 77
poverty, 48, 55, 111, 189, 328
pre-fabricated dressers, 97, 112, 115–18
prehistoric houses, 42, 56
presses, **30**, 95, 138
Price & Sons Pottery, 258
Price Brothers Pottery, **149**
promontory forts, 42
pubs, 41, 60, 131, 132–3
purlin roofs, 181

quartz stones, 188

ramparts, 23
raths, 26
recycling

of building materials, 176, 185, 198, 199, 211, 233
of jars and bottles, 209, 211
refugees, 18
remote sensing techniques, 77–8
renovations, 15, 17, 77, 79, 103, 167, 182, 199
rental cottages, 36, 41, 59, 131–2, 158–9, 303, 320
replica buildings, 19, 20, 24–8, **25**, **28–9**
research ethics, 63–5
resiliency, 4, 13–14, 19, 91, 160, 189, 201, 234, 243,
    276, 313, 319
restaurants, 49, 60, 114–15, 128, 131, 132–3, 320
Rich, Adrienne, 163, 164
Ridgway Potteries, **148**, 242–3, **242–3**, **269**
Robb, John, 7
Robert Cochran & Sons Verreville Pottery, Glasgow,
    108
Roonagh, Co. Mayo, 59
rose patterns, 99, **101**, **109**, 111, **149**
Roundstone, Co. Galway, 261
Rowland, Robyn, 2, 17, 39
Royal Irish Constabulary, 44
Royal Tudor Ware, **297**
Rusheen, Inishbofin, 49, **104**, 322–5

Sadler Pottery, Staffordshire, **109**, 111, **143**
St Colman's church, Inishbofin, 49, 83–5, **320**
St Columba's church, Inishturk, 59
St Leo's church, Inishark, 234
Sarah, Inishbofin
    dresser, **96**, 113, **114**, 124, 303
    hearth, **96**, 99
    holy water, 124, **279**
    statues, **279**
saucers *see* teacups and saucers
school slates, 216, 224–7, **226–7**
schools, 48, 49, 59, 185, 226, 320
Scotland, 108, 144, 204, 216, 247, 249–50, 258, 260,
    270–3
Scuffle, Edmund, 85
Scuffle, Edward, 43
Scuffle, Mary Lacey, 43
Scuffle, Thomas, 43
sea delph, 111
seasonal labour, 230, 262, 273; *see also* migrant labour
Second World War, 243, 244
Seeley, Enid, 298
sensuous human practice, 11–12
settles, **30**, 32, 33, 95
sewing, 175, 180, 190, 263
sheep, 55, 173, 176–9, 183, 190, 263
shellfish, 190, 263
sherds *see* ceramic sherds; glass sherds

ship manifests, 81
shoes, 201, **203**
shop ledgers, 60–1, 82, 87, **90–1, 228, 261–5, 262–4, 266–7**
shops, 49, 59, 60, 87, 228, 242, 261–9, **262**
shoulders, **73**, 99, 115, 128, 316
shrines, 42, 50, **78, 188, 236, 258**; *see also house shrines*
sledge feet, 105, 115, 128, 292, 308
Smith, Barbara, 13
social capital, 287
social geography, 6, 63
social networks, 34
souvenirs, 146, 259, 261, 281–3
spectacles, 216, 224, **225, 280**
spinning, 175, 180
spongeware, **194, 203, 207, 216, 218, 220, 240–1, 241, 272, 273, 290, 291, 293**
sports pitches, 59
Springfield, Massachusetts, 100, 103
Staffordshire, 99, 108–11, 244, 249, 255, 294
Staffordshire Tableware, 255, **256**
Stanley's, Clifden, 108
Stannus, Anthony Carey, 192
state societies, 11–12
station masses, 8, 9–11, 287, **288–9**
statues, 106–7, **279, 280**
stickiness, 7–8, 12, 13, 33–4, 103, 128, 147, 165, 259, 315–16
stools, 32, 95
storytelling, 13, 121, 159–60, 240, 298
streets, 173, 189, 199
style, 15, 18, 33, 37, 115, 150, 160, 243, 301–7
sugar bowls, 8, **10**
SuperValu, Clifden, 107, 112
sustainability, 14, 37, 50, 91, 319–20, 327–9
symbolic capital, 287, 303
symbolic objects, 7, 12–13, 298–9
Syria pattern, **107**, 108, **271**, 273

tables, 32, 33, 95
taste, 18, 35, 37, 108, 115, 155, 229, 283–93, 298, 301–7
taste epiphanies, 303
taxidermy, **72**
tea sets, 249, **277**, 278, 287
teacups and saucers
    Arklow Pottery, 99, **295**, 296
    Bedelia, Inishturk, **151**, 152
    Booth's Pottery, **275**
    Catherine, Inishbofin, **252**, 255, **256**, 274, **275, 295**, 296
    ceramic sherds from, **195**, 197–8, **205–6, 216,**

    219, 227–8, **229**, 229–31, 284, **284**
Coalport Pottery, **252**
    for daily use, 303–4
    for display, 303–4
    frequency of occurrence in collections, 138–42, **140**, 146
    George, Inishbofin, 106, 107, 111, 112
    James and Margaret, Inishturk, 99, 100
    Johnson Brothers Pottery, **275**
    Julia, Inishbofin, 281, **281**
    Mary, Cashel, 155
    Michael, Inishbofin, **269**
    Myott Pottery, 255, **256**
    occurrence in archival dressers, 139, 150–2, **151**, **153**
    occurrence in dresser-less delph collections, **158**
    occurrence in post-1980 dressers, 139, **151**, **156**, 157–8, 298
    Ridgway Potteries, **269**
    rose pattern, 111
    whiteware, 99
    Willow pattern, 107, 112, **295**, 296
    see also dinner sets
teapots
    Celia, Inishturk, **149**
    ceramic sherds from, 197–8, 229–31
    for daily use, 303–4
    for display, 303–4
    Ellen, Inishbofin, 9, **10**
    frequency of occurrence in collections, 138–40, **140**, 144
    George, Inishbofin, 107, **109**, 111
    James and Margaret, Inishturk, 100, 155, 269
    Mary, Cashel, 155
    Michael, Inishbofin, 144
    occurrence in archival dressers, 139, 150, **151**, **153**
    occurrence in dresser-less delph collections, **158**
    occurrence in post-1980 dressers, 139, **151**, **156**
    Price Brothers Pottery, **149**
    Sadler Pottery, **109**, 111
tenant farmers, 169–70, 189–90; *see also* farming
thatched roofs, 173, 179, 181, 188, 200, 211
thing-heaviness, 7, 8, 12
Thomas Cone Pottery, **294**
Thompson, Tok, 188
Tierney, James, 85
Times, 58–9
Toole family, 172
tools, 4, 7, 11, 27, 104, 112, 147, 203
Tolson, Louise, 8
tourism, 49–50, 59, 60, 320–2
transfer-printed decoration, 108, **137, 144**, 145, **194,**

196, 203–5, **205**, **207**, 216, **221**, 250, **252**,
   258, 273, 290, 293–6, **294**, **297**
Tully Cross, Co. Galway, 61, 87, 261
turas monuments, 42, 236
tureens
   Anne, Clifden**, 300**, 301–2
   Argyle pattern**, 294**, 296
   Booth's Pottery, 146, **147**
   for daily use, 303–4
   Delia, Inishbofin, 146, **147**
   for display, 303–4
   Eternal Beau pattern, **31**, 33
   flow blue decoration**, 300**, 301–2
   Ford & Sons Pottery, **294**
   frequency of occurrence in collections, 139–40,
      140
   occurrence in archival dressers, 139, 150, **151**, 152,
      153
   occurrence in dresser-less delph collections, **158**
   occurrence in post-1980 dressers, 139, **151**, **156**
   Patrick, Cashel, **31**, 33, **294**, 296
   W. H. Grindley & Company Pottery, **300**
turf racks, 232, 233

United States, 82, 100, 103, 111, 131, 240, 249, 260,
   281, 312–13, 316
US Immigration records, 82

valuation records, 36, 46, **47**, 48, 55, 57, 81, 83, 167,
   170–2, 179, 200, 212–14, 233
varnished dressers, 8, 101, 104, 115, 124, 128, 292, 308
vases, 146, 155, 159
vernacular architecture, 14–15, 48–9, 62, 96
vernacular furniture, 95–6
Vincentelli, Moira, 301, 303

Viney, Michael, 63
Virgin Mary statues, 146, **279**
voicefulness, 8, 12, 13, 33–4, 103, 128, 147, 259

W. H. Lockitt Pottery, **141**
Wade Pottery, Staffordshire, **109**, 111
Walsh, Colman, 85
Walsh, Margaret, 85
wardrobes, 32, 33, 108, 133
water glasses, **145**
weaving, 190, 224
Webster, Jane, 8
wedding sets, 99, 103, 155, **278**
Westport, Co. Mayo, 8, 46, 61, 87, 129, 145, 176, 228,
   261, 265
Westquarter, Inishbofin, 46, 49, 85, 265
white quartz stones, 188
whiteware, 99
Wilberforce, Henry William, 46
Wilkie, Laurie, 13
Willets Manufacturing Company, 241
William and Peggy, Inishbofin
   bowls, **145**, 145
   dresser, 113, 131, **145**, 145, 246, 303
   mugs, **145**, 145
   plates, **145**
   water glasses, **145**
Willow pattern, 107, **110**, 111, 112, **149**, 250, **256**,
   269, **271**, **295**, 296
Wilner, Eleanor, 276
Wolff, Nicholas, 2
Woodward, Ian, 303
woodworm, 97, 127

Yeats, Jack B., 261, **262**